HISTORY OF THE
CHOCTAW, CHICKASAW
AND
NATCHEZ INDIANS

H. B. Cushman

HISTORY

OF THE

Choctaw, Chickasaw
and Natchez Indians

BY

H. B. CUSHMAN

EDITED, WITH A FOREWORD, BY
ANGIE DEBO

INTRODUCTION BY
CLARA SUE KIDWELL

UNIVERSITY OF OKLAHOMA PRESS
NORMAN

Library of Congress Cataloging-in-Publication Data

Cushman, H. B. (Horatio Bardwell), b. 1822.
    History of the Choctaw, Chickasaw, and Natchez Indians
/ by H. B. Cushman ; edited, with a foreword, by Angie
Debo ; introduction by Clara Sue Kidwell.
        p. cm.
    "First edition published in 1899; abridged edition by
Angie Debo published in 1962 by Redlands Press"—T.p.
verso.
    Includes index.
    ISBN 0-8061-3127-6 (paper : alk. paper)
    1. Choctaw Indians—History. 2. Chickasaw Indians—
History. 3. Natchez Indians—History. I. Debo, Angie,
1890– . II. Title.
E99.C8C92 1999
976.2'004973—dc21   98-44030
                                                                CIP

Published by the University of Oklahoma Press, Norman, Pub-
lishing Division of the University. First edition published in
1899; abridged edition by Angie Debo published in 1962 by
Redlands Press. Introduction by Clara Sue Kidwell copyright
© 1999 by the University of Oklahoma Press. All rights reserved.
Manufactured in the U.S.A. First printing of the University of
Oklahoma Press edition, 1999.

2   3   4   5   6   7   8   9   10

DEDICATION

To the memory of my parents, Calvin and Laura Cushman, as Heralds of the Cross of Christ, they, with a few other congenial spirits, left their homes in Massachusetts, A. D. 1820, as missionaries, and went to the Choctaw Indians, then living in their Ancient Domains east of the Mississippi River. Devoted their lives to the moral and intellectual improvements and spiritual interests of that peculiar and interesting race of mankind, living and dying the sincere and abiding friends of the Red Man of the North American Continent.

ALSO

To the Choctaw and Chickasaw people, each the now feeble remnant of a once numerous, independent, contented and happy people, whose long line of ancestry dates back to the prehistoric ages of the remote past, it is inscribed in loving remembrance of the writer's earliest and most faithful friends, whom he has a just cause to cherish for their many long known and tested virtues.

INTRODUCTION

This reprinting of Angie Debo's edition of H. B. Cushman's *History of the Choctaw, Chickasaw and Natchez Indians* represents two generations of scholarship on American Indians. Cushman, son of missionaries sent in 1820 by the American Board of Commissioners for Foreign Missions to work with the Choctaws, was born and grew up in the Choctaw nation in Mississippi. His knowledge was gained firsthand from personal observation and stories he heard from Choctaw people. He was passionate in his respect for the nobility of Indian people and deeply affected by their degradation in American society.

Angie Debo came to Oklahoma Territory in a covered wagon with her family in 1899, at the age of nine. Although her family was very poor, she received one book every Christmas, and she took advantage of the limited educational opportunities at rural schools to become a teacher herself. She enrolled at the University of Oklahoma in 1915 with the thought of majoring in English but became enthralled with history and graduated with a degree in that subject in 1918. She completed a master's degree in history at the University of Chicago in 1924, and after a stint of college teaching she returned to the University of Oklahoma, where she received one of the first doctorates awarded by the history department. Her dissertation on the history of the Choctaw nation, published in 1934 by the University of Oklahoma Press as *The Rise and Fall of the Choctaw Republic*, won the John H. Dunning Prize of the American Historical Association. It was meticulously researched in primary documents generated by the Choctaw tribal government and the federal government, as well as in newspaper accounts and secondary sources, including Cushman's *History*. Although Debo mentioned "local color" provided by living Choctaws who had served on the tribal council, her work was based primarily on archival research, and it documented what Debo considered the extinction of Choctaw tribal identity. Even in 1971, in a preface to a new edition of *The Rise and Fall of the Choctaw Republic*, she maintained her belief: "The incorporation of tribal citizenship and the merging of tribal history into the composite life of the state of Oklahoma may be said to have ended the separate history of this gifted people." (p. x)

Although Cushman and Debo both wrote with the idea that Choctaw tribal culture had largely disappeared, Choctaw identity is far from extinct in contemporary America. The Choctaw tribal governments in Oklahoma and Mississippi today are flourishing entities that operate their own health facilities and business enterprises, which employ significant numbers of tribal members. Although the funeral customs, religious beliefs, and stickball games that Cushman described in historical Choctaw culture are no longer a part of the daily lives of most Choctaws in Oklahoma, the Choctaw language is still a vital part of life in some communities, and it is widely spoken among the Mississippi Choctaw communities. The tribe in Oklahoma also subsidizes tour buses to take tribal members to the headquarters of the Mississippi Band of Choctaw Indians at Pearl River, Mississippi, and to Nanih Waiya, the large mound about twenty miles northeast of Pearl River that is the focus of tribal origin stories.

Cushman gives a long account of the Choctaw and Chickasaw versions of their origin and the importance of Nanih Waiya, and he also explores significant events of their history. Although he often embroiders the facts and sometimes fabricates events, such as the supposed treaty Peter Pitchlynn made with the Osages in 1828, there is still much of value in the work. His vignettes of tribal customs (such as courting rituals), the biographical information on leading men of the tribes, and his acquaintance with the territory and place-names are all important for tribal histories. Cushman's narrative and language reflect an earlier era of historical interest in American Indians. They take the reader beyond the purely objective facts of history and into the author's richly remembered experiences and personal connections with members of the Choctaw and Chickasaw tribes. Angie Debo recognized the worth of

Cushman's book when she edited and indexed it in 1961, thereby making a valuable source of knowledge about the Choctaws, Chickasaws, and Natchez much more accessible. The Choctaw language is taught as a regular course at the University of Oklahoma and in a number of community settings for adult learners. These courses demonstrate an ongoing interest in the preservation of Choctaw identity. The interest of Oklahoma Choctaw people in traveling to their original homeland in Mississippi reveals the importance of the past to current generations of tribal members. This reprint of Cushman's book will help new generations to learn more about their history and culture, and it will also facilitate renewed scholarly efforts to document the histories of thriving Indian nations in American society.

CLARA SUE KIDWELL

University of Oklahoma
July 1998

FOREWORD

Horatio Bardwell Cushman's History of the Choctaw, Chickasaw and Natchez Indians has long been recognized as important source material for scholars in the field of Indian history. Of the Choctaws especially, he had unique opportunities for first-hand knowledge "having been reared among them," as he says in his preface, "and intimately acquainted with them during the vicissitudes of a life extending to nearly four score of years . . . With many of their illustrious men (long deceased) whom I have brought into this history, I was personally acquainted . . . ; with others, though not personally, yet I knew their minds and the motives of their actions . . . "

He was born at Mayhew, a station recently established for the Choctaws in Mississippi by the American Board of Commissioners for Foreign Missions, where his parents began their work in 1820. He spent much of his childhood at a newer station known as Hebron. When the Choctaws were removed from their ancient homeland to the present southeastern Oklahoma in the early 1830's, one of their mustering places was close to Hebron and he retained a vivid memory of their heartbreak. The American Board, which lost much of its Mississippi investment, was unable to reestablish the work on its former scale in the new location, and the Cushmans accordingly were left in Mississippi.

But the younger Cushman continued his association with the people his parents had served. Two of them were his classmates and intimate friends at Marietta College, Ohio, in 1839-42. He spent his mature years at Greenville, Texas, across the Red River from the new homeland of the Choctaws and the kindred Chickasaws. From 1884 to 1890, probably in preparation for writing his book, he rode over their country, renewing his contacts with elderly men who had been his boyhood playmates, reading familiar names on cemetery headstones, and visiting the legislatures (Councils) of both tribes. He also spent much time throughout his long life in the study of general Indian history.

The result of his labors was this book, published by the Headlight Printing House at Greenville, Texas, in 1899. (One suspects that he was the Headlight Printing House, and that the work was done by the local newspaper.) The title on the spine — *History of the Indians* — is somewhat more accurate than that on the title page; for he was unable to stay with his subject. He begins with general comments, works down to Columbus, and traces Indian-white relations from Quebec to Central America, with side excursions to Peru and the West Indies.

At the time of his writing his beloved Choctaws and their neighbors were at a new crisis in their affairs — the final destruction of their nationality. All of present Oklahoma except the Panhandle had been set apart as an Indian Territory, a refuge for tribes driven from their former homelands; but the Government had yielded to popular clamor, and these last enclaves were being broken up and opened to white settlement. Cushman resented the wrongs, centuries-old and current, inflicted upon the Indians by the white man's cupidity; but he was perhaps even more indignant at the biased portrayals of their history and institutions by uninformed or prejudiced writers. This last he set out to correct.

He leaned as far in the opposite direction. His Indians are not mere human beings deserving objective treatment before the bar of history, but impossibly Noble Red Men. It was natural that he should idealize them. His early years had been spent in a boy's dream of paradise, roaming through a lovely, unspoiled woodland, playing and hunting with Indian boys, petted by Indian mothers, listening to the tales of the elders.

Thus in spite of its sentimentality the book contains much information not available elsewhere. I used it in writing The Rise and Fall of the Choctaw Republic. John R. Swanton, foremost authority on the ethnology of the Southern Indians, quoted from it extensively, although he was plainly annoyed at the writer's "emotionalism" and "verbosity."

But for many years it has been virtually unavailable. The paper used in the original edition was newsprint, and it has become so fragile that it crumbles at a touch. When a copy came into the possession of John W. Hinkel, well known printer and book dealer of Stillwater, he decided to preserve it by a new printing, this time on permanent paper. As he and I discussed the project it seemed to us that much of the text was of no value, and I undertook the task of pruning.

Altogether I deleted about half of the original book. So far as I was able without destroying its continuity I eliminated repetition, religious moralizing, and literary and Biblical allusions, often entirely irrelevant. I discarded much general Indian history; some of this was interesting and fairly accurate, but it is easily available elsewhere. This left only the portion dealing with the two tribes Cushman knew personally and their close neighbors, the Natchez. These in fact are the Indians whose history Cushman set out to relate.

Except for these deletions I took few liberties with the text. I did change the spelling of a few proper names, notably those of Pushmataha, Apukshunnubbee, and Moshulatubbee, the great district chiefs of the early nineteenth century. Cushman insisted that his version was linguistically correct, but the "corrupted" form he scorned has come into general usage. Pushmataha, in particular, is a well known historical character. Oklahoma even has a county carrying his name. Few would recognize him as Apushamatahaubih, or could find him in an index with that spelling. Also I corrected some misspelled words — such as his John Elliot (instead of John Eliot) and the Elliot Mission named for him — and obvious typographical errors.

The reader may feel that I should have been more ruthless in my pruning. Doubtless I would have been except for the perishable quality of the newsprint, and the conviction that even a shade of meaning lost would be lost forever. For example, I retained three almost identical descriptions and two briefer accounts of the Choctaw mortuary customs because each had some small detail not found in the others. Like Cushman himself I felt a strong responsibility to preserve all possible clues to the history and institutions of a people deserving to be remembered.

ANGIE DEBO

Marshall, Oklahoma
October, 1962

CONTENTS

HISTORY

OF THE

Choctaw, Chickasaw and Natchez
INDIANS.

[THE CHOCTAWS]

[The first sixty-one pages deal with general characteristics of the Indian race and speculations regarding its origin. Only a few excerpts have any possible value in connection with the Choctaws and Chickasaws. Regarding the hypothesis that the Indians are descended from the Lost Tribes of Israel, as indicated by a word resembling Jehovah used by the Creeks in their green corn festival —]

I often heard the Choctaws, when engaged in their ancient dances at their former homes east of the Mississippi River, utter in concert and in solemn tone of voice Yar-vo-hah, Yar-vo-yar-hah! and when asked its signification, replied: "It is the name of the Great Spirit we worship." According to an ancient tradition of the Choctaws, the ancient Choctaws, Chickasaws and Muscogees (now Creeks) were once the same people, and today the Creeks have many pure Choctaw words in their language.

[A people known as Hitchitees had long constituted an important element in the Creek Confederacy. Cushman believed them to be Choctaws, and he had the mistaken impression that they had only recently joined the Creeks. Refering to a current theory that the Aztecs of Mexico were identical with the ancient Hittites —]

There is a clan of Choctaws now living among the Creeks in the Creek Nation, who did not move in 1832 with the Choctaws east of the Mississippi River until the exodus of the Creeks and then came with them to the present Creek Nation where they have remained to this day. They were known when living east of the Mississippi River as the Hitchiti or Hichitichi clan. Both words (as given above) are corruptions of the two Choctaw words Hish-i (hair) It-ih (mouth).

Now if the Aztecs be of Hittite origin, and the Choctaws of Aztec origin, of which there is great probability (if their ancient traditions may be relied on) may not the Choctaw words Hishi Itih, the name of one of their ancient iksas (clans) be itself a corruption of the word Hittite, and pointing back to their ancient origin in the eastern world?

[Regarding the integrity of the Indians —]

Despotism, oppression, avarice, fraud, misrepresentation in trade, were things absolutely unknown in all their own tribal relations, and in their dealings with neighboring tribes. Therefore were they, at first, so easily swindled in trade by unprincipled white men. Though it was easy to cheat an Indian once, to accomplish it the second time was a more difficult task. I recollect a little incident of this nature among the Choctaws when living east of the Mississippi River. A young Choctaw was cheated in a trade with a white man, and when censured for making the trade, he calmly replied: "Pale-face cheat me, me sorry; pale-face cheat me twice, me big fool." After that as a matter of course, he would never believe a word that a white man would say.

[Regarding the warrior's private medicine bag —]

Every warrior had his totem; i.e. a little sack filled with various ingredients, the peculiarities of which were a profound secret to all but himself; nor did any Indian ever seek or desire to know the contents. I have more than once asked some particular warrior friend concerning the contents of his totem but was promptly refused with the reply:

"You would not be any the wiser thereby." Every warrior kept his totem or medicine about his person.

[Refuting a passage in Ridpath's History of the United States, Cushman describes the village life of many tribes, with this reference to the Choctaws and their Southern neighbors —]

The missionaries, when they established Christian missions among the Cherokees in 1815, the Choctaws in 1818, and Chickasaws in 1821, found them living in prosperous towns and villages scattered from two to six miles apart all over their then vast territories, and to which I testify from actual, personal knowledge; and no people with whom I was ever acquainted, or of whom I ever read, exhibited more real social virtues, true contentment and genuine social happiness than they, yet Ridpath's doleful and stereotyped edition of misrepresentation and ignorance says: "But the Red Man was, at his best estate, an unsocial, solitary, and gloomy spirit. He communed only with himself and the genius of solitude. He sat apart; the forest was better than the village."

[Referring to his opportunity to learn Choctaw traditions —]

Their traditions, which form the connecting link between truth and romance, throw but a glimmering light upon the unwritten history of their past, which has so long been forgotten, as well as upon their ancient habits and customs, of which there can be no reliable information, therefore all must be left to conjecture. But I came in possession of many traditions seemingly founded more in truth than in fiction, as I oft sat among the Choctaws and Chickasaws in youth and early manhood and listened with romantic emotions to the narrations of the aged.

[Regarding the theory of some philologists that diversity of Indian languages was caused by corruption in dialects —]

This may seem more plausible from the following incident. Shortly after the Choctaws were removed from their
ancient domains east of the Mississippi River to their present places of abode, a small tribe of strange Indians was
discovered occupying a portion of their western territory,
now the Chickasaw Nation. A party of Choctaws, under
the command of Peter P. Pitchlynn, was sent out to ascertain who they were. When the delegation arrived at one of
the villages of the unknown tribe, they were totally unable
to communicate with them only through the sign language,
so well understood by all the Indians, and them alone.
However, it was soon observed that the villagers, in conversation with each other, used a few words that were decidedly of Choctaw origin, and now and then one or more
purely Choctaw words. This but increased the interest of
the now deeply interested delegates. Upon further investigation by means of the sign language, it was ascertained
that the name of the little tribe of strangers was Baluhchi,
a pure Choctaw word signifying hickory bark (formerly
used by the Choctaws in making ropes and whips when
peeled from the hickory bush in the spring). It was also
learned that they originally came from a country, to their
pleasant place of abode, that lay beyond the "Big Waters,"
and this was all that could be learned concerning them.
Being anxious to ascertain something more definite, the
delegates, upon further inquiry, learned that there lived in
another village a few miles distant, an aged man who was
formerly their chief but owing to his advanced age he no
longer acted in that capacity, but was regarded by the
tribe as their national Seer or Prophet. To him the delegation immediately went, and found to their agreeable surprise that the venerable old patriarch, for such he truly
was, could speak the Choctaw language fluently. He corroborated the statement of the villagers in regard to the
migration, and also claimed that he and his tribe were
Choctaws. When asked how long since he left his people
east of the "Big Waters," he replied: "Long ago, when a

little boy," and further stated that he was the only survivor of the little company that had wandered away years ago from the parent stock. But to fully test the matter, he was questioned as to the name of the Choctaw iksas (clans[1]) and their ruling chiefs at the time of his boyhood and the departure of the company to the far west. He readily gave the name of several clans and their then ruling chiefs, together with the names of the clan (Baluhchi) to which his parents belonged; also many memorable incidents connected with the Choctaws in his boyhood together with the general features and outlines of their territory. All of which was known to be true. The test was satisfactory. The delegates returned; made their report, and the Choctaw Nation at once received its long wandering prodigals into its paternal embrace, and without hesitation took them into full fellowship as children of one and the same family. About fifty families of this once lost clan, numbering about two hundred souls still survive, with a few of whom I am personally acquainted. The little band, I was informed, still adheres to the ancient customs of their clan with that tenacity peculiar to the North American Indians alone, but has returned to the use of the Choctaw language proper.

Here then, in this little band of strayed Choctaws, who had wandered from the parent stock scarcely a century before, is found a case in which their language had become so blended or mixed with that of the languages of other adjoining tribes, and thereby so corrupted and changed as not to be understood by their own people from whom they had wandered but a generation or two before. The ancient Baluhchi Clan of Choctaws was first made known to the whites by La Salle, who visited them on his voyage of discovery down the Mississippi River in 1682.

[1] Cushman did not understand the meaning of the word *clan*. He used it indiscriminately to designate the three tribal divisions or districts of the Choctaw Nation, the two great moieties into which the whole people was divided, groups of towns, bands, and actual clans. It is obvious that this Baluchi band was not a clan. Probably Cushman was confused because the Choctaws employed their word *iksa* as loosely as he did. After the missionaries came, they even used it to distinguish the different religious denominations.

[In a long account of French exploration and colonization in America, the following relates to the Choctaws —]

In 1699, the French, under the command of Lemoyne
de Iberville, also a French Canadian, founded Biloxi, in
Mississippi, which was named after a clan of the ancient
Choctaws called Baluhchi (Hickory Bark), of whom I have
already spoken. New Orleans was founded by the French
under Bienville, in 1718. Fort Rosalie among the Natchez
Indians, which was destroyed by them in 1729, who had
become exasperated by the oppressions of the French, of
whom I will again more particularly speak. In 1722, Bienville also founded Mobile, in Alabama. A chain of forts was
then built by the French between Montreal and New
Orleans.

[Finally on page 62 Cushman begins his Choctaw
history —]

The ancient traditional history of the Choctaws and
Chickasaws claims for them a Mexican origin, and a migration from that country at some remote period in the past,
under the leadership of two brothers, respectively named
Chahtah and Chikasah both noted and influential chiefs to
their possessions east of the Mississippi. Adair, in his
"American Indians," says: "The Choctaws and Chickasaws
descended from a people called Chickemacaws, who were
among the first inhabitants of the Mexican empire; and at
an ancient period wandered east, with a tribe of Indians
called Choccomaws; and finally crossed the Mississippi
river, with a force of ten thousand warriors." It is reasonable to suppose that the name Choctaw has its derivation
from Choccomaw, and Chickasaw, from Chickemacaw
(both corrupted); as they claim, and no doubt justly, the
names Choctaw and Chickasaw to be their ancient and true
names.

Their tradition, in regard to their origin as related by
the aged Choctaws to the missionaries in 1820, was in substance as follows: In a remote period of the past their

ancestors dwelt in a country far distant toward the setting sun; and being conquered and greatly oppressed by a more powerful people resolved to seek a country far removed from the possibility of their oppression.

A great national council was called, to which the entire nation in one vast concourse quickly responded. After many days spent in grave deliberations upon the question in which so much was involved, a day was finally agreed upon and a place of rendevous duly appointed whence they should bid a final adieu to their old homes and country and take up their line of march to seek others, they knew not where. When the appointed day arrived it found them at the designated place fully prepared and ready for the exodus under the chosen leadership of two brothers, Chahtah and Chikasah, both equally renowned for their bravery and skill in war and their wisdom and prudence in council; who were to lead them from a land of oppression to one of peace, prosperity and happiness. The evening before their departure a "fabussa" (pole, pro. as fa-bus-sah) was firmly set up in the ground at the centre point of their encampment, by direction of their chief medicine man and prophet, whose wisdom in matters pertaining to things supernatural was unquestioned and to whom, after many days fasting and supplication, the Great Spirit had revealed that the fabussa would indicate on the following morning, the direction they should march by its leaning. At the early dawn the following morn many solicitous eyes were turned to the silent but prophetic fabussa, Lo! It leaned to the east. Enough. Without hesitation or delay the mighty host began its line of march toward the rising sun, and followed each day the morning directions given by the talismanic pole, which was borne by day at the head of the moving multitude, and set up at each returning evening in the centre of the encampment, alternately by the two renowned chiefs and brothers, Chahtah and Chikasah. For weeks and months they journeyed toward the east as directed by the undeviating fabussa, passing over wide extended plains and through forests vast and abounding with game of many varieties seemingly undisturbed before by the presence of man, from which their skillful hunters bountifully supplied their daily wants. Gladly would they have accepted, as their future asylum, many parts of the country through which they traveled, but were forbidden, as each returning morn the unrelenting pole still gave its silent but comprehended command: "Eastward and onward." After many months of wearisome travel, suddenly a vast body of flowing water stretched its mighty arm athwart their path. With unfeigned astonishment they gathered in groups upon its banks and gazed upon its turbid waters. Never before had they even heard of, or in all their wanderings stumbled upon aught like this. Whence its origin? Where its terminus? This is surely the Great Father the true source of all waters, whose age is wrapt in the silence of the unknown past, ages beyond all calculation, and as they then and there named it "Misha Sipokni" (Beyond Age, whose source and terminus are unknown).

But what now says their dumb talisman? Is Misha Sipokni to be the terminus of their toils? Are the illimitable forests that so lovingly embraced in their wide extended arms its restless waters to be their future homes? Not so. Silent and motionless, still as ever before, it bows to the east and its mandate "Onward, beyond Misha Sipokni" is accepted without a murmur; and at once they proceed to construct canoes and rafts by which, in a few weeks, all were safely landed upon its eastern banks, whence again was resumed their eastward march, and so continued until they stood upon the western banks of the Yazoo River and once more encamped for the night; and, as had been done for many months before, the fabussa was set up; but ere the morrow's sun had plainly lit up the eastern horizon, many anxiously watching eyes that early rested upon its straight, slender, silent form, observed it stood erect as when set up the evening before. And then was borne upon that morning breeze throughout the vast sleeping encamp-

ment, the joyful acclamation, "Fohah hupishno Yak! Fohah
hupishno Yak! (pro., as Fo-hah, Rest, hup-ish-noh, we all
of us, Yak, here.)

Then, as commemorative of this great event in their
national history, they threw up a large mound embracing
three acres of land and rising forty feet in a conical form,
with a deep hole about ten feet in diameter excavated on
the top, and all enclosed by a ditch encompassing nearly
twenty acres. After its completion, it was discovered not to
be erect but a little leaning, and they named it Nunih
Waiyah (mountain or mound, leaning, pro. as Nunih Waiyah). This relic of the remote past still stands half buried in
the accumulated rubbish of years unknown.

Several years afterward, according to the tradition of
the Choctaws as narrated to the missionaries, the two
brothers, still acting in the capacity of chiefs, disagreed in
regard to some national question, and Chikasah proposed
that they should leave it to a game of chance, to which
Chahtah readily acquiesced. Thus it was played: They
stood facing each other, one to the east and the other to the
west, holding a straight pole, ten or fifteen feet in length, in
an erect position between them with one end resting on the
ground; and both were to let go of the pole at the same
instant by a pre-arranged signal, and the direction in which
it fell was to decide the direction in which Chikasah was to
take. If it fell to the north, Chikasah and his adherents
were to occupy the northern portion of the country, and
Chahtah and his adherents, the southern; but if it fell to the
south, then Chikasah, with his followers, was to possess the
southern portion of the country, and Chahtah with his, the
northern. The game was played, and the pole decreed that
Chikasah should take the northern part of their then vast
and magnificent territory. Thus they were divided and became two separate and distinct tribes, each of whom assumed and ever afterwards retained the name of their re-
pective chiefs, Chahtah and Chikasah.

Mr. Gaines, United States agent to the Choctaws in 1810, asked Apushamatahaubi[2] (pro. Ar-push-ah-ma-tar-hah-ub-ih), the most renowned chief of the Choctaws since their acquaintance with the white race, concerning the origin of his people, who replied: "A hattaktikba bushi-aioktulla hosh hopaki fehna moma ka minti" (pro. as Arn (my) hut-tark-tik-ba (forefather) hush-ih ai-o-kah-tullah (the west) mo-mah (all) meen-tih (came) ho-par-kih (far) feh-nah (very). And the same response was always given by all the ancient Choctaws living east of the Mississippi River, when the inquiry was made of them, whence their origin? By this they only referred to the country in which their forefathers long dwelt prior to their exodus to the east of the Mississippi River; as they also had a tradition that their forefathers come from a country beyond the "Big Waters" far to the northwest, crossing a large body of water in their canoes of a day's travel, thence down the Pacific coast to Mexico, the same as the .Cherokees. In conversation with an aged Choctaw in the year 1884, (Robert Nail, a long known friend,) upon the subject, he confirmed the tradition by stating that his people first came from Asia by way of the Behring Straits. He was a man well versed in geography, being taught in boyhood by the missionaries prior to their removal from their eastern homes to their present abode north of Texas[3].

The Choctaws were first made known to the European world by the journalists of that memorable adventurer, Hernando De Soto, who invaded their territory October, 1540, and introduced the civilized (so-called) race of mankind to the Choctaws in the following manner: A manly young Indian of splendid proportions, and with a face extremely attractive and interesting, visited De Soto after he had left Tallase. He was the son of Tuscaloosa (corruption of the

Choctaw words Tushka, warrior, Lusa, black), a renowned chief whose territories extended to the distant Tombigbee in the west. (Tombigbee is a corruption of the Choctaw words Itombi, box, ikbi, maker), a name given to a white man, it is said, who, at an early day, settled on the banks of the river and made boxes for the Choctaws, in which were placed the bones of their dead, which will be particularly noticed elsewhere.

The young warrior bore an invitation from his father to De Soto to visit him at his capital. The next day De Soto, advancing to within six miles of where the great chief awaited him, made a halt, and sent Louis de Mascosso with fifteen horsemen to inform Tush ka Lusa of his near approach. Mascosso and his troopers soon appeared before Tush ka Lusa, who was seated upon an eminence commanding a broad and delightful view. He was a man of powerful stature, muscular limbs, yet of admirable proportions, with a countenance grave and severe, yet handsome. When De Soto arrived Tush ka Lusa arose and advanced to meet him with a proud and haughty air, and said: "Great Chief; I receive you as a brother, and welcome you to my country. I am ready to comply with your requests." After a few preliminaries, in company with Tush ka Lusa and his followers, De Soto took up his line of march for Mobila the capital of the mighty chief. (Mobila is a corruption of the two Choctaw words moma, all, binah, a lodge, literally a lodge or encampment for all.)

On the third day of their march from Piache, (a corruption of the Choctaw word Pi-a-chih, to care for us), they passed through many populous towns, well stored with corn, beans and other provisions. On the fourth morning, De Soto, with a hundred cavalry and as many infantry, made a forced march with Tush ka Lusa in the direction of Mobila, leaving Mascosso to bring up the rear. At eight o'clock the same morning, October 18, 1540, De Soto and Tush ka Lusa reached the capital. It stood by the side of a large river, upon a beautiful plain, and consisted of eighty handsome houses, each large enough to contain a thousand men, and all fronting a large public square.

A high wall surrounded the town, made of immense trunks of trees set close together and deep in the ground, and made strong with heavy cross timbers interwoven with large vines. A thick mud plaster, resembling handsome masonry, concealed the wood work, while port-holes were abundant, together with towers, capable of holding eight men each, at the distance of fifteen paces apart. There were two gates leading into the town, one on the east, the other on the west. De Soto and Tush ka Lusa were escorted into the great public square with songs and chants, and the dancing of beautiful Indian girls. They alighted from their horses, and were given seats under a canopy of state. Having remained seated for a short time, Tush ka Lusa now requested that he should no longer be held as a hostage; to which De Soto giving no heed, the indignant chief at once arose and walked off with an independent attitude to where a group of his warriors stood. De Soto had scarcely recovered from his surprise at the independent conduct of Tush ka Lusa, when Jean Ortez followed the chief and stated that breakfast awaited him at De Soto's table; but he refused to return, and added, "If your chief knows what is best for him, he will immediately take his troops out of my territory." At this juncture De Soto secretly sent word to his men to be prepared for an attack. Then, hoping to prevent an attack until he could again get in possession of the chief, De Soto advanced toward him with assumed smiles and words of friendship, but Tush ka Lusa scornfully turned his back upon him, and was soon hidden among the multitude of now highly excited warriors. Just then a warrior rushed out of a house, denouncing the Spaniards as robbers and murderers and declared that they should no longer impose on their chief, by holding him as a prisoner. His words so enraged Baltaserde Gallagas, that he cut the warrior in twain with one sweep of his broad sword. At the sight of their slain warrior, the Choctaws, with their defiant war whoop, at once rushed upon De Soto and his men. De Soto, placing himself at the head of his men, fighting and retreating, slowly made his way out of the town into the plain; and continued to retreat until he had reached a considerable distance upon the plain. In the mean time the troopers rushed to secure their horses, which had been tied outside of the walls. The Choctaws at once knocked the chains from the hands and feet of the Indian prisoners whom De Soto had brought with him, giving them weapons and bade them help destroy the perfidious strangers. In the first rush the Choctaws killed five of the Spaniards, who had been left outside of the walls, and were loudly exulting over their seeming good fortune in dense masses before the gate. At that moment, De Soto with his cavalry, closely followed by his infantry, made a fearful charge upon the disordered mass of the Choctaws, who were still on the outside of the enclosures, and with a terrible slaughter drove them back into the town. Immediately the Choctaws rushed to the port-holes and towers, and hurled clouds of arrows and spears upon the Spaniards, and again drove them from the walls. Seeing the Spaniards again retreat, again the Choctaws rushed through the gate and fearlessly attacked the Spaniards fighting them hand to hand and face to face. Three long hours did the battle rage, the Spaniards now retreating, then the Choctaws. De Soto seemed everywhere hewing down on the right and left, as if his arm could never tire. That sword, which had been so often stained with the blood of the South American, was now red with that of the North American, a still braver race. Above the mighty din was heard the voice of Tush ka Lusa, encouraging his warriors; his tomahawk, wielded by his muscular arm, ascended and decended in rapid strokes, like a meteor across a starry sky. But could the feeble bow and arrow and the tomahawk avail against the huge lance and broadsword, the unprotected body of the Choctaw warrior against the steel clad body of the Spanish soldier? At length the Choctaws were forced to make a permanent

retreat within the enclosure of their town, closing the gates
after them; and at the same time the Spaniards made a
desperate charge against the gates and walls, but were met
with showers of arrows and other missiles. But the infantry,
protected by their bucklers, soon hewed the gates to pieces
with their battle-axes, and rushed into the town, while the
cavalry remained on the outside to cut to pieces all who
might attempt to escape. Then began a carnage too awful
to relate. The Choctaws fought in the streets, in the square,
from the house top, and walls; and though the ground was
covered with their dead and dying relatives and friends,
still no living one entreated for quarter. Hotter and hotter,
and more bloody waxed the desperate conflict. Often the
Choctaws drove the Spaniards out of the town, but to see
them return again with demoniac fury. To such a crisis had
the battle now arrived, that there could be no idle spectators; and now were seen women and girls contending side by
side with the husbands, fathers and brothers, and fearlessly
sharing in the dangers and in the indiscriminate slaughter.
At length the houses were set on fire, and the wind blew the
smoke and flames in all directions adding horror to the
scene. The din of strife began to grow fainter. Then all was
hushed. Mobila was in ruins, and her people slain. For
nine long hours had the battle raged. Eighty-two Spaniards
were killed and forty-five horses. But alas, the poor Choctaws, who participated in the fight were nearly all slain.

Garcellasso asserts that eleven thousand were slain;
while the "Portuguese Gentleman" sets the number at
twenty-five hundred within the town alone. Assuming a
point between the two, it is reasonable to conclude that six
thousand were killed in and outside of the town. Tush ka
Lusa perished with his people. After the destruction of
Mobila, De Soto remained a few days upon the plains
around the smoking town; sending out foraging parties,
who found the neighboring villages well stocked with provisions. In all these foraging excursions, females of great
beauty were captured, and added to those taken at the close

of the battle. On Sunday the 18th of November, 1540, this monster and his fiendish crew took their departure from the smouldering ruins of Mobila, and its brave but murdered inhabitants; and with the poor Mobila girls resumed their westward march.

Thus the Europeans introduced themselves to the Native Americans nearly four centuries ago as a race of civilized and Christian people, but proving themselves to be a race of fiends utterly devoid of every principle of virtue known to man. And thus the Native Americans introduced themselves to the Europeans as a race unknown to civilization and Christianity, yet proving themselves possessed of many virtues that adorn man, together with a spirit of true and noble patriotism that has never been surpassed.

That the Mobilians, as they have been called by the early writers, were a clan of the ancient Choctaws there can be no doubt whatever. The early French colonists established in the south under Bienville called the Choctaws, Mobilians and Pifalaiah (corruption of the Choctaw words pin, our, okla, people, falaiah, tall), and also called the Chickasaws Mobilians; they also state that the Choctaws, Pifalaiahs or more properly, Hottak falaiahs (long or tall men) and Mobilians spoke the same language. The present city of Mobile in Alabama was named after the Mobila "iksa," or clan of Choctaws by Bienville at the time he laid its foundation. Moma binah, or Mobinah (from which Mobile is derived) and Pifalaiah are pure Choctaw words. According to the ancient traditions of the Choctaws, and to which the aged Choctaws now living still affirm, their people were, in the days of the long past, divided into two great iksas; one was Hattak i holihtah (Pro. har-tark, men, i, their holihta, ho-lik-tah, fenced; i.e. Their men fortify). The other, Kashapa okla (as Ka-shar-pau-oke-lah): Part people. i.e. A divided people. The two original clans, subsequently divided into six clans, were named as follows: Haiyip tuk lo hosh, (The two lakes); Hattak falaiah (as, Hartark fa-lai-yah hosh, The long man or men); Okla hun-

nali hosh (as Okle-lah hun-nar-lih hosh, People six the);
Kusha (koon-shah) Being broken; Apela, (A help); Chik a
sah ha, (A Chickasaw).[4]

In 1721, a remnant of the Mobilians were living at the
junction of the Alabama and Tombigbee rivers, but finally
united with other clans of the Choctaws, their own people,
and thus became extinct as an iksa. The laws of the great
iksas or families, Hattak i holahta and kash ap a okla,
forbade the marriage of any person, either male or female,
belonging to the same clan; and to this day, the same laws
relating to marraige are strictly observed.

From the destruction of Mobila by De Soto, a long,
starless night of nearly two centuries throws its impenetrable veil over the Choctaws shrouding their history in the
oblivion of the past. But that they, with other southern
tribes, were a numerous and also an agricultural people as
far back as the fifteenth century there is no doubt; though
agricultural to a small extent in comparison with the whites;
yet to a sufficient degree to satisfy the demands of any
people to whom avarice was an entire stranger, and who
adhered to the maxim "Sufficient unto the day is the evil
thereof."

But the six great southern tribes, Choctaws, Chickasaws, Cherokees, Muscogees, Seminoles and Natchez possessed too grand a country not to attract the eyes of the
fortune hunters of all Europe, and excite their cupidity to
the highest degree; therefore, the French in Louisiana, the
Spaniards in Florida, and the English in Virginia and the
Carolinas, early sought to establish a foothold in the territories of those warlike and independent tribes by securing,
each for himself, their trade, with a view of ultimately con-
quering them and thus getting possession of their territories
and country. As early as 1670 the English traders and emissaries had also found their way to the Choctaws, Chick-

---

[4] Here Cushman gives the two great moieties of the Choctaws. This separation was
rigidly observed in marriage as he states, and also ran throughout their entire social life. But
when he attempts to subdivide these moieties into clans he confuses them with tribal divisions. It is probably impossible at this date to determine the ancient Choctaw clans.

asaws and Muscogees; and but few years had passed before
their designs, together with those of the French and Spaniards, were plainly manifested.

By each exciting the Indians and influencing them to
drive the others from their territories; each hoping thus to
ultimately secure these regions for their own country and
their personal interests. As the French had artfully gained
and held the friendship and confidence of the Choctaws, so
had the English secured and held that of the Chickasaws;
hence those two brave, and then powerful tribes, were
induced to make frequent wars upon each other, and thus
each foolishly but ignorantly furthering the designs of their
mutual foes against themselves.

In 1696, Bienville convened the chiefs of the Choctaws
and Chickasaws in council, that he might conciliate their
good will by presents; and, with a view of impressing them
with his power and greatness by an imposing display, he
also called together all the colonists within his reach; but
his effort to impress the Choctaws and Chickasaws with an
idea of his greatness proved more humiliating than flattering to the pride of Bienville, as they manifested to him their
utter contempt of such a farcical evidence of power and
greatness, by propounding a question to him, through one
of their chiefs, which was a humiliating proof of the low
estimation in which they held him as well as the entire
French people; it was, "If his people at home were as numerous as those who had settled in their country"? In reply,
Bienville, who had learned to speak their language to some
extent, attempted to describe to them by various compari-
sons the great numbers and power of the French. But still
the chiefs proved not only to be doubting Thomases, but
wholly established in the belief that all he had said was
false, by finally propounding the following questions: "If
your countrymen are as thick, as you say, on their native
soil as the leaves on the trees of our forests, why have they
not sent more of their warriors here to avenge the death of
those whom we have slain in battle? When they have the

power to avenge their death and then fail to do so, it is an evidence of great cowardice or a mean spirit. And why is it that the places of the strong and brave soldiers that first came with you, but now dead, are filled by so many little, weak and bad looking men, and even boys? If your nation is so great and your people so numerous, they would not thus act, and we believe that our white brother talks with a forked tongue." Thus was Bienville fully convinced that the Choctaws and Chickasaws did not tremble through fear of his boasted power; and that they also well knew that he had only about fifty soldiers at his command, and that his attempted display of power had but convinced them of his weakness. And had the Choctaws and Chickasaws been so disposed, they could, with a little handful of their warriors, have wiped out the French colony, Bienville, soldiers and all.

In 1702, Bienville, then commander of the French at Mobile, secretly sent out a small party to the Choctaws and Chickasaws to solicit their friendship, and thus secure their trade. A few chiefs returned with the party to Mobile, whom Bienville welcomed and entertained with affected friendship and assumed hospitality, bestowing presents and soliciting their friendship; yet, "In January, 1704," says Barnard de la Harpe, pp. 35, 83, "Bienville induced several war parties of the Choctaws to invade the country of the Indian allies of the English, and having taken several scalps they brought them to Bienville, who rewarded them satisfactorily," thus involving the Choctaws, whose interests he professed to have so much at heart, in destructive warfare so greatly detrimental to their national interests; and proving the shallowness of his professed friendship for the Indians and the perfidy of his nature, in a letter to the French minister, October 12, 1708, in which he suggested the propriety of the French colonists in North America, being allowed the privilege of sending Indians to the West India Islands to be exchanged as slaves for Negroes, asserting that "those Islanders would give two Negroes for three Indians."

There was a tradition of the Choctaws related to the missionaries over seventy-five years ago by the old warriors of the Choctaws of that day, who for many years before had retired from the hardships of the warpath, which stated that a two years' war broke out between their nation and the Chickasaws, over a hundred years before (about 1705) the advent of the missionaries among them, resulting in the loss of many warriors on both sides and finally ending in the defeat of the Chickasaws; whereupon peace was restored to the mutual gratification of both nations wearied with the long fratricidal strife. This war had its origin as the tradition affirms, in an unfortunate affair that occurred in Mobile (then a little French trading post) between a party of Chickasaw warriors (about seventy) who had gone there for the purpose of trade, and a small band of Choctaws who had preceded them on the same business. While there together, a quarrel arose between some of the different warriors resulting in a general fight, in which, though several Chickasaws were killed and wounded, the entire little band of Choctaws was slain as was supposed; but unfortunately for the Chickasaws a Choctaw happening to be in another part of the town at the time of the difficulty, escaped; and learning at once of the killing of his comrades, fled for home, where arriving safely he informed his people of the bloody tragedy at Mobile. Without delay the Choctaws adopted measures of revenge. Knowing that the company of Chickasaws would have to return home through their country, they laid their plans accordingly. The Chickasaws, not without fears, however, lest the Choctaws might have heard of the unfortunate affair, secured an escort from Bienville of twenty-five Canadians under the command of Boisbriant. As they approached a village, the Choctaws sent a small company to invite and escort them to a council pretendedly to be in session; which the Chickasaws, feeling safe under their escort, accepted. They were escorted to the sham council, and were given as was customary on such occasions, the inside circles, all seated on the ground; while the Chotaws formed a circle completely hemming them in. A Choctaw chief then arose and advanced with great solemnity and dignity to the speaker's place in the centre, with a tomahawk concealed under his dress, which, when he drew from its place of concealment, was the signal for the work of death to begin. The speaker went on for a few minutes in a strain of wild eloquence, but saying nothing that would awaken the least suspicion in the minds of his still unsuspecting guests; when suddenly he snatched the fatal tomahawk from its concealment and in an instant hundreds of tomahawks, heretofore concealed, gleamed a moment in the air and then descended upon the heads of the doomed Chickasaws, and, ere they had time for a second thought, all were slain. The Choctaws knowing that the Chickasaws would hear of the destruction of their brethren and would retaliate upon them, rushed at once into their country and destroyed several villages ere the Chickasaws could recover from their surprise. But the brave and dauntless Chickasaws, ever equal to any and all emergencies, soon rallied from their discomfiture, and presented a bold and defiant front. Then commenced a two years' war of daring deeds and fatal results between those two nations of fearless warriors, known and to be known to them alone. The creek, dividing that portion of their territories that lay contiguous to the place where the band of Chickasaws were slain on their return from Mobile, now in the northern part of Oktibbiha county, Mississippi, and known as Line Creek, was named by the Choctaws, after the two years' war, Nusih (sleep or slept, Chiah, yau-yau slept, that is, you were taken by surprise) in memorial of those two tragical events, the surprise and destruction of the Chickasaw warriors, and the disquiet and discomfiture of their nation at the unexpected attack upon them by the Choctaws, Nusih Chia has been erroneously interpreted by some as meaning "Where acorns abound." Nosi aiasha means where acorns abound.

The killing of this little band of Chickasaws under the circumstances, together with that of being under the escort and protection of the French, caused the Chickasaws to believe it was done through the connivance of the French, and ever afterwards they were the most inveterate and uncompromising enemies of the French, among all the Indian tribes, north and south, except the Iroquois, and in which, as a matter of course, they were encouraged by the Carolina traders from the English settlements.

That the southern Indians were friendly to their foreign intruders and disposed to live in peace with them, and were not such a bloodthirsty people as they have been represented, is clearly demonstrated by the fact that, in 1710 there was such a scarcity of provisions, that Bienville had to scatter his men among the Indians in order to obtain food for them, and so informed his government; a plan to which he had been driven before; and had not the Indians preferred peace to war with the whites, they surely would have embraced such favorable opportunities to destroy the unwelcome invader of their country.

In 1711, through the machinations of the English, who were ever ready to embrace every opportunity to enhance their own interests, though at the destruction of the Indians, the Choctaws and Chickasaws, were again involved in a fratricidal war, at the beginning of which there was a little company of thirty Chickasaw warriors instead of Choctaws, in Mobile, and fearing to return home through the Choctaw nation, they too earnestly requested Bienville to send a company of his soldiers with them for protection. Bienville, seeing so favorable an opportunity of winning the friendship of the Chickasaws, and hoping thus to seduce them from their alliance to the English to that of the French, cheerfully complied with their request by sending his brother, Chateaugne, to escort them through the Choctaw nation, which he safely did. But the cause and result of this war have long since passed with its participants into the silence of the unknown past.

Charles Gayarre (Vol. 1, p. 91) says: "In 1714 twelve English men, with a large number of Muskogees, came among the Choctaws, and were kindly received by all the towns except two, who fortified themselves and, while beseiged by the Muskogees, one night made their escape to Mobile." From the above, it appears that the visit of the twelve Englishmen to the Choctaws was attributed to an invitation extended to them by a Choctaw chief; since in the following year, July 1715, Bienville sent messengers to the Choctaws, demanding the head of Outoct-chito, a corruption of his true name, Oktak (oketark, Prairie) Chitoh (Big), or Big Prairie "who had persuaded the English traders to visit their nation, and had thereby caused to be driven off the inhabitants of two Choctaw towns, who were still in Mobile. The messengers returned to Mobile with the head of the unfortunate Oktak Chitoh, which had been stricken off by the Choctaw chiefs, who now were afraid of Bienville."

In 1741, Bienville was superseded by Marquis de Vaudreuil, to whom the Chickasaws sent a delegation to New Orleans to treat for peace. But Vaudreuil refused to treat unless the Choctaws, allies of the French, were made parties to the treaty. The Chickasaws then made an effort to induce the Choctaws to form an alliance with them, supported by the English, against the French. But their design was discovered and thwarted by the secret intriguing of Vaudreuil with Shulush Humma (Red Shoe), then a noted Choctaw chief and shrewd diplomat, and belonging to the clan called Okla Hunnali, (Six People) and living in the present Jasper County, Mississippi, who had been favorably disposed toward the English for several years; and finally, in 1745, through personal interest alone it was thought, he went over to the English; and, at the same time, influenced a chief of the Mobelans (properly, Moma Binah, or Mobinah, a clan of the ancient Choctaws) to do the same with his warriors, and also some of the Muscogees, all of whom were, at that time, allies of the French. Shortly after,

Vaudreuil went from New Orleans to Mobile, and there met twelve hundred Choctaw warriors in council assembled, with whom he made renewed pledges of friendship bestowing upon them many presents of various kinds. But Shulush Humma stood aloof and refused to participate in any of the proceedings; and to place beyond all doubt the position he occupied, he, a few weeks after, slew a French officer and two French traders, who unfortunately ventured into his village.

Thus the Choctaws were divided into two factions; at first peaceable, but which finally culminated into actual civil war through the instigations and machinations of both the French and English. In 1750, still infatuated with the belief that the white race sought their interests, the Choctaws still remained in two hostile factions, thirty of their villages adhering to the French, and only two to the English, who, in a terrible battle which ensued, had one hundred and thirty of their warriors slain, and soon after, were again defeated by the French, with a party of Choctaws, and compelled to sue for peace, while the English stood aloof and left them to fight alone against fearful odds, though their accepted friends.

Three years after (1753), De Vaudreuil was succeeded by Kerlerec, who, in one of his dispatches, thus spoke of the Choctaws: "I am satisfied with them. They are true to their plighted faith. But we must be the same in our transactions with them. They are men who reflect, and who have more logic and precision in their reasoning than is supposed."

November 3rd, 1762, the king of France ceded to the king of Spain his possessions in North America known under the name of Louisiana; and at which time, a treaty of peace was signed between the kings of Spain and France of the one party, and the king of England of the other, by which France was stripped of all her vast landed possessions. When the Indians learned of this treaty of cession, and were told that they had been transferred from the jurisdiction of the French to that of the English, whom they feared and dreaded tenfold more than they did the French, they were greatly excited and justly affirmed that the French possessed no authority over them by which to transfer them to the English, as if they were but so many horses and cattle.

In November, 1763, the Choctaws, Chickasaws, Cherokees, and Muscogees were, through their representative chiefs, assembled in council at Augusta, Georgia, with the representative governors of Virginia, North and South Carolina, and Georgia. But two years later, August, 1765, the Choctaws and Muscogees — inveterate enemies — commenced a fearful and devastating war, which, according to their traditions, continued six years with unabated hostility; and during which many battles were fought and heavy losses sustained on both sides, yet each displayed the most undaunted and heroic bravery. But as they had no native historians, the cause, the progress, the successes, the defeats, as Dame Fortune alternately bestowed her favors upon the one and the other, will never be known; for the long period of those six years of bloody strife is wrapt in the silence of the unknown past, and all that now may be written is contained in "They lived; they fought." Nor has much more been recorded concerning the vicissitudes of the North American Indian race, by their white historians; though "they killed, they robbed" is but a counterpart of the mutations of the white race also.

Be it as it may, we find the Choctaw people, amid all their vicissitudes and misfortunes, occupying, all along the line of their known history, a prominent place as one of the five great southern tribes, who have been justly regarded as being the most to be dreaded in war of all the North American Indians, for their skill and invincible bravery; and the most to be admired in peace for the purity of their friendship and fidelity to truth. And to compare the present enfeebled, oppressed, broken hearted, down-trodden, the still surviving little remnant, to their heroic, free, independent, and justly proud ancestors of two centuries ago, or even less than one century ago, is to compare the feeble light of the crescent moon lingering upon the western horizon to the blaze of the sun in the zenith of its power and glory. But what has wrought the fearful change? Truth points its unerring finger to these United States. And yet we claim to advocate the right of freedom and self government to all nations of people; and boldly hurl our anathemas against the iron heel of England's oppression of Ireland, and curse the greedy avarice of a heartless and grasping landlordism that for years has sapped the vitals of that unfortunate country and broken the spirit of its noble people; while we are guilty of the same greedy avarice that has broken the spirit of as noble a people as ever lived; and against whom we have long cherished and still cherish the basest and most unjust prejudice.

Pickett, in his History of Alabama, states: "In 1771, the eastern district of the Choctaw Nation was known as Oy-pat-oo-coo-la, signifying the 'Small Nation'; and the western district was called Oo-coo-la Falaya, Oo-coo-la Henete and Chickasaha." The four names are fair samples of the miserable corruption of the languages of the North American Indians everywhere, by the whites.

And in the above, Pickett is greatly in error in the word Oy-pat-oo-coo-la signifying "Small Nation," if he uses it as a Choctaw or Chickasaw word. In the first place there is no such word in either of their languages, and even admitting there is, it cannot signify "small nation." The words of both for small nation are Iskitini Pehlichika, small nation or kingdom. "And the western district was called Oo-coo-la Falaya, and Oo-coo-la Hanete and Chickasaha." It is evident also that these three names are corruptions from Choctaw words. The first being a corruption of the words Okla Falaiah, Tall People; the second, "Oo-coo-la Hanete," from Okla Hunnali, People Six, or Six People.

The third, Chickasaha, from Chikasah, Rebellion, all of which were names of different clans of the ancient Choctaws. There was also an ancient clan named Okla Isskitini, People Small, or Small People, which, no doubt, was corrupted to Oy-pat-oo-coo-la; if not, some linguist, other than a Choctaw, or Chickasaw, will have to give its signification.

[It should be stated, however, that the names of the districts as given here are recognizable. The Chickasaws (Chickasha) of course had long been a separate people; but the other three divisions—each with its own chief—were basic in the Choctaw government. By Cushman's spelling there were the Okla Falaiah (Tall People) in the west and the Okla Hunnali (Sixtown People) in the south, and according to Pickett the Oy-pat-oo-coo-la (Ahepat Okla) in the east. During the constitutional development of the nineteenth century these districts gradually lost their autonomy, but they persisted as administrative divisions as long as the Choctaws maintained their government.]

Alas; If the errors of our race were confined alone to the orthography, orthoepy and signification of various Indian languages, though as inconsistent and absurd as they are in that of the Choctaw, we might be excusable; but when they enter into every department of our dealings with that people, there can be no excuse whatever offered in justification of them.

See the gross errors set forth in the publications regarding the Indians from first to last, and all in direct opposition to known truth and common sense. The newspapers and periodicals of the present day are full of the same old stereotyped edition of vile caluminations against that hapless people. Even that class of literature devoted to the instruction of the young, books and papers bearing the title of "School History of the United States," "Youth's Companion," etc., are contaminated with falsehoods and defamitory articles against the Indians.

Before me lies a book bearing the title, "School History of the United States," under the signature of "W. H. Venable," by which its author has displayed as much knowledge of the North American Indians as might reasonably be expected to be found in a Brazilian monkey if writing its views upon the characteristics of the Laplanders in their icy homes. On page 17 is found the following absurdities: "The American Indians were fit inhabitants of the wilderness. Children of nature, they were akin to all that is rude, savage, and irredeemable. Their number within the limits of what is now the United States was at no time, since the discovery of America, above four hundred thousand individuals, for the Indian hopelessly unchanging in respect to individual and social development, was as regarded tribal relations and local haunts, mutable as the wind."

Again (page 19), he affirms: "Stratagem, surprise, and the basest treachery were approved and practiced even by the bravest." But what of the white race? Did not Washington and his generals "approve and practice deception, surprise and stratagem" upon the British in fighting for the independence of these United States? Did not Lee and Grant, yea, every officer from general down to captain, "approve and practice stratagem, deception and surprise," during our Civil War? And when an advantage, by these means, was gained, was it not acknowledged as a grand display of superior generalship? When practiced and approved by the whites, they are virtues; but when by the Indians, in their wars of resistance against our oppression and avarice, they at once become odious characteristics. But when and upon whom, did the Indians approve and practice stratagem, surprise and the basest treachery? Alone upon their enemies in war; never elsewhere. But we have alike "approved and practiced stratagem and surprise" in our wars with them always and everywhere; and have, in numerous instances, "approved and practiced the basest treachery" upon them by false promises, misrepresentations and absolute falsehoods when trying to influence them to enter into treaties with us by which we would secure for ourselves their landed possessions, and all under the disguise of declared disinterested friendship, and deep-felt interest in their prosperity and happiness; and I challenge anyone to successfully refute the charge. Yet this man would contribute his mite of misrepresentation and falsehood to assist others of his own congeniality, to hand down the Indians to the remotest posterity as a race of people the most infamous.

Therefore, he thus continues his lecture to the children, "Language cannot exaggerate the ferocity of an Indian battle, or the revolting cruelty practiced upon their captives of war. The very words tomahawk, scalping knife, and torture scaffold fill the fancy with dire images; and to say 'as savage as an Iroquois warror' is to exhaust the power of simile." But in impressing the youthful "fancy with dire images" he is scrupulously careful not to mention, or even drop a hint, in regard to the foul massacre of the friendly Cheyenne chief, Black Kettle, and his band by Gen. Custer and his soldiers, November 27, 1868; and of the "horrible" butchery of the Piegan Indians, on the 23rd of January, 1870, who were helplessly afflicted with the small pox, and guilty of no offense except being Indians, but in which assassination, one hundred and seventy-three Indians were slaughtered in cold blood by the whites, without the "loss of a man; ninety of whom were women, and fifty-five of them children, none older than twelve years, and many of them in their mothers' arms"; and though the butchery of these unoffending and helpless human beings merits the execration of all men, yet the actors in the bloody scene lived to boast among their fellows "I too have killed an Indian," though that Indian was an infant in its mother's arms; while their head was honored as the "Great" General Sheridan, backed by General Sherman. If the very words "tomahawk, scalping knife and torture fill the fancy with dire images; and to say as savage as an Iroquois warrior is to exhaust the powers of simile," does not the butchery of helpless and unoffending Indian women and children by civilized whites equally "fill the fancy with dire images"? And to say as savage as a Sheridan and Sherman in the blood-thirsty wars of extermintaing the Indians of the western plains "is to exhaust every power of simile."

On the 16th of February, 1763, the whole of Louisiana, for which they had so long struggled, passed entirely from under the dominion of the French to that of the English[5]; and all evidences of their occupancy of the sea coast of Mississippi, since Iberville first landed there on the 16th of February, 1693, are now only remembered as matters of history and traditions of the long past.

In 1765, through the solicitation of Johnstone, then acting as governor, the Choctaws and Chickasaws convened in general council with him at Mobile, at which time were confirmed the former treaties of peace and friendship, and also regulations of trade were established between them and the English; and in 1777, the Choctaws, the first time ever before sold a small portion of their country then known as the Natchez District, to the English Superintendent of Indian Affairs, which lay on the Mississippi River and extended north from the bluff then known as Loftus Cliffs to the mouth of the Yazoo River, 100 miles above.

In June, 1784, the Choctaws, Chickasaws and Muscogees convened in council at Pensacola, (corrupted from the Choctaw words Puska Okla, People with abundant bread) and there made a treaty of peace with Spain.

At this time, the United States set up her claim over the entire territories of the southern Indians by virtue of the English title, while Spain claimed, at the same time, the lion's part of their territories by virtue of her treaties, not with the Indians, the legal owners, but with England and France.

That the Choctaws were once a numerous people, even years after the destruction of Mobinah by De Soto, there can be but little room for doubt. Their ancient traditions affirm they were at one time one hundred and fifty thousand strong, but some allowance perhaps should be made upon that statement. However, their territory, as late as

---

[5] Cushman here refers to the French territory east of the Mississippi River.

1771, extended from middle Mississippi south to the Gulf of Mexico; and from the Alabama River west to the Mississippi River, embracing as fine a country as the eye could behold; and De Soto states he passed through towns and villages all along his route through their territory, as well as through the territories of other southern tribes. Roman states, in his travels through the Choctaw Territory in 1771, he passed through seventy of their towns. Rev. Cyrus Byington, who was a missionary among the Choctaws for many years previous to their exodus to the west, and had traveled all over their country in his labors of love and mercy, computed their number, all told, at the time of their removal, at forty thousand, but at which time six thousand died en route many with cholera, and others with various other diseases contracted on the road. I was informed, when traveling over their country in 1884, by an old Choctaw with whom I was personally acquainted when living east of the Mississippi, that many, when they first moved to their present homes, settled contiguous to the pestilential Red River, and in a few years four hundred of the colony had died, and the rest moved away from that stream of death to other parts of their territory.

Pickett, in his History of Alabama, says: "In 1771 there were two thousand three hundred warriors registered upon the superintendent's books at Mobile, while two thousand were scattered over the country, engaged in hunting." But as it is safe to say, the French did not register a fifth of the warriors, for several reasons: first, from their great aversion to their numbers being known to the whites; second, their dread and superstitious fear of having their names written in the "white man's books"; third, the great distance that the homes of thousands lay from Mobile, but few of whom ever saw the place; fourth, the missionaries who traveled all over their country found their villages and towns everywhere. And if the French had twenty-three hundred Choctaw warriors' names registered upon the pages of their

books, I feel confident, from my own knowledge of the
Choctaws over seventy years ago, in saying very few, if any,
of the owners of those registered names knew they were
recorded there. And if all be taken into consideration, the
six thousand, the lowest estimate, slain in the destruction
of Mobinah, then the great number that must have perished
in their wars with the English and French, as allies first to
the one and then to the other; and their wars with various
other tribes; and the many that were killed and died from
disease when engaged in our Revolutionary War; and the
six thousand that died on their removel to the West in
1832-33; and the multiplied hundreds that died soon after
their arrival to their present place of abode, from diseases
contracted en route and from not being acclimated to their
new country; and in addition to all this, the many depressing influences they have labored under since they have had
to do with the white race, and the terrible dispensation
under which they have lived, they must, at an early period
have been a numerous people, or long since they would
have become totally extinct.

"The Severalty Bill!" [6] I was in the Indian Territory
and read a letter from an Indian delegate in Washington
City, to a friend in the Territory and was forcibly struck
with the shameful truth of one sentence, "Congress can and
will pass any bill to destroy the Indians." I also read another letter written by an Indian in the Territory to a
delegate of his people, then (February 15, 1887) in Washington from which, by request and permission, I copied the
following without alteration:

[6] This bill became law in 1887. It provided that Indians should hold their land in
severalty, that is in individual rather than tribal ownership. Under this and subsequent acts
all the reservations in the Indian Territory and many of those in other parts of the United
States were broken up, and at the same time the tribal governments were abolished. After
each tribal member had received his individual farm—his "allotment"—any land remaining
was opened to white settlement. In some tribes all the land was allotted, but much of it
soon passed from the allottees to white owners, so that the final result was the same. The
severalty policy was adopted in response to popular demand for the Indians' land, but even
their friends—like Henry L. Dawes of Massachusetts, chairman of the Senate Committee on
Indian Affairs—believed that it would advance their welfare, and President Cleveland was
guided by the advice of the "experts." The Indians fought it desperately, but Cushman
stands almost alone among the white men of his day in his championship of their cause. The
effect of the policy has been disastrous to the Indians|

"Dear old friend:

"Wounded and grieved over the action of Congress and the President, who gave the Indians his word to stand by us, when our rights were trespassed upon. Behold now, his actions in the severalty bill. Are there no honest men, citizens of the United States? Alas, even the highest in power has no regard for his word! There must be very little honesty among them, and if God forsake us, we will soon be remembered only in story. God knows, if we had only the power that the United States have I would be willing to resent the wrong and insult, if it should be at the sacrifice of every drop of Indian blood that is circling [sic] in our race. Cleveland thinking he might lose the next nomination for President, is willing to sacrifice his word of honor to be on the popular side. Away with such hypocrisy! He should be a man of some principle and stamina, but he lacks all of it.

"Dawes[7], when here, said he would do everything to advance our cause; that he was surprised to see the intelligence and evidence of progress existing among us. See too, what he has done! God will surely damn such hypocrites. Poor Mr. Brown, I feel sorry for him, standing alone, as it were, in the cause of humanity and justice; but I hope he will not feel disheartened in the good cause, but will gather strength from the ruins of broken treaties and shattered pledges made and violated by his so-called great and magnanimous government. All honor and peace be his.

"We will ever feel grateful to him for the active part he took in our behalf. Had there been a few more honest and fearless men like him in Congress, we might have fared better. Inch by inch, does Congress trespass upon and violate the solemn vows it has made. Surely such an outrage is almost enough to drive us to raise the tomahawk, and die, every one of us, in fighting for justice against such

[7] Senator Dawes with four members of his committee had visited the Indian Territory in 1885, and had given the Indians a sympathetic hearing; but this did not change his determination to liquidate their tribal affairs. As this delegate pointed out, the policy was in direct violation of the treaties and guarantees given the Choctaws and their neighbors when they were removed to the Indian Territory.

high-handed tyranny and insupportable oppression of our helpless and hopeless race."

On June 22, 1784, the Spaniards convened a council at Mobile, Alabama, in which the Choctaws and Chickasaws were largely represented, also a few other smaller tribes came with their families. As usual on all such occasions, the Spaniards, unexcelled only by the Americans afterwards, lavished upon the Indians their flattery and presents, each of equal value, thus to induce them to form a treaty of alliance and trade, which was successfully consummated. The last article of this treaty confirmed, in the name of the Spanish king, the Indians in the peaceable possession of all their territories within the king's dominions; and furthermore, it was stipulated, should any of them be deprived of their lands by any of the king's enemies, he would repossess them with other lands within his territories equal in extent and value to those lost. But as stipulations and promises were the means adopted by the foreign nations that contended with each other for a portion of the North American Continent, so they, as the vicissitudes of war dictated, withdrew their protection from the Indians and unhesitatingly assumed the right of transferring them to any nation which their interest demanded; thus proving that they used every effort to secure and maintain the good will of the Indians only for the purpose of interposing them between themselves and their encroaching rivals.

The Spaniards again induced thirty-six of the most prominent and influential chiefs of the Choctaws and Chickasaws to visit them at New Orleans in 1787, where they were received and entertained with the greatest manifestations of respect and friendship, by escorting them to public balls and military parades, and the usual bestowal of presents and flattery; thus they were induced to renew their pledges of peace and friendship to the Spaniards, by smoking the pipe of peace in confirmation of their former treaty, by judging the actions of the Spaniards from the standpoint of the integrity and honesty of their own hearts.

The first treaty made with the Choctaws by the United States was at Hopewell, on January 3, 1786; and between this and January 20, 1825, seven additional treaties were made with them; the second being December 17, 1801, in which it was mutually agreed between the Choctaw Nation and the United States Government, "that the old line of demarcation heretofore established by and between the officers of his Brittanic Majesty and the Choctaw Nation, shall be retraced, and plainly marked in such a way and manner as the President may direct, in the presence of two persons to be appointed by the said nation; and that the said line shall be the boundary between the settlements of the Mississippi Territory and the Choctaw Nation."

James Wilkerson, as commissioner of the United States, and Push-kush Miko (Baby Chief), and Ahlatah Humma (Mixed Red, i.e. Mixed with Red), as commissioners of the Choctaw Nation, did run and mark distinctly this division line[8], and made a report of the same, August 31, 1803, as follows: "And we, the said commissioners plenipotentiary, do ratify and confirm the said line of demarcation, and do recognize and acknowledge the same to be the boundary which shall separate and distinguish the land ceded to the United States, between the Tombigbee, Mobile, and Pascugola Rivers, from that which had not been ceded by the said Choctaw Nation."

The names of the ancient Choctaws, as well as their entire race, as far as I have been enabled to learn, were nearly always connotative referring generally to some animal, and often predicating some attributes of that animal. Such names were easily expressed in sign language; as the objectiveness of the Indian proper names with the result is that they could all be signified by gesture, whereas the best sign talker among deaf mutes, it is said, is unable to translate the proper names in his speech, therefore resorts to the dactylic alphabet. The Indians were generally named, or

---

[8] Cushman is mistaken here. The Hopewell treaty fixed the southwestern boundary of the Choctaw country; these commissioners marked the southeastern boundary according to a treaty made in 1802.

rather acquired a name, and sometimes several in succession, from some noted exploit or hazardous adventure. Names of rivers, creeks, mountains, hills, etc., were given with reference to some natural peculiarity; for the Indian had a literature of his own, which grew every year in proportion and value; it was the love of nature.

As below stated, the first treaty was made by the United States with the Choctaw Nation on January 3, 1786. The following articles of this treaty were concluded at Hopewell, on the Keowee River, near a place known as Seneca Old Town between Benjamin Hawkins, Andrew Pickens, and Joseph Martin, commissioners plenipotentiary of the United States of America, of the one part, Yockenahoma, (I give the names of the Choctaws as recorded in the treaty, and also give their corrections and significations), corruption, Yoknahoma; Orig., Yoknihumma Land; Hommar, Red, great medal chief of Soanacoha, corruption of Sanukoah, pro. as Sar-nook-o-ah (I am mad); Yackehoopie, corruption of Yakni Hopaii, pro. as Yark-nih, (Land); Ho-py-ye (Land of the war chief), leading chief of Bugtoogoloo, corruption of Bok Tuklo, pro. as Boke (Creek) Took-lo (Two); Mingohoopari, corruption of Miko Hopaii, pro. as Mik-o (Chief) Ho-py-ye (Leader as War Chief), leading chief of Hashoopua, corruption of Hashokeah, pro. as Harsh-oh-ke-ah (Even the aforesaid); Tobocoh, corruption of Tobih Eoh, pro. as Tone-bih Eoh (All Sunshine) great medal chief of Congetoo, utterly foreign to the Choctaw language; Pooshemastuby[9], corruption of Pasholih-ubih, pro. as Par-sha-lih (To handle) ub-ih (and kill) gorget captain of Senayazo; cor. of Siah (I am) Yo-shu-ba (as ah) Lost; and thirteen small medal chiefs of the first-class, twelve medal and gorget captains, commissioners plenipotentiary of all the Choctaw Nation, of the other part.

The commissioners plenipotentiary of the United States of America give peace to all the Choctaw Nation, and

---

[9] This may have been the first official act of the young Pushmataha. Elsewhere Cushman spells his name *Apushamatahaubi*. The ending—here spelled ub-ih and tubi and signifying "killer"—was a war title often appended to Choctaw names.

receive them into favor and protection of the United States of America, on the following conditions:

Article 1st.—The commissioners plenipotentiary of all the Choctaw Nation, shall restore all the prisoners, citizens of the United States (useless demand, as the Choctaws were never at war with the United States, and never held any citizen of the United States as a prisoner, but always were their faithful allies) or subjects of their allies, to their entire liberty, if any there be in the Choctaw Nation. They shall also restore all the Negroes, and all other property, taken during the late war, from the citizens, to such person, and at such time and place, as the commissioners of the United States of America shall appoint, if any there be in the Choctaw Nation.

Article 2nd.—The commissioners plenipotentiary of all the Choctaw Nation, do hereby acknowledge the tribes and towns of the said Nation, and the lands with the boundary allotted to the said Indians to live and hunt on, as mentioned in the Third Article, to be under the protection of the United States of America, and of no other sovereign whatsoever.

Article 3rd.—The boundary of the lands hereby allotted to the Choctaw Nation to live and hunt on, within the limits of the United States of America, is and shall be the following, viz.: Beginning at a point on the thirty-first degree of north latitude, where the eastern boundary of the Natchez district shall touch the same; thence east along the thirty-first degree of north latitude, being the southern boundary of the United States of America, until it shall strike the eastern boundary of the lands on which the Indians of the said nation did live and hunt on the twenty-ninth of November, 1782, while they were under the protection of the King of Great Britain; thence northerly along the said eastern boundary, until it shall meet the northern boundary of the said lands; thence westerly along the said northern boundary until it shall meet the western boundary thereof; thence southerly along the same, to the beginning[10]; saving and reserving for the establishment of trading posts, three tracts or parcels of land, of six miles square each, at such places as the United States, in Congress assembled, shall think proper; which posts, and the lands annexed to them, shall be to the use and under the government of the United States of America.

Article 4th.—If any citizen of the United States, or other person, not being an Indian, shall attempt to settle on any of the lands hereby allotted to the Indians to live and hunt on, such persons shall forfeit the protection of the United States of America, and the Indians may punish him or not as they please.

Article 5th.—If any Indian or Indians, or persons residing among them, or who shall take refuge in their nation, shall commit a robbery or murder, or other capital crime, on any citizen of the United States of America, or person under their protection, the tribe to which such offender may belong, or the nation, shall be bound to deliver him or them up to be punished according to the ordinances of the United States in Congress assembled: provided, that the punishment shall not be greater than if the robbery or murder, or other capital crime, had been committed by a citizen on a citizen.

Article 6th.—If any citizen of the United States of America, or person under their protection, shall commit a robbery or murder, or other capital crime, on any Indian, such offender or offenders shall be punished in the same manner as if the robbery or murder, or other capital crime, had been committed on a citizen of the United States of America; and the punishment shall be in the presence of some of the Choctaws, if any will attend at the time and place; and that they may have an opportunity so to do, due notice, if practicable, of the time of such intended punishment shall be sent to some one of the tribe.

[10] The southwestern boundary of the Choctaws' country, as thus defined, left the "Natchez district" outside their limits.

Article 7th.—It is understood that the punishment of the innocent, under the idea of retaliation, is unjust, and shall not be practiced on either side, except where there is a manifest violation of this treaty; and then it shall be preceded, first by a demand of justice; and if refused, then by a declaration of hostilities.

Article 8th.—For the benefit and comfort of the Indians, and for the prevention of injuries or oppressions on the part of the citizens or Indians, the United States in Congress assembled shall have the sole and exclusive right of regulating the trade with the Indians, and managing all their affairs in such manner as they think proper.

Article 9th.—Until the pleasure of Congress be known, respecting the 8th article, all traders, citizens of the United States of America, shall have liberty to go to any of the tribes or towns of the Choctaws, to trade with them, and they shall be protected in their persons and property and kindly treated.

Article 10th.—The said Indians shall give notice to the citizens of the United States of America, of any designs which they may know or suspect to be formed in any neighboring tribe, or by any person whomsoever, against the peace, trade, or interest, of the United States of America.

Article 11th.—The hatchet shall be forever buried, and the peace given by the United States of America, and friendship re-established between the said States on the one part, and all the Choctaw nation on the other part, shall be universal, and the contracting parties shall use their utmost endeavors to maintain the peace given as aforesaid, and friendship established.

In witness of all and every thing herein determined, between the United States of America and all the Choctaws, we, the underwritten commissioners, by virtue of our full powers, have signed this definitive treaty, and have caused our seals to be hereunto affixed.

Done at Hopewell, on the Keowee, third day of January, 1786 L. S. (Locus Sigilli) Place of the Seal.

[Cushman then continues with the text of succeeding treaties made with the Choctaws. A summary of these seems sufficient, for Cushman has made some errors in copying and the correct text is easily available in Government documents. His interpretation of proper names has been retained, however. By the treaty concluded December 17, 1801, at Fort Adams on the Mississippi the Choctaws consented to the construction of a road through their country. This became the famous Natchez Trace, continuing through the lands of the Chickasaws and Cherokees to Nashville, Tennessee. Again he attempts to correct and translate the names of the Choctaw signatories—]

Corruption: Tuskana Hopia, his x mark. Original: Tushka hopaii, Warrior of the War Chief.

Corruption: Toota Homo, his x mark. Original: Tobu humma, made red.

Corruption: Mingo Hom Massatubby[11], his x mark. Original: Miko humma ubi (i, as ib) Red chief killer.

This treaty was also signed by twenty-two other Choctaws, whose names are omitted.

[Then follows the treaty signed at Fort Confederation on the Tombigbee, October 17, 1802, which provided for the commission that retraced and re-marked the old British boundary on the southeast of the Choctaw country—] which begins on the left bank of the Chickasaw-hay river, and runs thence in an easterly direction to the right bank of the Tombigbee River, terminating on the same, at a bluff, well known by the name of Hacha Tiggeby (corruption of Hacha toh bichi. You are very White.)

[And as usual Cushman gives his interpretation of Choctaw names—]

In behalf of the lower towns and Chickasaw-hay.

Corruption: Tuskona Hoopopio, his x mark. Original: Tushkahopaii. Warrior of the Prophet.

[11] This seems to be the name of the great district chief, Moshulatubbee.

Corruption: Mingo Hoopoio, his x mark. Original: Mikohopaii. King of War-chief.

The names of twelve Choctaws are omitted who signed this treaty.

[Cushman then quotes the report of the boundary commission (involving also a small land cession) as confirmed August 31, 1803—] Beginning at the channel of the Hatche at the point where the line of limits between the United States and Spain crosseth the same, thence up the channel of said river to the confluence of the Chickasaw-hay (corruption of Chikasahha) and Buckhatannee (corruption of Buchchah, a range of hills) and Hantah (to be bright) rivers, thence up the channel of the Buchhatannee to Boque Hooma (corruption of Bokhumma), Red Creek, thence up said creek to a pine tree standing on the left bank of the same, and blazed on two of its sides, about twelve links southwest of an old trading path, leading from the town of Mobile to the Hewanee towns, much worn, but not in use at the present time. From this tree we find the following bearings and distances, viz: south 54 degrees 30 minutes west, one chain, one link, a blackgum, north 39 degrees east, one chain, 75 links, water oak; thence with the old British line of partition in its various inflections to a mulberry post, planted on the right bank of the main branch of Sintee Bogue, (cor. of Sinti Bok and pro. as Seen-tih Boke, Snake Creek) where it makes a sharp turn to the southeast, a large broken top cypress tree standing near the opposite bank of the creek, which is about three poles wide, thence down the said creek to the Tombigbee and Mobile Rivers to the above mentioned line of limits between the United States and Spain, and with the same to the point of beginning; and we, the said commissioners plenipotentiary, do ratify and confirm the said line of demarkation, and do recognize and acknowledge the same to be the boundary which shall separate and distinguish the land ceded to the United States, between the Tombigbee, Mobile and Pascagola Rivers, from that which has not been ceded by the said

Choctaw Nation. (Tombigbee, corruption of Itombiikbi, Boxmaker; Mobile, corruption of Momabinah, A lodge for all; Pascagola, corruption of Pushkaokla, Bread people). In testimony whereof, we hereunto affix our hands and seals, this 31st day of August, 1803, to triplicates of this tenor and date. Done at Hoe-Buck-intoopa, (corruption of Hoburk, coward intakobi lazy) the day and year above written, and in the 27th year of the independence of the United States.

JAMES WILKERSON.

Corrupted: Mingo Pooscoos, his x mark; Original: Mikopuscus (pro. Mik-o Poos-koosh) Infant King.

Corrupted: Alatala Hooma, his x mark. Original: Alatalihhumma, (pro. Ar-lah-tah-lih hoom-mah.)

Witnesses present: Joseph Chambers, U. S. Factor.

Young Gaines, Interpreter.

John Bowyer, Capt. 2nd U. S. Regt.

We the commissioners of the Choctaw Nation, duly appointed, and the chiefs of the said nation who reside on the Tombigbee River, next to Sintee Bogue, do acknowledge to have received from the United States of America, by the hand of Brigadier General James Wilkerson, as a consideration in full for the confirmation of the above concession, the following articles, viz.: fifteen pieces of strands, three rifles, one hundred and fifty blankets, two hundred and fifty pounds of powder, two hundred and fifty pounds of lead, one bridle, and man's saddle, and one black silk handkerchief.

Mingo Pooscoos, his x mark,

Alatala Hooma, his x mark,

Commissioners of the Choctaw Nation.

Corrupted: Pio Mingo, his x mark; Original: Pin Miko, Our chief.

Corrupted: Pasa Mastubby Mingo, his x mark. Original: Pisahmiahubih[12] Miko, (pro. Pe-sah-me-ah-ub-ih Miko. To see, go ahead and kill the chief).

---

[12] This apparently is Pushmataha. His home seems to have been near St. Stephens in the ceded area. Cushman locates him there in 1811.

In November, 1805, another portion of their country was ceded to the United States; and in October, 1816, still another portion; and October 18, 1820, another portion was ceded for and in consideration of a tract of country west of the Mississippi River, being between the Arkansas and Red Rivers. Then in September, 1830, the climax of the white man's greediness as far as the Choctaws were involved, was reached, by forcing that people to cede the last acre of land they possessed east of the Mississippi River. And thus by hypocrisy, deception, fraud, misrepresentation and unblushing falsehood, has the octupus arm of white avarice seized the Indians' country from Maine to California; and yet, year by year, generation by generation, the grasp widens and tightens, and creeps further and further upon them until with its stiff-necked, incorrigible brutishness, its hissing is heard, throughout the length and breadth of the land, vibrating upon that harp of a thousand strings that still remains in tune to the same old howl "Open to white settlement, open up to white settlement."[13]

[By the treaty of November 16, 1805, the Choctaws ceded to the United States a huge tract of land across the southern part of their country, for which they received $50,500 and a permanent annuity of three thousand dollars in goods. Again Cushman gives his interpretation of Choctaw place names along the new boundary—]

Beginning at a branch of the Humecheeto (Cor. of Humma chitoh, being greatly red), where the same is intersected by the path leading from Natches to the county of Washington, usually called McClary's path, thence eastwardly along McClary's path, to the east or left bank of Pearl River, thence on such a direct line as would touch the lower end of a bluff on the left bank of Chickasaw-hay river, the first above Hiyoo wunnee (corruption of Hiohlih, Standing, uni, berries) towns, called Broken Bluff, thence in

---

[13] In the demand for the opening of the Indian Territory the land hunger of the American frontier had reached the greatest intensity in its long history and its white settlement was in rapid and dramatic process at the time of Cushman's writing.

a direct line nearly parallel with the river, to a point whence an east line of four miles in length will intersect the river below the lowest settlement at present occupied and improved in the Hiyoo wunnee town, thence still east four miles, thence in a direct line nearly parallel with the river to a point to be run from the lower end of the Broken Bluff to Falukta bunnee (corruption of Falakna, a fox squirrel, and bunna, one who wants) on the Tombigbee river, four miles from the Broken Bluff, thence along the said line to Falukta bunnee, thence east to the boundary between the Creeks and Choctaws on the ridge dividing the waters running into the Alabama from those running into the Tombigbee, thence southwardly along the said ridge and boundary to the southern point of the Choctaw claim. Reserving a tract of two miles square, run on meridians and parallels, so as to include the houses and improvements in the town of Fuket chee poonta (corruption of Fakit chipinta, and pro, as Fah-kit che-pin-tah, Turkey very small), and reserving also a tract of 5120 acres, beginning at a post on the left bank of Tombigbee River opposite the lower end of Hatch a tigbee (corruption of Hachotukni—pro. Harcho-tuk-nih, Loggerhead turtle) Bluff, thence ascending the river four miles front and two back; one half for the use of Alzira, the other half for the use of Sophia, daughters of Samuel Mitchell, by Molly, a Choctaw woman.

[The names of all three of the great district chiefs— Apukshunnubbee, Moshulatubbee, and Pushmataha—appear here for the first time in recognizable form, as the United States engaged—] to give to each of the three great medal Mingoes Puckshunnubbee (corruption of Apucksheubih) Mingo Hoomastubbee (corruption of Hummaubi, Red Killer) and Poosshamattaha (corruption of Anumaishtayaubih, a messenger of death), five hundred dollars, in consideration of past services in their Nation, and also to pay to each of them an annuity of one hundred and fifty dollars during their continuance in office.

[In the provision following and in the signatures are additional Cushman translations of proper names—]

Article 4.—The Mingoes, chiefs, and warriors of the Choctaws, certify that a tract of land not exceeding fifteen hundred acres, situated between the Tombigbee River and Jackson's Creek, the front or river line extending down the river from a blazed white oak, standing on the left bank of the Tombigbee, near the head of the shoal, next above Hobukenloopa (corruption of Hobachit Yukpa, a laughing echo), and claimed by John McGrew, was, in fact, granted to the said McGrew by Opiomingo Hesmitta, (corruption of the words Hopoamikohimmittah, The hungry young chief) and others, many years ago, and they respectfully request the government of the United States to establish the claim of the said McGrew to the said fifteen hundred acres.

*   *   *   *   *   *   *   *   *   *

Done on Mount Dexter, in Pooshapukanuk (corruption of Pashiakona, Unto the dust) in the Choctaw country, this the 6th of November, 1805, and of the independence of the United States of America the thirtieth.

James Robertson,
Silas Dinsmore,
Commissioners.

Puchunnubbee, his x mark,
Mingo Hoomastubbe, his x mark,
Pooshamattah, his x mark,

Great Medal Mingoes.

Chiefs and Warriors:—

Corruption Ookchummee, his x mark; original, Okchulih, Tiller of the land.

Corruption Tushamiubbee, his x mark; Tusuhahmutubih, to whoop and also kill, and thirty-one others.

[A treaty concluded October 24, 1816, and signed by the three district chiefs ceded all the remaining Choctaw land east of the Tombigbee, a large tract—] lying east of the following boundary, beginning at the mouth of Oakti-

buha (corruption of O-ka, water, it-tib-ih, having fought)
River, the Chickasaw boundary, and running thence down
the Tombigbee River, until it intersects the northern boundary of a cession made to the United States by the Choctaws at Mount Dexter, on the 16th of November, 1805.

[By the important treaty signed October 18, 1820, near
Doak's Stand on the Natchez Trace, the Choctaws exchanged the southwestern one-third of their remaining
homeland for a wild tract beyond the Mississippi between
the Canadian-Arkansas and Red Rivers, comprising the
southern half of the present Oklahoma and a large area in
Arkansas. Cushman's translation of proper names appears
in only one boundary location—"Black Creek, or Bogue
Loose (original Bok Lusa)." The object of the exchange
was stated in the preamble—]

Preamble: Whereas, it is an important object with the
President of the United States, to promote the civilization
of the Choctaw Indians, by the establishment of schools
amongst them; and to perpetuate them as a nation, by
exchanging, for a small part of their land here, a country
beyond the Mississippi river, where all, who live by hunting, and will not work, may be collected and settled together: And whereas, it is desirable to the State of Mississippi, to obtain a small part of the land belonging to said
nation; for the mutual accommodation of the parties, and
for securing the happiness and protection of the whole
Choctaw nation, as well as preserving that harmony and
friendship which so happily subsists between them and the
United States, James Monroe, President of the United States
of America, by Andrew Jackson, of the State of Tennessee,
Major General in the army of the United States, and General Thomas Hinds, of the State of Mississippi, commissioners plenipotentiary of the United States, on the one part,
and the Mingoes, head men, and warriors, of the Choctaw
Nation, in full council assembled, on the other part, have
freely and voluntarily entered into the following articles.

[The new boundary in Mississippi should be plainly marked, and should remain—] without alteration until the period at which said Nation shall become so civilized and enlightened as to be made citizens of the United States, and Congress shall lay off a limited parcel of land for the benefit of each family included in the Nation.

[To assist in establishing those who should elect to remove to the new home on the frontier the United States engaged—] to give to each warrior a blanket, kettle, rifle gun, bullet mould and nippers, and ammunition for hunting and defense, for one year. Said warrior shall also be supplied with corn to support him and his family, for the same period, and whilst travelling to the country above ceded to the Choctaw Nation.

[Of the land ceded in Mississippi the United States undertook to sell fifty-four mile-square sections for the establishment of a Choctaw school fund, three-fourths to be used in Mississippi, one-fourth in the West. Cushman, looking back on the development and subsequent disruption of these schools when the remaining Choctaws were driven West only ten years later, makes the bitter comment—]

But what was the result of this appropriation? In ten years after, when hundreds of dollars, proceeds of the sale of the fifty-four sections of their own lands, had been used in establishing schools, and these schools were flourishing all over their country, I speak of that east of the Mississippi River, and though, in spite of embarrassment, adversities and misfortunes, they were making the most rapid progress in civilization and Christianity, a quietus was placed upon everything by the United States forcing them to sell their entire land possessions to them, and driving them to the distant wilderness in the west where they had driven the former, there to civilize themselves by means of a "blanket, flap, kettle, rifle gun, moulds and nippers," while their schools and the "fifty-four sections of land" became things of the past to the Choctaw, to be heard of no more by them.

[The treaty stipulated that Choctaws owning improvements in the ceded land should receive compensation. (This included Apukshunnubbee.) Also a company of Choctaws had served under Andrew Jackson in the capture of Pensacola during the War of 1812, and apparently had not received their pay. Now the treaty stated that they should "be paid whatever is due them over and above the value of the blanket, shirt, flap, and leggins, which have been delivered to them." Provision was also made for the successor of Moshulatubbee, the district chief who had received an annuity under the treaty of 1805—]

Whereas the father of the beloved chief Mushulatubbee, (original Mosholatubil, with whom I was personally acquainted), of the lower towns, for and during his life, did receive from the United States the sum of one hundred and fifty dollars annually; it is hereby stipulated, that his son and successor, [14] Mushulatubbee, shall annually be paid the same amount during his natural life, to commence from the ratification of this treaty.

[As usual Cushman has his own way of writing the names the signers. Apparently in this case he failed to recognize the name of Pushmataha—]

Medal Mingoes:—

Corrupted: Puckshenubbee, his x mark. Original: A-pak-foh-li-chihub-ih.

Corrupted: Poohawattaha, his x mark. Original: Arnoom-pah-ish-tam-yah-ub-ih.

One hundred and twenty-eight names of Choctaws, who signed this treaty are omitted.

[14] This is puzzling. Choctaw children belonged to the moiety of their mother; thus they were under the authority of their mother and their maternal uncles rather than their father, and inheritance was from maternal uncle to nephew rather than from father to son. The second Moshulatubbee must have been a nephew rather than a son of his predecessor, or else descent was disregarded in his selection as district chief.

Dr. Gideon Lincecum who lived in Columbus, Mississippi, several years prior to the exodus of the Choctaws, was present at the treaty held by General Jackson and General Hinds at a place known as Doak's Stand, in the Choctaw Nation, in the fall of 1820. The object of the United States in holding this treaty was to exchange all that country where the five civilized tribes now reside south of the Canadian River for a strip of territory from the lower and western part of the then Choctaw Nation, known as the Huch-chalusachitoh—pro. as Huch-chah (River) loo-sah (black) che-toh (big) i. e. Big Black River country. A great many Choctaws were in attendance, and after General Jackson had read the commission and the President's letter to them, in a lengthly speech he explained the object and purpose for which they had been called together. He declared to them, that "to promote their civilization by the establishing of schools among them, and to perpetuate them as a nation, was a constant solicitude with the president of the United States." (But the sequel soon proved that "solicitude" to be false.)

"To enable the President to effect this great national and very desirable object to accommodate the growing state of Mississippi and thereby secure greater safety and protection to the Choctaws and their seminaries of learning at home, it was proposed by him to exchange for a small part of their lands here, a large country beyond the Mississippi River, where all who live by hunting and will not work, and who by the nature of their mode of life are widely scattered, may be collected and settled together in a country of tall trees, many water courses, rich lands and high grass, abounding in game of all kinds—buffalo, bear and deer, antelope, beaver, turkeys, honey, and fruits of many kinds, in this great hunting ground they may be settled near together for protection and to be able to pursue their peculiar vocation without danger.

"Another great benefit to be derived from this arrangement would be the removal from among the people at home who are already inclined to progress and civilization of the bad example of those who, in their wild wandering propensities do not care for improvement. The project recommends itself to the thinking portion of the industrious community, while it will provide ample means for the protection of the careless stragglers of the Nation.

"The tract of territory which the President proposes to exchange for the Big Black River country here, lies between the Arkansas and Red Rivers. It is a large and extended country. Beginning where the lower boundary line of the Cherokees strikes the Arkansas River, thence up the Arkansas to the Canadian River fork; thence up the Canadian to its source, thence due south to Red River, thence down Red River to a point three miles below the mouth of Little River which enters into Red River from the north, thence on a direct line to place of beginning.

"This extensive rich territory is offered in exchange by the President for the little strip of land in the lower part of the present Choctaw Nation. It is a much larger territory than the whole of your possessions this side of the Mississippi River, and is certainly a very liberal proposition. What say the chiefs and Choctaw people to this great offer?"

After the pipe lighters had finished handing the pipes around and order was again restored, Pushmataha arose and, addressing himself to his own people first, told them the man who had just finished his big talk was the great warrior, General Jackson, of whom they had all so often heard. Many of them had, no doubt, seen him and, like himself, had served under him in many successful battles. His great character as a man and warrior, in addition to the commission he bore from the President of the United States, demanded from the Choctaw people respectful replies from his propositions, and for that purpose he moved that the council adjourn until the middle of the day, tomorrow, which motion was carried and the council adjourned.

The chiefs and head men went into secret council that night, where they very deliberately discussed the merits of the propositions that had been made by the United States commissioners. They considered it a wise and benevolent proposition, and, notwithstanding that the land they offered to exchange the large tract of western territory for was worth more to them at this time than two such countries as the one they were offering, with the Choctaws, "the thing stood very differently, particularly in relation to the fixing of a home for our wandering hunters in the midst of a game country. However, good as the proposition is, we must in this case adopt the white man's rules in the transaction and get all we can from them. General Jackson is a great man, but in his talk in making the proposition to exchange countries he has been guilty of misrepresentations which he knows are such, and others which, perhaps, he is not apprised of their being false. Our plan is to meet him in the treaty with his own policy and let the hardiest reap the profits. If we can do no better we will take them at the offer already made." This much and the appointment of Pushmataha to do the talking, next day was the result of the secret council.

When at 12 o'clock the next day the council had assembled, the commissioners inquired of the chiefs if they had come to any conclusion on the subject of the propositions made to them yesterday in relation to the exchange of countries? Pushmataha arose and said that the chiefs and leaders of his people had appointed him to reply to the commissioners on the subject. He remarked that he fully appreciated the magnitude of the proposition and his incompetency to do it justice, especially while in contact with two such master minds as he would have to deal with. He further remarked that when any business was intended to be fairly and honestly transacted it made no difference as to the capacity of the contracting parties. One party might be a great man like General Jackson, the other a fool, but the result would be the same. The wise man in such cases would protect the rights of the fool, holding him firm on safe ground. From what he had already heard he had discovered that the great transaction now about to take place between friendly nations, was not to be conducted on those equitable principles, and that it would not be safe for him, fool as he was, to rely upon any such expectations. He was to come to the contest with such powers as he possessed, do the best he could, and his people must be satisfied and abide the results and consequences.

The object and benefits to be derived by the United States were very great and desirable, or they would not have sent two of their greatest warrior generals to conduct the treaty in their behalf. He was friendly toward the United States, and particularly to their two distinguished agents, for he had served under them and side by side in the hour of peril and deadly strife, had aided them in the acquisition of Florida and a considerable portion of the Muscogee country with his manhood, and as many of his countrymen as he could persuade to take part in the dangers of the enterprise. Under all these considerations he intended to strike the bargain in the exchange of countries with them if he could. He thought it was one of those kind of swaps, if it could be fairly made, that would accommodate both parties. He should do his best, and he hoped to succeed in presenting the thing in such a form as to convince the commissioners that further misrepresentation would be entirely unnecessary. He then sat down.

General Jackson arose and gravely remarked: "Brother Push, you have uttered some hard words. You have accused me of misrepresentation, and indirectly, of the desire to defraud the red people in behalf of my government. These are heavy charges, charges of a very serious character. You must explain yourself in a manner that will clear them up or I shall quit you." Pushmataha then arose and made a long explanatory speech, but its length precludes its production here.

The closing portion was, "I shall take much pleasure in my explanation to render a plain and irrefutable interpretation of what I have said, and which will present in a very

clear light the misrepresentations in relation to the quality
of the country west of the Mississippi and the size of the
country on this side of the great river.

"In the first place, he speaks of the country you wish to
obtain in the swap as a little slip of land at the lower part
of the present Choctaw Nation, whereas it is a very considerable tract of country. He has designated the boundaries
of it, and I am very familiar with the entire tract of land it
will cut off from us.

"In the second place, he represents the country he
wishes to exchange for the 'little slip' as being a very extensive country 'of tall trees, many water courses, rich lands
and high grass, abounding in game of all kinds, buffalo,
bear, elk, deer, antelope, beavers, turkey, honey and fruits
of many kinds.' I am also well acquainted with that country. I have hunted there often, have chased the Comanche
and Wichita over those endless plains, and they too have
sometimes chased me there. I know the country well. It is
indeed a very extensive land, but a vast amount of it is poor
and sterile, trackless and sandy deserts; nude of vegetation
of any kind. As to tall trees, there is no timber anywhere,
except on the botom lands, and it is low and brushy even
there. The grass is everywhere short; as for the game, it is
not plenty, except buffalo and deer. The buffalo, in the
western portion of the tract described, and on the great
plains into which it reaches, are very numerous and easily
taken. Antelopes, too, are there, and deer almost everywhere, except in the dry grassless, sandy desert. There are
but few elk, and the bear are plenty only on the Red River
bottom lands. Turkey are plentiful on all the water courses.
There are, however, but few beaver, and fruit and honey
are a rare thing. The bottoms on the river are generally
good soil, but liable to inundation during the spring season,
and in summer the rivers and creeks dry up or become so
salty that the water is unfit for use. It is not at these times
always salty, but often bitter and will purge a man like
medicine.

"This account differs widely from the description given by my friend yesterday, and constitutes what, in my reply to him, I styled a misrepresentation. He has proven to me by that misrepresentation and one great error that he is entirely ignorant of the geography of the country he is offering to swap, and therefore I shall acquit him of an intentional fraud. The testimony that he bears against himself, in regard to his deficiency of a knowledge of that far-off country manifests itself in the fact that he has offered to swap to me an undefined portion of Mexican territory. He offers to run the line up the Canadian River to its source, and thence due south to the Red River. Now, I know that a line running due south from the source of the Canadian would never touch any portion of Red River, but would go into the Mexican posessions beyond the limits even of my geographical knowledge."[15]

General Jackson interrupting him, said: "See here, Brother Push, you must be mistaken. Look at this map. It will prove to you at once that you are laboring under a great geographical error yourself," and he spread out the map.

Pushmataha examined it very minutely, while General Jackson traced out and read the names of the rivers for him. Pushmataha said: "The paper is not true." He then proceeded to mark out on the ground with the handle of the pipe hatchet, which he held in his hand while speaking, the Canadian and the upper branches of Red River, and said, holding the end of the hatchet handle on the ground, "there is the north;" then rapidly tracing a deep line on the ground, "here is the south, and, you see, the line between the two points does not touch any portion of Red River, and I declare to you that it is the natural position of the country and its water course."

[15] This analysis is correct except that Cushman inadvertently uses the word "Mexican" instead of "Spanish" in referring to a time before Mexican independence. The Canadian heads much farther west than the Red River; hence a line drawn south from the former would never strike the latter. And according to the treaty made with Spain the previous year, which fixed the boundary at the hundredth meridian, both rivers headed in Spanish territory. This geographical misconception was embodied in the treaty, but of course it had no legal effect; the United States could not grant Spanish land to the Choctaws.

"You must be mistaken," said General Jackson; "at any rate, I am willing to make good the proposition I have named."

"Very well," replied Pushmataha, "and you must not be surprised nor think hard of me if I call your attention to another subject within the limits of the country you designate west of the Mississippi, which you do not seem to be apprised of. The lower portion of the land you propose to swap to us is a pretty good country. It is true that as high up the Arkansas river as Fort Smith the lands are good and timber and water plenty, but there is an objectionable difficulty in the way. It was never known before, in any treaty made by the United States with the Red people, that their commissioners were permitted to offer to swap off or sell any portion of their citizens. What I ask to know in the stipulations of the present treaty is, whether the American settlers you propose to turn over to us in this exchange of countries are, when we get them in possession, to be considered Indians or white people?"

General Jackson replied and told the speaking chief that, "As for the white people on the land, it is a mere matter of moon-shine. There are perhaps a few hunters scattered over the country, and I will have them ordered off."

"I beg your pardon," said Pushmataha, "there are a great many of them, many of them substantial, well-to-do settlers, with good houses and productive farms, and they will not be ordered off."

"But," said General Jackson, "I will send my warriors, and by the eternal, I'll drive them into the Mississippi or make them leave."

"Very well," replied the chief, "and now the matter is settled as far as the land west of the Mississippi River is concerned. We will now consider the boundary and country the Choctaws are to give to you for it, and if we can agree upon that the trade will be completed. You have defined its boundaries and they include a very valuable tract of country of considerable extent, capable of producing corn, cotton, wheat and all the crops the white man cultivates. Now, if we do agree on terms and run this line, it must, as a part of this contract, be very clearly understood, and put on paper in a form that will not die or wear out, that no alternation shall be made in the boundaries of that portion of our territory that will remain, until the Choctaw people are sufficiently progressed in the arts of civilization to become citizens of the States, owning land and homes of their own, on an equal footing with the white people. Then it may be surveyed and the surplus sold for the benefit of the Choctaw people."

"That," said General Jackson, "is a magnificent arrangement and we consent to it readily."

An adjournment of the council was then made until 10 o'clock next day to allow the chiefs and warriors time to discuss the treaty, and the secretary of the commissioners for preparing his big paper, the treaty, ready for the seal.

Next day at the appointed time the council met and General Hinds, one of the commissioners of the United States, made a long talk to the chiefs and warriors.

Pushmataha was the speaking chief, and demanded the following additional remuneration:

1st—"That the United States furnish each of those who chose to go to the new country a good rifle, bullet mould, camp-kettle, one blanket and powder and lead to last one year. Also corn for one year."

2nd—"Out of the land about to be swapped, fifty-four sections of a mile square shall be surveyed and sold to the best bidder by the United States for the purpose of raising a fund to support Choctaw schools, all to be placed in the hands of the President of the United States to be dealt out by him for school purposes only in the Choctaw Nation."

3rd—"The United States to pay for military services of all the Choctaw warriors during the campaign to Pensacola."

4th—"Payment to all having good houses and residing on the ceded territory."

All the propositions were agreed to by the United States commissioners. The commissioners first signed the treaty, then Moshulatubbee, Apukshunnubbee and Pushamataha, the head chiefs of the upper, middle and lower districts of the Choctaw Nation. Then 100 leaders and warriors signed with their names or x mark. All were pleased and satisfied.

Pushmataha was then requested to speak. His effort, now on record, would equal Daniel Webster in any of his famous orations.

He concluded as follows: "I most solemnly declare that on my part the sacred words 'perpetual friendship,' included in the last article of the treaty, shall never be violated or suffer the slightest infringement. We have made many treaties with the United States, all conducted in peace and amicably carried out, but this last one, the greatest of all, has been peculiar in its stipulations, giving another and a stronger proof of the fostering care and protecting intentions of the United States toward their Choctaw friends. In all our treaties we have been encouraged by them to institute schools, urging us to prepare ourselves as fast as possible to become citizens and members of that great Nation. In the treaty which has been concluded today the subject of schools has been more particularly urged, and appropriations more extensively provided than any other former treaty. The applauding murmurs on that subject have passed through the camps of the Red people. It meets their approbation. They will most certainly succeed. It is a peculiar trait in the Choctaw character, that all the national movements turn out to be successes. I am pleased to hear so many speaking favorably of school institutions. It tells me that they will have them. It is a national sentiment, and I here venture the prediction, for I am considered a sort of prophet anyway, that the time will come, and there are many children and some grown men here today, who will live to see it, when the highly improved Choctaw shall hold office in the councils of that great Nation of white people, and in their wars with the Nations of the earth, mixed up in the armies of the white man, the fierce war whoops of the Choctaw warrior shall strike terror and melt the hearts of an invading foe. Mind that; Pushmataha has this day declared it and his words of prophecy are not uttered foolishly. To the chiefs, leaders and warriors of my countrymen I may say: Return to your homes and forget not the words of this great treaty to which so many of you subscribed your names with your white brothers to the same big paper, this bright day. Perpetual friendship is placed on that paper. You have all agreed to stand to it and manifested your consent by having your names placed on the big paper, where they will remain long after you have all passed away to the good hunting grounds."

See the low duplicity and misrepresentation adopted by Jackson to mislead Pushmataha, in regard to the country west of the Mississippi River that he was endeavoring to exchange with the Choctaws; for a portion of their west; and today, after three quarters of a century has past, it stands as a living testimony of the honesty and truthfulness of the noble Choctaw chief. And when he pointed to the white settlers occupying a part of the offered land—mark the threat of Jackson, "I will send my warriors, and, by the eternal, I'll drive them into the Mississippi or make them leave"; which was never executed; and after remaining five years, the quiet of the Choctaws was again disturbed on October 20, 1825, by the voice of the white man howling: "More land!" "More land!" Again were they summoned from their peaceful homes by their "Great Father at Washington" to cede to the United States that portion of their land still occupied by the aforesaid settlers. And in ten years after Pushmataha had made the treaty of 1820 (the last he ever made) the United States Government had defrauded the Choctaws out of every acre of their country east of the Mississippi. The old hero had died in Washington City six years before.

[Cushman then gives the text of the treaty signed at Washington, January 20, 1825, by which the Choctaws for a perpetual annuity of six thousand dollars retroceded to the United States that part of their Western grant lying in the present Arkansas and filled with white settlers; and the United States undertook to remove all the settlers west of the new boundary—a provision that was subsequently enforced in spite of the outraged protests of the squatters. Of the three district chiefs who had been called to Washington to negotiate this treaty Apukshunnubbee had died on the way and Pushmataha after arriving at the capital. The Choctaw delegates recommended Robert Cole as Apukshunnubbee's successor, and the treaty accordingly provided that Cole should —] receive the medal which appertains to the office of chief, and, also, an annuity from the United States of one hundred and fifty dollars a year, during his natural life, as was received by his predecessor.

[Again Cushman gives his version of the names of the signers —]

Corrupted: Mooshulatubbee, his x mark. Original: Mosholihubih.

> Robert Cole, his x mark.
> Daniel McCurtain, his x mark.
> Tushka Anumpuli Shali, his x mark.
> Pro. Tush-kah (warrior) shah-lih (messenger.)
> Red Fort, his x mark.

Corrupted: Nittuckachie, his x mark. Original: Nitak (a, as ah) a chih—To suggest the day.

> David Folsom.
> J. C. McDonald, Talkative warrior.

Tradition affirms there were several missionaries (Roman Catholic) among the Choctaws in 1735; and that the Reverend Father Baudouin, the actual superior general of the mission, resided eighteen years among the Choctaws. I have seen no record of the White Race ever manifesting any further interest in the southern Indians' welfare either of a temporal or spiritual nature, down through slowly revolving years to that of 1815; at which time may be dated the establishment of the first Protestant mission among the southern Indians. This mission, which was named Brainard, was established among the Cherokees by Rev. Cyrus Kingsbury, under the jurisdiction of the Old School Presbyterian Board of Foreign Missions, in Boston, Massachusetts, who arrived in that Nation, in company with his assistant laborers, Mr. and Mrs. Williams, January 13, 1815.

In 1818, Mr. Kingsbury, in company with Mr. and Mrs. Williams, left Brainard in the charge of Rev. Daniel S. Buttrick (who arrived there January 4, 1818, and remained as a missionary among the Cherokees until 1847, when his health failing, he went to Dwight Mission also in the Cherokee Nation, where he died June 8, 1851) and arrived in the Choctaw Nation near the last of June, 1818, and established a mission in a vast forest of lofty trees, three miles south of Yello Busha River (corruption from the Choctaw words Yaloba aiasha; Tadpoles abounding) and about thirty miles above its junction with the Yazoo (corruption of the Choctaw word Yoshuba—pro. as Yoh-shu-bah, and sig. Lost), and 400 miles distant from Brainard, which he named Eliot, in honor of the Rev. John Eliot, that distinguished missionary among the Indians of the New England States.

They went from Brainard to the Tennessee River, seven miles distant, by private conveyance, and there went by way of a boat, which had been engaged to carry them to the Muscle Shoals. A wagon was also placed upon the boat, by which they went from Muscle Shoals to the Chickasaw agency, two hundred miles away, where they abandoned the wagon, and crossed the country on horseback, directed alone by little paths that led through thickets and canebrakes, and safely arrived at the Yalobaaiasha settlement, where they were hospitably received by Capt. Perry (a half

breed) and many native families. On the following Sabbath
Mr. Kingsbury held a religious meeting and proclaimed
salvation through the Son of God, for the first time ever
proclaimed in the Choctaw Nation by the Protestant minister. Capt. Perry also supplied them with a house until
they were able to build for themselves.

In June, 1818, Moses Jewell and wife, John Kanouse
and wife, and Peter Kanouse left New York for New Orleans, and reached the Choctaw Nation, in the following
August. The first tree for the establishment of the Mission
was felled on August the 15th, 1818.

The Choctaws seemed to comprehend the benevolent
designs of the missionaries and received them with every
manifestation of friendship and good will; though some
misapprehension was indicated owing to the debased lives
of the white men (without a single white woman), with
whom the Choctaws had long associated.

Soon after came A. V. Williams (brother of L. S. Williams, who came with Cyrus Kingsbury) and Miss Varnum
and Miss Chase, whom Mr. Kingsbury met in New Orleans,
and there married Miss Varnum, with whom he had been
under matrimonial engagement before he entered the mission. They all returned to Eliot in February, 1819; then a
mission church was organized on the last Sabbath of the
following March, and the Lord's supper administered—the
first ever witnessed in the Choctaw Nation. Ten persons
composed the number of that church (all connected with
the mission), and the ten partook of that supper—a strange
and incomprehensible scene to the Choctaws, who gazed at
the novel sight with unassumed wonder.

Within ten months from the time Mr. Kingsbury and
Mr. Williams and Mrs. Williams arrived at the Ya-lo-ba-ai-
a-sha settlement, seven log houses had been erected and
completed, the largest 20x22, and the smallest, 12x16; and
also, had nearly completed a mill, stable and store-house,
and had nearly prepared timber enough for a school house,
kitchen, and dining-room, and had sawed by hand 9,000

feet of cypress and poplar plank with which to make furniture, floors, doors, etc., the principal labor of all which was done by employed Choctaws directed by the missionaries—so eager were they to assist their white friends who had come to live among them and bless them by their benevolent teachings; and before the school house was completed, eight children, through a false rumor that the school was opened, were brought over 160 miles to be entered. And thus the mission, without a school house, and also pressed by a great scarcity of provisions, was greatly perplexed; since, if the children were rejected, an unfavorable impression would be the inevitable result, and if they were received, those in the neighborhood would claim their equal rights to the same favor. However, it was resolved, upon due reflection, to receive them as the less of the two evils, and a little cabin was appropriated for a school house, and the school opened on the 19th of April, 1819, with ten pupils.

On the first of August, 1819, the mission was strengthened by the arrival of Dr. Pride and Isaac Fish, who was a farmer and blacksmith. Shortly after, the Choctaws convened in national council, which Mr. Kingsbury, through earnest solicitation of the Choctaws, attended. The subject of schools was discussed during the session of the council, in which Mr. Kingsbury took part, and among the other things suggested, also proposed that all who desired to have a school established among them should signify that desire by subscribing money, or live stock, as they preferred. At once a subscription was opened in the council, and a considerable amount of money was subscribed; Apakfohlichihubi[16] (sig. One who encircles to kill), the ruling chief, giving $200 of the same, while others gave 90 cows and calves, with the promise of as many more yearly, which was faithfully fulfilled; and thus the mission was, at once, amply stocked with cattle. A farm was soon opened and every

[16] Elsewhere I have changed the spelling of this name to Apukshunnubbee to conform to later Choctaw usage.

effort made to prepare for the reception and accommodation of as many pupils as might seek to enter the school.

The Chickasaws, learning of the school, made application for their children to attend the school, also, to which the Choctaw chiefs, though knowing that the children of the applicants of their own nation could not all be accommodated, finally gave their consent, fearing if they refused they would wound the feelings of their Chickasaw friends, but with the following proviso: That all Chickasaw children whose father or mother were Chickasaws, would be received into the school, and no others. Such was the zeal manifested for schools and churches among the Choctaws, from the opening of the first to the closing of the last, when despoiled of their ancient homes and driven to seek others in the distant west.

Soon after the opening of the schools a deep gloom threw its dark mantle over the mission in the sudden and unexpected killing of an aged Choctaw woman, named Illichih (pro. as Illich-ih, and sig, to cause to die,) and who lived about two miles from Eliot with a son (20 years of age) two daughters and two little grand-daughters, and had endeared herself to the missionaries by her many acts of kindness and much valuable assistance. The tragic affair happened thus:

A Choctaw girl, who lived about thirty miles distant, came, a short time before Mr. Kingsbury arrived, to visit some friends living near where Eliot was located. The girl was taken sick, and an old Choctaw woman—a conjuring doctress—proposed to cure her. She was at once employed in the case. After giving her patient a variety of root and herb decoctions, internally and also externally applied for several days, at the same time chanting her incantations and going through her wild ceremonies over and around her patient, she pronounced the girl convelescent and would recover; the father was duly informed of the happy change, and came to take his daughter home; he remunerated the apparently successful physician by giving her a pony, and retired for the night intending to start for home with his daughter the next day; but during the night, the daughter suddenly became worse and expired in 24 hours. It was at once decided that her sudden demise was the result of a isht-ul-bih (witch ball) shot from an invisible rifle in the hands of a witch. Without delay her physician was consulted, who pronounced Illichih to be the witch who had shot the fatal bullet. Immediately the father with several other men, all armed, went to the home of Illichih and entered her cabin. She displayed her hospitality, so universal among all Indians, by setting before them the best she had; and after they had partaken of her scanty refreshments, the father suddenly sprang to his feet and, seizing her by the hair, cried out "Huch-ish-no fiopa uno chumpa; aholh-kun-na chish-o yokut, cha ish ai illih, (your life I bought; a witch you are, and must die)." To which Illichih, realizing her inevitable doom, calmly replied: "Chomi holubih, Cha ish moma yimmih (others lie, and you all believe)." In a moment she was stretched upon the floor a bleeding corpse.

When her son, who was absent from home at the time of the tragedy, returned, his feelings may be imagined but not described. He at once hastened to the missionaries, for whom he had often worked, and told them his tale of woe. Mr. Kingsbury immediately went to the tragic scene of death. He found the mangled corpse of his old friend lying upon the floor, partially covered with a blanket, with the two daughters and granddaughters sitting around it in the deepest grief, and their wailings but feebly expressed the anguish of their hearts. Mr. Kingsbury had a coffin made, and the missionaries, with the five children, laid poor Illichih in her humble grave. The missionaries performed religious ceremonies at the grave and after they had placed the coffin in its last resting place, the relatives and friends of the deceased placed all her clothing and the little money she possessed, and her bedding upon the coffin and filled up the grave—an ancient custom of the Choctaws, as well as of all North American Indians, who believed their deceased friends will have need of those things in the world beyond the grave.

On the following Sabbath after the tragic death of Il-lich-ih, Mr. Kingsbury preached from the appropriate text, "The dark places of the earth are full of the habitation of cruelty." He spoke fearlessly but calmly to his Choctaw audience of the errors and wickedness of their superstitions, and the abhorrence of the Great Spirit in the slaying of their own people through the belief that they are witches, who listened in profound silence and with the deepest attention; and though a few old women in the Yalobaaiasha district fell as sacrifices before the superstition of witchcraft, after the establishment of the Eliot mission, yet by the influence and exertions of the missionaries the horrible practire was soon forever stopped. Though they believed that there were white witches also, yet they never attempted to kill a white witch, upon the ground that the whites eat so much salt, that a witch ball fell harmless when shot against an Indian by a white witch.

But the kindness and interest displayed by the missionaries to and for Il-lich-ih quickly spread over the country, and so won the respect and confidence of the Choctaws that all who were in affliction sent for one or more of them; and also manifested great interest in their teachings and anxiety for the success of all improvements both in churches and schools, as suggested by those men and women of God.

In 1820, Mr. Kingsbury started from Eliot for the purpose of establishing a mission near the It-oom bih River, and arrived at the home of David Folsom, sixty miles distant, and then known by the name of "Puch-i A-nu-si," (pro. as Push-ih (Pigeon) Ar-noos-ih (Sleep) or Pigeon Roost) from the vast numbers of that beautiful bird that formerly roosted there. There Mr. Kingsbury secured the voluntary assistance of Colonel Folsom in the selection of a proper situation for the contemplated mission; after the second day's travel they reached Major John Pitchlynn's—a white man who, by marrying a Choctaw woman, had been adopted by the Choctaws according to their custom, and who, at that time, was acting as interpreter for the Unietd States Government, and, in conjunction with Colonel Folsom and others, was a zealous advocate of the civil and religious improvement of his people; while both expressed the utmost gratitude to Mr. Kingsbury for his interest manifested toward their people, and the bright prospect of the Choctaws' future as presented by the missionaries in schools and their preaching among and in behalf of their long neglected people.

After many days riding over the country, Mr. Kingsbury, Col. Folsom, and Major Pitchlynn selected a place for the mission station on a high point overlooking a grand prairie towards the south and west, and on the south banks of a stream flowing into a stream now known as Tibi (corruption of the Choctaw word It-tib-ih—to fight or having fought), where they at once erected a camp, preparatory to the establishment of the missionary station—to which Mr. Kingsbury gave the name Mayhew. A log cabin or two were soon erected by the aid of the neighboring Choctaws, also a garden and cornfield opened and planted, when Mr. Kingsbury retraced his steps to Eliot and safely arrived there March 29.

Soon the news of the establishment of another station, and the opening of another school, echoed and re-echoed throughout the Nation with astonishing rapidity; and applications were immediately made from various parts of the Nation for stations and schools also. And to prove the sincerity of their applications, councils were held, and appropriations were made in various parts of the Nation, for churches, schools, blacksmith shops, etc., and in 1820, annuities were appropriated to these objects to the amount of six thousand dollars annually to run for sixteen years. These annuities were for large tracts of land sold by the Choctaws to the United States. Their country was at that time divided into three districts, known as the western, northeastern and southern; called Upper Towns, Lower Towns, and Six Towns. Each district had a ruling chief, and each town a subordinate chief, captain, and warriors, who managed the local affairs of the people. Eliot was located in the western district, over which, at that time, Pushmataha was the ruling chief; Mayhew, in the northeastern, over which Apuk-shunnubbee was the chief and Moshulatubbee of the southern.

About this time (1820) the mumps followed by the measles desolated many families and even towns and villages in different parts of the nation owing to the ignorance of the Choctaws concerning the nature of the new diseases and their proper treatment.

In the same year Apukshunnubbee and Moshulatubbee, with seven other chiefs, visited Eliot and were highly elated at the progress of the pupils, and exhorted the children in strains of native eloquence to learn the teachings of the Holisso Holitopa (pro. as Ho-lis-soh Ho-le-to-pah, and sig. Book Holy (Bible), which told them how to be good. In a social conversation with Moshulatubbee while at Eliot, Mr. Kingsbury referred to the evils resulting to his people by the use of whiskey; after listening attentively for some time, he replied: "I never can talk with you good missionaries without hearing something about the drunkenness and laziness of the Choctaws. I wish I had traveled over the white man's country; then I would know whether my people are worse than every other people. But I am determined it shall no longer be thus said. I will summon a council, have a big talk and stop the whiskey; for I am tired of hearing my people called everywhere lazy and drunkards." He was as good as his word. The council was convened; the "big talk" had, and the whiskey banished from the Choctaw Nation, and kept away, until the Mississippi legislature in 1830 abrogated their laws, and turned, by the hand of arbitrary power, the corrupting and devastating channel of Whiskey River into their country, as the quickest means of securing their remaining lands, knowing their horror of the white man's laws with his whiskey as the protector and sustainer of human "Personal Liberty".["]

Early in the year 1820, an English traveller from Liverpool, named Adam Hodgson, who had heard of the Eliot mission when at home, visited the mission, though he had to turn from his main route of travel the distance of sixty miles. He, at one time on his sixty miles route, employed a Choctaw to conduct him ten or twelve miles on his new way, which he did, then received his pay and left him to finish his journey alone. Of this Choctaw guide Mr. Hodgson, as an example of noble benevolence and faithful trust, states: "After going about a mile, where we became confused in regard to the correct direction and were halting upon two opinions, my guide suddenly and unexpectedly appeared at my side, and pointed in the direction I should go, as he could not talk English. I thanked him and again we parted; but again becoming confused by a diverging path, half a mile distant, as suddenly and unexpectedly appeared again my guide who had still been, silently and unobserved, watching my steps. Again he set me right. and made signs that my course lay directly toward the sun, and then disappeared"; and by carefully keeping the course as directed by the Choctaw, Mr. Hodgson safely reached the mission, where he was warmly received by the missionaries.

Mr. Hodgson was duly introduced to the members of the mission, and then to the school of native American pupils, and expressed his surprise as well as heartfelt gratification with the account the teachers gave of the uncommon facility with which they acquired knowledge. After remaining a few days, Mr. Hodgson left, and was accompanied several miles on his way to Brainard by Mr. Kingsbury.

Mr. Hodgson, in a letter written shortly after he left Eliot, thus spoke his interview with Mr. Kingsbury in his own room at Eliot: "A log cabin, detached from the other

[17] At the time of Cushman's writing "Personal Liberty" was a favorite slogan of those who opposed prohibition of the liquor traffic.

wooden buildings, in the middle of a boundiess forest, in an
Indian country, consecrated, if I may be allowed the expression, by standing on missionary ground, and by forming at once the dormitory and the sanctuary of a man of
God; it seemed to be indeed the prophet's chamber, with
the 'bed and the table, the stool and the candlestick.'

"It contained, also, a little book-case, with a valuable
selection of valuable books, periodicals, biographical, and
devotional; among which I found many an old acquaintance
in this foreign land, and which enabled Mr. Kingsbury, in
his few moments of leisure, to converse with many, who
have long since joined the 'spirits of just men made perfect,'
or to sympathize with his fellow-laborers in Staheite, Africa,
or Hindoostan. About midnight we became thirsty with
talking so much; and Mr. Kingsbury proposed that we walk
to the spring, at a little distance. The night was beautifully
serene after the heavy showers of the preceding night; and
the coolness of the air, the fresh fragrance of the trees, the
deep stillness of the midnight hour, and the soft light which
an unclouded moon shed on the log cabins of the missionaries, contrasted with the dark shadows of the surrounding
forest, impressed me with feelings which I can never forget." In regard to the mission family, he said: "I was particularly struck with their humility, with their kindness of
manner towards one another, and the little attentions which
they seemed solicitous to reciprocate. They spoke very
lightly of their privations, and of the trials which the world
supposes to be their greatest; sensible, as they said, that
these are often experienced in at least as great degree, by
the soldier, the sailor, or even the merchant.

"Yet, in this country these trials are by no means
trifling. Lying out for two or three months, in the woods,
with their little babes in tents which cannot resist the rain
here, falling in torrents such as I never saw in England,
within sound of the nightly howling wolves, and occasionally visited by panthers, which have approached almost to
the door, the ladies must be allowed to require some cour-

age; while, during many seasons of the year, the gentlemen can not go 20 miles from home (and they are often obliged to go 30 or 40 for provisions) without swimming their horses over four or five creeks. Yet, as all their inconveniences are suffered by others with cheerfulness, from worldly motives, they would wish them suppressed in the missionary reports, if they were not calculated to deter many from engaging as missionaries, under the idea that it is an easy, retired life. Their real trials they stated to consist in their own imperfections, and in those mental maladies, which the retirement of a desert cannot cure. I was gratified by my visit to Eliot, this garden in a moral wilderness; and was pleased with the opportunity of seeing a missionary settlement in its infant state, before the wounds from recent separation from kindred and friends had ceased to bleed, and habit had rendered the missionaries familiar with the peculiarities of their novel situation. The sight of the children also, many of them still in Indian costumes, was most interesting. I could not help imagining, that, before me, might be some Alfred of this western world, the future founder of institutions which are to enlighten and civilize his country, some Choctaw Swartz or Eliot, destined to disseminate the blessings of Christianity from the Mississippi to the Pacific, from the Gulf of Mexico to the Frozen Sea. I contrasted them in their social, their moral, and their religious conditions, with the staggering white hunters and their painted faces, who occasionally stare through the windows, or, with the half-naked natives, whom we had seen a few nights before, dancing around their midnight fires, with their tomahawks and scalping knives, rending the air with their fierce war whoops, or making the woods thrill with their wild yells.

"But they form a still stronger contrast with the poor Indians, whom we had seen on the frontier, corrupted, degraded, debased by their intercourse with English, Irish, or American traders. It was not without emotions, that I parted, in all human probability forever in this world, from my kind and interesting friends, and prepared to return to

the tumultuous scenes of a busy world from which, if life
be spared, my thoughts will often stray to the sacred solitudes of Yallow Busha, as a source of the most grateful and
refreshing recollections."

Soon after Mr. Hodgson left Eliot, a reenforcement of
missionaries arrived at Eliot and Mayhew from Massachusetts, viz: Messrs. Smith, Cushman, Bardwell, with their
families, Byington, Hooper, Misses Frisselle and Thacher
from Pennsylvania. They travelled together as far as Pitts-
burgh, Pennsylvania, where (November 4, 1820) they took
passage on a large flatboat called, at that day, an Ark, and
reached the Walnut Hills (now Memphis, Tennessee) about
the last of December. There Mr. Cushman and his family,
and Mr. Hooper, took a wagon, and safely arrived at Mayhew after being about three weeks upon the road; while
Mr. Smith and family and Mr. Byington and Miss Thacher
remained on the boat until they reached the mouth of the
Yoh-shu-bah (Yazoo); and Mr. Bardwell and his family and
Miss Frisselle remained at the Walnut Hills to look after
the interests of the property of the mission, which had
been there deposited to await the arrival of the Choctaw
packet to carry it to Eliot and Mayhew. But the river rising
to such a height as to render it impracticable to travel by
water, Mr. Bardwell, after waiting many days for the falling
of the river, procured horses upon which he and his family
and Miss Frisselle rode to Eliot through the wilderness by
way of little paths alone.

A short time before the arrival of the above mentioned
missionaries at Eliot and Mayhew, Mr. Loring S. Williams,
who came with Mr. Kingsbury to the Choctaw Nation, trav-
alled over that Nation to learn the views of the Choctaw
people in regard to the establishment of churches and
schools among them, whom he found everywhere delighted
with the idea. In his travels he visited, among many others,
a point on the Old Natchez Trace, (to which I will again
refer) called French Camp, about half way between Eliot
and Mayhew where he eventually settled with his family,

opened a school and both preached to and taught the Choctaws, and God greatly blessed him in his glorious work.

In the meantime Mr. Kingsbury met all their chiefs in
a great council near and explained to them the nature and
design of the missions being established in the Nation; to
which a chief thus responded: "I be not used to make a
talk before white man, but when my heart feel glad, me can
say it. Me and my people have heard your talk before, but
never understood this business so well as now, that the
missionaries work for Choctaws without pay; that they
leave their homes, and all for good of Choctaws. We are
ignorant. We know when day come, and when night come.
That be all they know."

Thus was manifested the eagerness of those ancient
Choctaws, as well as all their race from the days of Eliot,
the early Apostle to the Red man of North America, down
to Cyrus Kingsbury, the Apostle of the Choctaws; and thus
it would have been down to the present day, but for the
interference with and pulling down the labors of those men
of God, by the hands of those white men of the devil, whose
howls are heard from the centre to circumference of the
land, even this day, "Open up to white settlement! Open
up to white settlement!"

But now missions began to be established in various
parts of the Choctaw Nation, and now was also seen the
long closed gates of an age of moral and intellectual darkness swinging open to the first echo of the approaching
footsteps of those pioneers of the Cross. But the ever
watchful and closely observing Choctaws at once learned
to justly appreciate the simple beauty of such lives as
theirs, never before seen nor even heard of, in all their
knowledge of and intercourse with the White Race. Consequently, they held them in great respect and reverence; and
even to this day, though all have passed from their toils
below to their rewards above, Mr. Cyrus Kingsbury, the
last of that noble little band of Christian heroes and hero-
ines, dying June 27, 1871, aged 83 years, 7 months and 4

days, while their names live in the memory of the present
generation of the Choctaws; since, in all the years of their
long lives of labor and love among them, they did them no
wrong, but only good.

Many parents and friends attended the closing exercises of the first session of the Mayhew school, and were
delighted at the improvement of the children, and the day
was a happy one both to parents and pupils. Moshulatubbee accompanied by many of his chieftains and warriors,
also attended the examination, and made the following remarks to the school: "Such a thing was not known here
when I was a boy. I had heard of it, but did not expect to
see it. I rejoice that I have lived to see it. You must mind
your teachers, and learn all you can. I hope I shall live to
see our councils filled with the boys who are now in this
school, and that you will then know much more than we
know and do much better than we do." And he did live to
see it. All returned to their homes highly pleased. At the
opening of the next session of the school, Moshulatubbee
brought two of his sons and a nephew to enter the school;
also an aged Choctaw man brought his grandson and
daughter to enter the school, and said to Mr. Kingsbury:
"I now give them to you, to take them by the hand and
heart, and hold them fast. I will now only hold them by
the end of their fingers."

To the examination at Mayhew in 1822, many Choctaws came from a long distance, and the whole Nation,
from centre to circumference, seemed awake upon the subject of improvement, morally, intellectually, and religiously.
But alas, the devil was not asleep, but secretly busy in
trying to thwart the good efforts of both the Choctaws and
missionaries, by influencing his abandoned white subjects,
who had fled from the religious restraints of their homes in
the States, to misrepresent the designs of the missionaries
and, in a few instances, succeeded in inducing parents to
take their children from under the care and instruction of
the schools. But many Choctaws came the distance of 70

miles to learn the truth of the reports; and, as might be expected, returned satisfied of their falsity, and better pleased with the missionaries, their churches and schools, than ever before; and thus was the devil and his white subjects gloriously defeated in their nefarious designs.

Soon after, a brother of Captain Cole (who died ten or twelve miles east of Atoka in the present Choctaw Nation, Indian Territory, in the year 1884, at the advanced age of nearly four score and ten years) sent five children to school, and a few months later sent another, but the school was so crowded that the sixth could not be admitted, and for causes not known, the father sent and took away the five, who manifested the greatest sorrow in having to leave the school. But Captain Cole, after more room had been provided, sent a petition with the signature of himself and eight chiefs urging the propriety of returning all the six children to the school; and not only the six were returned, but also six others, besides application for two others, one of whom was his son, whom he gave to the missionaries, with the words: "I want him to remain with you until he obtains a good education, if it takes ten years."

Mrs. Kingsbury died at Mayhew, on the 15th day of September, 1822, and was buried in the Mayhew cemetery—a true self-sacrificing Christian woman, who gave up all for the sake of assisting to lead the Red Man of North America into the fold of her Divine Master. Her noble husband's body rests from its earthly labors, in a Choctaw cemetery near Old Boggy Depot, Indian Territory, among the people he loved so well, and for whose good he labored so faithfully for 53 long and eventful years. She left two little boys, Cyrus and John. The last mentioned also lies in the same cemetery near the grave of his noble father; the former, if alive, I know not where he is. The last I heard of him, (years ago) he was living in Iowa. Both were the playmates of my childhood's years, never to be forgotten.

Ah! How those names stir the memories that still cluster around my early youth! We were five missionary boys,

Cyrus and John, my two brothers and myself, all playmates. But life soon taught its realities to us as to all poor humanity whose days are full of sorrow, and lives but a span. But it rests me, to pause, here and there, in the midst of hurry and care, to sit in this my angle-nook, among the present Choctaws in Indian Territory, and ponder o'er the joys of bygone days, when I was a fifth part of the happy, boyhood group that each day gathered together in the long ago.

Though the death of Mrs. Kingsbury was a great bereavement and trial to Mr. Kingsbury, yet he faltered not in the cause of his Divine Master among his loved Choctaws. But two weeks after he started upon a long journey in the southern part of the nation to find suitable points for establishing churches and schools among the Choctaws, that their children might receive an education near home, and also relieve the missions from all expenses except that of the support of teachers. After several days' travel, he arrived at the home of the celebrated chief of Choctaws, Pushmataha, where he met Mr. Jewell; thence, they journeyed together to a point one hundred miles distant, called by the Choctaws Oktak Falaiah (Ok-tark, Prairie), (Far-laiah, Long). There they laid the foundations for the establishment of a school, which was afterwards named Emmaus, and was near the line between Mississippi and Alabama. At Oktak Falaiah they made the acquaintance of Henry Nail, an aged white man, who had been adopted by the Choctaws by his marriage, many years before, to a Choctaw woman. He told Mr. Kingsbury and Jewell that he had twelve children living and one dead. He was a chief among the Choctaws for many years, and is the progenitor of the Nail family among the Choctaws. But I will speak of him again more definitely. Thence the two missionaries, in company with Joel Nail, a son of Henry Nail, who lived near his father with a wife and several small children, went to Okla Hunnali pro. Ok-lah (people) Hun-nar-lih (Six). While en route, they unexpectedly came upon a large company of Choctaws assembled for a ball play. As soon as

they ascertained that one of the white men was "Na-sho-ba-
An-o-wa," (Nar-sho-bah, Wolf), (Arn-o-wah, Walking) (a
name given to Mr. Kingsbury by the Choctaws, though one
foot was badly deformed by the cut of a scythe when a
boy) of whom they had heard, they postponed their ball
play, and both chiefs and warriors gathered at once around
him, and urgently solicited him to give them "a talk" about
schools. He willingly complied, while they listened with
the deepest interest and in profound silence to his propositions, and manifested unassumed joy at the prospect of a
school. Mr. Kingsbury then bade them a friendly adieu,
and the three continued their journey thence to Okla Hunnali, which comprised six clans, and contained 2164 inhabitants.

Aboha Kullo Humma, (pro. Ar-bo-hah) (House) Kullo
(strong) Humma (red) or, in our phraseology—(Strong red
house—but in the Choctaw, Red Fort) was the chief of
Okla Hunnali. The clans of the Choctaws were all perpetu-
ated in the female line. When a man married, he was
adopted into the family of his wife, and her brothers had
more authority over her children than her husband; therefore, when a lover wished to marry a girl, he consulted her
uncles, and if they consented to the marriage, the father
and mother approved. Those of the same clan were never
allowed to intermarry. A Choctaw regarded marrying a
girl of his own clan with the same horror as the white man
did to marry his own sister; and equally so did the Choctaw
girl.

Aboha Kullo Humma was highly elated at the proposition of Mr. Kingsbury to establish a school among his clans,
or people; and earnestly importuned Mr. Kingsbury to establish two in his district; and such were his pleadings that
Mr. Kingsbury finally agreed to write a letter to the Pru-
dential Committee, solicit more teachers, and Aboha Kullo
Humma also wrote a letter, and sent it with Mr. Kingsbury's, a true copy of which I here insert:

Six Towns, Choctaw Nation, October 18, 1822.

Brothers:

"The first law I have made is, that when my warriors go over the line among the white people, and buy whiskey, and bring it into the Nation to buy up the blankets, and guns, and horses of the Red people, and get them drunk; the whiskey is to be destroyed. The whiskey drinking is wholly stopped among my warriors. The Choctaw women sometimes killed their infants, when they did not want to provide for them. I have made a law to have them punished, that no more children be killed."

This law had actually been passed and was then in full force, as had been exemplified in the case of a woman who had been tried and convicted for killing her infant, a short time prior to Mr. Kingsbury's visit to Okla Hunnali. She was tied to a tree and whipped by the officers of justice until she fainted; and not only the woman was whipped, but her husband also received the same punishment for not restraining his wife in the destruction of the child. But thus continues Aboha Kullo Humma.

"The Choctaws formerly stole hogs and cattle, and killed and ate them. I have organized a company of faithful warriors to take every man who steals, and tie him to a tree, and give him thirty-nine lashes."

This law of punishing theft by whipping has never been repealed; but has been amended to this extent, and so stands today—being fifty lashes on the bare back for the first theft; a hundred for the second, and death by the rifle for the third.

"The Choctaws have, sometimes, run off with each other's wives. We have now made a law, that those who do so, shall be whipped thirty-nine lashes; and if a woman runs away from her husband with another man, she is also to be whipped in the same manner. The number of men, women, and children in the Six Towns, is 2164. I want the good white people to send men and women to get up a school in my district; I want them to do it quick, for I am growing old and want to see the good work before I die. We have always been passed by. Other parts of the Nation have schools; we have not; we have made the above laws because we wish to follow the ways of the white people. We hope they will assist us in getting our children educated. This is the first time I write a letter. Last fall the first time we make laws. I say no more. I have told my wants. I hope you will not forget me."   "Aboha Kullo Humma."

Mayhew, the second mission established among the Choctaws, as before stated, was located on the eastern border of a magnificent prairie that stretched away to the west and south in billowy undulations presenting a scene of fascinating loveliness unsurpassed, when arrayed in its dress of summer's green, dotted with innumerable flowers of various colors; and the country in all directions for miles away, was rich in all the boundless extravagance of picturesque beauty, where Nature's most fascinating features everywhere presented themselves carelessly disposed in wild munificence, unimproved, and indeed unimprovable by the hand of art. Truly the lovely situation of that mission is still fresh in memory, though more than a half century has passed away; and today, as of that long ago, the eye of memory sees the far extending prairie on the south and west, and the boundless forests on the north and east, with their hills and vales of romantic loveliness, and creeks and rivulets combining to give a moral interest to the pleasure derived from the contemplation of Nature in her brightest, happiest and most varied aspect.

Their horses, cattle and hogs, which they possessed in great numbers, were fed alone from Nature's ample storehouse filled at all times with the richest varieties of provender-grass, cane, acorns and nuts; while game of many varieties roamed over their forests undisturbed only as necessity demanded their destruction. Birds of many kinds, and of various plumage, added their enchantment to the scene.

Those early missionaries (both men and women), who offered their lives to the cause, were of strong character,

firm resolution and of fine tastes and ideals; and of those
missionary women it may be truthfully added, they were
intelligent and elegant as they were heroic; and the lovers
of missionary lore oft read with delight the ideal romance
of their lives. They first studied and made themselves acquainted with the various dialects of the Indians' complicated languages—difficult because of the combination of
signs and words that cannot be reduced to any known rule;
they administered to the wants of the sick and dressed
the wounded; they braved sickness and death and preached
the tidings of peace on earth and good will to men.

"They found the Indians' confidence was easily gained,
and as easily retained by just and humane treatment, they
found that he was not vicious nor bloodthirsty, an untam-
able savage, as he was and ever has been so unjustly represented to be; they found that, unlike his white defamer, he
never was profane. He took not in vain the name of his
God, the Great Spirit, nor the names of the subordinate
deities, to whom his religion taught him the supreme Great
Spirit delegated supernatural powers among men. Whatever he loved, he called it good; whatever he hated, he
called it bad. Of whiskey he said: "O-ka-ki-a-chuk-ma,
Water not good," that was all.

They found the men to be, to a great extent, even as
the whites, good husbands, loving fathers, and the most
faithful of friends; the women, devoted wives, adoring
mothers, and equally true as friends, and both men and
women, truthful to the letter, all scorning a lie and a liar.

There were many things which served to awaken in the
minds of the early missionaries to the present Five Civilized
Tribes[18], when living in their ancient domains east of the
Mississippi River, sad and melancholy reflections. They
beheld all around them indubitable evidence of the former
existence of a large population who lived long prior to the
people among whom they labored, and had in the years of

---

[18] This designation was applied to the Southern Indians—Choctaws, Chickasaws,
Cherokees, Creeks, and Seminoles—after their removal to the Indian Territory to distinguish
them from the hunting tribes native to the region.

the long ago performed their part upon the stage of life, and unremembered, passed into the secret chambers of oblivion. They felt that they walked over the graves of a long succession of generations ages before mouldered into dust; the surrounding forests were once animated by their labors, (as their rude and moundering fortifications testified), their huntings and wars, their songs and their dances; but silence had drawn its impenetrable veil over their entire history; no lettered page, no sculptured monument told who they were, whence they came, or the period of their existence.

And the missionaries found them, to their agreeable surprise, as little meriting the title, savages, which ignorance, prejudice and imbecile egotism had applied to them, as any race of unlettered people that were ever known to exist; and, in viewing them in the light of a true catholic spirit, saw much that was touching and beautiful in their manners and customs. They also found them to be a people with immovable faith in a Supreme Being, and possessing a great reverence for powers and abilities superior to those of earth; though, to some extent, materialistic in their conception, but totally ignorant of the white man's ideas and views of Christ and the Father. They regarded the Great Spirit as the source of general good, of whom they asked guidance in all undertakings, and implored aid against their enemies, and to whose power they ascribed favors and frowns, blessings, successes and disappointments, joys and sorrows; and though their faith may have seemed cold to us, and their ceremonies, frivolous, ridiculous, and even blasphemous in our eyes; but in such light as they had truly walked, with ready and sincere acknowledgement of human dependence on superhuman aid and mercy. Can we say as much for ourselves? Do we walk according to the light we have as truly and faithfully as the unlettered Indians did?

But among the many things that are associated with the North American Indians as topics of conversation and subjects of the printer's ink—more talked about and less understood — is the "Medicine-Man." On November 14, 1605, the first French settlement was made in America, on the northeast coast of Nova Scotia, and they gave the name Acadia to the country; and on July 3, 1808, Samuel Champlain laid the foundation of Quebec. The character "Medicine-Man" had its origin, according to tradition, among those early French colonists who corrupted the word "Meda"—a word in the language of one of the Indian tribes of that day signifying chief, into "Medicine-Man," and also called the religious ceremonies of the Indian "making medicine," which was afterwards called, as the result, "medicine," and which finally became in use among the Indians themselves, and has so continued to the present day.

It was a religious ceremony for the propitiation of invisible spirits and practiced by all of the North American Indians, with scarcely an exception. The ancient Choctaws and Chickasaws had their Medicine-Men, with many of whom I was personally acquainted in the years of the long ago.

There were two kinds of Medicine (religious ceremonies) among the Choctaws and Chickasaws, the same as among all other tribes of their race, the tribal medicine and the individual, each peculiar to the individual tribe and individual person of that tribe. What the different ingredients were, which composed the tribal medicine, no one knew, or ever tried to know, except he who secretly collected and stored them away in the carefully dressed, highly ornamented and sacred deer-skin sack; yet it was held as sacred in the hearts of the entire tribe of all ages and sexes, as was the ark of the covenant among the ancient Jews. And equally so was that of the individual, whose ingredients were known only to its maker and possessor. More than once did my boyish curiosity induce me to ask a Choctaw warrior what was in his medicine sack, but only to get the repulsive reply: None of your business.

Indeed, the mission of the tribal medicine was to the Indians the same, to all intents and purposes, as that of the sacred ark to the ancient Jews when borne through the wilderness in those days of their historical pilgrimage. It was regarded as the protector of the tribe; in fact, the visible embodiment of the promise of the good Great Spirit to provide for the tribe all the necessaries of life, and protect them from all enemies. So too was that of the individual medicine which he had made for himself alone, and which was indeed a part of his life, — his assurance in danger, his safety in battle, and his success amid all the vicissitudes of his earthly career. If the sacred and secret articles that composed the contents of the tribal medicine bag, or those of the individual medicine bag, should become known to others, than the one who collected and placed them therein, the mystic bag at once became powerless. And was it captured in war or otherwise fell into the hands of an enemy the greatest consternation fell upon the entire tribe, and superhuman efforts were made to recover it. If they failed in this, overtures soliciting peace, even to humiliation, were made at once to the enemy.

But, if an individual was in any way deprived of his, which he always kept about his person, he made another. The making of another may seem an easy matter to the uninformed. But not so. It entailed upon the maker a long period of utter seclusion in the solitude and silence of the forest far away from the abodes of mankind, with long continued fasting, meditation and prayer, followed by long protracted labor in finding and securing the necessary articles, such as earths of different colors, the ashes of various weeds, bones of certain birds and snakes, and various other things which his fancy might suggest. These were placed in a vessel of water prepared for the purpose, and the vessel was then placed upon a fire and the contents continually stirred with a stick as it became more and more heated. During this process he obtained a sign from some developed peculiarity which he regarded as infallible, and which enabled him to interpret signs and omens, both of good and evil. A small portion of the contents of the vessel was placed in his mystic sack and accompanied him everywhere. In time of peace, the tribal medicine was placed in the care of a chief noted for his bravery, who carefully guarded it from all profanation; but in the time of war, the war-chief carried it in front of his warriors, as they marched upon the war-path. The youthful warrior was always instructed in the art of making medicine by the aged men of the tribe, of which he made good use and never forgot.

The philosophy of the ancient Indian ever taught him to concentrate his mind upon the spirit land; and that the influences which surrounded him in Nature, above, beneath, around, are sent direct by the spirits that dwell in an invisible world above; that there are two kinds of spirits—the good and the bad, who are continually at war with each other over him, the good directing all things for his prosperity and happiness, the bad directing all things against his prosperity and happiness; that within himself he can do nothing, as he is utterly helpless in the mighty contest that is waged over him by the good and bad spirits. Therefore, he exerts his greatest energies of mind and body to the propititaion of the bad spirits rather than the good, since the former may be induced to extend the sceptre of mercy to him, while the latter will ever strive for his good, and his good alone. Therefore, when he is fortunate he attributes it to some good spirit; when unfortunate, to some bad spirit. So, when he said it is "good medicine," he meant that the good spirit had the ascendency; and when he said it is "bad medicine" he meant that the bad spirit had the ascendency.

Therefore, all things in nature, as a natural consequence, indicated to him the presence of the spirits, both good and bad, — as each made known their immediate nearness through both animate and inanimate nature. The sighing of the winds; the flight of the birds; the howl of the lone wolf; the midnight hoot of the owl, and all other sounds heard throughout his illimitable forests both by day and by night, had to him most potent significations; and, by which, he so governed all his actions that he never went upon any enterprise before consulting the signs and omens; then acted in conformity thereto. If the medicine is good, he undertakes his journey; if bad, he remains at home, and no argument can induce him to change his opinion, which I learned from personal experience.

The missionaries found the precepts of the Choctaws to be moral; and also that they respected old age, and kept fresh in memory the wise councils of their fathers, whose lessons of wisdom the experience of the past, taught their youthful minds to look upward, and whose teachings they did not forget in their mature years.

Their tenderness to and watchful care of the aged and infirm was truly remarkable; they looked upon home and regarded their country as sacred institutions, and in the defense of which they freely staked their lives; they also inculcated a high regard for parents, and were always courteous by instinct as well as by teaching; they held in high veneration the names of the wise, the good, and the brave of their ancestors, and from their sentiment toward the dead grew sweet flowers in the heart. They believed that integrity alone was worthy of station, and that promotion should rest on capacity and faithfulness; they also had swift and sure methods of dealing with the incorrigible, official or private; nor were they impatient of the slow processes of the years but knew how to wait in faith and contentment; and if they were not as progressive, as our opinion demands in its rush for gain and pompous show, they had at least conquered the secret of National and individual steadfastness. Today we are a prodigal and wasteful people, the Indians are frugal and economical.

In 14 months after the location of the mission at Eliot by the indefatigable perseverance of Mr. Kingsbury, a sufficiency of houses were erected, a school was opened, and that then young pioneer of the Cross proclaimed the Gospel of the Son of God, where it never before had been proclaimed; and at the time the Choctaws were so cruelly driven from their ancient domains to make room for our cruel and unchristian venality called "Progress," the Eliot and Mayhew missions together with the eleven others established in various parts of the Choctaw Nation, were in a flourishing condition; and this earliest effort to evangelize this worthy people was highly encouraging from the readiness, yea, absolute eagerness, on their part to receive instruction. A considerable and suitable literature both educational and religious was soon prepared; a school system was also founded through which many young Choctaws, both male and female, received the elements of a good education. Many of the useful arts of civilized life were introduced; and the missionaries had gathered many Christian congregations of whom not a few had received the good seed in an honest heart. And of those noble, self-sacrificing missionaries, it may truly be said, "Their works do follow them"; and today the names Kingsbury, Byington, Williams, Cushman, Polly, Hotchkins, Hawes, Bardwell and Smith, are still held in grateful rememberance by the Choctaws, as the names of some of those who were their true, their noblest and best earthly friends, to which the following will truthfully attest.

In his first annual report of the Eliot Mission, bearing date October 28, 1819, Mr. Kingsbury says: (I copy from the original M.S.) "The first tree was felled on the 13th day of August, 1818. Since we arrived, (himself and Mr. and Mrs. Williams) we have been joined by the following persons:

"Mr. Peter Kanaise, Mr. John Kanaise and wife, carpenter, Mr. Moses Jewell and wife, Mr. N. Jersey, Mr. N. York, carpenter and millwright, Mr. A. V. Williams, laborer, Mrs. Kingsbury, Miss Chase, Mr. Isaac Fisk, blacksmith, Mr. W. W. Pride, physician.

"All these came out to labor gratuitously for the benefit of the Choctaws.

"It would be trespassing unnecessarily on the time of the secretary to detail the principal circumstances and difficulties which have attended the progress of our labors. They have been similar to what must always attend such enterprises in an uncivilized country far removed from those places where the necessaries, comforts, and conveniences of life can be obtained.

"Since our arrival, we have been principally occupied in erecting buildings. This devolved upon us much labor and greatly retarded our other business, but by the blessing of a kind Providence, we have been prospered in our work, much beyond our expectations.

"Within about fourteen months there have been erected at Eliot seven commodious cabins which are occupied as dwelling houses.

"A dining room and kitchen contiguous, (54 x 20) with hewed logs and a piazza on each side.

"A school house 36 ft. x 34 hewed logs; and finished on the Lancastrian plan.

"A millhouse 34 x 30 ft., and also a lumberhouse and granary, each 18 x 20 ft.

"A blacksmith shop, stable, and three outhouses, all of which are nearly completed.

"On the plantation between 30 and 40 acres have been cleared and fenced; and between 20 and 30 acres have been cultivated, which have produced a considerable quantity of corn, potatoes, beans, peas, etc.

"Besides the above, considerable time has been spent in cutting roads in different directions, and constructing several small bridges, which were necessary for transporting with a wagon.

"The stock at present belonging to the mission, consists of 7 horses, 10 steers, 75 cows, 75 calves and young cattle, and about 30 swine. Of the above, 54 cows and calves, and 6 steers and young cattle have been presented by the Choctaws for the benefit of the school.

"There is no private property attached to the mission. All is sacredly devoted to the various purposes of instructing the Choctaws.

"Urged by the importunity of the natives, the school was commenced under many disadvantages in April last, with ten pupils. As accommodations and means of support have increased the school has been enlarged, and there are fifty-four students who attend regularly — males and females. All these board in our family. They are of different ages—from 6 to 20, and could not speak our language when they came. More pupils are expected to join the school shortly. In addition to the common rudiments of education, the boys are acquiring a practical knowledge of agriculture in its various branches, and the girls, while out of school, are employed under the direction of the female missionaries in different departments of domestic labor. We have also a full-blooded Choctaw lad learning the blacksmith trade; and another, now in school, wishes to engage in the same employment, so soon as there is opportunity. All the children are placed entirely under our control, and the most entire satisfaction is expressed as to the manner they are treated.

"The school is taught on the Lancastrian plan, and the progress of the children has exceeded our most sanguine expectations. Thirty-one began the A. B. C.'s. Several of these can now read the Testament, and others in easy reading lessons. Most of them have also made considerable progress in writing.

"There have been instances of lads 14 to 16 years old, entirely ignorant of our language, who have perfectly learned the alphabet in three days, and on the fourth day could read and pronounce the abs. We have never seen the same number of children in any school, who appeared more promising. Since they commenced, their attention has been constant. No one has left the school, or manifested a wish to leave it.

"Want of accommodations, but more particularly want of funds, has obliged us to refuse many children who wish to enter the school. If adequate means can be obtained, we design to increase the number to 80 or 100. It is our intention to embrace in their education, that practical industry, and that literary, moral and religious instruction, which may qualify them for useful members of society; and for the exercise of those moral principles, and that genuine piety, which form the basis of true happiness.

"The expenditures of the mission, including the outfit and traveling expenses of the missionaries, and exclusive of their services (which have all been gratuitous) have been more than $9000. About $2000 of this has been on account of buildings. It has been our constant endeavor to impress on the people of this nation the advantages of instruction, and the propriety of their contributing towards the education of their own children; and by commencing on a labored and extensive scale for their improvement we have drawn forth a spirit of liberality as unexpected as it is encouraging.

"At a council in August, which by invitation I attended, the natives subscribed ninety-five cows and calves, and more than $1300 in cash for the benefit of the school. At a lower town district, in September, they unanimously voted to appropriate $2000 (their proportion of the money due from the United States for the last purchase of land) to the support of a school in that district. It has been proposed in this district to make a similar appropriation for the benefit of this school.

"These measures disclose the disposition of the Nation and evince that under the influence and direction of the Executive a fund might be established, which eventually would be adequate to the instruction of the Nation. We feel a confidence that in future treaties with the Nation, this subject will, without any suggestion of ours, receive that attention which its consideration demands."

"To bring this people," continues that true Christian, "within the pale of civilization and Christianity is a great work. The instruction of the rising generation is unquestionably the most direct way to advance. Nothing is now wanting to put the great mass of children in this Nation, in a course of instruction but efficient means.

"It may be proper to observe that the Chickasaws are anxious to have similar institutions in their Nation, and two more are earnestly desired and much needed by the Choctaws. For the support of one of them, two thousand dollars for 17 years annually ($34,000) have already been appropriated by the Choctaws. It is the intention of the American Board to commence one or more of the establishments as soon as they can command the means. It is therefore desirable that the one already commenced here should be completed without delay and placed on a permanent foundation.

"Before closing this report, I beg leave to remark on two points relative to the improvement of the Choctaws.

"First: We think the introduction of a few respectable mechanics of good moral character, would be of great advantage in civilizing and introducing industry among them. We have a blacksmith of this description, who came out at the expense of the American Board, and the profits of his work are devoted to the support of this establishment. Many of the mechanics found in the Indian countries are of little advantage in any respect; and the conduct of some is an outrage on barbarism itself.

"Second.—Could the missionaries be relieved from the labor of erecting the buildings, it would enable them much sooner to direct their attention to the improvement of a plantation and other necessary preparations for commencing the school.

"With sentiments of sincere respect, I am, dear sir, your obedient and very humble servant.   Cyrus Kingsbury."

From a letter (now before me) written to the then young missionary, Rev. Cyrus Kingsbury, bearing date, October 2, 1819, I take the following extract: "In a situation like yours, it must be an unspeakable comfort to know that you have the prayers of God's people. Many are daily supplicating the Throne of Grace for you, and the object in which you are engaged; but I presume you can hardly realize the extent of the interest which is awakened for our missions among the Southern Indians. The eyes of all our churches are turned toward them with the earnest expectation, which is the offspring of faith and prayer. The Indian character in the estimation of even those who have hitherto deemed them too savage to be civilized; and those who acknowledge the excellency of many of the native traits of their character, but were faithless as to the practicability of making them good citizens, are now convinced by the experiments made at Brainard, that the Indians can be educated, became good citizens and devout Christians.

"Truly, you have seen more to rejoice your heart than is witnessed by one in ten of our New England ministers. You have witnessed the Christian devotion of characters once degraded. You have witnessed the wilderness and the solitary place, in one year, became glad before you, and the desert blossom as the rose. After such experience of the smiles of heaven do not faint or become discouraged. God's promises are established in truth, and they are all yours. Blessed promises! Thus far the Lord has favored you more than any Indian missionary for sixty or seventy years past. The public are waking up with wonderful rapidity to the wants of the Indians. You may be distressed and perplexed for a season, but it will not last always. The Lord will come and will not tarry."

For the first few years the good and glorious work of reform went on for the most part quietly though steadily. Then there was manifested a greater spirit of inquiry, not only about the truth as a matter of speculation, but after salvation through the Lord Jesus Christ. It was truly affecting to see the deep and unaffected interest manifested by those unlettered warriors, as they listened for the first time to the wonderful story of the Cross—a theme to them incomprehensible and almost beyond human belief. That a friend might peradventure die for a friend was to them a possible thing; but for a father to give his only son to die for the benefit of his enemies, and that son also be willing to accept the ordeal of dying the most excruciating death that their mutual enemies might be benefitted thereby, seemed too incredible for belief, and filled them with wondering astonishment. Yet hundreds of them yielded to the regenerating influences and power of the Divine Spirit years before they were driven from their ancient homes to seek others in a distant wilderness that the progress of the white man in his strife for gain might not be impeded by their presence, and lived the exemplary lives of the true Christian, and died the death of the righteous in bright hopes of a blissful immortality.

The first conversion among the full-blooded Choctaws was that of an aged man, who lived near Col. David Folsom, chief of the Choctaws, named Tun-a pin a-chuf-fa, (Our one weaver) hitherto as ignorant of the principles of the religion of Jesus Christ as it is possible to conceive. He manifested an interest in the subject of religion about six months before any other of his people in the neighborhood, and soon began to speak publicly in religious meetings, and gave evidence by his daily walk and conversation, of a happy and glorious change, to the astonishment of his people, who could not comprehend the mystery. The old man, but now a new one, lived the life of a true and devoted Christian the few remaining years of his life, and then died leaving bright evidence of having died the death of the righteous. When he was received into the church, he was baptized and given the name of one of the missionaries, viz.: William Hooper, by his own request, to whom Mr. Hooper had endeared himself by many acts of kindness conferred upon the aged appreciative Choctaw.

Shortly after he professed religion, he dictated a letter to Col. David Folsom, his nephew, which was written and translated into English by Mr. Loring Williams, of which the following is a copy:

"Ai-ik-hum-a, (A place of learning), January 30, 1828.

"Brother:—Long time had we been as people in a storm which threatened destruction, until the missionaries came to our land; but now we are permitted to hear the blessed Gospel of truth. You, our brother and chief, found for us a good and bright path, and we would follow you in it. You are as our good father, and your words are good. Your messengers (the missionaries), that you sent to us, we hear. When we think of our old ways, we feel ashamed. This blessed day I have given a true talk. The black and dirty clothes I used to wear I have taken off and cast away. Clean and good clothes, I now put on. My heart, I hope, had been made new. My bad thoughts I throw away. The words of the great Father above I am seeking to have in my mind.

"The missionaries, in the Choctaw Nation, salute. The missionaries, chiefs, and people, I salute. O my chief, I, your uncle, salute you. I am your warrior. You must remember me in your love. The letter which I send you, you must read to your captains, leaders, and warriors. As I feel today, I wish to have all my Choctaw brothers feel. I am the first of the Choctaws that talk the good talk. My chief, as you go about among your people, you must tell them this, the dark night to me has gone, and the morning has dawned upon me. The missionaries at Mayhew, I salute you. Mr. Kingsbury, when this letter you see, you will forward it to Miko (chief) Folsom.   Tunapinachuffa."

Soon after the writing of this letter, Mr. Williams visited the venerable ex-chief and retired warrior of the Choctaws. As he drew near the humble log cabin his attention was attracted by the voice of singing. He halted a moment to listen. It was Tunapinachuffa singing a song of Zion; and when Mr. Williams came up he found him sitting at the opposite side of his little cabin, resting his head on one hand and holding a catachism in the other, holding holy and sweet communion with his newly found Savior; and so absorbed was he in his meditations, that the presence of Mr. Williams was not known, until announced by the barking of the dogs; and yet, so deep and pleasant was his reverie, that he remained seemingly unconscious of everything around him until Mr. Williams came to his side and spoke to him. He then looked up, sprang to his feet and greeted Mr. Williams with unfeigned manifestations of the greatest joy; and, at once, inquired after Mr. Kingsbury with expressions of the greatest affection; then requested Mr. Williams to tell Mr. Kingsbury, that "he did love the Savior with all his heart and soul"; that "he took great delight in the Sabbath, and loved to pray"; that, "today heaven is near; it is not far away—I know it is near—I feel it." Mr. Williams and the new born babe in Christ though feeble and alone with the weight of nearly three score years and ten, joined in a song together, in praise to Him who has said: "Come unto me, ye that are heavy laden, and I will give you rest"; and then Tunapinachuffa offered up a prayer to Him who is the Indian's God as well as the white man's.

Mr. Williams stated, in speaking of the interview with the venerable Choctaw, that, he prayed with the deepest sincerity for his family; then, that all his people "might be united to Christ in peace and love as with an iron chain; and that they might take hold of the Savior with their hands." At morning and at night this redeemed Choctaw child of God called his household around the family altar, nor ever permitted business or company to interfere with those sacred devotions.

But Tuna pin a chuffa was not an isolated case. Hundreds of similar cases could be mentioned among the young, as well as the aged, of those Choctaw converts under the teachings of the missionaries when living in their ancient possessions.

After the conversion of Tuna pin a chuffa, a great and wonderful change for the better was soon seen in not only Tuna pin a chuffa's district, but also in other districts— both in outward appearance and moral condition. The men soon began to acquire habits of industry, cultivating cotton and enlarging their corn fields. Temperance rapidly gained ground all over the Nation; and in nearly every house throughout the country soon were found the cotton card, the spinning wheel and the loom, with here and there blacksmith and wood-shops.

Soon large quantities of various cotton cloths were made by the Choctaw mothers and daughters; while the father and son raised corn, sweet potatoes, peas, beans, and various kinds of vegetables; and their willingness to work ran parallel with their progress and advancement in Christian knowledge. Nor was there any difficulty experienced by the missionaries in hiring Choctaws to work for them, both men and women, and even boys and girls; many of the men with their families, went to the adjoining States and picked cotton for the white farmers, after they had gathered their own crops. As cotton pickers, both in quantity and quality, day by day, they had no superiors; therefore, the white farmers paid them one dollar per hundred pounds, and also boarded them; and a thousand have been known to leave their Nation at one time to pick cotton in the States; and before they were driven to the wild wilderness far away to the west by the inexorable law of the whites, that "Might is Right," when dealing with the North American Indian; fifty, yea a hundred and fifty, drunken white men could be found in the contiguous States, to where one Choctaw would be found in the Nation most distant from the neighborhood of the white settlements. Much has been said to prove the drunken Indian to be a fiend incarnate; and though I have seen drunken Indians, yet my experience has taught me that a drunken white man is far worse than a drunken Indian, and more to be feared ten to one, than the Indian.

After Tunapinachuffa, followed the conversion of Col. David Folsom, and many other leading men of the Nation, together with the common warriors and their wives; and to that extent was the interest in the subject of religion manifested by all that a special meeting was appointed in the woods by the missionaries; and at which, Col. David Folsom and others, together with the now zealous and good old Tunapinachuffa, took an active part. Though there were few Choctaws present, yet the Spirit of God was there; and one evening an unusual solemnity seemed to pervade the entire little company of worshippers, and so deeply felt by old Tunapinachuffa, that he was unable to longer restrain himself. He arose and commenced an exhortation to his people present, and continued for thirty or more minutes in such sublime Indian eloquence, such deep pathos, and such irresistible arguments, as are seldom heard anywhere.

At the close of his exhortation, he, in a persuasive tone of voice, said: "All you who desire and are willing to receive these good tidings from above into your hearts and go with me to the good land above, come and sit on this log." What a moment was that to the noble-hearted and pious missionaries who were so fortunate as to be present! Who can justly describe it? First one, and then another and another, came forward and took their seats on the forest log, until it was covered; and there and then twelve adults became living, active witnesses for the cause of the world's Redeemer. That little religious meeting, in the deep solitudes of a Mississippi forest, closed; but the tidings of its strange proceedings and its more wonderful results spread far and wide, and it became the subject of conversation and inquiry for miles away; and soon was awakened such a feeling of curiosity and desire to learn more of this, to them strange and incomprehensible thing, that other meetings were appointed, to which hundreds gathered, and the result was they were multiplied all over the land and scores flocked to and around the standard of Christianity.

But this interest was confined for several months, almost excusively, to the northern part of the Nation contiguous to Mayhew, whence the missionaries went out among the Choctaws and taught and preached to them. The converts were at first gathered into one church organization though widely separated; hence their sacramental meetings were held in the woods under the wide extended branches of the mighty forest oaks of that day, where many hundreds would congregate and spend several days worshipping God; and a more humble and devout assembly of worshippers of the living God (without an indifferent or idle spectator) was never anywhere beheld. At one of these forest meetings, where the wind, sighing amid the trees had for ages untold received no response but that of the defiant warwhoop, now was mingled the praise of human tongues in anthems sweet with nature to nature's God; ninety Choctaws both men and women, were enrolled in the army of the Cross; and at another over a hundred.

Messrs. Williams, Smith, Howse and Bardwell, shortly after the establishment of the Mayhew mission, took charge of the one established in the southern part of the Nation among a clan of Choctaws called Okla Hunnali, (people Six), distant seventy or more miles from Mayhew, leaving Messrs. Kingsbury (to whom the Choctaws gave the name Na-sho-ba No-wah (Walking Wolf), Byington (whom they named La-pish O-la-han-chih, Sounding Horn), Cushman and a few others at Mayhew.

Soon after the close of the revival meetings in the northern part of the Nation, several new converts, in company with Col. David Folsom and a few missionaries of the Mayhew mission, made a journey to the Okla Hunnali mission to attend a religious meeting previously appointed. The Choctaws of that district, expecting them, came in large numbers from the surrounding villages to the appointed place to welcome them, and manifested the greatest delight regarding it as a great favor conferred upon them by their friends who had come so far to attend their meetings. They assembled without ostentation, yet in all the paraphernalia of Choctaw custom, presenting a novel appearance to the eye of the novice. But the "tidings of great joy—peace on earth and good will to man"—to the red as well as the white, proclaimed and urged upon them with such evidence of truth, sincerity and deep feeling, was to them something new indeed, unseen and unfelt before.

Calm reflection assumed (as at the meetings in the northern section of the Nation) the place of thoughtlessness and indifference (for an Indian can and does reflect as well as a white man), and soon were seen on many a painted face trickling tears (though not given to weeping) forming little channels through the vermillion as they coursed their way down. And this meeting was also blessed with a gracious visitation of the Holy Spirit, and many precious souls (though Choctaws) were gathered into the fold of the Great Shepherd as had been done in the northern portion of their country. At once a mighty change began all over their Nation wherever the missionaries went; and soon, one by one their ancient customs and habits were forever laid aside, culminating in a general change of things well adapted to their then, it may be truthfully stated, progressive condition. But among the most prominent features indicating a speedy reformation at this time (1826), was the enacting of a law forever banishing that curse of all curses O-ka Humma (Red Water) or properly O-ka Ho-mi (Strong Water), which stands today unrepealed, and will so continue as long as they are permitted to exist as a Nation.[19]

Many of the ancient Choctaws were adepts in the art of singing their native airs, of which they had many; but all effort to induce one of them to sing alone one of his favorite songs was fruitless. They invariably replied to the solicitation in broken English, "Him no good." Then sing me a war-song. "Him heap no good," with an ominous shake of the head. Then sing me a hunting song. "No good; he no fit for pale face." Well, sing me a love song. "Wah!" (an ancient exclamation of surprise—now obsolete) much love song, him had, no good for pale face." Though this was somewhat tantalizing yet it had to be endured.

---

[19] It is true that the Choctaws' prohibition law—which antedated the Maine law by many years—remained in force throughout the rest of their tribal history.

Like all their race, the Choctaws never forgot an act of kindness be it ever so trivial; and many a white man overtaken by misfortune when traveling over their country, and weak beneath the remorseless grasp of hunger, has felt that the truth of the eastern proverb has been brought home to him: Cast thy bread upon the waters, and thou shalt find it after many days. More than once has it fallen to my lot to contribute to an Indian's immediate necessities, in days of their individual want and weakness; and, in after days— the incident by me long forgotten; they have returned the favor thirty fold; and for many favors have I become indebted to them, when I had nothing to return. Their great delicacy in conferring a favor was not the least admirable part of their conduct, often they would leave a large wild turkey upon the door-sill, or place a venison ham just within it, and steal away without saying a word, as if they feared you might suspect them of trying to buy your friendship, when not enabled to secure it alone by merit; or that, to accept a present from a poor Indian might be humiliating to the pride of the receiver and they would spare him mortification of returning thanks. Never was a race of people more sensitive to kindness, or more grateful for any little act of benevolence exercised toward them, or practiced the great Christian principle, Charity to a greater degree of perfection, especially in regard to strangers, than did the North American Indians. The missionaries everywhere and among all tribes, met them with kindness and confidence, and conducted themselves by the rules of strict integrity in all their dealings with them; and no instance has been recorded, where their confidence in the Indians was betrayed, or their good opinion of them destroyed.

The Choctaws were great imitators, and possessed a nice tact in adopting the manners of those with whom they associated. An Indian, however, is Nature's gentleman— never familiar, coarse or vulgar. If he takes a meal with you, he quietly waits to see you make use of the unaccustomed implements on the table, and the manner in which you eat, he exactly imitates with a grace decorum and as much apparent ease, as if he had been accustomed to the same usages from childhood. He never attempts to help himself or demand more food, but patiently waits until you perceive what he requires. This innate politness is natural to all Indians. But the mixture of white blood, while it may be said to add a little to the physical beauty of the half-race, yet produces a deplorable falling off from the original integrity of the Indian character; which, however, may be attributed wholly to the well known fact, that the young half-breeds mingle with the whites ninety per cent more than the full-bloods; and ever retain that peculiar characteristic of the Indian i. e. confidence in all professions of friendship until proved false, then never again to be trusted; thus are they easily made the dupes of the whites, and are ignorantly, and therefore unconsciously, led step by step down to a level with their destroyers, and too late awake to the consciousness that they are the victims.

No Indian was ever so selfish as to smoke alone in the presence of others. I have oft attended their social gatherings where, seated on the ground in little groups forming little circles, the personification of blissful contentment, I invariably saw the pipe on its line of march, and so continued until the talk was ended. If but two were seated together, and one lighted his pipe, he only drew a few whiffs and then handed it to his companion, who also drew a whiff or two and returned it; and thus the symbol of peace, friendship and good will passed back and forth until the social chat was terminated.

The Choctaw women did not indulge in the use of tobacco in any way whatever when living east of the Mississippi, except a few in advanced years; and it was regarded as great a breach of female decorum for a Choctaw woman to use the weed, as it is with the white women of the present day to chew or smoke; and even the men confined its use exclusively to the pipe. But now they seem to have deviated to some extent from that good custom; for in my travels over their country during the last few years, I have frequently fallen in company with Choctaws, and when offered a chew of tobacco it was accepted by a few fullbloods, and chewed with as much gusto as we rode along together, as I dared to assume with all my long years of experience; and thus I ascertained that those of the present day do not confine the use of tobacco exclusively to the pipe as did their fathers of the long ago, proving the truthfulness of the adage, "Evil communications corrupt good manners," and also good habits.

The innate politeness of the Indians, when in their strength and independence east of the Mississippi River, was truly remarkable. The early explorers were surprised at the perfection of this characteristic in the Choctaw Indians, and many expressed their admiration in their writings. If a Choctaw of the long ago met a white man with whom he was acquainted and on terms of social friendship, he took his proffered hand, then with a gentle pressure and forward inclination of the head, said, in a mild and sweet tone of voice: "Chishno pisah yukpah siah it tikana su," I am glad to see you my friend, and if he had nothing of importance to communicate, or of anything to obtain information, he passed on without further remarks.

But one of the many noble traits among the Choctaws was that of unfeigned hospitality; and to that extent that it became proverbial—deservingly so. When any one entered their house or hunting camp, be he a friend, mere acquaintance or entire stranger, they extended the hand of welcome—and it was sincere,—and after exchanging a few words of greeting the visitor was invited to take a seat; after which, they observed the most profound silence, waiting for their visitor to report his business. When he had done this, the silent but attentive wife brought what food she might have prepared (they were seldom found without something on hand), and her husband said to his guest: "Chishno upah" "you eat." To exhibit a true knowledge of Choctaw etiquette, it became your duty to partake a little of every thing the hospitable wife had placed before you; otherwise you would, though unwittingly, cause your host and hostess to regard your neglect of duty as a plain demonstration of contempt for their hospitality — purposely intended and offered.

Whether the Choctaws assembled for social conversation or debate in council, there never was but one who spoke at a time, and under no circumstances was he interrupted. This noble characteristic belongs to all the North American Indians, as far as I have been able to ascertain. In the public councils of the Choctaws, as well as in social gatherings and religious meetings, the utmost decorum always prevailed, and he who was talking in the social circle or addressing the council or lecturing in the religious meeting, always had as silent and attentive hearers as ever delighted and blessed a speaker. And when a question had been discussed, before putting it to a vote, a few minutes were always given for meditation, during which the most profound silence was observed; at the expiration of the allotted time, the vote of the assembly was taken; and which, I have been informed, is still kept up to this day. For many years after they had arrived from their ancient homes to the present place of abode, no candidate for an office of any kind ever went around among the people soliciting votes; the candidates merely gave notice by public announcement, and that was all; and had a candidate asked a man for his support, it would have been the death knell to his election.

On the day of the election, the names of all the candidates were written in regular order upon a long strip of paper, with the office to which each aspired written opposite to his name; and when the polls were opened, this paper was handed to the voter when he presented himself at the polls to vote, who commenced at the top of the list and called out the name of the candidate he wished to support for the different offices; if the voter could not read, then one of the officers in charge of the election, who could read, took the paper and slowly read the names and the office each aspirant desired; and the voter called out the name of each candidate for whom he wished to vote as he read; and no candidate ever manifested any hard feelings toward those who voted against him. Here was exhibited true liberty and free suffrage.

The Choctaw warrior, as I knew him in his native Mississippi forest, was as fine a specimen of manly perfection as I have ever beheld. He seemed to be as perfect as the human form could be. Tall, beautiful in symmetry of form and face, graceful, active, straight, fleet, with lofty and independent bearing, he seemed worthy in saying, as he of Juan Fernandez fame: "I am monarch of all I survey." His black, piercing eye seemed to penetrate and read the very thoughts of the heart, while his firm step proclaimed a feeling sense of his manly independence. Nor did their women fall behind in all that pertains to female beauty. I have seen among the Choctaws and Chickasaws, when living east of the Mississippi, as beautiful young women as could be found among any nation of people—civilized or uncivilized. They were of such unnatural beauty that they literally appeared to light up everything around them. Their shoulders were broad and square and their carriage true to Nature, which has never been excelled by the hand of art, their long, black tresses hung in flowing waves, extending nearly to the ground; but the beauty of the countenances of many of those Choctaw and Chickasaw girls was so extraordinary that if such faces were seen today in one of the parlors of the fashionable world, they would be considered as a type of beauty hitherto unknown. It was the wild untrammeled beauty of the forest, at the same time melancholy and splendid. The bashful calm in their large, magnificent eyes, shaded by unusually long, black eye-lashes, cannot be described; nor yet the glance, nor the splendid light of the smile which at times lit up the countenance like a flash, exposing the loveliest white and even teeth.

But alas! what a change has seventy-five years wrought upon this once free and happy people! How different the present generation from that happy, independent spirit that characterized their people when living in their ancient domains now the State of Mississippi! That manly bearing has given place to weakness and dejection; that eye, once so bright, bold and piercing, is now faint and desponding. The Choctaws once looked you straight in the eye with fearless yet polite, manly independence; his descendants now scarcely raise their heads to greet you. I have frequently met, here and there, a few Choctaws in Texas bordering on Red River. They seemed as strangers wandering in a strange land among whose people no voice of sympathy could be heard; no word of commiseration to be found; no smile of encouragement to be seen. With each different little band I tried to introduce a conversation only to be disappointed; and though I addressed them in their own native language, I could only obtain a reply in a few scarcely audible monosyllables. They remembered the past and were silent, yet how eloquent that silence.

In 1832, at Hebron, the home of the missionary, Calvin Cushman and his family, was the place appointed for the assembling of all the Choctaws in that district preparatory to their exodus from their ancient domain to a place they knew not where; but toward the setting sun as arbitrary power had decreed. Sad and mournful indeed was their gathering together—helpless and hopeless under the hand of a human power that knew no justice or mercy.

I was an eye witness to that scene of despairing woe and heard their sad refrain. I frequently visited their encampment and strolled from one part of it to another; while there came, borne upon the morn and evening breeze from every point of the vast encampment, faintly, yet distinctly, the plaintive sounds of weeping. It was the wailing of the Choctaw women. Around in different groups they sat with their children from whose quivering lips sobs and moans came in subdued unison; now, in wild concert united, their cries quivered and throbbed as they rose and fell on the night air, then dying away in pathetic wail.

The venerable old men, who long had retired from the hardships and fatigues of war and the chase, expressed the majesty of silent grief; yet there came now and then a sound that here and there swelled from a feeble moan to a deep, sustained groan—rising and falling till it died away just as it began. Their upturned faces mutely, but firmly spoke the deep sorrow that heaved within, as they sat in little groups, their gray heads uncovered in the spray of dancing sunshine which fell through the branches of the trees from above, while pitiful indeed was the feeble semblance of approval of the white man's policy which they strove to keep in their careworn countenances; while the heart-piercing cries of the women and children, seated upon the ground with heads covered with shawls and blankets and bodies swinging forward and backward, set up day and night, sad tones of woe echoing far back from the surrounding but otherwise silent forests; while the young and middle-aged warriors, now subdued and standing around in silence profound, gazed into space and upon the scattered clouds as they slowly swept across the tender blue. While here and there was heard an inarticulate moan seeking expression in some snatch of song, which announced its leaving a broken heart.

But why dwell upon such bitter memories? My soul finds no pleasure in them. Deep down to undiscovered depths has my life among, and study of the North American Indians during over three score and ten years, enabled me to penetrate their human nature with all their endurances and virtues: What the world ought to know, that I have written; and especially for those who desire more light on that unfortunate race of people, and feel an interest in truth, justice, and what concerns humanity the world over. To me was offered the mission, and I accepted it because my conscience approved it as right; and I have thus far, exerted every power to fulfill even to the letter and shall so continue to the end; allowing each reader to freely think his or her own thoughts.

Every missionary among the Choctaws, when he entered the mission gave a pledge that he would devote his or her life to the service of God in the cause of civilizing and Christianizing the Choctaw people, with no remuneration whatever except that of food and clothing for himself and family. This was supplied by the Board of Foreign Missions established at Boston, Massachusetts, to which Board everything pertaining to the mission in the way of property belonged—the missionaries owning nothing. This Board had spent a great deal towards the missions, and, in the removal of the Choctaws west, was unable to build up new missions there of sufficient number to supply labor for all of the missionaries; hence, all but three were absolved from their pledge, who soon returned to their friends in Massachusetts, while the three—Messrs. Kingsbury, Byington and Hotchkins, with their families, followed the exiled Choctaws to their unknown homes to be found in the wilderness of the west. Mr. Calvin Cushman was one of the two who remained in Mississippi, and died at his old missionary post, Hebron, a few years after the banishment of his old and long tried friends the Choctaws, for whose moral and intellectual benefit he had so long and faithfully labored; and the other was Mr. Elijah Bardwell, who labored at Ok-la Hun-na-li, sixty miles southwest of Hebron, but who, after the banishment of the Choctaws, moved to a point a mile and a half east of the present town of Starkville, Mississippi. He too, with all the rest of his co-laborers, has long since also gone to his reward.

As an example of the faithfulness with which those ancient missionaries adhered to every principle inculcated in the religion they professed among and preached to the Choctaws of the long ago, I will here relate the following as worthy of remembrance.

In the early days of the town of Starkville, Mississippi, a blacksmith (John McGaughey) established a shop in the embryo city, and, in connection with his smithing, also traded in horses, keeping a few on hand all the time. Mr. Bardwell knowing this, and wishing to purchase a horse, called at Mr. Gaughey's shop one morning and asked him if he had a horse for sale that would be suitable for a farm. Mac. replying in the affirmative, they went to the stable, where Mr. Bardwell, after examining the animal, asked the price. To this Mr. McGaughey replied: "Eighty-five dollars." "I regard that as too high a price," said Mr. Bardwell. Mr. McGaughey, well knowing the aged missionary and having unlimited confidence in his integrity, asked him what he believed the horse to be worth. To which Mr. Bardwell replied: "Sixty-five dollars." "You can have him at that price," responded Mr. McGaughey. Mr. Bardwell paid the money and took the horse. The trade was made in the spring of the year. Early in the following autumn, Mr. Bardwell called at the shop and, after the usual salutation, handed Mr. McGaughey twenty dollars, saying: "Here is that money that I owe you." Mr. McGaughey, in much astonishment, replied: "You are certainly mistaken. You do not owe me a dollar, you have always paid me the cash for all the work I have done for you in my shop." "True!" said Mr. Bardwell. "But this is not for work done in the shop, but is due you in a trade we made last spring." "What trade?" asked Mr. McGaughey in unfeigned surprise. "Why! in the purchase of a horse from you," replied Mr. Bardwell. "But you paid me the sixty-five dollars cash, the price for which I told you, you could have him." "True," replied Mr. Bardwell, "But you judged the horse to be worth eighty-five dollars, while I estimated his worth at only sixty-five; upon trial I have found him to be well worth the eighty-five dollars, the price you first asked for him. Here is your money." "But, Mr. Bardwell, I cannot accept the money. It was a fair trade." "Not so," replied the aged missionary, "you were right, Mr. McGaughey, in your judgment as to the correct value of the horse, and I was wrong. I insist upon your accepting that which is your just due." Mr. Mc-Gaughey finally accepted the twenty dollars but only through his great respect for Mr. Bardwell, whose feelings he knew would be wounded if he did not accept the proffered twenty dollars.

Mr. John McGaughey, many years afterwards, frequently related this horse trade.

Seventy years ago, the Choctaw hunter generally hunted alone and on foot; and when he killed his game, unless small, he left it where it had fallen, and turning his footsteps homeward, traveled in a straight line, here and there breaking a twig leaving its top in the direction he had come, as a guide to his wife whom he intended to send to bring it home. As soon as he arrived, he informed her of his success and merely pointed in the direction in which the game lay. At once she mounted a pony and started in the direction indicated, and guided by the broken twigs, she soon arrived at the spot, picked up and fastened the dead animal to the saddle, mounted and soon was at home again; then soon dressed and prepared a portion for her hunter lord's meal, while he sat and smoked his pipe in meditative silence. No animal adapted for food was ever killed in wanton sport by any Indian hunter.

As a marksman the Choctaw could not be surpassed in the use of the rifle. It mattered not whether his game was standing or running; a bullet shot from his rifle, when directed by his experienced eye, was a sure messenger of death. A shotgun was regarded with great contempt, and never used. The rifle, and the rifle alone, would he use. To surprise a Choctaw warrior or hunter in the woods—see him before he saw you—was a feat not easily accomplished; in fact, impossible by an inexperienced white woodsman, and extremely difficult even by the most experienced. His watchful and practiced eye was always on the alert, whether running, walking, standing or sitting; and his acute ear, attentive to every passing sound, heard the most feeble noise, which, to the white man's ear was utter silence.

Years ago I had a Choctaw, (full-blood) friend as noble and true as ever man possessed. Oft in our frequent hunts together, while silently gliding through the dense forests ten or fifteen rods apart, he would attract my attention by his well-known ha ha (give caution) in a low but distinct tone of voice, and point to a certain part of the woods where he had discovered an animal of some kind; and though I looked as closely as possible I could see nothing whatever that resembled a living object of any kind. Being at too great a distance to risk a sure shot, he would signal me to remain quiet, as he endeavored to get closer. To me that was the most exciting and interesting part of the scene; for then began those strategic movements in which the most skillful white hunter that I have ever seen, was a mere bungler. With deepest interest, not unmixed with excitement, I closely watched his every movement as he slowly and stealthily advanced, with eyes fixed upon his object; now, crawling noiselessly upon his hands and knees, then as motionless as a stump; now stretched full length upon the ground, then standing erect and motionless; then dropping suddenly to the ground, and crawling off at an acute angle to the right or left to get behind a certain tree or log, here and there stopping and slowly raising his head just enough to look over the top of the grass; then again be hidden until he reached the desired tree; with intense mingled curiosity and excitement, when hidden from my view in the grass, did I seek to follow him in his course with my eyes. Oft I would see a little dark spot not larger than my fist just above the top of the grass, which slowly grew larger and larger until I discovered it was his motionless head; and had I not known he was there somewhere I would not have suspected it was a human head or the head of anything else; and as I kept my eyes upon it, I noticed it slowly getting smaller until it gradually disappeared; and when he reached the tree, he then observed the same caution slowly rising until he stood erect and close to the body of the tree, then slowly and cautiously peeping around it first on the right, then on the left; and when, at this juncture, I have turned my eyes from him, but momentarily as I thought, to the point where I thought the game must be, being also eager to satisfy my excited curiosity as to the kind of animal he was endeavoring to shoot, yet, when I looked to the spot where I had just seen him—lo! he was not there; and while wondering to what point of the compass he had so suddenly disappeared unobserved, and vainly looking to find his mysterious whereabouts, I would be startled by the sharp crack of his rifle in a different direction from that in which I was looking for him, and in turning my eye would see him slowly rising out of the grass at a point a hundred yards distant from where I had last seen him. "Well, old fellow," I then ejaculated to myself, "I would not hunt for you in wild forest for the purpose of obtaining your scalp, knowing, at the same time, that you were somewhere about seeking also to secure mine; I would just call to you to come and take it at once and save anxiety."

Frequently have I proposed to exchange guns with George (that was his name—simply George and nothing else) my double barreled shot-gun for his rifle, but he invariably refused; and when I asked for his objection to my gun, he ever had but one and the same reply—"Him push." He did not fancy the reaction or "kicking" so oft experienced in shooting the shot-gun which George, no doubt, once experienced to his entire satisfaction. Generous and faithful, George! I wonder where you are today? If on the face of God's green earth, I am sure—humble though you may be—there is one true heart above the sod that still beats in love for me.

It was truly wonderful with what ease and certainty the Choctaw hunter and warrior made his way through the dense forests of his country to any point he wished to go, near or distant. But give him the direction, was all he desired; with an unerring certainty, though never having been in that part of the country before, he would go over hill and valley, through thickets and canebrakes to the desired point, that seemed incredible. I have known the little Choctaw boys, in their juvenile excursions with their bows and arrows and blow-guns to wander miles away from their homes, this way and that through the woods, and return home at night, without a thought of fear of getting lost; nor did their parents have any uneasiness in regard to their wanderings. It is a universal characteristic of the Indian, when traveling in a unknown country, to let nothing pass unnoticed. His watchful eye marks every distinguishing feature of the surroundings—a peculiarily leaning or fallen tree, stump or bush, rock or hill, creek or branch, he will recognize years afterwards, and use them as landmarks, in going again through the same country. Thus the Indian hunter was enabled to go into a distant forest, where he never before had been, pitch his camp, leave it and hunt all day—wandering this way and that over hills and through jungles for miles away, and return to his camp at the close of the day with that appeared ease and unerring certainty, that baffled all the ingenuity of the white man and appeared to him as bordering on the miraculous. Ask any Indian for directions to a place, near or distant, and he merely points in the direction you should go, regarding that as sufficient information for any one of common sense.

In traveling through the Choctaw Nation in 1884, at one time I desired to go to a point forty miles distant, to which led a very dim path, at times scarcely deserving the name, and upon making inquiry of different Choctaws whom I frequently met along my way, they only pointed in the direction I must travel and passed on; and being ashamed to let it appear that I did not have sense enough to go to the desired point after being told the direction, I rode on without further inquiry, and by taking the path, at every fork that seemed to lead the nearest in the direction I had been told to travel, I, in good time, reached my place of destination. So, after all, the Choctaws told me all that was necessary in the matter.

The ancient Choctaw warrior and hunter left the domestic affairs of his humble home wholly to the management of his wife and children. The hospitalities of his cabin, however, were always open to friend or stranger, before whom he ever assumed a calm and respectful reserve, though nothing escaped his notice. If questioned he would readily enter into a conversation concerning his exploits as a warrior and hunter, but was indifferent upon the touching episodes of home, with its scenes of domestic bliss or woe, though their tendrils were as deeply and strangely interwoven with the fibres of his heart as with those of any other of the human race. The vicissitudes of life, its joys and sorrows, its hopes and fears, were regarded as unworthy the consideration of a warrior and hunter; but the dangers, the fatigues and hardships of war and the chase as subjects only worthy to be mentioned. Yet, with all this, in unfeigned affection for his wife, children, kindred and friends; in deep anxiety for them in sickness and distress; in untiring efforts to relieve their necessities and wants; in anxiety for their safety in hours of danger; in fearless exposure of himself to protect them from harm; in his silent yet deep sorrow at their death; in his unassumed joy in their happiness; in these all Indians stand equal to any race of people that ever lived. And when roaming with him years ago in the solitudes of his native forests, and have looked upon him, whose nature and peculiar habits have been declared by the world to have no place with the rest of the human family, and these have gone with him to his humble, but no less hospitable, forest home, and there witnessed the same evidences of joy and sorrow, of hope and fear, of pleasure and pain that are everywhere peculiar to man's nature, I could but be more firmly established in that which I long had known, that the North American Indian, from first to last, had been wrongfully and shamefully misrepresented, and though in him are blended vindictive and revengeful passions, so much condemned by the civilized world, yet I found these were equally balanced by warm, generous, and noble feelings, as were found in any class of the human race.

To the ancient Choctaw warrior and hunter, excitement of some kind was indispensible to relieve the tedium of the nothing-to-do in which a great part of his life was spent. Hence the intervals between war and hunting were filled up by various amusements, ball plays, dances, foot and horse races, trials of strength and activity in wrestling and jumping, all being regulated by rules and regulations of a complicated etiquette.

But the tolik (ball play) was the ultimatum of all games—"the sine qua non" of all amusements to the Indians of the south; and to which he attached the greatest importance, and in the engagement of which his delight reached its highest perfection, and in the excelling of which his ambition fell not below that of him who contested in the Olympic games of ancient Greece.

A Choctaw tolik seventy years ago, was indeed a game that well might have astonished the Titan, and diverted them, pro. tem. at least, from their own pastime. But when I look back through the retrospective years of the long past to that animating scene, and then read in recent years the different attempts made by many through the journals of the day to describe a genuine Choctaw ball-play of those years ago, it excites a smile and only intensifies the hold memory retains of that indescribable game. No one, who has not witnessed it, can form a just idea of the scene from any description given; for it baffles all the powers of language and must be seen to be in any way comprehended. The baseball-play of the present day, so popular among the whites, in point of deep interest and wild excitement produced in the spectator, when compared to the chashpo tolik (ancient ball-play) of the Choctaws east of the Mississippi River, bears about the same relation that the light of the crescent moon does to the mid-day light of the mighty orb of day in a cloudless sky. However, I will attempt a description, though well aware that after all that can be said, the reader will only be able to form a very imperfect idea of the weird scene.

When the warriors of a village, wearied by the monotony of everyday life, desired a change that was truly from one extreme to that of another, they sent a challenge to those of another village of their own tribe, and, not infrequently, to those of a neighboring tribe, to engage in a grand ball-play. If the challenge was accepted, and it was rarely declined, a suitable place was selected and prepared by the challengers, and a day agreed upon. The hetoka (ball ground) was selected in some beautiful level plain easily found in their then beautiful and romantic country. Upon the ground, from three hundred to four hundred yards apart, two straight pieces of timber were firmly planted close together in the ground, each about fifteen feet in height, and from four to six inches in width, presenting a front of a foot or more. These were called aiulbi (ball posts). During the intervening time between the day of the challenge and that of the play, great preparations were made on both sides by those who intended to engage therein. With much care and unaffected solemnity they went through with their preparatory ceremonies.

The night preceding the day of the play was spent in painting, with the same care as when preparing for the war-path, dancing with frequent rubbing of both the upper and lower limbs, and taking their "sacred medicine."

In the meantime, tidings of the approaching play spread on wings of the wind from village to village and from neighborhood to neighborhood for miles away; and during the first two or three days preceding the play, hundreds of Indians—the old, the young, the gay, the grave of both sexes, in immense concourse, were seen wending their way through the vast forests from every point of the compass, toward the ball-ground; with their ponies loaded with

skins, furs, trinkets, and every other imaginable thing that
was part and parcel of Indian wealth, to stake upon the
result of one or the other side.

On the morning of the appointed day, the players, from
seventy-five to a hundred on each side, strong and athletic
men, straight as arrows and fleet as antelopes, entirely in a
nude state, excepting a broad piece of cloth around the
hips, were heard in the distance advancing toward the plain
from opposite sides, making the heretofore silent forests
ring with their exulting songs and defiant hump-hel (banter)
as intimations of the great feats of strength and endurance,
fleetness and activity they would display before the eyes of
their admiring friends. The curiosity, anxiety and excitement now manifested by the vast throng of assembled spectators were manifested on every countenance. Soon the
players were dimly seen in the distance through their majestic forests, flitting here and there as spectres among the
trees. Anon they are all in full view advancing from opposite sides in a steady, uniform trot, and in perfect order, as
if to engage in deadly hand to hand conflict; now they meet
and intermingle in one confused and disorderly mass inter-
changing friendly salutations dancing and jumping in the
wildest manner, while intermingling with all an artillery of
of wild shakuplichihi that echoed far back from the solitudes of the surrounding woods.

Then came a sudden hush—a silence deep, as if all
Nature had made a pause—the prophetic calm before the
bursting storm. During this brief interval, the betting was
going on and the stakes being put up; the articles bet were
all placed promiscuously in one place, often forming a vast
conglomeration of things too numerous to mention, and the
winning side took the pile. This being completed, the players took their places, each furnished with two kapucha
(ball-sticks), three feet long, and made of tough hickory
wood thoroughly seasoned. At one end of each ka-puch-a
a very ingenious device, in shape and size, very similar to
that of the hand half closed, was constructed of sinews of

wild animals, in which they caught and threw the ball. It was truly astonishing with what ease and certainty they would catch the flying ball in the cups of the sticks and the amazing distance and accuracy they could hurl it through the air. In taking their places at the opening of the play, ten or twenty, according to the number of players engaged, of each side were stationed at each pole. To illustrate, I will say, ten of the A party and ten of the B party were placed at pole C; and ten of the B party and ten of the A party at pole D. The ten of the B party who were stationed at the pole C were called fa-lo-mo-li-chi (throw-backs); and the ten of the A party also stationed at pole C were called hat-tak-fa-bus-sa (pole men), and the ten of the A party stationed at the pole D were called fala molichi, and the ten of the B party stationed at the pole D hattak fabussa. The business of the falamolichi at each pole was to prevent if possible, the ball thrown by the opposite party, from striking the pole C; and throw it back towards the pole D to their own party; while that of the hattak fabussa at pole C was to prevent this, catch the ball themselves, if possible, and hurl it against the pole C, and the business of the fala-molichi and hattak fabussa at the pole D was the same as that at the pole C. In the centre, between the two poles, were also stationed the same number of each party as were stationed at the poles, called middle men, with whom was a chief "medicine man," whose business was to throw the ball straight up into the air, as the signal for the play to commence. The remaining players were scattered promiscuously along the line between the poles and over different portions of the play-ground.

All things being ready, the ball suddenly shot up into the air from the vigorous arm of the medicine man, and the wash-o-ha (playing) began. The moment the ball was seen in the air, the players of both sides, except the falamolichi and hattak fabussa, who remained at their posts, rushed to the spot, where the ball would likely fall, with a fearful shock. Now began to be exhibited a scene of wild grandeur that beggared all description. As there were no rules and regulations governing the manner of playing nor any act considered unfair, each of course, acted under the impulse of the moment regardless of consequences.

They threw down and ran over each other in the wild excitement and reckless chase after the ball, stopping not nor heeding the broken limbs and bruised heads or even broken neck of a fallen player. Like a herd of stampeded buffaloes upon the western plains, they ran against and over each other, or any thing else, man or beast, that stood in their way; and thus in wild confusion and crazed excitement they scrambled and tumbled, each player straining every nerve and muscle to its utmost tension, to get the ball or prevent his opponent, who held it firmly grasped between the cups of his trusty kapucha, from making a successful throw; while up and down the lines the shouts of the players—"Falamochi! Falamochi!" (Throw it back! Throw it back) as others shouted "Hokli! Hoklio!" (Catch! Catch!). The object of each party was to throw the ball against the two upright pieces of timber that stood in the direction of the village to which it belonged; and, as it came whizzing through the air, with the velocity comparatively of a bullet shot from a gun, a player running at an angle to intercept the flying ball, and when near enough, would spring several feet into the air and catch it in the hands of his sticks, but ere he could throw it, though running at full speed, an opponent would hurl him to the ground, with a force seemingly sufficient to break every bone in his body—and even to destroy life, and as No. 2 would wrest the ball from the fallen No. 1 and throw it, ere it had flown fifty feet, No. 3 would catch it with his unerring kapucha, and not seeing, perhaps an opportunity of making an advantageous throw, would start off with the speed of a deer, still holding the ball in the cups of his kapucha—pursued by every player.

Again was presented to the spectators another of those exciting scenes, that seldom fall to the lot of one short life-time to behold, which language fails to depict, or imagination to conceive. He now runs off, perhaps, at an acute angle with that of the line of the poles, with seemingly superhuman speed; now and then elevating above his head his kapucha in which safely rests the ball, and in defiant exultation shouts "Hump-he! Hump-he!" (I dare you) which was acknowledged by his own party with a wild response of approval, but responded to by a bold cry of defiance from the opposite side. Then again all is hushed and the breathless silence is only disturbed by the heavy thud of their running feet. For a short time he continues his straight course, as if to test the speed of his pursuing opponents; then begins to circle toward his pole. Instantly comprehending his object, his running friends circle with him, with eyes fixed upon him, to secure all advantages given to them by any strategic throw he may make for them, while his opponents are mingled among them to defeat his object; again he runs in a straight line; then dodges this way and that; suddenly he hears the cry from some one of his party in the rear of the parallel running throng, who sees an advantage to be gained if the ball was thrown to him, "Falamolichi!" "Falamolichi!" He now turns and dashes back on the line and in response to the continued cry— "Falamolichi!" he hurls the ball with all his strength; with fearful velocity it flies through the air and falls near the caller; and in the confusion made by the suddenly turning throng, he picks it up at full speed with his kapucha, and starts toward his pole. Then is heard the cry of his hattak fabussa, and he hurls the ball toward them and, as it falls, they and the throw-backs stationed at that pole, rush to secure it; and then again, though on a smaller scale, a scene of wild confusion was seen—scuffling, pulling, pushing, butting—unsurpassed in any game ever engaged in by man. Perhaps, a throw-back secures the ball and starts upon the wing, in the direction of his pole, meeting the advancing throng, but with his own throw-backs and the polemen of his opponents at his heels; the latter to prevent him from making a successful throw and the former to prevent any interference, while the shouts of "Falamolichi!" "Fala-molichi!" arose from his own men in the advancing runners. Again the ball flies through the air, and is about to fall directly among them, but ere it reaches the ground many spring into the air to catch it, but are tripped and they fall headlong to the earth. Then, as the ball reaches the ground again is brought into full requisition the propensities of each one to butt, pull, and push, though not a sound is heard, except the wild rattling of the kapucha, that remind-ed one of the noise made by the collision of the horns of a drove of stampeding Texas steers. Oft amid the play women were seen giving water to the thirsty and offering words of encouragement; while others, armed with long switches stood ready to give their expressions of encourage-ment to the supposed tardy, by a severe rap over the naked shoulders, as a gentle reminder of their dereliction of duty; all of which was received in good faith, yet invariably elicited the response—"Wah!" as an acknowledgment of the favor.

From ten to twenty was generally the game. When-ever the ball was thrown against the upright fabussa (poles), it counted one, and the successful thrower shouted: "Illi tok," (dead) meaning one number less; oft accompany-ing the shout by gobbling vociferously like the wild turkey, which elicited a shout of laughter from his party, and a yell of defiance from the other. Thus the exciting, and truly wild and romantic scene was continued, with unbated ef-forts on the part of the players until the game was won. But woe to the inconsiderate white man, whose thoughtless curiosity had led him too far upon the hetoka (ball ground) and at whose feet the ball should chance to fall; if the path to that ball was not clear of all obstructions, the two hun-dred players, now approaching with the rush of a mighty whirlwind would soon make it so. And right then and there, though it might be the first time in life, he became a really active man, if the desire of immediate safety could be any inducement, cheerfully inaugurating proceedings by turning a few double somersets, regardless as to the scientific manner he executed them, or the laugh of ridicule that might be offered at his expense; and if he escaped only with a broken limb or two, and a first-class scare, he might justly consider himself most fortunate. But the Choctaws have long since lost that interest in the ball-play that they formerly cherished in their old homes east of the Mississippi River. 'Tis true, now and then, even at the present day, they indulge in the time honored game, but the game of the present day is a Lilliputian—a veritable pygmy—in comparison with the grand old game of three quarters of a century ago; nor will it be many years ere it will be said of the Choctaw tohli, as of ancient Troy—"Ilium fuit."

To any one of the present day, an ancient Choctaw ball-play would be an exhibition far more interesting, strange, wild and romantic, in all its features, than anything ever exhibited in a circus from first to last—excelling it in every particular of daring feats and wild recklessness. In the ancient ball-play, the activity, fleetness, strength and endurance of the Mississippi Choctaw warrior and hunter, were more fully exemplified than anywhere else; for there he brought into the most severe action every power of soul and body. In those ancient ball-plays, I have known villages to lose all their earthly possessions upon the issue of a single play. Yet, they bore their misfortune with becoming grace and philosophic indifference and appeared as gay and cheerful as if nothing of importance had occurred. The education of the ancient Choctaw warrior and hunter consisted mainly in the frequency of these muscular exercises which enabled him to endure hunger, thirst and fatigue; hence they often indulged in protracted fastings, frequent foot races, trials of bodily strength, introductions to the warpath, the chase and their favorite tolih.

They also indulged in another game in which they took great delight, called ulth chuppih, in which but two players could engage at the same time; but upon the result of which, as in the tolih, they frequently bet their little all. An alley,

with a hard smooth surface and about two hundred feet
long, was made upon the ground. The two players took a
position at the upper end at which they were to commence
the game, each having in his hands a smooth, tapering pole
eight or ten feet long flattened at the ends. A smooth round
stone of several inches in circumference was then brought
into the arena; as soon as both were ready, No. 1 took the
stone and rolled it with all his strength down the narrow
inclined plane of the smooth alley; and after which both
instantly started with their utmost speed. Soon No. 2 threw
his pole at the rolling stone; instantly No. 1 threw his at the
flying pole of No. 2, aiming to hit it, and, by so doing,
change its course from the rolling stone. If No. 2 hits the
stone, he counts one; but if No. 1 prevents it by hitting the
pole of No. 2, he then counts one; and he, who hits his
object the greater number of times in eleven rollings of the
stone, was the winner. It was a more difficult matter to hit
either the narrow edge of the rolling stone, or the flying
pole, than would be at first imagined. However, the ancient
Chahtah ulte chupih may come in at least as a worthy competitor with the pale-face ten-pin-alley, for the disputed
right of being the more dignified amusement.

Judge Julius Folsom of Atoka, Indian Territory, informed me that a friend of his, Isaac McClure, found an
ulth chuppih ball in a mound near Skullyville, Choctaw
Nation, Indian Territory, and not knowing what it was,
brought it to him for information. This proves that the
Indians who occupied the territory prior to the Choctaws
also indulged in the game of ulth chuppih.

The following was furnished me by my learned friend
H. S. Halbert, of Mississippi, a genuine philanthropist and
true friend to the North American Indian race:

"The Great Ball Play and Fight on Noxubee" (a corruption of the Choctaw word Nakshobih, a peculiarly offensive
odor), between the Creeks and Choctaws.

"In the fall of 1836, there died in the southern part of
Noxubee County an aged Indian warrior named Stonie

Hadjo. This old Indian had resided in the county for years and was very popular with the pioneers, who regarded him as an upright and truthful man. He was a Creek by birth, a Choctaw by adoption. This old warrior would often tell of a gre⸱' ball-play and fight which occurred between the Creeks and Choctaws in Noxubee County. This event, from date given by him, must have occurred about the year 1790.

"On Noxubee River there was anciently a large beaver pond, about which the Creeks and Choctaws had a violent dispute. The Creeks claimed it by priority of discovery, while the Choctaws asserted their right to it because it lay in their own territory. As the fur trade at Mobile and Pensacola, (corruption of the Choctaw words puska okla, bread people, then small places, but the main points of trade for the southern Indians) was lucrative, each party was loath to renounce the right to the beavers. The two Nations finally agreed to settle the matter by a ball-play. A given number of the best players were accordingly selected from each nation, who were to decide, by the result of the game, to which nation the exclusive right to the beaver pond should belong. Great preparations were made by each party for this important event. They commenced preparing on the new moon and it took them two whole moons and until the full of the third to complete preparations. Great quantities of provisions had to be procured, and the ball players had to subject themselves meanwhile to the usual requirement of practice, the athletic exercises customary on such occasions.

"Finally the day came, and Stonie Hadjo said that there were ten thousand Indians, Creeks and Choctaws, camped around the ball ground on Noxubee River. The Creek Chief who held the highest command, after seeing his people properly encamped left to pay a visit of ceremony to the great Chief of the Choctaws, who lived at some distance. Stonie Hadjo gave the names of those two chiefs, but these names cannot now be recalled." (If I mistake not, the Choctaw Chief was Himakubih, now to kill). "Every thing being now ready the play commenced, and it was admitted on all sides to have been the closest and most evenly matched game ever witnessed by either nation. Fortune vascillated from Creek to Choctaw and then from Choctaw to Creek. At last, it was a tied game, both parties standing even. One more game remained to be played which would decide the contest. Then occurred a long and terrible struggle lasting for four hours. Every Creek and every Choctaw strained himself to his utmost bent. Finally after prodigious feats of strength and agility displayed on both sides, fortune at least declared in favor of the Creeks. The victors immediately began to shout and sing! The Choctaws were greatly humiliated. At length a high spirited Choctaw player, unable longer to endure the exultant shouts of the victorious party, made an insulting remark to a Creek player. (Who, in retaliation, Choctaws state, threw a petticoat on the Choctaw—the greatest insult that can be offered to an Indian). The latter resented it, and the two instantly clutched each other in deadly combat. The contagion spread, and a general fight with sticks, knives, guns, tomahawks and bows and arrows, began among the ball players. Then warriors from each tribe commenced joining in the fight until all were engaged in bloody strife.

"The fight continued from an hour by the sun in the evening with but little intermission during the night, until two hours by the sun the next morning. At this juncture the great chiefs of the Creeks and the Choctaws arrived upon the ground and at once put a stop to the combat, runners having been dispatched at the beginning of the fight to these two leaders to inform them of the affair. The combatants upon desisting from the fight, spent the remainder of the day in taking care of the wounded; the women watching over the dead. The next day the dead were buried; their money, silver ornaments, and other articles of value being deposited with them in their graves. The third day a council convened. The Creek and the Choctaw chiefs made "talks" expressing their regrets that their people should have given way to such a wild storm of passion resulting in the death of so many brave warriors. There was no war or cause for war between the two nations and they councilled that all forget the unhappy strife, make peace and be friends as before. This advice was heeded. The pipe of peace was smoked, all shook hands and departed to their homes.

"Stonie Hadjo stated that five hundred warriors were killed outright in this fight and that a great many of the wounded afterwards died. The Creeks and Choctaws had had several wars with each other, had fought many bloody battles, but that no battle was so disastrous as this fight at the ball ground. For many long years the Creeks and Choctaws looked back to this event with emotions of terror and sorrow. For here, their picked men, their ball players, who were the flower of the two Nations, almost to a man perished. Scarcely was there a Creek or Choctaw family, but had to mourn the death of some kinsman slain. For several years the Creeks made annual pilgrimages to this ball ground to weep over the graves of their dead. The Choctaws kept up this Indian custom much longer. Even down to the time of their emigration in 1832 they had not ceased to make similar lamentations.

"After the fight, by tacit consent, the beaver pond was left in the undisputed possession of the Choctaws; but it is said that soon afterwards, the beaver entirely abandoned the pond. According to Indian superstition, their departure was supposed to have some connection with the unfortunate fight.

"In 1832, a man named Charles Dobbs settled on this ball and battle ground. Stonie Hadjo, who was then living in the vicinity pointed out to him many of the graves, wherein money and other valuables were buried. Dobbs dug down and recovered about five hundred dollars in silver, and about two hundred and fifty dollars worth of silver ornaments.

"This ground is situated on the eastern banks of Noxubee River, about five miles west of Cooksville and about
two hundred yards north of where Shuqualak (corruption
of Shohpakalih, Sparkling,) Creek empties into Noxubee.
The beaver pond, now drained and in cultivation, is situated
on the western bank of Noxubee, about half a mile north of
the ball-ground."

Frequently disputes between the ancient Choctaws
and Muscogees arose as a result of a ball-play, but which
too frequently terminated in a fearful fight, followed by a
protracted war. My friend, H. S. Halbert, informed me by
letter, of another, which was told to him by an aged Choctaw who remained in Mississippi with others at the time of
the Choctaw exodus in 1832. It is as follows:

"The war in 1800 between the Choctaws and Creeks
had its origin in a dispute about the territory between the
Tombigbee and Black Warrior Rivers, which both nations
claimed. It was finally agreed to settle the matter by a ball-
play. The play occurred on the west bank of the Black
Warrior, a mile below Tuscaloosa. The Creek chief was
named Tuskeegee, the Choctaw, Luee, (corruption of La
wih, being equal). Both parties claimed the victory. A violent dispute arose which resulted in a call to arms followed
by a furious battle in which many were killed and wounded
on both sides, but the Choctaws were victorious. This
occurred in the spring. The Choctaws after the fight withdrew to their homes. The Creeks, stung by defeat, invaded
the Choctaw Nation in the ensuing fall under Tuskeegee
and fought the second battle in the now Noxubee County,
in which the Creeks were victorious. Luee again commanded the Choctaws." But the Choctaws being reinforced,
another battle was soon after fought in which the Choctaws
under Himarkubih, were victorious and drove the Creeks
out of their country. I have been told that previous to our
Civil War the trees still showed signs of the ancient conflict.

The Choctaws, at the time of their earliest acquaintance with the European races, possessed, in conjunction

with all their race of the North American Continent, a
vague, but to a great extent, correct knowledge of the Oka
Falama, "The returning waters," as they termed it—The
Flood.

The Rev. Cyrus Byington related a little incident, as
one out of many interesting and pleasing ones that frequently occurred when traveling through their country
from one point to another in the discharge of his ministerial
duties, over seventy years ago. At one time he found night
fast approaching without any visible prospect of finding a
place of shelter for the night, safe from the denizens of the
wilderness through which his devious path was leading
him. Then and there roads were unknown and paths alone
led the traveler from place to place. Soon, however, he
discovered an humble cabin a few hundred yards distant,
directly to which the little path was leading him, and which
he readily recognized as the home of a Choctaw hunter.
Several little children were engaged in their juvenile sports
near the house, who, upon seeing the white stranger approaching, made a precipitate retreat into the house. The
mother hastened to the door to learn the cause of the
alarm—saw, gazed a moment, and then as suddenly disappeared. As Mr. Byington rode up, he observed an Indian
man sitting before the door, whose appearance betokened
his experience in the vicissitudes of life to have reached
four score years or more, who cheerfully extended the hospitality of his humble home to the solitary and wayworn
stranger.

Soon Mr. Byington was also seated before the cabin
door near the aged Choctaw, and very naturally took a
survey of the surroundings. It was a cloudless eve in May,
1825. After an exchange of a few words, and the aged man
had learned who his guest was, for he had heard of the
good missionaries, mutual confidence was at once established between the two; especially as the stranger was con-
versant, to some extent, in his native Choctaw tongue.
During the conversation of the evening, the good mission-

ary, true to his trust, narrated to his aged host the story of the Cross, with all its interesting bearings, and in conclusion set forth, with much eloquence, the importance and necessity of his host's immediate attention to the things that appertained to his interests beyond the sphere of time; to all of which the old man listened in profound silence, and with the deepest interest and attention; then rising from his seat and taking Mr. Byington by the hand and leading him to the corner of the little cabin where the setting sun could be seen in full view, he pointed to it and said: "Your talk is, no doubt, true and good, but it is strange and dark to me. See yonder is the sun of my life; it but lingers upon the western sky. It is now too late for me to follow your new and strange words. Let me continue in the path I long have walked, and in which my fathers before me trod; the Great Spirit tells me, it will lead me to the happy hunting grounds of the Indian, and that is sufficient for me." And who can say it was not? Then pointing to his children and grand-children, he continued: "Tell your new talk to them and to my young people. They have time to consider it. If it is a better way to the happy hunting grounds than the Indian's, teach them to walk in it, but persuade me not to now forsake my long known path, for one unknown and so strange to me." Mr. Byington, deeply interested in his aged friend, related, in connecton with other Bible truths, the account of the flood. Instantly the old veteran's countenance brightened up, and with a smile of self-confidence said: "You no longer talk mysteries. I know now of what you speak. My father told me when a boy of the Oka Falama." Mr. Byington then asked him, if he knew how long since it occurred. The old veteran, stooping, filled both hands with sand, then said: "As many seasons of snow ago, as I hold grains of sand in my hand."

During the fall of 1887, I was boarding at a Choctaw friend's in the territory, a man of noble characteristics, and one day related to him the above incident. I was struck with his remark. As I closed, he said in a slow and mourn-

ful tone of voice: "Ever thinking of the good of their people,—the young and rising generations coming after them."
I asked a more explicit explanation. He replied: "The aged
men of my people always expressed more concern for the
welfare of the young than they did for themselves. That
old Choctaw, of whom you have just spoken, seemed to realize that it was too late for him to be benefitted by the
teachings of the good white man, but still was anxious for
him to do all the good he could for the young and rising
generation of his nation. Why is the Indian so traduced by
the white man? Has my race no redeeming traits?"

The Choctaw hunter was famous as a strategist when
hunting alone in the woods; and was such an expert in the
art of exactly imitating the cries of the various animals of
the forests, that he would deceive the ear of the most experienced. They made a very ingeniously constructed instrument for calling deer to them, in the use of which they were
very expert; and in connection with this, they used a decoy
made by cutting the skin clear round the neck, about ten
inches from the head of a slain buck having huge horns, and
then stuffing the skin in one entire section up to the head
and cutting off the neck where it joins the head. The skin,
thus made hollow from the head back, is kept in its natural
position by inserting upright sticks; the skin is then pulled
upwards from the nose to the horns and all the flesh and
brains removed; then the skin is re-pulled to its natural
place and laid away to dry. In a year it has become dry;
hard and inoffensive, and fit for use. All the upright sticks
are then taken out except the one next to the head, which is
left as a hand-hold. Thus the hunter, with his deer-caller
and head decoy, easily enticed his game within the range of
his deadly rifle; for, secreting himself in the woods, he commenced to imitate the bleating of a deer; if within hearing
distance, one soon responds; but, perhaps, catching the
scent of the hunter, stops and begins to look around. The
hunter now inserts his arm into the cavity of the decoy and
taking hold of the upright stick within, easily held it up to

view, and attracted the attention of the doubting deer by rubbing it against the bushes or a tree; seeing which, the then no longer suspicious deer advanced, and only learned its mistake by the sharp crack of the rifle and the deadly bullet.

The antlers of some of the bucks grew to a wonderful size, which were shed off every February, or rather pushed off by the forthcoming new horns, a singularly strange freak of nature, yet no less true. There was also a strange and ancient tradition among the Choctaw and Chickasaw hunters, before their exodus to their present place of abode, that, as soon as the horns dropped off, the buck at once pawed a hole in the ground with his feet (it being always soft during the season of shedding, from the frequent rains) into which he pushed the fallen horns and carefully covered them up. This may seem fabulous, yet there are good grounds upon which to establish, at least a probability, if not its truth. I have heard of white hunters who had been attracted by the appearance of something being freshly covered up, with the tracks of deer alone at and around the spot, and, upon digging down, have found the horns of a deer. In many hunts in the forest of Mississippi, during many years, where the deer almost filled the woods, I have never seen a deer horn except those attached to a skull— left in the woods by the hunter, or those of a buck that had died a natural death. The forests were burnt off the latter part of every March, and thus the ground, was entirely naked and a deer's horn, if above ground, could have been seen a hundred yards distant, but they were not seen. The fires of the forest were not hot enough to burn them. Now what became of them if not buried by the bucks, as hundreds were shed yearly?

The Choctaw warrior was equally as expert in deceiving his enemy as he was in that of the wild denizens of his native forests. When upon the war-path the Choctaws always went in small bands, which was the universal custom of their entire race, traveling one behind the other in a straight line; and, if in the enemy's territory each one stepped exactly in the tracks of the one who walked before him, while the one in the extreme rear defaced, as much as possible, their tracks, that no evidence of their number, or whereabouts might be made known to the enemy. In these war excursions, the most profound silence was observed; their communications being carried on by preconcerted and well understood signs made by the hand or head; if necessary to be audible, then by a low imitative cry of some particular wild animal.

The dignity of chieftainship was bestowed upon him who had proved himself worthy by his skill and daring deeds in war; and to preserve the valiant character of their chief, it was considered a disgrace for him to be surpassed in daring deeds by any of his warriors; at the same time, it was also regarded as dishonorable for the warriors to be surpassed by their chief. Thus there were great motives for both to perform desperate deeds of valor—which they did; nor did they wait for opportunities for the display of heroism, but sought perils and toils by which they might distinguish themselves. These war parties, gliding noiselessly like spectres through the dense forests, painted in the most fantastic manner conceivable, presented a wild and fearful appearance, more calculated to strike terror to the heart of the beholder than admiration. Though they advanced in small bodies and detached parties, yet in their retreats they scattered like frightened partridges, each for himself, but to unite again at a pre-arranged place miles to the rear. No gaudy display was ever made in their war excursions to their enemy's country. They meant business, not display, depending on the success of their expedition in their silent and unexpected approach, patient watching, and artful stratagems. To fight a pitched battle in an open field giving the enemy an equal chance, was to the Choctaws the best evidence of a want of military skill. But unlike most of their race, they seldom invaded an enemy's territory from choice; but woe to the enemy, who attributing this to cowardice, should have the presumption to invade their country; like enraged bears robbed of their young, they would find the Choctaw warriors, to a man, ready to repel them with the most desperate and fearless bravery ever exhibited by any race of men. Yet, to them, no less than to the whites, strategy was commendable, and to outwit an enemy and thus gain an advantage over him, was evidence of great and praiseworthy skill.

Duels.—The duelist, according to the white man's code of honor, was regarded by the Choctaws with utmost contempt, the fool above all fools. That a man would stand up openly before his enemy to be shot at with the opportunity of getting an open shot at him, was a code of honor beyond their comprehension a piece of nonsense in the indulgence of which a Choctaw could not be guilty.

I did once hear, however, of a young Choctaw warrior accepting a challenge from a white man in their nation east of the Mississippi River. A white man, who had been living in one of their villages for several months, taking offense at something a young warrior had done, and well knowing the repugnance with which the Choctaws regarded the white man's code of honor, thought it a proper time to impress them with the belief that he was very brave, since he had but little to fear that he would be called upon to put it to the test; therefore, gave him a verbal challenge, in the presence of many other Choctaw warriors, to fight him a duel according to the white man's code; and to impress upon the minds of the bystanders that where there was so much bravery, there must be a proportional amount of honor, the heroic challenger informed the young Choctaw that, as he was the challenged party, the white man's code of honor nobly awarded to him the choice of weapons, time and place. To all of which the young Choctaw listened in meditative silence. All eyes were turned upon him expecting a negative reply; none more so than the "brave" pale-face. At that moment he sprang to his feet and with a nimble bound placed himself directly before the face, and within a few feet of his challenger, and, with his piercing eyes upon him, said in broken English, "You say, me hab choice of weapon, time, and place, too?" "Yes," responded the now dubious white brave. Then looking around upon all with a determined eye, to the astonishment of all, the challenger by no means excepted, the Choctaw exclaimed in a calm tone of voice: "Pale-face, me fight you tomarler wid rifle." Then turning to one of the bystanders he said: "You take him" (pointing to his challenger) "tomarler, sun so high," (pointing to the east) "one mile dis way, put him behind tree, den you come back." Then turning to another, continued: "You take me tomarler, sun same so high" (again pointing to the east) "one mile dis udder way, put me behind tree, too, den you come back." Then turning his penetrating black eyes fully upon the then astonished "man of honor," and looking him straight in the eyes, said: "Pale-face, you hunt me tomarler, and me hunt you tomarler; you see me first, den you shoot me first; me see you first, den me shoot you first." The pale-face warrior, quickly concluding that prudence then and there was evidently the better part of valor, wisely declined the honor with all the prospective pleasure of the morrow's hunt; to the great amusement of the Choctaws, who by their continued tantalizing, soon drove the would-be duellist from their territory.

Upon this subject, I here quote the following from the pen of Rev. Israel Folsom, a Choctaw, with whom I was personally acquainted east of the Mississippi River, and kindly furnished me by his amiable daughter, Czarena, now Mrs. Robb, a noble Christian lady living at Atoka, I. T. (from Ai-a-tuk-ko, a protection or shield).

"They had duels too; but they were quite different from any that has been practiced by any of the Indians of the continent or the whites; and which most commonly proved fatal to both parties. When a quarrel or difficulty occurred between two warriors, a challenge was sent by one to the other; not to meet and take a pop at each other with pistols, as is the case in civilized and refined nations, but in reality, it was a challenge for both to die. It was understood in no other way; this was the mode of trying the man's bravery, for they believe that a brave man, who possesses an honest and sincere heart, would never be afraid to die: It was usual for each one to select his own friend to dispatch him. If one should back out from the challenge, they considered it as a great mark of cowardice and dishonesty in him, and he would be despised by his relations and friends, and by the whole tribe. If a challenge was given and accepted, it was certain to end in the death of both parties. This mode of deciding difficulties had a strong tendency to restrain men from quarreling and fighting among themselves, for fear of being challenged and consequently compelled to die, or forever be branded with dishonesty and cowardice, and afterwards live a life of degradation and disgrace. Hence, it was a common saying among them, that a man should never quarrel, unless he was willing to be challenged and to die. On one occasion a sister seeing her brother about to back out from a challenge stepped forward and boldly offered herself to die in his stead, but her offer was not accepted, and she was so mortified at her brother's want of courage that she burst into tears."

Thus they fought the duel: When one Choctaw challenged another the challenge was given verbally, face to face, the time and place then and there designated. If accepted (and it was almost certain to be) the two went to the place each with his second. The two combatants then took their places unarmed about twenty feet apart, each with a second at his right side with a rifle in hand. At a given signal each second shot the combatant standing before him. That closed the scene. Each had proven himself a tush-ka siah (warrior I am) and that was satisfactory to all.

To have it said, "he died bravely," was the highest ambition of the Choctaw warrior, and thus it is even to the present day. He regards death as merely a transmigration to the happy hunting-ground, to which many of his friends have already gone. His rifle, so long his boon companion and trusty friend, together with his tomahawk, knife and tobacco, he only required to be deposited in the grave by his side as all the requisites necessary for him, when he arrived at the land of abundant game to resume the sports of the chase. Frequently a little corn and venison were also placed in the grave, by the hand of maternal foresight and love, that her warrior boy might not hunger during his long journey.

There was a peculiar custom among the ancient Choctaws, prior to 1818, which, according to tradition, was as follows: For many years after the marriage of her daughter, the mother-in-law was forbidden to look upon her son-in-law. Though they might converse together, they must be hidden the one from the other by some kind of screen, and when nothing else offered, by covering her eyes. Thus the mother-in-law was put to infinite trouble and vexation lest she should make an infraction upon the strange custom; since, when travelling or in camp often without tents, they were necessarily afraid to raise their heads, or open their eyes through fear of seeing the interdicted object.

Another peculiarity, which, however, they possessed in common with other tribes, was, the Choctaw wife never called her husband by name, but addressed him as "my son or daughter's father" or more commonly using the child's name, when if Shah-bi-chih (meaning, to make empty, the real name of a Choctaw whom I know) for instance, she calls her husband "Shah-bi-chih's father." Another oddity in regard to names was, the ancient Choctaw warriors seemed to have a strange aversion to telling their own names, and it was impossible to get it unless he had an acquaintance present, whom he requested to tell it for him.

The Choctaw ya-yahs; Cries Over the Dead.—Their manifested sorrow and wailing over the graves of their dead were affecting in the extreme. For twelve months, at various intervals, the women repaired to the grave of the last deceased relative or friend there to weep and express their unassumed, heart-felt griefs to the memory of the dead, loved in life and lamented in death, thus manifesting the tender sensibility of the Indian female.

There never lived a race of people more affectionate one to another than the Choctaws in their ancient homes. They actually seemed as one great brotherhood—one loving, trusting family; nor has there been any material change from that day to this. 'Tis true, they were subject to like passions with all imperfect humanity, and in momentary fits of passion, excited by the white man's "Personal Liberty," one sometimes killed another; but as soon as his drunken fit had worn off and momentary anger cooled, he manifested the deepest sorrow for the unfortunate affair; nor did he ever try to escape from the punishment attending the crime—never; but calmly offered himself as a voluntary sacrifice to the offended law.

They held specified cries for the dead, which to us of the present day would appear strange and even bordering upon the romantic, yet could not be witnessed without emotions of sadness. After the death and burial, the time was set by the near relations of the deceased for the cry, and notice was given to the neighboring villages for their attendance, to which all gave a ready response. When assembled, as many as could conveniently, would kneel in a close circle around the grave, both men and women; then drawing their blankets over their heads would commence a wailing cry in different tones of voice, which, though evident to a sensitive ear that the rules of harmony had been greatly overlooked, produced a solemnity of feeling that was indescribable, to which also the surroundings but added to the novelty of the scene: for here and there, in detached little groups, were seated upon the ground many others, who in solemn demeanor chatted in a low tone of voice and smoked the indispensible pipe; while innumerable children of all ages and sexes, engaged in their juvenile sports and in thoughtless glee mingled their happy voices with the sad dirge of their seniors; which added to the barking of a

hundred dogs intermingling with the tinkling chimes of the
little bells that were suspended upon the necks of as many
ponies, made a scene baffling all description. At different
intervals, one, sometimes three or four together, would arise
from the circle of mourners, quietly walk away and join
some one of the many little groups seated around, while the
vacancy in the mourning circle was immediately filled by
others, who promptly came forward, knelt, drew their
blankets over their heads, and took up the mournful strain;
and thus for several days and nights, the wailing voices of
the mourners, the gleeful shouts of thoughtless yet innocent
and happy childhood; the howling and barking of innumerable dogs, and the tinkling of the pony-bells of every tone
imaginable, in all of which dissonance was a prominent
feature, was heard for miles away. More than once have I
witnessed the scene and heard the wailing thereof. Oft, in
the calm still hours of a starry night, have I heard the dubious tones of a distant Choctaw Indian cry, and as the dis-
connected sounds, borne upon the night breeze, floated by
in undulating tones, now plainly audible, then dying away
in the distance, I must confess there was a strange sadness
awakened in my breast, unfelt and unknown before or
since. It must be heard to be comprehended. When the
time for the cry had expired, the mourning was exchanged
for a previously prepared feast; after the enjoyments af-
forded in the participation of which, all joined in a jolly
dance; thus happily restoring the equilibrium so long phys-
ically and mentally disturbed. Then each to his home
returned, while the name of the departed was recorded
among the archives of the past,—to be mentioned no more.

The relatives of the deceased, who lived at too great a
distance conveniently to cry over the grave of the dead set
up a post a short distance from the house, around which
they gathered.

The faces of the Choctaw and Chickasaw men of sixty
years ago were as smooth as a woman's, in fact they had no
beard. Sometimes there might be seen a few fine hairs (if

hairs they might be called) here and there upon the face, but they were few and far between, and extracted with a pair of small tweezers whenever discovered. Oft have I seen a Choctaw warrior standing before a mirror seeking with untiring perseverance and unwearied eyes, as he turned his face at different angles to the glass, if by chance a hair could be found lurking there, which, if discovered, was instantly removed as an unwelcome intruder. Even today, a full-blood Choctaw or Chickasaw with a heavy beard is never seen. I have seen a few, here and there, with a little patch of beard upon their chins, but it was thin and short, and with good reasons to suspect that white blood flowed in their veins.

It is a truth but little known among the whites, that the North American Indians of untarnished blood have no hair upon any part of the body except the head. My knowledge of this peculiarity was confined, however, to the Choctaws and Chickasaws alone. But in conversation with an aged Choctaw friend upon this subject, and inquiring if this peculairity extended to all Indians, he replied: "To all, I believe. I have been among the Comanches, Kiowas and other western Indians, and have often seen them bathing, men and women, promiscuously together, in the rivers of their country, and found it was the same with them, their heads alone were adorned with hair."

In conversation soon after with a Creek friend upon the subject in regard to the full-blood Creeks, he said, "They have no hair whatever upon the body, except that of the head, and the same is the case with all full-bloods that I have seen of other tribes." It is also the testimony of all the early explorers of this continent.

In their ancient councils and great national assemblies, the Choctaws always observed the utmost order and decorum, which, however, is universally characteristic of the Indians everywhere. In those grave and imposing deliberations of years ago convened at night, all sat on the ground in a circle around a blazing fire called "The Council Fire." The

aged, who from decrepitude had long retired from the
scenes of active life, the warpath and the chase, formed the
inner circle; the middle-aged warriors, the next; and the
young warriors, the outer circle. The women and children
were always excluded from all their national assemblies.
The old men, beginning with the oldest patriarch, would
then in regular succession state to the attentive audience all
that had been told them by their fathers, and what they
themselves had learned in the experience of an eventful
life—the past history of their nation; their vicissitudes and
changes; what difficulties they had encountered, and how
overcome; their various successes in war and their defeats;
the character and kind of enemies whom they had defeated
and by whom they had been defeated, the mighty deeds of
their renowned chiefs and famous warriors in days past,
together with their own achievements both in war and the
chase; their nation's days of prosperity and adversity; in
short, all of their traditions and legends handed down to
them through the successive generations of ages past; and
when those old seers and patriarchs, oracles of the past, had
in their turn gone to dwell with their fathers in the Spirit
Land, and their voices were no longer heard in wise counsel, the next oldest occupied the chairs of state, and in turn
rehearsed to their young braves the traditions of the past,
as related to them by the former sages of their tribe, together with their own knowledge; and thus were handed
down through a long line of successive generations, and
with much accuracy and truth, the events of their past
history; and when we consider the extent to which all
Indians cultivated that one faculty, memory, their connections in the history of the past is not so astonishing. I will
here relate a little incident (frequently published) in the
life of the famous Indian chief, Red Jacket, as an evidence
of strength and correctness of the Indian's memory. It is
said of Red Jacket, that he never forgot anything he once
learned. On a certain occasion, a dispute arose in a council
with his tribe and the whites, concerning the stipulations

made and agreed upon in a certain treaty. "You have forgotten," said the agent, "we have it written on paper." "The
paper then tells a lie," replied Red Jacket. "I have it written
down here," he added, placing his hand with great dignity
on his brow. "This is the book the Great Spirit has given
the Indian; it does not lie." A reference was immediately
made to the treaty in question, when, to the astonishment of
all present, the document confirmed every word the unlettered warrior and statesman had uttered. There can be
little doubt but that a large majority of their traditions are
based upon truth; though passing as they have through so
long a period of time, it is reasonable to suppose that many
errors have crept in.

An ancient Choctaw tradition attributes the origin of
the prairies along the western banks of the Tombigbee
River, to some huge animals (mammoths) that existed there
at the advent of their ancestors from the west to Mississippi.
Their tradition also states that the Nahullo, (Supernatural)
a race of giant people, also inhabited the same country,
with whom their forefathers oft came in hostile contact.
These mighty animals broke off the low limbs of the trees
in eating the leaves, and also gnawed the bark off the trees,
which, in the course of time, caused them to wither and die;
that they roamed in different bands, which engaged in desperate battles whenever and wherever they met, and thus
caused them to rapidly decrease in numbers; and that, in
the course of years all had perished but two large males,
who, separate and alone, wandered about for several
years—each confining himself to the solitude of the forest
many miles from the other. Finally, in their wanderings
they met, and at once engaged in terrible conflict in which
one was killed. The survivor, now monarch of the forests,
strolled about for a few years wrapt in the solitude of his
own reflections and independence—then died, and with
him the race became extinct.

That the Choctaw traditions of both the mammoth and
great men, was based on truth as to their former existence

in the southern and western parts of this continent is satisfactorily established by the many mammoth skeletons of
both men and beasts and fragments of huge bones that
have been, and are continually being found in different
parts of the country, and all of whom, according to their
tradition were contemporary with the ancient fathers of the
present Indian race. A huge skeleton of one of those ancient animals was found in March, 1877, four miles east of
the town of Greenville, Hunt County, Texas. I secured a
fragment of the skeleton, evidently a part of the femoral
bone, which measured twenty-one inches in circumference.
A tooth measured three inches in width, five inches in
length along the surface of the jaw bone and five inches in
depth into the jaw, and weighed the seemingly incredible
weight of eleven pounds. The teeth proved the monster
herbivorous, the enamel of which was in a perfect state of
preservation. The greater part of the frame crumbled to
dust, as soon as exposed to the action of the air.

Here then it had found a burial place, among others of
the prehistoric population of the various animals which
held possession of this continent before, perhaps, the advent of man, rising up before us like some old granite dome,
weatherbeaten and darkened by the lapse of ages past. But
death came to it, as to its predecessors, whose cemeteries
time has opened here and there, and revealed to the scru-
tiny of the curious, the testimony of a vanished age. Many
citizens of the immediate neighborhood visited the place of
disinterment, and viewed the solitary grave and looked
with wondering interest upon this stranger of hoary antiquity arising from his forest tomb where he had so long
slept in silence, unknown and unsung; whose history, as
that of his mighty race, is wrapt in the eternal silence of the
unknown past. Yet, to one who seeks to muse o'er the mysteries of the unwritten long ago, this fossil tells a story of
the mystic days of yore and of the multiplied thousands of
years since old Mother Earth commenced to bear and then
destroy her children.

"Hupimmi hattak tikba a mintih hushi aiokatula" (our forefathers came from the west), declare the ancient Choctaws through their tradition, and "they saw the mighty beasts of the forests, whose tread shook the earth; but our forefathers' ancestry came from the northwest beyond the big water."

" 'Tis but the tradition of the ignorant Indian—a foolish fable," responded he of the pale-face, of boasted historical attainments. When lo! accident unearths the long hidden monster of traditional record, and the truth of the rejected declaration of the despised Indian is established, and with equal truth establishing the fact that, mid all our boasted ancient pedigree, theirs is more ancient, and perhaps more honorable, reaching back through the vista of prehistoric times to the dim and hazy regions of ages past and unknown.

Also of the tradition of the Choctaws which told of a race of giants that once inhabited the now State of Tennessee, and with whom their ancestors fought when they arrived in Mississippi in their migration from the west, doubtless Old Mexico. Their tradition states the Nahullo (race of giants) was of wonderful stature; but, as their tradition of the mastodon, so this was also considered to be but a foolish fable, the creature of a wild imagination, when lo! their exhumed bones again prove the truth of the Choctaws' tradition. In the fall of 1880, Mr. William Beverly, an old gentleman 84 years of age living near Plano, Collin County, Texas, and who was born in west Tennessee and there lived to manhood, stated to me that near his father's house on a small creek were twenty-one mounds in consecutive order forming a crescent, each distant from the other about fifty feet and each with a base of seventy-five or eighty feet in diameter, and rising to an average height of forty feet; that he, when a boy twelve years of age, was present with his father, when an excavation was made in one of the mounds in which human bones of enormous size were found, the femoral bones being five inches longer than the ordinary length, and the jaw bones were so large as to slip over the face of a man with ease. This statement was confirmed by Rev. Mr. Rudolph of McKinney, Texas, and several others, all men of undoubted veracity, which places the truth of the former existence of the mounds, their excavations and results, as well as the Choctaw tradition, beyond all doubt and even controversy.

In regard to the race of giants that once occupied the now State of Tennessee and mentioned in the tradition of the ancient Choctaws. Mr. H. S. Halbert, an esteemed friend, says in a letter to me, January 22, 1878, "I will give you some facts which modern researchers have thrown upon the ancient occupancy of this continent.

"The Delawares, or Leni Lenape as they style themselves in their native tongue, have a tradition that they came from the west. When they came to the Great River, perhaps, somewhere in the latitude of St. Louis, they found a people of tall stature, and living in towns. This people the Delawares called Allegewi. They asked the Allegewi for permission to cross the river, which was granted. The Allegewi, however, seeing the Indians constantly coming from the west in such large numbers, and fearing they would ultimately dispossess them of their country, commenced war upon them. After years of fighting, the Allegewi were defeated and driven out of their country—retreating southward, and the Delawares and other tribes took possession of their country. Now these Allegewi are without doubt the same stock of people spoken of in Choctaw tradition as the Nahoolo."

The word Nahoolo is a corruption of the Choctaw word Nahullo and is now opplied to the entire White Race, but anciently it referred to a giant race with whom they came in contact when they first crossed the Mississippi River. These giants, says their tradition, as related to the missionaries occupied the northern part of the now states of Mississippi and Alabama and the western part of Tennessee. The true signification of the word Nahullo is a superhuman or supernatural being, and the true words for white man are Hattak-tohbi. The Nahullo were of white complexion, according to Choctaw tradition, and were still an existing people at the time of the advent of the Choctaws to Mississippi; that they were a hunting people and also cannibals, who killed and ate the Indians whenever they could capture them, consequently the Nahullo were held in great dread by the Indians and were killed by them whenever an opportunity was presented; by what means they finally became extinct tradition is silent.

"Chemical analysis of the bones of this giant race in Tennessee and elsewhere," says Mr. H. S. Halbert, in a letter of January 3, 1878, "indicates the ravages of one of the most terrible diseases to which flesh is heir. Bones exhumed from these ancient cemeteries indicate with painful certainty that syphilis was at least one cause of the extinction of this ancient people. It was long supposed that syphilis was imported into this continent by the European race. That may have been the case, in the historical period, but I have no doubt it prevailed with awful fatality among that ancient people, who dominated a large portion of this continent before the advent of the Indian race."

I admit, with friend Halbert, that, possibly the Allegewi of Delaware tradition may be the Nahullo of Choctaw tradition,—if they were of white complexion, as the word Nahullo is emphatically applied to the white race and no other. If white, may they not be of the Northmen, who, it is said, "established a few colonies upon the Atlantic coast A. D. 1000"?

Some have believed that the Nahullo were the Carib Indians, as they were said to be of gigantic stature and also cannibals, and who once inhabited our Gulf coast. They were found by Columbus in the West Indies, and they are still found in the isles of the Carribean Sea and Venezuela. The early French writers of Louisiana called the Caribs by their Indian name Attakapas, and Attakapas Parish in Louisiana took its name from that tribe. The French

translated Attakapas, Man-eater. Attakapas is a corruption
of the Choctaw words Hattakapa, (man eatable) which they
(the French), no doubt, got from the Choctaws, who gave
the tribe that name. I am inclined to believe that the
Nahullo of the Choctaw tradition were not regular cannibals, but that they sacrificed human victims in their religious ceremonies, which in extreme cases may, perhaps,
have required their officiates to eat a portion of the victim's
flesh. The same also of the Caribs,—hence Hattakapa,
(man eatable) instead of Hattakupa, eater.

The Choctaws' endurance of pain—even to excruciating torture—and to him the true exponent of every manly
virtue, was equal to that of any of his race and truly astonishing to behold; and he who could endure the severest
torture with the least outward manifestation of suffering,
was regarded by his companions as most worthy of admiration and adulatory praise, the bravest of the brave.

Even the little Choctaw boys took delight in testing
the degrees of their manhood by various ways of inflicting
pain. I have often seen the little fellows stir up the nests of
yellow jackets, bumble-bees, hornets and wasps; and then
stand over the nests of the enraged insects which soon
literally covered them, and fight them with a switch in each
hand; and he who stood and fought longest without flinch-
ing—fore-shadowed the future man—was worthy the appellation of Mighty Warrior. But the business ends of
the hornets, bees and wasps universally effected a hasty
retreat of the intruder upon their domiciles, sooner or
later—much to the delight of his youthful companions and
acknowledged by an explosion of yells and roars of laughter. But the discomfitted embryo warrior consoled himself
by daring any one of his merry-making companions to
"brave the lion in his den," as he had and endure longer
than he did the combined attacks of the valiant little
enemy. The challenge was most sure to be accepted, but
invariably with the same result, a retreat at the expense of
a hearty laugh. From one to three minutes was the average

length of a battle, the insects holding the field invariably. I have also seen them place a hot coal of fire on the back of the hand, wrist and arm, and let it burn for many seconds—bearing it with calm composure and without the least manifestation of pain; thus practicing those first lessons of endurance which were to enable them, when arrived to manhood, to undergo the most dreadful tortures without manifestation of pain, or experience the deepest sorrow without the slightest emotion.

Patience was also considered among the Choctaws a bright and manly virtue and in connection with that of endurance, formed the basis from which they derived all the other qualities of their characters; and they estimated their success, both in war and hunting, as depending almost exclusively upon their unwearied patience and the ability of great and long endurance.

The ancient Choctaws were as susceptible to all the pleasing emotions produced by the sweet concords of sound as any other people, yet their musical genius, in the invention of musical instruments, never extended beyond that of a cane flute and a small drum, which was consructed from a section cut from a small hollow tree, over the hollow part of which was stretched a fresh deer skin, cleansed from the hair, which became very tight when dried; and when struck by a stick made a dull sound, little inferior to that of our common snare-drum; which could be heard at a considerable distance; and though uncouth in appearance, and inharmonious in tone, as all drums, still its "voice" was considered an indispensable adjunct as an accompaniment to all their national and religious ceremonies. Yet the ancient Choctaw, in all his solemn ceremonies, as well as amusements and merry-makings, did not depend so much upon the jarring tones of the diminutive drum, as he did upon his own voice; which in concert with the monotonous tones of the drum,—to the cultivated and sensitve ear a mere jargon of sound,—was to the Indian ear the most exciting music, and soon wrought him to the highest state

of excitement. In all their dances they invariably danced to
the sound of the indispensable drum, accompanied with the
low hum of the drummer, keeping exact step with its monotonous tone. In the social dance alone were the women
permitted to participate, which to the youthful maiden of
"sweet sixteen," was truly the ultimate of earthly bliss.

But little restraint, parental or otherwise, was placed
upon their children, hence they indulged in any and all
amusements their fancy might suggest. The boys in little
bands roamed from village to village at their own pleasure,
or strolled through the woods with their blow-guns and
bow and arrows, trying their skill upon all birds and squirrels that were so unfortunate as to come in their way. They
were but little acquainted with the principles of right and
wrong, having only as their models the daring deeds of
their fathers in war and the chase, they only yearned for the
time when they might emulate them in heroic achievements; and one would very naturally infer that these boys,
ignorant of all restraint from youth to manhood, would
have have been, when arrived to manhood, a set of desperadoes, indulging in every vice and committing every crime.
But not so. No race of young people ever grew up to manhood in any nation who were of a more quiet nature and
peaceful disposition than the youths of the old Mississippi
Choctaws. They seldom quarreled among themselves even
in boyhood, and less, when arrived to the state of manhood.
To them in youth as well as in advanced years, as to all of
their race, the dearest of all their earthly possessions from
childhood to manhood, from manhood to old age, and from
old age to the grave, was their entire and unrestrained freedom; and yet there seemed to exist in their own breasts a
restraining influence, a counteracting power, that checked
the ungoverned passions of their uncultivated natures
through life, and kept them more within the bounds of
prudence and reason, than any race of uneducated people
I ever knew.

To the Choctaws, as well as to all Indians, the voice of the distant muttering thunder that echoed from hill to hill through their wide extended forests; the roaring wind and lightning flash that heralded the approaching storm, were but the voice of the Great Spirit, and they made them the themes that filled their souls with song and praise. They ever heard the voice of that unseen Great Spirit throughout all nature—in the rustling leaf and the sighing breeze; in the roaring cataract and the murmuring brook; and they expressed their souls' adoration; understood and comprehended by them alone, in their songs and dances. To them all nature ever spoke in language most potential, and their immortality and future existence in another world they never doubted, though their ideas of future rewards and punishments beyond the tomb were feeble and confused.

It was their ancient custom to leave the murderer in the hands of the murdered man's relatives and friends; and, as "an eye for an eye, and a tooth for a tooth" was recorded upon their statute book, he was, sooner or later, most sure to fall by an unknown and unseen hand. Sometimes, however, the slayer appeased the avenger by paying a stipulated amount; but this was of rare occurrence. Soon after the missionaries were established among them, a company of armed and mounted police, called "light horsemen," were organized for each district. They were continually riding over the country settling all difficulties that arose among parties or individuals, and arresting all violators of the law. The custom of leaving the murderer to be disposed of as the relatives of the deceased saw proper, was then set aside, and the right of trial by the light horse who acted in a three fold capacity—sheriff, judge and jury, was awarded to all offenders. The light horse were composed of a brave and vigilant set of fellows, and nothing escaped their eagle eyes; and they soon became a terror to white whiskey peddlers who invaded the Choctaw territories at that time. When caught, the whiskey was poured upon the ground and the vender informed that his room was preferable to his company.

When a murder was committed, the light horse at once took the matter into consideration, and after hearing all the testimony pro and con, pronounced the verdict in accordance thereto. If the person accused was found to be guilty, there and then, the time and place of his execution was designated, and the doomed man was informed that his presence would accordingly be expected. He never failed to make his appearance at the appointed place and hour, and all things being ready, a small red spot was painted over his heart for the executioner; and, being placed in position, calmly received the fatal bullet. Sometimes the condemned would request a short respite, a few days' extension of time, assigning as a reason for the desired delay, that a grand ball-play, dance or hunt, was soon to take place, in which he desired to paritcipate. The request was seldom refused. The doomed man then designated the day and hour on which he would return and attend to the matter under consideration. He went to the ball-play, the dance, or the hunt, engaged in and enjoyed his anticipated fun, then returned true to his promised word and paid the penalty of the violated law. The rifle was invariably used as the instrument of execution, for the soul of the Choctaw who had been executed by hanging was regarded as accursed—never being permitted to join his people in the happy hunting grounds, but his spirit must forever haunt the place where he was hung. Hence their horror of death by hanging, and the gallows has ever been unknown among them. If the condemned should fail to appear, which was never known to be, at the time and place of his execution, or should manifest any emotion of fear during his execution, it was regarded as a disgrace to himself, his relatives, and his nation as a Choctaw warrior, which no length of time could ever efface; hence their honor, resting upon their firmness in the hour of death, was watched with jealous

care. Never was a full-blood Choctaw known to evade the
death penalty, passed upon him by the violated law, by
flight, hence all places of imprisonment were unknown. For
minor offenses, whipping was the punishment; fifty lashes
for the first offense, one hundred for the second, and death
by the rifle for the third offense in case of theft, and so it
is today.

He who had been condemned to receive this punishment never attempted to evade it; but promptly presented
himself, or herself, at the designated place of punishment.
This punishment was inflicted several times at the mission
of Hebron, to which I was an eye witness. Before the hour
appointed the neighborhood assembled around the church
which stood about forty rods distant from the mission-
house, where they indulged in social conversation and
smoking; never, however, mentioning, or even hinting the
subject which had brought them together. The culprit was
as gay and cheerful as any of them, walking with an air of
perfect indifference, chatting and smoking with the various
groups sitting around on blankets spread upon the ground.
Precisely at the moment designated, the lighthorse would
appear. The crowd then went into the church, closed the
door and commenced singing a religious hymn, taught them
by the missionaries, which they continued until the tragedy
outside was over. At the same time the culprit shouted "Sa
mintih!" I have come! then ejaculated "Sa kullo!" (I am
strong!) He then elevated his arms and turned his back to
the executioner and said: "Fummih (whip). When he had
received fifteen or twenty blows, he calmly turned the
other side to the Fum-mi (one who whips); and then again,
his back, uttering not a word nor manifesting the least sign
of pain. As soon as the whipping was over, the church door
was opened and the whole assembly came out and shook
hands with the "Fum-ah" (whipped), thus reinstating him to
his former position in society, and the subject was then and
there dropped, never to be mentioned again, and it never
was.

The Choctaws had great pride of race. The warrior's proudest boast was Choctaw Siah! (I am a Choctaw!) and he still clings to it with commendable tenacity even as he does to his native language. It has been said that no people have been truly conquered who refuse to speak the language of the conqueror; therefore the North American Indians, that subdued, yet unsubduable people, have never ceased to speak their native tongue.

As an illustration of this peculiar characteristic of the Indians—so different from that of any race of whom I have heard—i. e., never fleeing from, or in any way attempting to evade the penalties of the violated law, I here introduce the sad scene in the execution of Chester Dixon, a Choctaw youth convicted of murder at a term of the circuit court of the Choctaw Nation in December, 1883.

Chester Dixon was a young, full-blood Choctaw, about 17 years of age. He was subject to fits, during which he seemed to be unconscious of his acts. Aside from this malady, he was considered rather a bright boy. He lived with his mother and step-father, five or six miles from Atoka. Their nearest neighbors were a Choctaw known as Washington and Martha, his wife. One evening Washington, on his return home from Atoka, was shocked in finding the body of his wife lying on the floor of his cabin fearfully mangled, the head severed from the body, with several frightful gashes, evidently inflicted with an ax, which lay by the side of the corpse. The alarm was given, and it was soon ascertained that Chester Dixon was seen coming from the house in which the deed had been committed, covered with blood. He was arrested, tried by the Choctaw law, condemned, and sentenced to be shot on an appointed day, at noon. He was neither confined nor guarded, but went where he pleased, having pledged his word of honor, however, that he would be at the place of execution punctual to the hour appointed. A few days before the execution he came with his step-father to Atoka for the purpose of order-

ing his coffin. He had his measure taken for the grave, and
then calmly informed his step-father where he wished to
be buried.

The day of execution came; and a few, mostly whites,
assembled at the place of execution to witness the sad
scene. The doomed boy did not make his appearance to
within twenty or thirty minutes of the appointed time, and
many of the whites, judging from their own standpoint,
began to doubt the integrity of the Choctaw, and expressed
those doubts one to another. But true to his plighted word,
the truthful youth soon rode up; and, dismounting from his
horse, quietly walked up to a little group of Choctaws, who
were sitting around a fire, without taking any notice whatever of the surroundings, and calmly took his seat upon the
ground, with his head bowed between his knees as if lost in
meditation. An aged Choctaw man soon approached him,
and, speaking to him in his own language, encouraged him
to bravely meet his fate as a young Choctaw brave; and to
die willingly, since nothing but his life could atone for the
one he had taken; and also to feel that his people had been
just in condemning him. He spoke not a word nor raised
his head during his old friend's conversation; but at its conclusion he looked up and around for a moment, then
grasped the old man's hand, as if to say, I'll be firm, and he
was to the last. Then his Choctaw friends, both men and
women, came up and bade him their last earthly adieu;
with all of whom he shook hands, but spoke not a word.
After which, the sheriff brought the unfortunate boy a
change of clothing, in which he clothed himself for the
grave, without the least discernible sign of agitation; he
then took his seat on a blanket spread for him, and his
mother combed his hair with calm composure—her last act
of maternal love; and though, with a heart bleeding at
every pore, no outward manifestation was made, yet her
face told the storm of grief that raged within; while, true to
her nature, she clung to her boy to the last moment, to console him with a mother's presence and a mother's love.

The sheriff then told Chester that the hour of execution had come. He arose at once and quietly walked to the spot pointed out to him by the sheriff, and stopped facing his coffin—the personification of calm composure and firm resignation. His step-father and cousin then walked up, the former taking him by the right hand and the latter by the left. The same venerable old man who had first approached him, again came forward and made a little black spot upon his breast, just over the heart, and once more whispered a few words of parting encouragement, then walked away. The sheriff then bound a handkerchief over his eyes, asked him to kneel, and beckoned to a man who had until then kept himself concealed. This man was a cousin of Chester Dixon, and had been chosen by Chester to do the shooting. He now advanced, and taking his position five or six paces from the poor boy, leveled his winchester rifle and fired. The ball went to the mark. At the report of the rifle Dixon fell forward, and died without a struggle. The mother now came forward, took charge of the lifeless body of her boy, and with the assistance of friends, laid it away in the grave. No confusion nor even the semblance of excitement disturbed the solemn proceedings. And when contrasted to the civilized mode of punishment that of hanging—the Choctaw method is certainly more humane and effective, to say the least of it.

I will state another instance that took place among the Choctaws when living in their ancient domains.

A Choctaw unfortunately killed another in a fit of passion. He was duly tried, convicted, and sentenced to be shot on a certain day; but requested a stay of the execution, upon the plea that his wife and little children would be left in a destitute condition unless he was allowed to return home and finish making his crop. His request was granted with no other assurance than his pledged word that he would return and receive his death sentence. The day of execution was fixed at a time when the crop would be matured, and the doomed man returned to his home and family. The fatal day came and found the necessary labor on the crop finished and also the noble Choctaw at the appointed hour and place, where he calmly received the fatal bullet which at once closed his earthly career.

Thus sacred was held the noble virtue. Truth among the ancient Choctaws when they lived east of the Mississippi River; and thus sacred is it still held among the full-bloods west of the same river; and I have never known or heard of a full-blood Choctaw or Chickasaw, during my personal acquaintance with that truly grand and noble people for seventy-five years, who violated his pledged word of honor by failing to appear at the time and place designated, to suffer the penalties of the violated law, be it death by the rifle or fifty or a hundred lashes at the whipping post. And truly it may be said: No race of people ever adhered with greater tenacity to truth, or the greater hatred for the falsehood, than did and do the Choctaws. They truly abhorred and still abhor a liar. Years before the advent of the missionaries among them, one of their chiefs was strangely addicted to lying; and so great did their disgust finally become that they, in council assembled, banished him from their Nation under pain of death if he ever returned. This exiled chief then settled with his family in the now parish of Orleans, Louisiana, on a small tract of land which projects into lake Pontchartrain, and erected his lonely cabin near a bayou which is connected with the lake. And to this day, that small tract of land, it is said, is called Ho-lub-i Miko (Lying Chief), having taken its name from the exiled Choctaw chief.

The territories of the Choctaws in 1723, in which year the seat of the French government in Louisiana, then under Bienville, was definitely transferred from Natchez to New Orleans, then containing about one hundred houses and three thousand inhabitants, extended from the Mississippi River to the Black Warrior, east; and from Lake Pontchartrain to the territories of the Natchez, west, and Chickasaws, north. They possessed upwards of sixty principal towns, and could muster, as was estimated, twenty-five thouand warriors.

The Choctaws called all fables shukha anump (hog talk) as a mark of derision and contempt. Some of their fables, handed down by tradition through unknown generations, were similar in the morals taught by those of the famous Aesop. One of these shukha anumpas was that of the turkey and the terrapin:—A haughty turkey gobbler, with long flowing beard and glossy feathers, meeting a terrapin one bright and beautiful spring morning, thus accosted him with an expression of great contempt: "What are you good for?" To which the terrapin humbly replied "many things." "Name one," continued the turkey. "I can beat you running," said the terrapin. "What nonsense! I thought you were a fool, now I know it," continued the turkey.

"I repeat it, I can beat you running, distance half a mile," continued the terrapin. "To prove you are a fool in believing such an absurdity, I'll run the race with you," responded the turkey with marked disgust. The day was appointed, the distance marked off, and the agreements entered into, one of which was, the terrapin was to run with a white feather in his mouth by which the turkey might be able to distinguish him from other terrapins; another was, the turkey was to give the terrapin the advantage of one hundred yards in the start. In the intervening time of the race, the wily terrapin secured the assistance of another terrapin to help him. Therefore, he secretly placed his assistant, with the white insignia also in his mouth, at the terminus to which the race was to be run. Early on the morning of the day agreed upon, the competitors were at their posts—the contemptuous turkey at the goal, and the dispassionate terrapin a hundred yards on the line. The turkey was to give the signal for starting by a loud gobble. The signal was given, and the race was opened. The turkey soon came up with the terrapin, who had gotten but a few feet from his goal, and shouted derisively as he passed by "What a fool!"

To which the terrapin ejaculated—"Not as big as you imagine." The confident turkey ran on about half way, and then stopped and turned off a little distance to secure his breakfast, but kept an eye on the track that the terrapin might not pass unobserved. After feeding about some time and not seeing anything of the terrapin, he began to fear he had passed him unobserved; therefore, he started again at full speed; and not overtaking the terrapin as he expected, he redoubled his exertions and reached the goal breathless, but to fiind the terrapin with the white feather in his mouth (his supposed opponent) already there. Moral.—The scornful are often outwitted by those upon whom they look with contempt.

In the disposition of their dead, the ancient Choctaws practiced a strange method different from any other nation of people, perhaps, that ever existed. After the death of a Choctaw, the corpse wrapped in a bear skin or rough kind of covering of their own manufacture, was laid out at full length upon a high scaffold erected near the house of the deceased, that it might be protected from the wild beasts of the woods and the scavengers of the air. After the body had remained upon the scaffold a sufficient time for the flesh to have nearly or entirely decayed, the hattak fullih nipi foni, (bone picker) the principal official in their funeral ceremonies and especially appointed for that duty—appeared and informed the relatives of the deceased that he had now come to perform the last sacred duties of his office to their departed friend. Then, with the relatives and friends, he marched with great solemnity of countenance to the scaffold and, ascending which, began his awful duty of picking off the flesh that still adhered to the bones, with loud groans and fearful grimaces, to which the friends below responded in cries and wailings.

The bone-picker never trimmed the nails of his thumbs, index and middle fingers which accordingly grew to an astonishing length—sharp and almost as hard as flint—and well adapted to the horrid business of their owner's calling. After he had picked all the flesh from the bones, he then tied it up in a bundle and carefully laid it upon a corner of the scaffold; then gathering up the bones in his arms he descended and placed them in a previously prepared box, and then applied fire to the scaffold, upon which the assembly gazed uttering the most frantic cries and moans until it was entirely consumed. Then forming a procession headed by the bone-picker the box containing the bones was carried, amid weeping and wailing, and deposited in a house erected and consecrated to that purpose and called a-bo-ha fo-ni, (bone-house) with one of which all villages and towns were supplied. Then all repaired to a previously prepared feast, over whch the bone-picker, in virtue of his office, presided with much gravity and silent dignity.

As soon as the bone-houses of the neighboring villages were filled, a general burial of the bones took place, to which funeral ceremony the people came from far and near, and, in a long and imposing procession, with weeping and wailing and loud lamentations of the women, bore off the boxes of bones to their last place of rest, and there depositing them in the form of a pyramid they were covered with earth three or four feet in depth forming a conical mound. All then returned to a previously designated village and concluded the day in feasting.

Thus many of the mounds found in Mississippi and Alabama are but the cemeteries of the ancient Choctaws, since, as often as the bone-houses became filled, the boxes of bones were carried out to the same cemetery and deposited on the previously made heap commencing at the base and ascending to the top, each deposit being covered up with earth to the depth of three or four feet, and thus, by continued accession through a long series of ages, became the broad and high mounds, concerning which there has been so much wild speculation with so little foundation for truth or common sense. Even at the time the missionaries were established among them (1818), many of the mounds were of so recent date that not even bushes were growing upon them, though the custom of thus laying away their dead had become obsolete; still a few bone-pickers had survived the fall of their calling, and were seen, here and there, wandering about from village to village as ghosts of a departed age, with the nails of the thumb, index and middle fingers still untrimmed, and whose appearance indicated their earthly pilgrimage had reached nearly to a century, some of whom I personally knew.

Shortly before the advent of the missionaries, the custom of placing the dead upon the scaffolds was abolished, though not without much opposition; and that of burial in a sitting posture was adopted, with also new funeral ceremonies, which were as follows: Seven men were appointed whose duty it was to set up each a smooth pole (painted red) around the newly made grave, six of which were about eight feet high, and the seventh about fifteen, to which thirteen hoops (made of grape vines) were suspended and so united as to form a kind of ladder, while on its top a small white flag was fastened. This ladder of hoops was for the easier ascent of the spirit of the deceased to the top of the pole, whence, the friends of the deceased believed, it took its final departure to the spirit land.

They also believed that the spirits of the dead, after their flight from the top of the pole to the unknown world, had to cross a fearful river which stretched its whirling waters athwart their way; that this foaming stream has but one crossing, at which a cleanly peeled sweet-gum log, perfectly round, smooth and slippery, reached from bank to bank; that the moment the spirit arrives at the log, it is attacked by two other spirits whose business is to keep any and all spirits from crossing thereon. But if a spirit is that of a good person, the guardians of the log have no power over it, and it safely walks over the log to the opposite shore, where it is welcomed by other spirits of friends gone before, and where contentment and happiness will forever be the lot of all.

But alas, when the spirit of a bad person arrives at the log-crossing of the fearful river, it also is assailed by the ever wakeful guards, and as it attempts to walk the slippery log they push it off into the surging waters below, to be helplessly borne down by the current to a cold and barren desert, where but little game abounds and over which he is doomed to wander, naked, cold and hungry.

When a death was announced, which was made by the firing of guns in quick succession, the whole village and surrounding neighborhood—almost to a man—assembled at once at the home of the deceased, to console and mourn with the bereaved. On the next day a procession was formed headed by the seven men called fabussa sholih (pole-bearer), each carrying on his shoulder a long, slender pole painted red, and all slowly and in profound silence marched to the grave, where the poles were at once firmly set up in the ground—three on each side of the grave, and one at the head, on which the thirteen hoops were suspended. The corpse was then carefully placed in its last earthly place of rest, the grave filled up, and all returned to the former home of the departed. They had specified cries at the grave of the deceased, which continued for thirteen moons. At the termination of each cry, a hoop was taken off of the pole, and so on until the last one was removed; then a grand funeral ceremony was celebrated called fabussa halut akuchchih, (pole to pull down). And the manager of the pole-pulling was called hattak iti i miko, (their chief man); and the hunters sent out to provide venison for the company on that occasion were called hattak (man) illi (dead) chohpa (meat). That is, meat for the dead man; or, more properly, meat for the obsequies of the dead man.

To this celebration, or last commemoration of the dead, when all had assembled, the fabussa halulli, (the same fabussa sholih who had set up the poles) under the command of the hattak iti i miko (the same who bore and set up the long pole upon which was attached the hoops and flag) slowly and silently marched in solemn procession to the grave and pulled up the poles, and carried them off together with the hoops and concealed them in a secret place in the forest where they were left to return to dust forever undisturbed.

As soon as the fabussa hallulli had disposed of the poles and hoops, preparations were begun for the finale—a feast and the grand aboha hihlah, home dancing, or dancing home of the deceased good man to the land of plenty and happiness, and the bad man to the land of scarcity and suffering.

The festivities continued during the day and the night following the pole-pulling. On the next morning all returned to their respective homes; and from that day he or she of the grave became a thing of the past, whose names were to be mentioned no more. And they were not.

Among the ancient Choctaws, a mare and colt, cow and calf, and a sow and pigs were given to each child at its birth, if the parents were able so to do,—and all, with few exceptions, were able; this stock, with its increase under no circumstances whatever, could be disposed of in any way; and when he or she, as the case might be, became grown, the whole amount was formally conveyed over to him or her. Thus when a young couple started out in life they had a plenty of stock, if nothing more.

Diseases, they believed, originated in part from natural causes, therefore their doctors sought in nature for the remedies. Graver maladies, to them, were inexplicable, and for their cures they resorted to their religious superstitions and incantations. They were very skillful in their treatment of wounds, snake bites, etc. Their knowledge of the medicinal qualities of their various plants and herbs, in which their forests so bountifully abounded, was very great. 'Tis true they were powerless against the attacks of many diseases—importations of the white race, such as small-pox, measles, whooping-cough, etc.; yet, they did not exhibit any greater ignorance in regard to those new diseases, to them unknown before, than do the doctors of the white race, who have had the experience of ages which has been handed down to them through the art of printing, manifest in regard to the new diseases that so oft attack their own race. The art of blood-letting and scarifying was well understood and practiced by many of their doctors, as well as the virtue of cold and warm baths; and in many of the healing arts they fell not so far below those of the white race as might be supposed.

In cases of bowel affections they used persimmons dried by the heat of the sun and mixed with a light kind of bread. In case of sores, they applied a poultice of pounded ground ivy for a few days, then carefully washed the afflicted part with the resin of the copal-tree. For fresh wounds they made a poultice of the root of the cotton-tree which proved very efficacious; to produce a copious perspiration, a hot decoction of the china root swallowed, had the desired effect. They possessed an antidote for the bite and sting of snakes and insects, in the root of a plant called rattlesnake's master, having a pungent yet not unpleasant odor. The root of the plant was chewed, and also a poultice made of it was applied to the wound, which at once checked the poison and the patient was well in a few days. The medical properties of the sassafras, sarsaparilla, and other medicinal plants, were known to them. They possessed many valuable secrets to cure dropsy, rheumatism, and many other diseases, which, no doubt, will ever remain a secret with them, proving that their powers of observation, investigation and discrimination, are not, by any means, to be regarded as contemptible; while their belief, that the Great Spirit has provided a remedy in plants for all diseases, and never refuses to make it known to those who seek the knowledge of it by proper supplications, is praiseworthy in them to say the least of it.

Their doctors were held in great veneration, though they oft practiced upon their patrons many frauds. Millfort, p. 298, says: "when one of them had a patient on hand a long time, and the poor sick fellow's means had been exhausted he privately told the relatives that his skill was exhausted, that he had done all in his power to no avail, and that their friend must die within a few days at farthest; and, with great seeming sympathy, set forth the propriety of killing him, and so terminate his sufferings at once. Having the utmost confidence in the doctor's judgment and knowledge of the case, and also believing the case hopeless, the poor fellow was at once killed." In proof of this, he states that in 1772 a doctor thus advised concerning one of his patients. "The sick man," he says, "suspecting, from the actions of his physician, that he was advising the propriety of ending his suffering by having him killed, with great effort succeeded one night in crawling out of the house and making good his escape. After much suffering he succeeded in making his way into the Muscogee Nation, and fortunately went to the house of Col. McGillivry, who, Samaritan-like, took him into his house, and soon restored him to his usual health. At the expiration of several months he returned to his home, and found his relatives actually celebrating his funeral by burning the scaffold which they had erected to his memory, with the accustomed weeping and waling,—believing him to be dead. His unlooked-for appearance among them, at that solemn hour and place, threw them into the greatest consternation, and, in horror and wild dismay, all fled to the woods. Finding himself thus received by his own relatives and friends, he returned in disgust to the Muscogees and spent the remainder of his days among them. But when his relatives had become truly satisfied that he did not die, and was actually alive and well, they made the doctor pay heavily for the deception he had practiced upon them, by killing him."

The greatest mortality among them was most generally confined to the younger children; while longevity was a prominent characteristic among the adults. After the age of six or eight years the mortality of disease among them was less than among the white children of the present day after that age. But after those baneful diseases, scarlet fever, measles, mumps, whooping-cough, diseases unknown to them before, had been introduced among them, the fatality among the children was distressing, frequently destroying the greater number of the children in a village or neighborhood;—being wholly ignorant as they were of the proper mode of treatment was a great cause of the fearful fatality. Mental or nervous diseases were unknown to the ancient Choctaws; and idiocy and deformity were seldom seen. But of all the "diseases" introduced among them by the whites, the most pernicious and fatal in all its features, bearings, and consequences, to the Choctaw people, was, is, and ever will be, okahumma (red water or whiskey); which, when once formed into habit, seemed to grow to a species of insanity equal even to that so often exhibited among the whites.

The medicine man was a dignitary who swayed his scepter alike among all Indians, but was altogether a very different personage from the common physician. The medicine man professed an insight into the hidden laws of nature; he possessed a power over the elements, the fish of the waters and the animals of the land; he could cause the fish to voluntarily suffer themselves to be caught, and give success to the hunter by depriving the denizens of the forest of their natural fear of man; he could impart bravery to the heart of the warrior, strength and skill to his arm and fleetness to his feet; yea, could put to flight the evil spirits of disease from the bodies of the sick. He could throw a spell or charm over a ball player that would disenable him to hit the post; or over the ball-post that would prevent its being hit by anyone whom he wished to defeat. Such were the professed attainments of the Indian medicine man. But whether he possessed all or any of the supernatural powers he professed, it matters not; it is certain, however, that he possessed one thing, the power, art, or skill, call it which you may, to make his people believe it, and that was all-sufficient for him—even as it is with all humbugs. The Choctaws regarded dreams as the direct avenues to the invisible world, the divine revelations of the Great Spirit. If a vision of the spirt of an animal appeared to the hunter in his dream, he felt confident of success on the morrow's hunt. But though he invoked the friendship, the protection and the good will of spirits, and besought the mediation of the medicine man, he never would confess his fear of death. But chide not too harshly, reader, the poor, unlettered Indian for his superstitions and wild beliefs, for the same long existed among the civilized nations of the world, nor are they entirely exempt even at the present day, nor is it likely they ever will be.

They lived in houses made of logs, but very comfortable; not more rude or uncouth, however, than many of the whites even of the present day. Their houses consisted generally of two rooms, both of which were used for every domestic purpose—cooking, eating, living and sleeping; nor was their furniture disproportionate with that of the dwelling—for the sitting room, a stool or two; for the kitchen, a pot or kettle, two or three tincups, a large and commodious wooden bowl, and a horn spoon, constituted about the ultimate—'twas all they needed, all they wanted, and with it they were perfectly contented and supremely happy.

Tafula; (pro. tarm-ful-ah, hominy; corrupted to tom-fuller), is made of pounded corn boiled, using lye for fermentation, and tafula tobi ibulhtoh (boiled corn mixed with beans) were, and are to the present day, favorite dishes among the Choctaws; nor need it be thought strange, as they are dishes worthy the palate of the most fastidious. But little pains was taken in the preparation of their food, which was as rude, though clean and nice, as the means of preparing it. Having no tables or dishes, except the wooden bowl, nor knives and forks, they squatted around the pot of boiled meat and bowl of tafula, and each used his or her fingers in extracting the contents of the pot, and conveying it to the mouth, and the horn spoon by turns in doing obeisance to the tafula—all in perfect harmony and jollity.

They use another preparation for food called botah kapussa (cold flour), which was made of parched corn pounded very fine; an ounce of which mixed with a little water would in a few minutes become as thick as soup cooked by a fire. Two or three ounces of this were sufficient to sustain a man for a day. In their war expeditions it was an indispensable adjunct to the bill of fare, as they could not shoot game with the rifle when upon the warpath in their enemy's territories for fear of giving notice of their presence. Bunaha was another food much used in the long ago. It was made of pounded meal mixed with boiled beans to which is added a little lye, then made into a dough wrapped in corn husks and boiled. Oksak (hickory nut), atapah (broken in) is still another; this was made of pounded meal mixed with the meat of the hickory nut instead of boiled beans, and cooked as bunaha. I have eaten the three kinds, and found them very palatable.

They were great lovers of tobacco; yet never chewed it, but confined its use exclusively to the pipe, in which they smoked the weed mixed with the dried leaf of the aromatic sumac, which imparted to the smoke a delightful flavor, agreeable even to the most fastidious nose. But they now have learned to chew, which I ascertained by actual observation, when riding over their country visiting them during the years 1884 to 1890. However, I could state that the habit is not as universal, by great odds, as among the whites.

All the drudgery work about the house and the hunting camp was done by the wife assisted by her children; and as the wife of the Choctaw warrior and hunter was regarded as the slave of her husband, so likewise may equally be regarded the unfortunate wives of many of the boasted white men of this 19th century.

With the Choctaw wife, as with all Indians, parturition was a matter that gave no uneasiness; nor did it interfere with her domestic affairs, but for a few hours. Unlike her civilized sister, she neither required nor desired, nor accepted any assistance whatever. I have known them to give birth to a child during the night, and the next morning would find them at the cowpen attending to the affairs of the dairy. To have a man physician, on such occasions, was as abhorrent to her sense of modesty and revolting to her feelings, as it was wholly unnecessary. And the old custom is still adhered to by the present Choctaw wife and mother. After a child was born, after undergoing the usual necessary preliminaries, it was placed in a curiously constructed receptacle called ullosi afohka, (infant receptacle) where it spent principally the first year of its life, only when taken out for the purpose of washing and dressing. This curiously made little cradle (for such it may truly be called) was often highly ornamented with all the paraphernalia that a mother's love and care could suggest or obtain. The little fellow's face, which was always exposed to view, was carefully protected by a piece of wood bent a few inches above and over it. The babe would remain in its little prison for hours without a whimper; part of the time asleep, and part of the time awake looking around in its innocence with calm and tranquil resignation. According to her convenience, the mother suspended her thus cradled child on her back, when walking, or the saddle when riding; or stood it up against a neighboring tree, if a pleasant day, that it might enjoy the fresh and pure air, and exhilarating sunshine; or suspend it to the projecting limb of a tree there to be rocked to sleep and pleasant dreams by the forest breeze. As soon as it was old enough to begin to crawl, it bade an informal adieu to its former prison, but to be found perched upon its mother's back, where it seemed well contented in all its journeys— long or short. It was truly astonishing with what apparent ease the Choctaw mother carried her child upon her back. The child was placed high up between the shoulders of the mother, and over it was thrown a large blanket, which was drawn tightly at the front of the mother's neck, forming a fold behind; in this the child was placed and safely carried, with seemingly little inconvenience to either mother or child. When the little chap had grown to such proportions as to be no longer easily thus transported, he was fastened to the saddle upon the back of a docile pony, which followed the company at pleasure; though here and there stopping momentarily to bite the tempting grass that grew along the pathway, then briskly trotting up until it had again reached its proper place in rank and file, indifferent to the jolting experienced by the youthful rider tied upon its back, who, however, seemed to regard it with stoical indifference. When arrived at the age of four or five years, he was considered as having passed through his fourth and last chrysalis stage, and was then untied from the saddle and bid ride for himself; and soon did the young horseman prove himself a true scion of the parent tree, as a fearless and skillful rider.

Though the allosi afohka has long since passed away with other ancient customs, still the Choctaw mother carries her child upon her back as she of a century ago, and loves it with the same fond and strong love; and though she did not, nor does not, express it by any outward manifestations, yet her love was and is real, perfect and constant; nor was she ever known to trust her babe to a hired nurse. The love for their children and untiring devotion to their homes and families, and their profound regard for the aged, were indeed beautiful and touching traits in the characteristics of the Choctaw women. In fact, the great respect and uniform kindness paid by the Indians everywhere, and under all circumstances, to the aged of their people, might justly bring the blush of shame upon the face of many of the young twigs of the professed enlightened white race. The Choctaw women of years ago were a merry, light-hearted race, and their constant laugh and incessant prattle formed a strange contrast to the sad taciturnity of the present day. The easily conjectured cause precludes the necessity of being mentioned here.

Adair (p. 89) says: "The Choctaws, in an early day, practiced the custom of flattening the heads of their infants by compression, and were first known to the whites by the name of Flat Heads." Be that as it may, the custom had long ceased to be practiced, when later known.

Wherever they went, distant or otherwise, many or few, they always traveled in a straight line, one behind the other. They needed no broad roads, nor had they any; hence, they dispensed with the necessity of that expense, road-working, so grudgingly bestowed by all white men. Paths alone, plain and straight, then led the Choctaws where now are broad roads and long high bridges, from village to neighborhood, and from neighborhood to village, though many miles apart; and so open and free of logs, bushes, and all fallen timber, was their country then, rendered thus by their annual burning off of the woods, it was an easy matter to travel in any direction and any distance, except through the vast cane-brakes that covered all the bottom lands, which alone could be passed by paths.

On hunting excursions, when a party moved their camp to another point in the woods, whether far or near, they invariably left a broken bush with the top leaning in the direction they had gone, readily comprehended by the practiced eye of the Choctaw hunter. They kept on a straight line to where a turn was made, and whatever angle there taken, they travelled it in a straight line, but left the broken bush at the turn indicating the direction they had taken. If a wandering hunter happened to stumble upon the late deserted camp and desired to join its former occupants, the broken but silent bush gave him the information as to the direction they had gone. He took it and traveled in a straight line perhaps for several miles; when suddenly his ever watchful eye saw a broken bush with its top leaning in another direction. He at once interpreted its mystic language—"Here a turn was made." He too made the turn indicated by the bush; and thus traveled through the unbroken forest for miles, directed alone by his silent but undeviating guide, which was sure to lead him to his desired object.

All North American Indians, have always held their lands in common; occupancy alone giving the right of possession. When a Choctaw erected a house upon a spot of ground, and prepared a few acres for his corn, beans, potatoes, etc., so long as he resided upon it as his home, it was exclusively his, and his rights were strictly respected by all; but if he left it and moved to another place, then his claim to his forsaken home was forfeited; and whoever saw proper could go and take possession; nor was the second occupant expected to remunerate the first for the labor he had done. However, if No. 1 afterward should desire to return to his previous home he could do so, provided no one had taken possession. The present time, if one improves a place and leaves it, no one has the right to take possession of the deserted place without permission of the one who improved it.

The famous little Choctaw pony was a veritable forest camel to the Choctaw hunter. His unwearied patience, and his seemingly untiring endurance of hardships and fatigue, were truly astonishing—surpassing, according to his inches, every other species of his race—and proving himself to be a worthy descendant of his ancient parent, the old Spanish war-horse, introduced by the early Spanish explorers of the continent. In all the Choctaws' expeditions, except those of war in which they never used horses, the chubby little pony always was considered an indispensable adjunct, therefore always occupied a conspicuous place in the cavalcade. A packsaddle which Choctaw ingenuity had invented expressly for the benefit of the worthy little fellow's back, and finely adapted in every particular for its purpose, was firmly fastened upon his back, ready to receive the burden, which was generally divided into three parts, each weighing from forty to fifty pounds. Two of these were suspended across the saddle by means of rawhide rope one-fourth of an inch in diameter and of amazing strength, and the third securely fastened upon the top, over all of which a bear or deerskin was spread, which protected it from rain. All things being ready, the hunter, as leader and protector, took his position in front, sometimes on foot and sometimes astride a pony of such diminutive proportions, that justice and mercy would naturally have suggested a reverse in the order of things, and, with his trusty rifle in his hand, without which he never went anywhere, took up the line of march, and directly after whom, in close order, the loaded ponies followed in regular succession one behind the other, while the dutiful wife, and children brought up the rear in regular, successive order, often with from three to five children on a single pony—literally hiding the submissive little fellow from view. Upon the neck of each pony a little bell was suspended, whose tinkling chimes of various tones broke the monotony of the desert air, and added cheerfulness to the novel scene. Long acustomed to their duty, the faithful little pack-ponies seldom gave any trouble, but in a straight line followed on after their master; sometimes, however, one here and there, unable to withstand the temptation of the luxuriant grass that offered itself so freely along the wayside, would make a momentary stop to snatch a bite or two, but the shrill, disapproving voice of the wife in close proximity behind, at once reminded him of his dereliction of order and he would hastily trot up to his position; and thus the little caravan with the silence broken only by the tinkling pony bells, moved on amid the dense timber of their majectic forests, until the declining sun gave warning of the near approaching night. Then a halt was made, and the faithful little ponies, relieved of their wearisome loads were set free that they might refresh themselves upon the grass and cane that grew and covered the forests in wild abundance. Late next morning—(for who ever knew an Indian, in the common affairs of life, to be in a hurry or to value time? Time! He sees it not; he feels it not; he regards it not. To him 'tis but a shadowy name—a succession of breathings, measured forth by the change of night and day by a shadow crossing the dial-path of life) the rested and refreshed ponies were gathered in, and, each having received his former load, again the tinkling chimes of the pony bells alone disturbed the quiet of the then far extending wilderness, announcing in monotonous tones the onward march, as the day before, of the contented travelers; and thus was the journey continued, day by day, until the desired point was reached.

The Indian, unlike the white man, often received a new name from some trivial incident or some extraordinary adventure, which frequently occurred, especially in their wars. Anciently the Choctaws and Muscogees were uncompromising enemies, ever making raids into each others territories At one time a Muscogee party invaded the Choctaw country, and made a sudden and unexpected attack upon a band of Choctaw warriors. The Choctaws, though surprised, made a brave resistance, and, after a short but furious fight, defeated and put their assailants to flight. A vigorous pursuit at once ensued in which a fleet young Choctaw warrior named Ahaikahno, (The Careless) had gone far in advance of his comrades, killed a Muscogee, and was in the act of scalping him, when two Muscogee warriors turned and rushed toward him with their utmost speed. The Choctaws in the rear, seeing the danger of Ahaikahno, who was ignorant of his two fast approaching foes, shouted to him with all the strength of their voices— Chikke-bulilih chia! Chikke bulilih chia! (pro. Chik-ke (Quickly) bul-elih (run) che-ah (you!). Ahaikahno, hearing the shout and seeing his danger, was not slow in heeding the advice. Ever afterwards Ahaikahno bore the additional name Chikke Bulilih Chia. Both parties lost many warriors in this short but bloody fight, and the little mound erected by the Choctaws over the common grave of their slain warriors was still to be seen down to the year of the Choctaw migration west, in 1831-32.

Nearly every river, creek, lake, rock, hill and vale, was endeared to them, by a name given to it from some peculiarity, some incident or adventure of the past, that was significant of the same; and in which were embodied the remembrance of the heroic achievements of a long line of ancestry; some in nature's rocks, mountains, hills, dells, woods, and waters; while others took substantial form in the impressive memorials reared by loving hearts and willing hands in the form of mounds over their dead. Many of those names were beautifully significant; but alas, how corrupted by the whites, to that extent indeed, that not even one has retained its original purity. Think you, reader, it was an easy matter for the Choctaws, with such a country as they then possessed, endeared to them by ten thousand times ten thousand ties as strong as were ever interwoven around the human heart, to cut loose from this their ancient home, and set sail on an unknown sea for distant ports in an unknown land, and under the pilotage of those pretended friends, who they had found could not be trusted.

Of all the wild animals of the cane-brake, the wild boar truly merited the name of being the most dangerous, when brought to bay, the panther or bear not excepted, and in attacking him, coolness and a steady nerve were as necessary as perfect marksmanship. In this kind of sport a novice would always find it the better part of valor to keep in mind that "distance lends enchantment to the view"; for he seldom made a charge without leaving his mark, since that charge I can attest by frequent observation, was no child's play. One stroke with his long, keen tusks, was all he wanted to kill an offending dog, or even disembowel a horse; and woe to the hunter that carelessly or with foolhardiness approached too near; if he failed to make a dead-shot, his life was the forfeit; for with the rush of a whirlwind, and the agility of a cat, he sprang from his lair, and more sure and fatal was his stroke as he passed, than the stroke of a dagger in the hands of an enraged man. An effectual shot was only made by shooting him through the

brain, as his shoulders were protected by a massive shield
extending from his short neck two-thirds of the way to the
hips, and impervious even by a ball shot from the rifle of
that day; his enormous head, set off by ears about the size
of a man's hand, standing straight up, and his powerful
jaws, armed with four fearful tusks, two short stubby ones
protruding from the upper and two long, dagger-like ones
from the lower lips, with a backward curve, combined with
his strength and activity, rendered him a formidable foe,
and made him truly the monarch of the Mississippi cane-
brake seventy years ago. From his short legs and sluggish
appearance, when secretly seen from a distance moving
about at his leisure, one would have supposed him slow in
point of speed; but such was not the case. For as soon as
you gave him a good cause to bestir himself, he did it to
such a good purpose that it was hard for a common horse to
escape his pursuit for a short distance, or to overtake him in
his flight. But of the two contingencies the latter, so far as
the hunter was concerned, was immeasurably the safer;
since his temper was as short as his legs, and very little
indeed sufficed his boarship's philosophy to constitute sufficient provocation, to make a sudden whirl, present and
about face, and instantly make a furious charge; then, if the
horseman was not as quick to make the turn, there was a
collision, always to the great advantage of the boar.

To intrude upon his retreat when at bay was madness;
and though his progeny were styled the "racers, razor
backs, subsoilers, jumpers, and rail splitters," by the early
white settlers, yet his majesty was justly styled the undisputed monarch of the Mississippi cane-brakes. He often
wandered companionless, then he became more morose and
and malignant, and more dangerous to intrude upon. One
of this character, for reasons best known to himself, ventured under the cover of a dark night, to sleep with the
tame hogs belonging to the missionary station, Hebron,
over which Mr. Calvin Cushman had jurisdiction, soon after
the exodus of the Choctaws. At that early day, hounds were

a protective necessity against the carnivorous wild animals that numerously abounded in the forests, though Mr. Calvin Cushman was never known to fire a gun at a wild animal of any kind, or to go into the woods as a hunter, but left that wholly to others, among whom his three sons were generally found. The visitor had overslept himself, or, at least, was a little dilatory the next morning in starting for his home in the cane-brake, and thus was discovered about daybreak, by one of the hounds between whom and his boarship uncompromising hostility existed. At once the hound gave notice to his companions in the yard of the presence of their hated and dreaded enemy by loud and vociferous barking, to which the whole pack, gave immediate response by rushing headlong over the yard fence, and in full cry hastened to the call of their fellow. At once they rushed for the wild intruder, who, taking in the surroundings, broke at once for his citadel in the swamp two miles away across an intervening forest with no undergrowth in which to shelter himself in case of being overtaken by his pursuing foes. My brother and I, knowing from the wild outcry of the hounds that they had discovered some wild animal of merit, seized our rifles, rushed to the barn, saddled our hunting horses and mounted; then listened a moment to ascertain the bearings of the hounds whose cry was now faintly heard in the distance, but gave evidence that the object of their pursuit was no small matter. At once we started at full speed through the open forest, and, after running a mile or more, stopped to listen when we ascertained they had overtaken the night intruder, whatever he was, and brought him to bay, but still nearly a mile distant. Again we put our horses at full speed, and thus continued until we had reached the top of a high ridge, where came into full view, about three hundred yards distant, the hounds encircling a huge wild boar. For a minute we silently stood and gazed upon the exciting scene.

The hounds (eight in number) knowing, from sad experience, the characteristics of their foe, were running this way and that around the old monarch of the canebrake, but observing the judicious caution to keep twenty or thirty feet distant from him, who defiantly stood in the center of the circle and boldly solicited closer quarters. No undergrowth obstructed our view, and the whole play was being enacted before us. Now a hound would make a dash at his rear only to be met by the about face of the agile boar, which caused the hound to also make an about face followed by a hasty retreat, then one would succeed in giving him a snap in the rear, which caused the boar, not only to make a quick turn, but also to make a rush for a few paces after the now retreating dog, but to be again pinched in the rear by some one of his more venturesome assailants. Finally one made a dash at the rear of the boar with high expectations of securing a good bite; but poor Pete was not quick enough in his whirl, for the boar, in his sweep, struck him with his curving tusks upon the thigh making an ugly wound three or four inches in length and to the bone. Pete at once acknowledged his defeat by a shrill cry and immediate retreat to the rear. Thinking it time to take a hand in the fray, we dismounted, and leaving our horses concealed, cautiously advanced to the scene of action, but taking care not to let his boarship learn of our proximity. But not much danger of that, as his attention was wholly engaged with the still tormenting dogs. When we had approached within a hundred yards, we halted behind a large tree and formed our plan of attack, as we silently peeped from our hiding place and viewed the scene. The boar was still ignorant of our presence; but the hounds had evidently suspected our presence somewhere, by frequently looking back and sniffing the air, and then barking more vigorously at the boar and making bolder and more frequent attacks upon his rear.

He was truly a magnificent specimen of his race, of a sandy color, full grown, and in fine condition. His huge head was adorned with enormous, curving tusks with one sweep of which he could cut a man, dog or horse into threads. His little red eyes, nearly covered with shaggy hair, now glowed like coals of fire, beneath a pair of ears about the size of a man's hand which stood perfectly erect; his tail, though curled once at his body, nearly touched the ground with its long shaggy hairs; his cavernous mouth was white with foam—proof that he was mad all over; his bristles about four inches long, extended from his ears to his tail, and stood up erect and stiff, while every hair upon his body seemingly quivered with rage; the massive sinews of his great chest stood out like small ropes as he turned from side to side, exposing also to view the outlines of the almost inpervious shield that enveloped his shoulders. He was truly an incarnation of immense strength, activity, courage, and brutal ferocity.

Our curiosity being satisfied in viewing his dimensions and appearance, it was resolved that my brother, who was the more courageous and the better marksman, should crawl to a large tree that stood exactly between us and the boar, which would bring him within fifty or sixty yards of his boarship, and also, the sure range of his rifle, while I was to keep my position as a rear guard in case of a compulsory retreat. By good fortune he gained the tree unobserved by hound or boar; then arose to his feet and brought his rifle to his shoulder, with the barrel resting against the right side of the tree, thus being enabled to keep his body wholly concealed. Soon I saw the boar turn his head exactly toward the tree and instantly the crack of the rifle mingled with the baying of the hounds, and the fierce brute pitched over on his nose to be instantly covered with exultant dogs who bit and snapped their fallen foe. We hurried up, only to see a convulsive shiver run through the huge mass of flesh and bone, and the fierce glare of the eye as it died out slowly, like a coal fading in the sunlight as the white ashes cover it. The rifle ball had accomplished its mission of death.

In conclusion, I will but add: If those, who today talk about dangerous game, would like to enjoy a rough and tumble encounter, I would, could I recall the last seventy years, recommend to them a wild boar of the Mississippi cane-ᵇreaks, with strong testimonials; nor would they have far to go, at that day, to find him.

O-ka-it-tib-ih-ha County, Mississippi, as well as its sister counties, has been the scene of many hard struggles between the contending warriors of the different tribes, who inhabited the noble old state in years of the long past; not only from the statements and traditions of the Choctaws, who were among the last of the Indian race whose council-fires lit up her forests, and whose hoyopatassuha died away upon her hills, but also from the numerous fortifications and intrenchments, that were plainly visible, ere the ploughshare had upturned her virgin soil, and her native forests still stood in their primitive beauty and grandeur. From those rude fortifications, plainly identified many years after the advent of the missionaries, strong positions were evidently held by each contending party; yet they seemed to have been constructed with no regard to mathematical skill, but rather as circumstances demanded or would admit. Such at least were the intrenchments enclosing the Shakchi Humma old fort; and the many evidences, such as rusted tomahawks, arrow-heads, human bones, teeth and fragments of skulls that were continually being ploughed up for many years, proved the hard contested fight of the Shakchi Hummas and the allied Choctaws and Chickasaws; and that the brave but greatly outnumbered Shakchi Hummas had disputed every inch of the ground, and had only yielded to the superior numbers of the combined Choctaw and Chickasaw warriors. The ancient Choctaws, as well as all other Indians, did not confine their battles to forts and intrenchments, but fought as circumstances offered, oftener in small bodies than in large. Hence, they never drew out their forces in open field, but fought from behind trees, stumps and logs; each seeking every possible advantage of

his enemy, regarding all advantages gained as wholly at-
tributable to superior skill; all advantages lost, to want of it.

According to the statements made by the Choctaws to
Mr. Calvin Cushman, when first established among them as
a missionary, nearly eighty years ago, the Shakchi Hummas,
a warlike and very overbearing tribe of Indians, were
wholly exterminated by the combined forces of the Choctaws and Chickasaws about the year 1721.

I was personally acquainted with a remarkable old
Choctaw warrior, by the name of Ish-iah-hin-la, (you liable
to go) who claimed to have fought through the Shakchi
Humma war. He was said to be the last surviving Choctaw
warrior of that memorable conflict, and died in 1828 at the
advanced age of 107 years, so he claimed to be. Indeed the
old warrior's white locks, wrinkled face, shriveled and decrepit body, indicated life's journey to have reached that
point, and, as longevity was frequent at that time (as even
to-day) among the Indians, many then living whose ages
reached eighty and ninety years, I did not doubt the old
man's statement. He took great delight in relating many
incidents of that war and oft amused my boyish fancy in
telling many thrilling scenes in which he participated. This
war had its origin from the overbearing disposition of the
Shakchi Hummas, and the frequent murders committed by
their war parties upon the Choctaws and Chickasaws. The
account, as related by the Choctaws to the missionaries, is
in substance, about as follows: Many years after the Choctaws and Chickasaws had established themselves east of
the Misissippi River, a Choctaw chief, named Shakchi
Humma (Crawfish Red), recrossed the Mississippi River,
with his family and a large number of his adherents, and
established a colony (under the name of their chief, Shakchi
Humma) in now the state of Arkansas.

In the course of years this colony became greatly enlarged by constant accessions; and, with increasing numbers
and strength, also became insolent and overbearing to that
extent that a war arose between them and another tribe,

in which they were defeated and driven back over the Mississippi to their former country. After being established there, (not as Choctaws but as Shakchi Hummas disregarding their ancient kindred ties) they adopted an arrogant and aggressive policy towards both the Choctaws and Chickasaws, who, provoked beyond longer endurance, formed a secret alliance in an exterminating war against the Shakchi Hummas.

Then followed a three years' war of extermination (famous in Choctaw tradition) culminating at the battle of Oski Hlopah and blotting out the Shakchi Humma nation. The Choctaws and Chickasaws took the warpath together, resolving to exterminate their insolent enemies or be exterminated themselves. At this juncture, several large parties of Shakchi Hummah hunters were camped on Noxubee Creek, as much game had congregated there owing to the destruction of the range in many parts of the country by the accidental fall fires. The Choctaws, being aware of the locality of the Shakchi Humma hunters, opened the war by making an unexpected attack upon them and slew the greater part, throwing their dead bodies into the creek which caused an awful stench, which gave the name Nahshobili to the creek, and opened hostilities in good earnest between the Choctaws and Chickasaws on one side and the Shakchi Hummas on the other.

Extermination being the war-cry adopted by the contestants, both parties fought with desperation. But, unexpectedly as the two allied tribes had rushed upon their unsuspecting and unprepared enemies (thus in the outset gaining great advantage) yet the Shakchi Hummas soon rallied from the discomfiture caused by their surprise; and then commenced one of those fierce and bloody conflicts, so oft engaged in by the Red Men in the years of the hoary past, but known only to themselves. In union there is strength, is an old but true adage; and thus it proved to the Choctaws and Chickasaws. Though fortune for a while appeared to waver, vacillating from the one side to the other and seeming at a loss on whom to bestow her smiles, but finally looked with favor upon the two allied tribes. The Shakchi Hummas, after many reverses and great losses, finally sought to protract the strong struggle by taking refuge in their intrenched villages. But one after another of these fell into the hands of the victorious Choctaws and Chickasaws, who now had become fearless by their success, and, ere the third year of the desperate conflict had closed, every village had been taken, and destroyed, and the majority of the inhabitants slain. The few who escaped united their strength and finally took their last stand at a point now known as Lyon's Bluff on Oski Hlopah (Cane stripped) River, known now as Trimcane, about nine miles northeast of Starkville, Mississippi, hopeless, yet determined to fight to the death. Sheltered by a few logs and banks of earth, the last of that once powerful and arrogant tribe, now fought as only men in despair can and do fight, sending many of their enemies to precede them to the hunting grounds in the great beyond. Surrounded on all sides without the possibility of escape, and sheltered only by a few logs and piles of dirt; yet they baffled all attempts of their enemies to dislodge them.

Like tigers at bay, they fought day and night, though hour by hour thinned in numbers, till at last but few remained; yet that handful yielded not, nor asked for quarter, but singing their death song, and ever and anon hurling back their defiant warwhoops, they continued to fight, killlog and mud fort successfully hold out, bravely driving back their assailants in every charge. At length, the Choctaws and Chickasaws, maddened at the obstinate resistance of the now desperate Shakchi Hummas, and the continued falling here and there of their own warriors, with a mighty rush broke over the feebly defended walls, but to be met by the little squad of still defiant Shakchi Hummas, who received them with the last shout of their still defiant warwhoop. Then, for a few moments, was heard the clashing and ringing of the tomahawks as the busy scene of death went on; each Shakchi Humma warrior fighting, not for life or for glory, but in mad despair—seeking to kill ere he was killed. But soon the last death-dealing blow was struck that blotted out forever the Shakchi Humma Nation. Only one of the whole tribe was left, and that one was a young girl about sixteen or eighteen years of age, who was spared on account of her wonderful beauty. She was adopted by the Choctaws, and lived to be nearly or quite a hundred years old, and was living some years after the advent of the missionaries among them. Mr. H. Peden, who lived fourteen miles from Hebron, the home of Mr. Calvin Cushman, stated that Mr. P. P. Pitchlynn, who had often spoken to him of this old Shakchi Humma captive, one day pointed her out to him at a religious meeting of the Choctaws. Mr. Peden stated that she was the oldest looking human being that he had ever seen, and from her appearance, he judged her to be over a century old. She died a few years before the venerable old warrior, Stahenka; but lived to hear the tidings of the Cross preached to her race, though the only survivor of her own tribe, exterminated in the bright morn of her youthful but eventful life. But such is the only history of the Shakchi Hummas whose blood still runs in the veins of a few Choctaws—descendants of the girl saved at the tragic destruction of her tribe—one of whom became a chief of the Choctaws and died in 1884 at his home a few miles east of Atoka, Choctaw Nation, Indian Territory. His name is Coleman Cole.

| The Choctaws, ~~like all of their race,~~ had no written laws, and their government rested alone on custom and usage, growing out of their possessions and their wants; yet was conducted so harmoniously by the influence of their native genius and experience, that one would hardly believe that human society could be maintained with so little artifice| As they had no money, their traffic consisted alone in mutual exchange of all commodities; as there was no employment of others for hire, there were no contracts, hence judges and lawyers, sheriffs and jails were unknown among

them. There were no beggars, no wandering tramps, no orphan children unprovided for in their country, and deformity was almost unknown, proving that nature in the wild forest of the wilderness is true to her type. Their chiefs had no crown, no sceptre, no body guards, no outward symbols of authority, nor power to give validity to their commands, but sustained their authority alone upon the good opinion of their tribe. No Choctaw ever worshipped his fellow man, or submitted his will to the humiliating subordinations of another, but with that sentiment of devotion that passed beyond the region of humanity, and brought him in direct contact with nature and the imaginary beings by whom it was controlled, which he divined but could not fathom; to these, and these alone, he paid his homage, invoking their protection in war and their aid in the chase.

The ancient Choctaws believed, and those of the present day believe, and I was informed by Governor Basil LeFlore, in 1884, (since deceased) that there is an appointed time for every one to die; hence suicide appeared to them as an act of the nearest cowardice. Though they regarded it as a sacrilege to mention the names of their dead, still they spoke of their own approaching death with calmness and tranquility. No people on earth paid more respect to their dead, than the Choctaws did and still do; or preserved with more affectionate veneration the graves of their ancestors. They were to them as holy relics, the only pledges of their history; hence, accursed was he who should despoil the dead. They had but a vague idea of future rewards and punishments. To them a future life was a free gift of the Great Spirit, and the portals of the happy hunting grounds would be opened to them, in accordance as their life had been meritorious as a brave warrior. They were utterly ignorant of the idea of a general resurrection, and it was difficult for them to be induced to believe that the body would again be raised up. But to-day finds the Choctaws advanced in knowledge and improvement, which has produced a revolution in their moral and intellectual condition and in the current of their thoughts and ideas.

As a proof of the Indian's love of country and the scenes of his childhood, so cruelly denied him by the oppressors, I will state that a few years after they had moved west, a few Choctaw warriors, seemingly unable to resist the desire of once more looking upon the remembered scenes of the unforgotten past, returned to the homes of their youth; for a few weeks they lingered around, the very personification of hopeless woe, with a peculiar something in their manner and appearance, which seemed to speak their thoughts as absently following a long dream that was leading them to the extreme limits of their once interminable fatherland. But their souls could not brook the change, or the ways of the pale-face. They gazed awhile, as strangers in a strange land, then turned in silence and sorrow from the loved vision they never would enjoy or look upon again, but which they never would forget, and once more directed their steps toward the setting sun and were seen no more.

The Indians have ever been termed a nomadic race, and as such have been represented by all who have written about them. There certainly never has a greater error been promulgated about any people. I refer to the southern Indians who formerly lived east of the Mississippi River. How far the Indians of the western plains may merit the title, I will not attempt to judge, being but little acquainted with their habits and customs, ancient or modern. Webster, the standard authority, gives the definition of nomadic as signifying, "Moving from place to place," and how that word could in any way justly be applied to the Choctaw, Chickasaw and Muscogee Indians is a difficult matter to comprehend. In 1832, the United States Government found them still where De Soto, the Virginians, the French, the Carolina traders, Adair, Roman, and the missionaries had found them, and moved them to their present place of

abode in 1882; and 1899, A. D., finds them just where the
government put them sixty-seven years ago. So they have
"moved from place to place," once in 359 years, and then
moved by the force of arbitrary power, they are called
nomadic.

They were truly men of the past, as well as men of the
woods, yet noble and true, glorying in their ancestors, and
living in their deeds by reverencing what they had handed
down to them.

Having no alphabet nor written language, their knowledge was conveyed to the eye by rude imitation. In the
pictures of various animals which had been drawn on a
smooth substance, a piece of bark, or tree, there he recognized a symbol of his tribe; and in these various figures
which he saw sketched here and there, he read messages
from his friends. The rudest painting, though silent and
unintelligible to the white man, told its tale to the Choctaws. They had no calendar, but reckoned time thus: the
months, by the full or crescents moons; the years by the
killing of the vegetation by the wintry frosts. Thus, for two
years ago the Choctaw would say: hushuk (grass) illi (dead)
tuklo (twice); literally, grass killed twice, or, more properly,
two killings of the grass ago. The sun was called Nittak
hushi—the Day-sun; and the moon, Neuak hushi, the
Night-sun and sometimes, Tekchi hushi—the Wife of the
sun. Their almanac was kept by the flight of the fowls of
the air; whose coming and going announced to them the
progress of the advancing and departing seasons. Thus the
fowls of the air announced to the then blessed and happy
Choctaw the progress of the seasons, while the beasts of the
field gave to him warning of the gathering and approaching
storm, and the sun marked to him the hour of the day; and
so the changes of time were noted, not by figures, but by
days, sleeps, suns and moons—signs that spoke the beauty
and poetry of nature. If a shorter time than a day was
required to be indicated two parallel lines were drawn on
the ground, a certain distance apart, then pointing to the

sun he would say: "It is as long as it would take the sun to move from there to there." The time indicated by the moon was from its full to the next; that of the year, from winter to winter again, or from summer to summer. To keep appointments, a bundle of sticks containing the exact number of sticks as there were days from the day of appointment to the appointed, was kept; and every morning one was taken out and thrown away, the last stick announced the arrival of the appointed. This bundle of twigs was called fuli (sticks) kauah (broken) broken sticks.

The abundant game of his magnificent and wide extended forests, which he never killed in wanton sport, no more than a white man would kill his cattle, but only as his necessities demanded, together with the fish of his beautiful streams, his fields of corn, potatoes, beans, with that of the inexhaustible supplies of spring and summer berries of fine variety and flavor, and winter nuts, all united to consummate his earthly bliss in rendering him a successful huntsman, a good fisherman, and cheerful tiller of the ground. The Choctaws have long been known to excel all the North American Indians in agriculture, subsisting to a considerable extent on the produce of their fields. In mental capacity the Choctaws, as a race of people, both ancient and modern, were and are not inferior to the whites; and their domestic life, as I knew them seventy years ago, would sustain in many respects, a fair comparison with average civilized white communities. Their perceptive faculties were truly wonderful; and the Choctaws of to-day, to whom the advantages of an education have been extended, have given indisputable evidence of as great capacity for a high order of education as any people on earth, I care not of what nationality.

There were no degrees of society among them, no difference in social gatherings; all felt themselves equal, of the same standing and on the same terms of social equality. And it is the same today . They had no surnames, yet their names were peculiar, and most always significant, expressive of some particular action or incident; even as the names given to their hills, rivers, creeks, towns and villages. As those of ancient, classic fame in the eastern world, so to the superstitious mind of the Choctaw of the western world, caused him also to regard the sudden appearance of certain birds and their chirpings and twitterings, the howl of the wolf and the lonely hoot of the owl, as omens of evil, while others as omens of good; the spiritual significance of which, however, he interpreted according to the dictation of his own judgment, instead of that of an augur differing in this particular from his ancient brothers of Rome and Greece; yet like them he undertook no important enterprise without first consulting his trusted signs, whether auspicious or otherwise. If the former, he hesitated not its undertaking; if the latter, no inducement could be offered that would prevail upon him to undertake it; but he returned to his cabin and there remained for favorable omens.

But how far may be found a more just cause for admiration of the religious superstitions of the ancient Romans and Grecians than that of the North American Indians it is difficult to see, since the Indians, alike with them, acknowledged, everywhere in nature, the presence of invisible beings; and it was the firm belief that his interests were under the special care of the Great and Good Spirit that the Choctaw warrior went upon the war-path, and the hunter sought the solitudes of his native forests in search of his game; and that his career in life was marked out for him by a decree that could not be altered. The mystery of nature had its influence upon the untutored minds of all Indians, as well as its phenomena upon his senses; which, to them, were represented by the inferior spirits that surround the Great Spirit, who was the all-controlling diety; and to Him they all turned in gratitude for blessings, and for aid in all the affairs of life. And though the rites and ceremonies of the Indians, by which they expressed their belief in their dependence on the Great Spirit, was made in offerings of corn, bread, fruits, etc., instead of the sacrifices of animals; and sought omens in the actions of living animals, instead of an augury in the entrails of dead animals; yet the sincere feelings of piety, of gratitude and dependence, which gave origin to those offerings, gave origin also to that universal habit ·f self-examination and secret prayer to the Great Spirit, so characteristic of the Indian race. They believed that the Great Spirit communicated his will to man in dreams, in thunder and lightning, eclipses, meteors, comets, in all the prodigies of nature, and the thousands of unexpected incidents that occur to man. Could it be otherwise expected from those who walked by the light of nature alone? But that they derived their religious beliefs from the common seed with which man first started, there can be no doubt; but ere it had developed to any extent they strayed from the parent stock, and it assumed different aspects under different circumstances, during the long period of isolation that ensued. Still, we find existing everywhere among mankind the same sensitiveness to the phenomena of nature, and the same readiness and power of imagining invisible beings as the cause of these phenomena.

The tendency of the Indian mind was thoroughly practical, stern and unbending, it was not filled with images of poetry nor high-strung conceptions of fancy. He struggled for what was immediate, the warpath, the chase and council life; but when not engaged therein, the life of the national games, under the head of social amusements, filled up the measure of his days—the ball play, horse-race, foot-race, jumping and wrestling—to them as honorable as the gymnastic exercises of the eastern nations of antiquity; enduring heat and cold, suffering the pangs of hunger and thirst, fatigue and sleeplessness. The object of the Indian boy also, was to gain all the experience possible in all manly exercises, therefore at an early age he went in search of adventures. Their tribal council consisted of the best, wisest and most worthy of the tribe. They had but few laws, but the few were rigidly enforced.

There were many natural orators among the ancient Choctaws when living in undisturbed prosperity and happiness east of the Mississippi River. Their orations were very concise, animating and abounding in many beautiful metaphors; and who, had they possessed the embellishments of a refined education, would have compared well with any race of mankind that ever existed.

The Choctaws, like all their race, deliberated with great dignity and solemnity on national affairs; and in all their assemblies, both, national and social, everything was carried on in the best order and unassumed decorum. Their treaties were ratified by smoking the pipe of peace—an emblem respected, honored, and held sacred by all Indians everywhere. As with all their race, so war was, in the estimation of the ancient Choctaws, the most patriotic avocation in which a man could engage; they seldom began a war with another tribe, but rather waited for an attack, then no braver or more resolute warriors ever went upon the warpath. The opening of hostilities was always preceded by the famous hoyopahihla, war-dance. Night was the chosen time for engaging in that time-honored ceremony; and as soon as evening began to spread her dark mantle o'er their forests, a huge pile of dry logs and brush previously prepared was set on fire, whose glaring and crackling flames intermingling with their hoyopataloah (war-songs) and soul-stirring hoyopa-tassuhah (warwhoops) presented a scene as wild and romantic as can possibly be imagined.

On the return of a successful warpath, the village at once became the scene of festivity and triumph. The varied trophies—scalps, painted shields, etc., were hung on poles near the houses. Then followed war-feasts, scalp-dances, accompanied with war-songs and shouts of victory, while the old men went from house to house rehearsing in a loud tone of voice the events of the battle and the various daring exploits of the warriors. But, amid all this, sounds of another kind were also heard mingling in discordant tones with those of joy; they were the piteous wailings of the women borne upon the air from the surrounding hills, where they had retired to mourn in darkness and solitude for their slain in battle.

Like all nations of the human family, so the Choctaws of both sexes delighted in ornaments. Though the Choctaw warrior, in his training for the duties of manhood, inured himself to fatigue and privation, and in defense of his country and home, and resenting an insult, was as brave as bravery itself; yet he was fond of admiring himself before a mirror when arrayed in the paraphernalia of Choctaw fashion; i. e. a red turban, highly decorated with the gay plumage of various kinds of birds encircling his head; with face painted according to Choctaw etiquette; with crescents of highly polished tin suspended from his neck and extending in regular order from the chin to the waist; with shining bracelets of the same metal encircling his wrists and arms above the elbows; with a broad belt around his waist, tastily interwoven with innumerable little beads of every gay and flashing color; with feet encased in moccasins soft and pliant, and highly decorated with little beads of sparkling hue, did the young Choctaw warrior walk forth among the admiring beauties of his tribe.

The Choctaws were strong in their belief in the existence of hat-tak holth-kun-a (witches); even as our own "enlightened" ancestors in the days of Cotton Mather—differing, however, in this particular; the Choctaws selected old and discrepit women as victims of their superstitions, while their white brothers, whose boasted civilization had rendered a little more fastidious, manifested their superiority in intellectual attainments over the Indians, by selecting the young as the victims of their wild theories. But ghosts and witches have long since been to the Choctaws as things of the forgotten past.

The restless and fertile imagination of the Choctaws, as well as all their race, peopled with beings of a higher order than themselves the mountains, plains, woods, lakes, fountains and streams. But in regard to the origin of man, the one generally accepted among the Choctaws, as well as many other tribes was that man and all other forms of life had originated from the common mother earth through the agency of the Great Spirit; but believed that the human race sprang from many different primeval pairs created by the Great Spirit in the various parts of the earth in which man was found; and according to the different natural features of the world in which man abode, so their views varied with regard to the substance of which man was created; in a country of vast forests, they believed the primeval pair, or pairs, sprang from the trees; in a mountainous and rocky district of country, they sprang from the rocks; in valleys and prairies, from the earth; but their views as to the time this creation of man took place, whether at the same time throughout the various inhabited regions or at different periods, their traditions are silent.

The Choctaws had several classes of dignitaries among them who were held in the highest reverence: The medicine man or prophet, the rain maker, the doctor—a veritable chip of Esculapius. Well indeed did each fill his allotted position in life, and faithfully discharge the mystic duties appertaining thereunto, both in their own opinion as well as that of their people. Their doctors relied much on dry-cupping, using their mouth alone in all such cases. Oft have I witnessed the Choctaw physician, east of the Mississippi River, administering to the necessities of his sufferng patient through the virtues found in the process of dry-cupping. Stretching the sufferer upon a blanket spread upon the ground, he kneeled beside him and began a process of sucking that part of the body of which the patient complained, or where, in his own judgment, the disease was located, making a gutteral noise during the operation that reminded one of a dog worrying an oppossum; at different intervals raising his head a few inches and pretending to deposit into his hands, alternately in the one and the other, an invisible something which he had drawn from his patient, by a magic power known alone to himself.

After sucking a sufficient length of time to fill both hands, judging from the frequent deposits therein made, with great apparent dignity and solemn gravity, this worthy son of Esculapius arose and stepping to the nearest tree, post, or fence, wiped the secret contents of his apparently full hands thereon; then with an air of marked importance walked away to the enjoyments of his own reflections, while the sufferer, in real or fancied relief, acknowledged the efficacy of the physician's healing powers by ceasing to complain, turned over and sought forgetfulness in sleep. If there ensued a change for the better he claimed the honor and praise as due the noble profession of which he recognized himself a worthy and important member; but if the disease proved stubborn and refused to yield to the medicinal virtues of his herbs, roots and dry-cupping, he turned to his last resort—the anuka, (hot-house). This edifice, an important adjunct in all Choctaw villages, was made of logs rendered nearly air tight by stopping all cracks with mortar. A little hole was left on one side for an entrance. A fire was built in the center of this narrow enclosure, and soon the temperature within was raised to the desired degree, then the fire was taken out and the patient instructed to crawl in; which being done, the little opening was closed. As a matter of course, the patient must bake or sweat; which, however, resulted in the latter; and when, in the opinion of the alikchi, (doctor) he had undergone a thorough sweating, the entrance was opened, and the patient bidden to come forth; who, upon his exit, at once runs to the nearest water into which he plunged head first; but if not of sufficient amount and depth for the correct performance of that ceremony to its fullest extent, he ducks his head into it several times. In case of common intermittent fever, the efficiency of this mode of proceeding (the sweat and cold bath) was truly astonishing, seldom failing to effect a cure.

But if the patient died—ah, then! with that shrewdness peculiar to all quacks the world over, he readily found a cause upon which to base his excuse for his inefficacy to effect a cure; differing somewhat, however, from his white brother alikchi, who attributes the cause of his failure to innumerable "whereases and ifs," while he openly acknowledged and emphatically declared the interposition of a hattak holth-kun-na (witch), who consequently was immediately slain by the relatives of the deceased; an illustration of which I have already given in the case of the unfortunate Il-lich-ih.

In the matter of rain, the Choctaw rainmaker truly swayed the sceptre of authority in that line of art, undisputed, and was regarded with reverential awe by his people. In all cases of protracted drouth, which was quite frequent at an early day in their ancient domains, the hut-tak um-ba ik-bi, (man rain maker) was regarded as the personage in whom alone was vested the power to create rain; therefore to him they went with their offerings and supplications. He without hesitation promised to head their solicitations, but gently hinting that, in his judgment, the offerings were not in as exact ratio to their importunities as they should have been. However, he now assumes an air of mysterious thoughtfulness and strolled from village to village, gazing at the sun by day and the stars by night, seeming to hold communion with the spirits of the upper worlds; finally he ventured his reputation by specifying a certain day upon which he would make it rain. The day arrived, and if haply came with it a rain the faith of his dupes was confirmed. But if otherwise, he did not as the alikchi, attribute his failure to the counteracting influence of a witch in the person of an old woman, but to that of a brother umba ikbi living in some remote part of the nation, with whom he was just then at variance. He now informs his people that an umba ikbi's mind must be free of all contending emotions while engaged in the mystic ceremonies of rain making; that he was now angry, too much mad to make it rain. Upon which announcement, the now despairing people earnestly solicited to know if they, in any

way could assuage his wrath. He replied in the negative;
but promised, however, to consider the matter as soon as
his anger abated. He now became more reserved; sought
solitude where undisturbed he might scan the sky and perchance discern some sign of rain. Sooner or later, he dis-
covers a little hazy cloud stretched along the distant western horizon; attentively and carefully watches it as broader
and higher it ascends, until he feels sure he can safely risk
another promise; then leaves his place of secret and though-
ful meditation, and announces his anger cooled and wrath
departed; that now he would bring rain without delay, yet
dropping a casual hint as to the efficacy of a coveted pony,
cow, blanket, etc., being added, as a surer guarantee. The
hint was comprehended and fully complied with in hopeful
expectation. Soon the sky is overcast with clouds of black-
est hue while the lightning's flash and the thunder's roar
seem to proclaim to the people their wonderful umba ikbi's
secret power; and, as the vast sheets of falling water wet
the parched earth they sing his praise. But all such delu-
sions soon vanished before the teachings of the missionaries.

In connection with this peculiar one of the Choctaws,
I will here relate an incident that took place during a great
drouth that prevailed in their Nation soon after the establishment of the mission called Hebron.

The rain maker had long been appealed to through
supplication and fees, but all in vain; and it seemed that
the stubborn drouth had united with more than one distant
brother umba ikbi in rendering his present worship prodig-
iously mad. Since wells and cisterns were luxuries then
unknown to the Indians, they depended upon their rivers,
creeks, lakes and ponds, which seldom failed to supply.
Amid the prevailing gloom an aged Choctaw widow named
Im-ai-yah (to go by) living two miles south of Hebron, came
one day, as she oft had done before, to talk with her pale-
face friend, Mrs. Cushman, concerning the drouth. She
soon stated that she believed there would be plenty of rain
in a few days. When asked upon what she based her belief,

she replied: "On my way here this morning, I sat down at the roots of a large tree; while sitting there these thoughts came to me. Our rain maker cannot make it rain, or he would. If he can make it rain, why should not I be able to make it rain too? Why should not anyone? Then I asked myself; who made this big tree? Somebody made it, and he who made it surely can make it rain too. I know he can; and I will ask him to please make it rain very soon. I then kneeled down at the roots of that big tree and earnestly prayed to him who made the big tree to please make it rain; and while I was praying a little cloud formed directly over the tree, and a little shower fell and many of the drops of water, passing through the leaves of the tree, fell on me. I know now who can make it rain." "Who?" earnestly asked the deeply interested pale-face listener. "He who made that tree. Is he your God of whom you have told me?" "He is," replied the poor widow's pale-face friend and spiritual teacher.

But what of that prayer at the roots of that "big tree?" It was heard and answered by the Maker of that "big tree"; who has said, "I will not bruise the broken reed nor quench the smoking flax." Yes, in a few days, an abundance of rain fell; yea, more. From that time the mystic power of the umba ikbis began to wane, and soon vanished as a summer dream from the Choctaw Nation. And he who cannot believe that Israel's God heard the humble request of that earnest petitioner and did not then and there acknowledge its virtue in the little shower of rain, and in a few days answer that prayer of faith by an abundant shower, is thrice welcome to his unbelief.

Their laws (for they had laws), though exceptional in some respects to the White Race, nevertheless, were good, and quite consistent with the nations of a primitive age. But like all others of their race, their severest law was that of blood revenge. "Whosoever sheddeth man's blood, by man shall his blood be shed" was a statute rigidly enforced among all North American Indians. It was ackuowledged

among all, not only to be the right, but also the imperative
duty of the nearest relative on the male side of the slain, to
kill the slayer wherever and whenever a favorable opportunity was presented. Under many existing circumstances
the law might, perhaps, have been just and salutary; but
unfortunately it went too far, as any male member of the
murderer's family, though innocent and even ignorant of
the crime, might become the victim of the avenger of
blood, if the guilty had fled; but such seldom occurred, as
the murderer rarely ever made any effort whatever to escape, but passively submitted to his fate. Still, this law,
revolting as it may appear to many, exercised a good influence among the Choctaws, as it had a salutary effect in
restraining them in the heat of passion, by rendering them
cautious in their disputes and quarrels, lest blood should be
shed; knowing the absolute certainty of murder being
avenged sooner or later upon the murderer himself, or some
one of his nearest male relatives; hence no man, or family,
would with impunity commit or permit, if they could avoid
or prevent it, an act that would be sure to be avenged, no
one could tell when or where. Days, weeks, and even
months perhaps, might pass, yet the avenger sleepeth not
nor has he forgotten; and, at an hour least expected and
from a source least apprehended, the blow at last falls, and
there the matter ends. Nor did the slayer find any protection from any source whatever, not even from his nearest
relatives. Yet calmly and with stoical indifference awaited
his certain doom; nor was the avenger, though known,
interrupted in any manner whatever, either before or after
he had accomplished his revenge. The avenger of blood
never took the life of a female of the slayer's family, but
satisfied himself in the death of the slayer himself or in the
person of some one of his nearest male relatives. If the
murderer had fled, and the life of one of his male relatives
had been sacrificed in lieu of his own, he then could return
without fear of molestation; but the name of coward was

given to him—an appellation more dreaded and less endurable than a hundred deaths to all North American Indians.

A few instances have been known among the Choctaws, where a relative proposed to die for the slayer, and was accepted on the part of the relatives of the slain; but such instances were very rare. I remember of an instance related, of undoubted authority, which deserves to be held in lasting remembrance if nothing more than to forever silence and put to eternal shame the foolish croakings of those who deny to the Indian the possession of any of the finer feelings and emotions of the heart, and to establish the fact that the height, depth, and breadth of an Indian mother's love can only be equalled by that of her white sister, both immeasurable, incomprehensible, unfathomable. The case which I here relate, was Toh-to Pe-hah (Red Elm Gathered Up), an aged Choctaw mother, who gave her life for that of her oldest son. This poor widowed Choctaw mother, came with others of her friends to the place of execution on the day her son was to be shot for killing an aged Choctaw man living many miles distant from that of his own home. This killing was done before the establishment of the law that the slayer should be tried by law, and no longer left in the hands of the "avenger of blood." Of her four children he was the oldest, her darling first-born, on whom she mainly depended for assistance in the support of her little family, and whom she had named Hoh-tak Lah-ba (Lukewarm).

When the mother arrived at the place of execution, she found many had already assembled; but she pressed through the throng to where her doomed boy stood, close to the executioner with the deadly rifle in hand, upon which Hohtak Lahba looked with steady eye and unshaken nerves. All were silent. The mother glanced a look of love at the erect form of her son; then turned them a moment upon the executioner with an appealing look for compassion; then beseechingly upon the relatives of the man slain, and at once broke the silence with an irresistible appeal to them to take her life instead of Hohtak Lahba's. "He is young, and I am old," she cried. "His wife and child, his two little sisters and brother, will suffer if he is taken from them. They cannot live without him, they can without me. I am old and can do but little for them, nor that little long. Your relative he killed was an old man. Why take a young life for an old life? Take mine in the place of Hohtak Lahba's.' A murmur of approval was heard in the crowd, and soon one of the nearest in kindred to the slain arose and accepted the offer in a firm and distinct tone of voice. A smile of joy lit up the countenance of Toh-to Pe-hah as she responded, " 'Tis well." A few moments were given her to bid an adieu to her loved ones, and give her last admonitions to her wayward boy; after which she calmly presented herself before the executioner. Then the sharp crack of the rifle broke the profound stillness of the moment, and the spirit of that loving Choctaw mother winged its flight to Him who has said: "Where little is given, little is required." Such was the custom of this peculiar people in the years of the long ago. "'An eye for an eye, and a tooth for a tooth," was ever found written in all Indians' code of laws, and to the execution of which they adhered with the strictest punctuality. The spirit of the murdered Indian could never take its flight from earth, or find rest anywhere in the eternal unknown, until blood had atoned for blood, a belief as firmly fixed upon the Indian heart as that upon the Christian's, that the blood of the Lord Jesus Christ, the Son of God, atoned for the sins of the world.

It is natural to suppose that Hohtak Lahba would have refused the offer of his devoted mother. But custom denied him the privilege of any action whatever in the matter. If the offer was made and accepted by the relatives of the slain, he no longer stood condemned before the violated law, or in the eyes of the avenger, and he or she, who had voluntarily assumed the position, could only make the atonement. The unfortunate Hoh tak Lahba, though the

avenger of the blood of his slain victim had been appeased
at a fearful cost to him, was afterwards often taunted by
the relatives and friends of the old man he had slain, with
the accusation of cowardice.

For several years he bore up under their taunts until
life to him had become a burden too great to be longer
borne. But what could he do? To take his own life would
not do, since that act would stamp the seal of woe upon his
eternal destiny. How then was he to secure for himself an
honorable death and wipe off the stain of cowardice that
had been attached to his name, and depart to the eternal
and happy home that awaited all brave warriors? His cogi-
tative mind at last suggested a plan; it was, only by killing
another man. This he adopted and put into immediate
execution; and to make his death the more certain, he
sought, found, and slew a son of the very man for whose
death his doting mother had so heroically atoned; and
though his victim lived many miles distant, he well knew
the deed would speedily bring the avenger to his side. But
that he might effectually wipe forever from his name the
stain of cowardice, to his own honor and that of his kindred,
he at once resolved to take his own life, since now it would
be blood for blood, and self sacrifice would no longer fix
upon him the penalty of eternal woe. Quietly but resolutely
he dug his own grave before putting his dreadful resolution
into effect; and when completed, calmly stretched himself
therein to ascertain if it was complete in every particular.
As soon as he had slain his victim he hastened home with
his utmost speed, and at once told his relatives and friends
what he had done, and then said: "You know that I have
long been accused of cowardice, but now I will prove to
you that I can also meet death like a brave warrior." Slowly
he went through with his preliminary death ceremonies:
the careful examination of his rifle, the singing of his death
song, and the farewell shaking of the hands of his relatives
and friends present, consisting of his wife, two sisters and
brother, who sat in a mournful group a little to one side;

while the old men of the neighborhood sat in little groups around, smoking their pipes in doleful silence. No wailing, not even a half smothered sigh, broke the silence of the solemn scene. Nothing was heard but the voice of Hoh tah Lahba, as he now and then chanted his death-song. When he had bidden all his last adieu, he seized his bottle of whiskey, that bright insignia of the white man's "Personal Liberty," drank a long draught, then hurled the bottle with its contents to the ground with all his strength, as if invoking a curse upon its maker and vendor, then snatched his rifle from its leaning position against a tree, rushed to his waiting grave, and the sharp crack of the rifle that immediately followed told but too plainly that Hohtah Lahba was dead. Then burst forth a long restrained wail of grief from his bereaved wife, sisters, and other female friends alone, (as an Indian man never expresses his grief by any external emotions) heretofore smothered in respect to Hoh tah Lahba's request, "that all emotions of grief be restrained in his presence," that echoed far back from the surrounding forests.

Truly may it be said of the North American Indian woman as a general thing, that they rank higher in those feminine virtues that so peculiarly belong to women than any unlettered race known in history or otherwise. And for that highest of all female virtues, chastity, the full-blood North American Indian woman can fearlessly challenge her white sisters of the entire United States, without the fear of the possibility of defeat. During my sojourn among the Choctaw and Chickasaw people in the years 1884 to 1890, I made frequent inquiries relative to this subject, both of native citizens and white citizens married among them, and whites living among them as renters of their farms, and they have spoken in the highest terms of praise of the chastity of the Choctaw and Chickasaw women, and to which I add my own, based upon a knowledge of over seventy years' personal acquaintance with these two branches of the Indian race, and also that of the missionaries who labored among them when living east of the Mississippi River.

The Choctaw women were of medium height, beautiful in form, strong and agile in body; strictly honest, truthful, light-hearted and gay, and devoted in their affection to family and friends, while common custom protected them against all offense, even as it does at the present day;—how commendable to the Choctaw men.

Curiosity was one of the chief characteristics of the Choctaws, and held a prominent position in their breasts. They were desirous to know everything peculiar or strange that was transpiring about them; not more so, however, than any others of the human race. Yet the Choctaw differed from his white brother in this particular; the white man expressed openly his curiosity at anything unusual or strange, and asked innumerable questions concerning it. and manifested the greatest excitement, until his curiosity was gratified; but the Choctaw asked no questions, nor manifested any surprise whatever, no matter how strange or incomprehensible to him, but walked around with an air of seemingly perfect indifference; yet was attentive to any and all explanations that were being made by others.

The ingenuity of the white man as displayed in his various inventions was, to him, as to all his race, the deepest mystery, an incomprehensible enigma that placed the pale-face, in his opinion, in close relationship to superhuman beings; and influenced an aged Indian chief to exclaim, when viewing the mysterious workings of a steam engine when once at Washington City, "I hate the avarice of the white man's heart, but worship the ingenuity of his mind." The astonishment sometimes depicted upon the countenances of the Indians when beholding the wonderful performances of the white man, audibly expressed by the ancient Choctaws in the sudden ejaculation, "Wah?" was often very diverting.

As an evidence of the tenacity with which the ancient Choctaws adhered to the veracity of their traditions handed down through a long line of ancestry, I will here relate a little incident in which my twin brother and myself (then seven years of age) were the chief actors, and shared all the glory. At that time, there was a remembered tradition of their ancestors which they truly believed, that pale-face twins (if boys) possessed the magic power of dispelling all depredating worms and insects from corn fields, gardens, etc., which, in some years, at that early day, proved quite destructive, especially to their corn during the milk stage. Now it so happened during one summer, that the corn-worms were unusually numerous and were committing great depredations upon their fields of green corn. This corn-worm, with which all southern farmers are well acquainted, is, when fully grown, about an inch and a half or two inches long, and about the size of a wheat straw, and commits its depredations only when the corn is in the milk stage, entering the ear at the top and gradually working downward, but leaving it as soon as the grain becomes hard. Now it also happened, they had learned that Mr. Cushman, the "good pale-face," as he was termed, had a pair of twin boys; a propitious opportunity (long desired) was now offered to secure for themselves, by an occular demonstration, the traditional efficacy of the pale-face twins' supernatural power, which they joyfully embraced.

Unexpectedly, one beautiful June morning, a company of fine-looking Choctaw warriors were seen approaching on horseback at full speed. They halted at the gate of Mr. Cushman's yard and called for him. He at once responded by walking out to them. After the usual friendly salutations had been passed, they inquired if he had a pair of twin sons, to which he replied in the affirmative. They then informed him of the depredations being committed upon their fields of green corn, and also of the traditions of their ancestors, requesting at the same time the loan of his twins. Mr. Cushman, ignorant of such a power having been be-

stowed upon his twin boys, at first demurred; but they
becoming more importunate in their request, he finally told
them he would give them an answer in a few minutes. He
then stepped into the house and presented the case to Mrs.
Cushman for consideration, who at once, from a mother's
natural apprehensions that would arise in such a novel case,
most positively refused her consent; but after a few minutes'
deliberation reluctantly yielded, to the great joy and satisfaction of the twins, who had been attentive spectators and
listeners to the whole proceedings, and had become eager
to test their attributed power (unknown before) and to
enjoy the anticipated novel sport so closely connected with
the horseback ride that was presented. Mr. Cushman at
once led his little twins to the gate and introduced them to
the now jubilant warriors, by telling them the respective
names of the "wonderfully gifted" twins; and then granted
their request upon the promise that they would return his
boys in the evening of the day, before the sun had set.

Mr. Cushman then set each of his boys upon a horse
before a warrior, accompanying the act with the parting
request: "Take good care of my little boys!" Unnecessary
appeal, as not a Choctaw in that little band but would have
shielded the entrusted twins from injury even at the expense of his life. At once we galloped off in the direction of
their village, three miles distant, called Okachiloho fah.
(Water falling, or Falling water). When we arrived in sight,
their success was announced by a shrill whoop to which the
villagers responded their joy by another. As soon as we
rode into the village, we were immediately surrounded by
an admiring throng, and being tenderly lifted from our
positions on the horses, we were handed over to the care of
several old men, who took us in their arms and with much
gravity carried us into a little cabin, which had previously
been set in order for our reception, where we found prepared a variety of eatables, to us seemingly good enough to
excite the appetites of the most fastidious twin epicures;
after which the venerable old seers of the village instructed

us in the mystic rites and ceremonies of their tribe, preparatory to calling into requisition the magic power of our
twinship in all its bearing upon the duties of the day. Then
showing us our weapons, which consisted of iron, wood and
fire, the two former in the shape of a frying-pan, in which
we were to burn the worms after picking them from the
corn, and a blazing chunk of fire, two stout and straight
sticks about six feet in length, with the proper instructions
in regard to the manner of using them effectually. Having
been thoroughly drilled in these preliminaries, the line of
march was taken up toward the field where the enemy were
said to be strongly entrenched; in profound silence and with
unfeigned gravity, the palokta tohbi, (twins white, or white
twins) led the van, borne upon the shoulders of two powerful warriors closely followed by three others bearing the
arms, while the villagers, headed by the veteran seers,
brought up the rear.

When the field was reached a halt was made, and two
venerable looking old men came to the front and, with
solemn mien, lifted us from our perches and gently placed
us over the fence into the field; then handing the frying
pan, chunk of fire, and sticks, our weapons, to us, with a
word of encouragement whispered in our ears to prove
ourselves valiant and worthy our traditional fame, they
bade us charge the foe. The plan of the campaign was to
attack the enemy first in the center; there build a hot fire
with the dry wood, previously prepared by the thoughtful
Choctaws, upon which place the frying pan and into which
throw all prisoners; and likewise also at the four corners of
the field. The centre was gained, the fire made, and upon it
placed the pan; then we made a vigorous attack upon the
strongholds of the enemy dislodging them and at the same
time taking them prisoners of war; then hurrying them to
the centre hurled them into the frying pan heated to a red
heat, and with our ready sticks stirred them vigorously,
while the wreathes of smoke that ascended from the scene
of carnage and floated away before the summer breeze,

together with the odor, gave undisputed evidence of our
victories; while our waiting Choctaw friends, acknowledged
their approval from the outside of the field, (since the tradition forbade them sharing in the dangers of the conflict—
the paloktas must fight alone) filling our youthful hearts
with heroic emotions unfelt before or afterwards.

After we had immolated two or three panfulls of the
enemy at the centre and at each corner of the field, nor lost
a man, we returned in triumph to our waiting friends, by
whom we were received with unfeigned manifestations of
affection and pride. Thence we were borne as before to other
fields, where were enacted the same prodigies of valor, with
similar results until the declining sun gave warning of their
promise not being fulfilled if the paloktas were not returned
ere the sun went down. Therefore we were carried from
our last field of slaughter back to the village in glorious
triumph, where never were offered to frail mortality more
sincere homage and unfeigned devotion than were bestowed upon the paloktas by those grateful Choctaws. They
seemed only to regret not being able to manifest a still
greater degree of gratitude, and to do more for us as a
manifestation of their appreciation of the great favor we
had conferred upon them. With zealous care they watched
over us while under their care, that no harm might befall
us. As we came so we returned, and safely reached home
ere the sun sank behind the western horizon. We were
afterwards frequently called upon, much to our gratification and delight, it was fun for us, to bring into requisition
our mysteriously delegated power in behalf of their corn-
fields; and we became the special favorites of that kind-
hearted and appreciative people; and woe to him or them
who should impose upon or attempt to injure their little
pets, the pale-face paloktas. But the boyish pride that filled
my heart on those occasions, though seventy years have
fled, is remembered to this day.

But curiosity might now be inquisitive enough to ask:
"Did the worms cease their depredations on the green

corn?" To which I reply: Many of them certainly did; and, as no further complaint was made by the Choctaws during that season, it is reasonable to suppose those that were left, after the immolation of so many of their relatives, took a timely hint and sought other quarters where pale-face paloktas were unknown; but whether actuated through fear of a similar fate as had befallen a goodly number of their companions, or because the corn had become too hard by age for easy mastication and healthy digestion, I will leave for future consideration and determination of those who feel more interested in its solution than I do just now.

There were many traditions among all North American Indians, many of which bordered on the poetical and from which I will select one or two more, which shall suffice as examples of a few of the peculiarities of this pecular yet interesting people.

Thus says the tradition of "Ohoyo Osh Chisba," (The Unknown Woman). In the days of many moons ago, two Choctaw hunters were encamped for the night in the swamps of the bend of the Alabama River. But the scene was not without its romance. Dark, wild, and unlovely as a swamp is generally imagined to be, yet it had its aspects of beauty, if not of brightness. I speak from long personal experience. Its mysterious appearance; its little lakes and islands of repose; its silent and solemn solitudes; its green canebrakes and lofty trees, all combined to present a picture of strange but harmonious combination. The two hunters having been unsuccessful in the chase on that and the preceding day, found themselves without anything on that night with which to satisfy the cravings of hunger except a black hawk which they had shot with an arrow. Sad reflections filled their hearts as they thought of their sad disappointments and of their suffering families at home. They cooked the hawk and sat down to partake of their poor and scanty supper, when their attention was drawn from their gloomy forebodings by the low but distinct tones strange yet soft and plaintive as the melancholy notes of the dove, but produced by what they were wholly unable to even conjecture. At different intervals it broke the deep silence of the early night with its seemingly muffled notes of woe; and as the nearly full orbed moon slowly ascended the eastern sky the strange sounds became more frequent and distinct. With eyes dilated and fluttering heart they looked up and down the river to learn whence the sounds proceeded, but no object except the sandy shores glittering in the moonlight greeted their eyes, while the dark waters of the river seemed alone to give response in murmuring tones to the strange notes that continued to float upon the night air from a direction they could not definitely locate; but happening to look behind them in the direction opposite the moon they saw a woman of wonderful beauty standing upon a mound a few rods distant. Like an illuminated shadow, she had suddenly appeared out of the moon-lighted forest. She was loosely clad in snow-white raiment, and bore in the folds of her drapery a wreath of fragrant flowers. She beckoned them to approach, while she seemed surrounded by a halo of light that gave to her a supernatural appearance. Their imagination now influenced them to believe her to be the Great Spirit of their nation, and that the flowers she bore were representatives of loved ones who had passed from earth to bloom in the Spirit-Land.

The mystery was solved. At once they approached to where she stood, and offered their assistance in any way they could be of service to her. She replied she was very hungry, whereupon one of them ran and brought the roasted hawk and handed it to her. She accepted it with grateful thanks; but, after eating a small portion of it, she handed the remainder back to them replying that she would remember their kindness when she returned to her home in the happy hunting grounds of her father, who was Shilup Chitoh Osh—The Great Spirit of the Choctaws. She then told them that when the next midsummer moon should come they must meet her at the mound upon which she was then standing. She then bade them an affectionate adieu, and was at once borne away upon a gentle breeze and, mysteriously as she came so she disappeared. The two hunters returned to their camp for the night and early next morning sought their homes, but kept the strange incident a profound secret to themselves. When the designated time rolled around the midsummer full moon found the two hunters at the foot of the mound but Ohoyo Chishba Osh was nowhere to be seen. Then remembering she told them they must come to the very spot where she was then standing, they at once ascended the mound and found it covered with a strange plant, which yielded an excellent food, which was ever afterwards cultivated by the Choctaws, and named by them Tunchi, (corn).

Somewhat similar to the tradition of the Ohoyo Chishba Osh is that of the Hattak Owa Hushi Osh, (The Man Hunting for the Sun).

The Choctaws once, a great amount of corn having been made and as a manifestation of their appreciation and gratification and gratitude to the Great Spirit, their benefactor, held a Great National Council at which their leading prophet spoke at great length upon the beauties of Nature which contributed so much to their pleasure, and the various productions of the earth and the enjoyment derived therefrom, attributing much of all to the effects of the sun. That great lighter and heater of the earth came from the east, but whence it went after it had passed behind the western hills, had long been a subject of debate, never satisfactorily determined. Again the mooted question was brought up by the prophet in his speech, who, in a strain of wild eloquence, cried out, "Is there not a warrior among all my people who will go and find out what becomes of the sun when it departs in the west?" At once a young warrior, named Oklanowah, (Walking People) arose in the assembly and said: "I will go and try to find where the sun sleeps, though I may never return." He soon took his departure on his dubious errand leaving behind him one sad heart at least, to whom he gave a belt of wampum as a token of remembrance.

But after an absence of many years he returned to the home of his nativity, only to find himself an entire stranger among his people. After many days' search, however, he found one in the person of an aged and decrepit woman, who remembered the circumstances connected with the young hunter who had gone many years before on his adventurous exploit to find the sleeping place of the sun; and though he was satisfied that she was his identical betrothed—the loved one of his youth—oft spoke with the deepest affection of her long lost Oklanowah, yet no arguments could induce her to acknowledge the old man before her as her lover of the past. The unfortunate and forlorn Hattak Owa Hushi Osh spent his few remaining days in narrating his adventures to his people, the vast prairies and high mountains he had crossed; the strange men and animals he had seen; and, above all, that the sleeping place of the sun was in a big, blue water. Still after hearing all this, the old woman refused to believe, but secluded herself in her lonely cabin, and alone occupied the sad hours of the days and years that came and went in counting the wampum in her belt, the sacred memento of her Oklanowah—loved, but lost; lost, yet loved. Spring returned, but ere the leaves were grown Hattak Owa Hushi Osh died, and was buried near the ancient mound Nunih Waiyah, and ere the moon of the corn planting had come, the old woman also died, and she too was buried at the sacred Nunih Waiyah by the side of her unrecognized yet faithful Oklanowah.

Another specimen of their love legends is exhibited in that of Chahtah Osh Hochifoh Keyu—the Nameless Chahtah. In the days of the long past there lived in the Choctaw village Aiasha, (Habitation), the only son of a great war-chief. This son was noted for his wonderful beauty of form and features and manly bearing. The aged men of the Nation predicted, on account of his known and acknowledged bravery, he would become a renowned warrior. But as he had not distinguished himself in war either by slaying an enemy, taking a prisoner, or striking the dead (a feat accompanied with the greatest danger, as every effort is made by the friends of the fallen warrior to prevent such an insult to the dead) he was not permitted to occupy a seat in the councils of the tribe, though respected and honored, and his bravery undoubted by all.

According to the custom of the ancient Choctaws, a boy was not given a specific name in childhood unless he merited it by some daring act, and the young warrior, by some unavoidable chain of circumstances, passed through his chrysalis stage of life without having won a reputation according to his youthful ability; therefore went by the general name Chahtah Osh Hochifoh Keyu, The Nameless Chahtah. In the same village Aiashah, there also lived, according to the legend, the most famous beauty of the tribe, the daughter of a noted warrior and skillful hunter, and the betrothed of Chahtah Osh Hochifo Iksho. Though they often met at the great dances and festivals of the tribe, yet she (whose name the legend does not state) treated him with distant reserve (then the universal custom of the Choctaw girls) though the ardent lover of the nameless hero. Still one cloud cast its gloomy shadow over their happiness; it was the knowledge of the stubborn truth, that the laws of their Nation were unalterable; and that they could never become husband and wife until he had acquired a name by some daring deed in battle with the enemies of his country. But time slowly rolled away and summer again came with a balmy day followed by its evening twilight, which witnessed the lovers seated together upon the summit of a hill shaded by the foliage of innumerable and immense forest trees. Far below from a distant plain ascended the light and smoke from the fire of a war-dance, around which danced in wild excitement four hundred Choctaw warriors, preparatory to a war expedition against the Osages, far distant to the west, and that night was the last night of their preparatory ceremonies. Previous to that night Chahtah Osh Hochifoh Keyu had acted as one of the most conspicuous in the dances engaged in the four previous nights before, but on the last night, had retired from the dance to enjoy a parting interview with his betrothed. There they parted, ere the morning's sun again lighted up the eastern horizon, the "sound of revelry by night" had ceased, while silence again resumed her sway o'er Nature's vast expanse, and bespoke the four hundred warriors with Chahtah Osh Hochifoh Keyu were many miles upon the warpath that led to the country of the Osages among the headwaters of the Arkansas River.

The hostile land was reached, and soon they discovered a large cave into which they entered, that concealed they might better arrange their plans for future operations, being then in the enemies' country. Two scouts, however, were sent out to reconnoitre, one to examine the surroundings east, the other west. The latter was Chahtah Osh Hochifoh Keyu. But alas for human hopes! The evening passed away and night came on bringing one Osage hunter who had oft before sought the cave and found a safe resting place for the night. But as he drew near the cave, his observant eyes, ever on the alert, discovered signs which told him of the presence of others; further examination revealed that they were his nation's most bitter and unrelenting enemies, the hated Choctaws. Silently he stole away undiscovered by the Choctaws, until safely distant, then sped away through the darkness on nimble feet to his village and told of his discovery; at once a large band of Osage warriors rushed for the cave, and as they drew near gathered up small logs, chunks, limbs and brush with which they silently and effectually closed the mouth of the cave, and to which they applied the torch, and the sleeping Choctaws awoke but to read their inevitable doom—all perished. The Choctaw scout who had gone east returned during the night, but ere he reached the cave the flames revealed to him the tale of woe; he approached near enough, however, to comprehend the whole; stood a moment and gazed in mazy bewilderment, then turned and fled for home where he safely arrived and revealed the sad intelligence of the wretched fate of his comrades to their relatives and friends. It was also believed by all that Chahta Osh Hochifoh Keyu had been discovered and had also been slain. The sad tidings fell heavily upon all and the wail of woe was heard in many a village and cabin; but upon one it fell with terrible weight; and the promised wife of "The Nameless Choctaw" at once began to droop and soon withered away; and ere another moon had passed she was laid away in a grave upon the very spot (by her request) where she had last shared the parting embrace with her adored Chahtah Osh Hochifoh Keyu.

But the supposition that he too had been slain proved untrue. Though he had been discovered by the Osages and vigorously pursued for several days and nights, he finally was fortunate enough to escape. During the chase his flight had been devious, and when he had gotten beyond the danger of further pursuit by his fearful foes, he found himself to be a bewildered man, wretched and forlorn. Everything appeared wrong, and even the sun appeared to rise in the wrong direction, all nature was out of order. After several days of dubious wanderings, hither and thither, he knew not where, he came to the foot of a mountain, whose sides were covered with a kind of grass entirely different from anything he had ever seen before. Then, in the course of his wanderings, he strayed, at the close of another day, into a lovely wooded valley, where he camped for the night, kindled a fire and cooked a rabbit he had killed, of which he made his supper, and then sought temporary forgetfulness of his woes in sleep. Morning again dawned, but to awake him to a stronger sensibility of his loneliness and wanderings he knew not where. Many moons came and passed away and left him a lost wanderer. Summer came, and he called upon the Great Spirit to make his paths straight, that they might lead him out of bewilderment. He then hunted for a spotted deer, found and killed one, and offered it a sacrifice to the Great Spirit, after reserving a small portion to satisfy his own immediate wants. Night again came on, and as he sat by his little campfire in lonely solitude, he heard the near approach of footsteps in an adjoining thicket, but before he could take a second thought, a snow-white wolf of immense size was crouching at his feet, and licking his moccasins with the utmost manifestations of affection. Then looking him in the face said: "Whence came you, and why are you alone in this wilderness?" To which Chahtah Osh Hochifoh Keyu gave a full account of his misfortunes. The wolf then promised to lead him safely out of the wilderness in which he had been so long wandering and return him to his country, and they started early on the following morning.

Long was the journey, and dangerous the route; but by the time that the corn-hoeing moon came the forlorn wanderer entered once more his native village, the anniversary of the day he had bidden his betrothed adieu; but alas, only to find his village in mourning for her premature death. Alas too, so changed was he that none recognized in the wayworn stranger the lost Chatah Osh Hochifoh Keyu; nor did he make himself known. Often, however, did he solicit them to rehearse to him the account of her death; and oft he chanted his wild songs, to the astonishment of all, to the memory of his loved one, dead yet loved, loved yet dead. During his frequent nightly visits to her lonely grave upon the hill which had witnessed their last parting, he once came on a calm, cloudless night—'twas his last—and stood by the grave that held his dead at a moment when the Great Spirit cast a shadow upon the moon, then fell upon it and died. They found him there, and then was he recognized as the long lost Chatah Osh Hochifoh Keyu, and there buried by the side of his earthly idol. For three consecutive nights the silence of the forests contiguous to the lovers' graves was broken by the continual wailing howl of a solitary wolf, then it ceased and was heard no more; but the same wail was taken up by the pine forest upon the hill where the lovers parted in hope, but there to be buried in despair, and that mournful, wailing sound they have continued from that day down to the present time.

The traditions of the Choctaws concerning the Oka Falama (Returned waters—the Flood) is as follows: In ancient time, after many generations of mankind had lived and passed from the stage of being, the race became so corrupt and wicked—brother fighting against brother and wars deluging the earth with human blood and carnage— the Great Spirit became greatly displeased and finally determined to destroy the human race; therefore sent a great prophet to them who proclaimed from tribe to tribe, and from village to village, the fearful tidings that the human race was soon to be destroyed. None believed his words, and lived on in their wickedness as if they did not care, and the seasons came again and went. Then came the autumn of the year followed by many succeeding cloudy days and nights, during which the sun by day and the moon and stars by night were concealed from the earth; then succeeded a total darkness, and the sun seemed to have been blotted out; while darkness and silence with a cold atmosphere took possession of earth. Mankind wearied and perplexed, but not repenting or reforming, slept in darkness but to awake in darkness; then the mutterings of distant thunder began to be heard, gradually becoming incessant, until it reverberated in all parts of the sky and seemed to echo back even from the deep center of the earth. Then fear and consternation seized upon every heart and all believed the sun would never return. The Magi of the Choctaws spoke despondently in reply to the many interrogations of the alarmed people, and sang their death-songs which were but faintly heard in the mingled confusion that arose amid the gloom of the night that seemed would have no returning morn. Mankind went from place to place only by torch-light; their food stored away became mouldy and unfit for use; the wild animals of the forests gathered around their fires bewildered and even entered their towns and villages, seeming to have lost all fear of man. Suddenly a fearful crash of thunder, louder than ever before heard, seemed to shake the earth, and immediately after a light was seen glimmering seemingly far away to the north. It was soon discovered not to be the light of the returning sun, but the gleam of great waters advancing in mighty billows, wave succeeding wave as they onward rolled over the earth destroying everything in their path.

Then the wailing cry was heard coming from all directions, Oka Falamah, Oka Falamah (The returned waters). Stretching from horizon to horizon, it came pouring its massive waters onward. Soon the earth was entirely overwhelmed by the mighty and irresistible rush of the waters which swept away the human race and all animals leaving the earth a desolate waste. Of all mankind only one was saved, and that one was the mysterious prophet who had been sent by the Great Spirit to warn the human race of their near approaching doom. This prophet saved himself by making a raft of sassafras logs by the direction of the Great Spirit, upon which he floated upon the great waters that covered the earth, as various kinds of fish swam around him, and twined among the branches of the submerged trees, while upon the face of the waters he looked upon the dead bodies of men and beasts, as they arose and fell upon the heaving billows.

After many weeks floating he knew not where, a large black bird came to the raft flying in circles above his head. He called to it for assistance, but it only replied in loud, croaking tones, then flew away and was seen no more. A few days after a bird of bluish color, with red eyes and beak came and hovered over the raft, to which the prophet spoke and asked if there was a spot of dry land anywhere to be seen in the wide waste of waters. Then it flew around his head a few moments fluttering its wings and uttering a mournful cry, then flew away in the direction of that part of the sky where the new sun seemed to be sinking into the rolling waves of the great ocean of waters. Immediately a strong wind sprang up and bore the raft rapidly in that direction. Soon night came on, and the moon and stars again made their appearance, and the next morning the sun arose in its former splendor; and the prophet looking around saw an island in the distance toward which the raft was slowly drifting, and before the sun had gone down seemingly again into the world of waters, the raft had touched the island upon which he landed and encamped, and being wearied and lonely he soon forgot his anxieties in sleep; and when morning came, in looking around over the island, he found it covered with all varieties of animals— excepting the mammoth which had been destroyed. He also found birds and fowls of every kind in vast numbers upon the island; among which he discovered the identical black bird which had visited him upon the waters, and then left him to his fate; and, as he regarded it a cruel bird, he named it Fulushto (Raven)—a bird of ill omen to the ancient Choctaws.

With great joy he also discovered the bluish bird which had caused the wind to blow his raft upon the island, and because of this act of kindness and its great beauty he called it Puchi Yushubah (Lost Pigeon).

After many days the waters passed away; and in the course of time Puchi Yushubah became a beautiful woman, whom the prophet soon after married, and by them the world was again peopled.

Whence this tradition with such strong resemblance to the account of the deluge as given in the Sacred Scriptures? It is not fiction or fable, but the actual tradition of the ancient Choctaws as related by them to the missionaries in 1818. Whence this knowledge of the flood of the Bible? Does one reply, they obtained it from the early European explorers of the continent? Not so; for the earliest explorers speak of the North American Indians' various traditions of the Flood. May it be possible that their ancestors, far back in the early dawn of the morn of Christianity, received it from some one or more of the apostles, as ours did—the ancient Britons? Who knows? It is a thing impossible, if we admit they drifted ages ago from Asia's shores to the western continent. If not, whence and how have they this knowledge of the flood?

Another Choctaw version of their traditional flood (Okla-falama) is as follows: In the far distant ages of the past, the people, whom the Great Spirit had created, became so wicked that he resolved to sweep them all from the earth, except Oklatabashih (People's mourner) and his family, who alone did that which was good. He told Oklatabashih to build a large boat into which he should go with his family and also to take into the boat a male and female of all the animals living upon the earth. He did as he was commanded by the Great Spirit. But as he went out in the forests to bring in the birds he was unable to catch a pair of biskinik (sapsucker), fitukhak (yellow hammer), bak bak, (a large red-headed woodpecker); as these birds were so quick in hopping around from one side to the other of the trees upon which they clung with their sharp and strong claws, that Oklatabashih found it was impossible for him to catch them, therefore he gave up the chase, and returned to the boat, and the door closed, the rain began to fall increasing in volume for many days and nights, until thousands of people and animals perished. Then it suddenly ceased and utter darkness covered the face of the earth for a long time, while the people and animals that still survived groped here and there in the fearful gloom. Suddenly far in the distant north was seen a long streak of light. They believed that, amid the raging elements and the impenetrable darkness that covered the earth, the sun had lost its way and was rising in the north. All the surviving people rushed towards the seemingly rising sun, though utterly bewildered, not knowing or caring what they did. But well did Oklatabashih interpret the prophetic sign of their fast approaching doom. Instead of the bright dawn of another long-wished-for day, they saw, in utter despair, that it was but

the mocking light that foretold how near the Oklafalama
was at hand, rolling like mountains on mountains piled and
engulfing everything in its resistless course. All earth was
at once overwhelmed in the mighty return of waters, except
the great boat which, by the guidance of the Great Spirit,
rode safely upon the rolling and dashing waves that covered the earth. During many moons the boat floated safely
o'er the vast sea of waters. Finally Oklatabashih sent a
dove to see if any dry land could be found. She soon returned with her beak full of grass, which she had gathered
from a desert island. Oklatabashih to reward her for her
discovery mingled a little salt in her food. Soon after this
the waters subsided and the dry land appeared; then the
inmates of the great boat went forth to repeople another
earth. But the dove, having acquired a taste for salt during
her stay in the boat continued its use by finding it at the
saltlicks that then abounded in many places, to which the
cattle and deer also frequently resorted. Every day after
eating, she visited a saltlick to eat a little salt to aid her
digestion, which in the course of time became habitual and
thus was transmitted to her offspring. In the course of
years, she became a grandmother, and took great delight in
feeding and caring for her grandchildren. One day, however, after having eaten some grass seed, she unfortunately
forgot to eat a little salt as usual. For this neglect, the Great
Spirit punished her and her descendants by forbidding them
forever the use of salt. When she returned home that evening, her grandchildren, as usual began to coo for their
supply of salt, but their grandmother having been forbidden
to give them any more, they cooed in vain. From that day
to this, in memory of this lost privilege, the doves everywhere, on the return of spring, still continue their cooing
for salt, which they will never again be permitted to eat.
Such is the ancient tradition of the Choctaws of the origin
of the cooing of doves.

But as to the fate of the three birds who eluded capture by Oklatabashih, their tradition states: They flew high

in air at the approach of Okafalama, and, as the waters rose higher and higher, they also flew higher and higher above the surging waves. Finally, the waters rose in near proximity to the sky, upon which they lit as their last hope. Soon, to their great joy and comfort, the waters ceased to rise, and commenced to recede. But while sitting on the sky their tails, projecting downward, were continually being drenched by the dashing spray of the surging waters below, and thus the end of their tail feathers became forked and notched, and this peculiar shape of the tails of the biskinik, fitukhak and bakbak has been transmitted to their latest posterity. But the sagacity and skill manifested by these birds in eluding the grasp of Oklatabashih, so greatly delighted the Great Spirit that he appointed them to forever be the guardian birds of the red men. Therefore these birds, and especially the biskinik, often made their appearance in their villages on the eve of a ball play; and, whichever one of the three came, it twittered in happy tones its feelings of joy in anticipation of the near approach of the Choctaws' favorite game. But in time of war one of these birds always appeared in the camp of a war party, to give them warning of approaching danger by its constant chirping and hurried flitting from place to place around their camp. In many ways did these birds prove their love for and friendship to the red man, and he ever cherished them as the loved birds of his race, the remembered gift of the Great Spirit in the fearful days of the mighty Oklafalama.

The French in making their voyages of discovery along the coast of the Gulf of Mexico in 1712, under the command of Iberville, anchored one evening near an island (now known as Ship Island) which they discovered to be intersected with lagoons and inhabited by a strange and peculiar animal seemingly to hold the medium between the fox and cat, and they gave it the name Cat Island, by which it is still known; thence they passed over the mainland, where they discovered a tribe of Indians called Biloxi, among whom they afterwards located a town and gave it the name Biloxi—now the oldest town in the State of Mississippi. This tribe of Indians proved to be a clan of the Choctaws, and the name Biloxi, a corruption of the Choctaw word Ba-luh-chi, signifying hickory bark. Thence going eastward they discovered another tribe which they called the Pascagoulas, which also proved to be a clan of the Choctaws, and the name Pascagoula, a corruption of the two Choctaw words Puska (bread) and Okla (people), i. e.: Bread People, or people having bread; but which has been erroneously interpreted to mean "Bread Eaters." A remnant of the Ba-luh-chis still exist among the Choctaws, while the Puskaoklas have been long lost by uniting with other Choctaw clans. There was an ancient tradition among the Puskaoklas, which stated that, in the years long past, a small tribe of Indians of a lighter complexion than themselves, and also different in manners and customs, inhabited the country near the mouth of the Pascagoula River, whose ancestors, according to the tradition, originally emerged from the sea, where they were born; that they were a kind, peaceful and inoffensive people, spending their time in public festivals and amusements of various kinds; that they had a temple in which they worshipped the figure of a Sea God; every night when the moon was passing from its crescent to the full, they gathered around the figure playing upon instruments and singing and dancing, thus rendering homage to the Sea God. That shortly after the destruction of Mobilla (now Mobile, Alabama) in 1541, by De Soto, there suddenly appeared among the Sea God worshippers a white man with a long, gray beard, flowing garments and bearing a large cross in his right hand; that he took from his bosom a book, and, after kissing it again and again, he began to explain to them what was contained in it; that they listened attentively and were fast being converted to its teachings when a fearful catastrophe put an end to all. One night, when the full moon was at its zenith, there came a sudden rising of the waters of the river, which rolled in

mighty wave, along its channel; on the crest of the foaming
waters sat a woman, with magnetic eyes, singing in a tone
of voice that fascinated all; that the white man, followed
by the entire tribe, rushed to the bank of the stream in wild
amazement, when the siren at once, modulated her voice to
still more fascinating tones, chanting a mystic song with the
oft repeated chorus, "Come to me, come to me, children of
the sea! Neither book nor cross, from your queen, shall win
ye." Soon, an Indian leaped into the still raging waters,
followed by the remainder in rapid succession, all disappearing as they touched the water, when a loud and exultant laugh was heard, and then the waters returned to their
usual level and quiet leaving no trace of their former fury;
the white man was left alone; and soon died of grief and
loneliness.

The belief of the ancient Choctaws in regard to the
eclipses of the sun was not more inconsistent than that of
any portion of the human family, whose minds had never
been enlightened by the rays of spiritual light from the
gospel of the Son of God. The Romans, the Celtics, the
Asiatics, the Finns of Europe, and, no doubt, Britons, too,
all had their views in regard to eclipses as absurd as the
Choctaws. The Choctaws attributed an eclipse of the sun
to a black squirrel, whose eccentricities often led it into
mischief, and, among other things, that of trying to eat up
the sun. When thus inclined, they believed, which was
confirmed by long experience, that the only effective means
to prevent so fearful a catastrophe was to favor the little,
black epicure with a first-class scare. As soon, therefore, as
the sun began to draw its lunar veil over its face, the cry
was heard from every mouth from the Dan to the Beer-
sheba of their then wide extended territory, echoing from
hill to dale, "Funi lusa hushi umpa! Funi lusa hushi umpa,"
according to our phraseology, the black squirrel is eating
the sun! Then and there was heard a sound of tumult
sufficient to have made him lose forever afterward all relish
for a mass of suns for an early or late dinner. The shouts of

the women and children mingling with the ringing of discordant bells as the vociferous pounding and beating of ear-splitting pans and cups mingling in "wild confusion worse confounded," yet in sweet unison with a first-class orchestra of yelping, howling, barking dogs gratuitously thrown in by them innumerable and highly excited curs, produced a din, which even a "funi lusa," had he heard it, could scarcely have endured even to have indulged in a nibble or two of the sun, though urged by the demands of a week's fasting.

But during the wild scene the men were not idle spectators, or indifferent listeners. Each stood a few paces in front of his cabin door, with no outward manifestations of excitement whatever—so characteristic of the Indian warrior—but with his trusty rifle in hand, which he loaded and fired in rapid succession at the distant, devastating squirrel, with the same coolness and calm deliberation that he did when shooting at his game. More than once have I witnessed the fearful yet novel scene. When it happened to be the time of a total eclipse of the sun, a sufficient evidence that the little, black epicure meant business in regard to having a square meal, though it took the whole sun to furnish it, then indeed there were sounds unsurpassed by any ever heard before. Then the women shrieked and redoubled their efforts upon the tin pans, which, under the desperate blows, strained every vocal organ to do its utmost and whole duty in loud response, which the excited children screamed and beat their tin cups, and the sympathetic dogs barked and howled; while the warriors still stood in profound and meditative silence, but firm and undaunted, as they quickly loaded and fired their rifles, each time taking deliberate aim if perchance the last shot might prove the successful one; then, as the moon's shadow began to move from the disk of the sun, the joyful shout was heard above the mighty din Funi-lusa-osh mahlatah! The black squirrel is frightened. But the din remained unabated until the sun again appeared in its usual splendor, and all nature again assumed its harmonious course; then quiet below again assumed its sway, while contentment and happiness resumed their accustomed place in the hearts of the grateful Choctaws—grateful to the Great Spirit who had given them the victory. But the scene of a total eclipse of the sun in the Choctaw Nation in those ancient years must be witnessed to be justly comprehended by the lover of the romantic, and heard by the highly sensitive ear to be fully appreciated and enjoyed.

On the road leading from St. Stephen, then a little town in Alabama, near which was the home of the renowned Choctaw Chief Pushmataha in 1812, to the city of Jackson, Mississippi, stood the mound Nunih Waiyah erected by the Choctaws in commemoration of their migration, as has been previously stated. I read an article published some years ago in a newspaper, which stated that an ancient tradition of the Choctaws affirmed that they derived their origin from Nunih Waiyah, their ancestors swarming from the hole on the top as bees swarming from the hive in summer, and thus was that part of the world peopled with Choctaws. The Choctaws did not so state their origin to the early missionaries of 1818. They always have claimed their origin from a country far to the West.

The Choctaws lived around their honored memento of the past for many successive generations, and some, even in large excavations made in its sides. And when interrogated by the whites with the question "Whence came they?" alluding to the origin of their race, the Choctaws, thinking their interrogator wished to learn from what part of their nation they came, replied: "From the Mound"; while those who dwelt in the excavations made in its sides, answered: "From out the Mound," meaning they lived in the mound. No Choctaw was such a fool as to believe, or even assert, their ancestors jumped out of the hole on the top of Nunih Waiyah full fledged warriors. And when speaking to them of this tradition, with seeming emotions of pity mingled with contempt, they have replied: "That fellow did not know what he was talking about." True, they held Nunih Waiyah in great reverence; but not it as the place of their origin, but as an ancient relic handed down to them through a long line of honored ancestry.

As an evidence of their admiration and veneration for this ancestral memento, the Choctaws, when passing, would ascend it and drop into the hole at its top various trinkets, and sometimes a venison ham, or dressed turkey, as a kind of sacrificial offering to the memory of its ancient builders, who only appeared to them through the mists of ages past; and as the highest evidence of their veneration for this relic of their past history, it was sometimes spoken of by the more enthusiastic as their Iholitopa Ishki, (beloved mother).

In 1810, the United States agent, George S. Gaines, was one day riding along the road that leads near Nunih Waiyah, and to satisfy his curiosity turned and rode to its base, then dismounted and walked to its top. While there, he noticed a large band of Choctaw warriors passing along the road; and being desirous of their company, he hastily descended, mounted his horse and soon overtook them. As he rode up, and the usual salutations had been exchanged, the chief, who was no less than the renowned Pushmataha, with a significant smile in which fun and innocent mischief were most prominent, said: "Well, friend Gaines, I see you have been up to pay your compliments to our good mother." "Yes, I concluded to pay her a visit as I was passing," replied Mr. Gaines. "Well, what did she say to you?" asked the great chief. "She said," responded Mr. Gaines, "that her Choctaw children had become too numerous to longer be prosperous, contented and happy in their present country, therefore, she thought it best for them to exchange their old country and lands for a new country and lands west of the Mississippi River, where the game was much more abundant, and the hunting grounds far more extensive." With a loud laugh in which his warriors also heartily joined Pushmataha then exclaimed, "Holobih! holubit ish nohowa nih! (It's a lie). Do not go about telling lies. Our good old mother never could have spoken such words to you." After the laugh of the joke was over, Pushmataha expressed himself freely with Mr. Gaines upon various subjects relative to his people as they rode along together; among many things that were mentioned, that of their origin was brought up; and to the inquiry of Mr. Gaines, "Whence they came to the country then occupied by them," the chief replied: "Our ancestors came from a country far to the west many suns and moons ago." And this was the invariable reply made by all the Choctaws when asked concerning their traditional origin.

The Choctaw Nation from its earliest known history to the present time has, at different intervals, produced many great and good men; who, had they had the advantages of education, would have lived upon the pages of history equally with those of earth's illustrious great.

Of the patriotism and undaunted bravery of Tushka Lusa, and his ability as a commander of his warriors, De-Soto had satisfactory proof at the battle of Momabinah. But so little of the history of those ancient Choctaws has escaped oblivion that in sketching a line of their history at such a distance of time we necessarily pass through unknown fields; while, as we approach our own times, merely the outline of their history, if accurately drawn, would fill many volumes; therefore, in the selection of objects to present to the reader, with a due regard for his pleasure and profit, I shall have continual reference to the power of association, and endeavor to present such as will be most likely to bring to my Choctaw and Chickasaw friends, for whom the work is especially written, the remembrance of many incidents and circumstances, which once were fresh, but now are fading in their minds by devoting here a few pages to the brief sketch of the lives of some of their eminent men now living, together with some of their distinguished dead.

Therefore, that the following biographical sketches may be as incentives and models to the young men of the Choctaw and Chickasaw people, has been one of the inducements that has actuated me in writing them. None but those who personally knew them, can form any just conception of the manly efforts put forth by those truly noble and honest patriots, in their exertions to elevate the standard of their Nation in the estimation of the Christian world. They sought and obtaned every useful information that could give them additional mental power in the pursuit of their favorite object, and studiously gathered the ripe experience of others, both by the study of books and observations in their travels among the whites, in their visits to Washington City on business of national affairs; and it is a matter of astonishment that amid the many difficulties they had to overcome in counteracting the evil influences of the lawless whites who invaded their country, that they accomplished what they did.

Tushka Lusa, the hero of Moma Bina, as before stated, is the only Choctaw chief whose name has been handed down from that tragic scene through the long line of historic silence, to the year 1745, when in the English and French wars, in which each was contending for supremacy upon the western continent, involving both the Choctaw and Chickasaw Nations, a few chiefs arose to the surface whose names have escaped oblivion by their daring achievements during those scenes of blood and carnage; the most prominent of the Choctaws were Shulush Humma and Ibanowa, (one who walks with) Miko (chief) whom I will more particularly speak in the history of the Chickasaws. From 1745 to 1785 no other names of Choctaw chiefs have been preserved, all alike having gone down into the silence of eternal forgetfulness, but from 1785 the names of many of their great chiefs have been preserved, though long since deceased; among which, as the most prominent, stand that of A-push-a-ma-ta-hah-ub-i" (a messenger of death, literally, one whose rifle, tomahawk, or bow alike fatal in war or hunting). A-pak-foh-chih-ub-ih,[21] (to encircle and kill,

[20] Pushmataha. *Supra* p. 21, note 2.
[21] Apukshunnubbee. *Supra* p. 73, note 16

corrupted by the whites to A-puck-she-nubee, and so used by the Choctaws of the present day). A-to-ni Yim-in-tah, (a watchman infatuated with excitement) Olubih, (to take by force); Coleman Cole, Greenwood La Flore, Nit-tak-a chih-ub-ih,[22] (to suggest the day and kill); David Folsom, Peter P. Pitchlynn, (the Calhoun of the Choctaws); Isaac Folsom, Silas Pitchlynn, Israel Folsom, (The Wesley of the Choctaws) and many others. With the last seven mentioned I was personally acquainted.

The distinguished warrior and chief of the Choctaws, Pushmataha, was born, as near as can be ascertained, in the year 1764. He was of the iksa, called Kun-sha (A reed—the name of the creek along whose banks the Kunsha Clan dwelt). Kunsha-a-he (reed—potato) is the full name of the clan, which took its name from the thick reeds and wild potatoes that grew together in the marshy ground along the banks of the creek—Cane and Potato Creek.

At an early age Pushmataha acquired great celebrity among his people as a brave warrior and successful hunter. His love for the fascinating excitement of the chase and daring adventures frequently led him into the deep solitudes of the then distant and wild forests west of the Mississippi River untrodden by the foot of the white man, to engage in hunting buffalo, a sport considered by the red man, and at a later period by the white also, as the noblest ever engaged in upon the North American continent. The buffalo, at that day, congregated in seemingly incredible numbers, and roamed over the entire wide extended western valley, grazing in countless multitudes upon the rich grasses of the west prairies that extended before the vision to where earth and sky seemed to embrace. But now that noble game is numbered with the things of the past.

In those distant hunting expeditions and daring adventures, accompanied only by a small number of youthful and congenial spirits, Pushmataha encountered many dangers and endured many privations and hardships.

At one time, while engaged in one of those hunts on Red River with a little party of Choctaw braves, his camp was unexpectedly and unceremoniously attacked, by a large band of Cal-lag-e-hah warriors, (Callage-hah is evidently a corruption of the words, Chah lih hihla, (fast dancers). These Indians may possibly have been a clan of the Choctaws before they left Mexico, and afterwards followed on to join the main body, but never crossed the Mississippi River, hence became forever lost from the parent stock) and being greatly outnumbered, Pushmataha and his little party, after a brief skirmish, were totally defeated, and but few escaped, each taking care of himself. Pushmataha, being one of the few, found himself alone. After experiencing great hardships and dangers in eluding the vigilance of his wily enemies, he fortunately stumbled upon a Spanish settlement, in which he remained many months, serving as a hunter for the Spaniards, and secretly preparing his plans for revenge against the Callagehahs for their unceremonious attack upon his camp, and which he successfully executed, as the sequel will show. At this time (1793) Missouri, Kansas and Arkansas were under Spanish dominion.

After he had thoroughly laid his plans of revenge, he bade his Spanish employers a formal adieu, and started for his distant and long absent home by devious paths, until he came upon a camp of his enemies, the Callagehahs, upon which he rushed at night with the ferocity of a tiger, and slew seven of its occupants and secured their scalps, ere they could recover from their surprise; then shouting back his warwhoop of defiance, he fled with the nimble feet of the antelope, directing his course homeward, where he, in the course of several weeks safely arrived, to the astonishment and joy of his relatives, who had regarded him among the number of the slain, who had fallen on the fatal night of the raid made upon their camp by the Callagehahs. He remained at home two or three years, but had not forgotten

the attack made upon his hunting camp in the distant solitudes of the forests west of the Mississippi River, and the
death of his comrades; while his proud spirit still chafed
under the imagined disgrace of his defeat, he yearned to
punish the Callagehahs still more severely for their audacity and insult; therefore, he again started with a select
company of warriors for his enemies' territories; where
again surprising one of their unsuspecting camps he slew
three warriors without sustaining loss; after which he withdrew from the Callagehahs' country, but remained west of
the Mississippi River for several months in the fascinating
amusements of the chase, that exciting occupation that
renders the hunter, both red and white, oblivious to all else.
Again he returned home with his little band; yet his restless
spirit could not rest in inactivity longer than a few weeks;
and once more, with another little company of congenial
spirits of about twenty-five in number, he started for the
land of his foes and was gone several months, when he
again returned home with a dozen or more Callagehah
scalps, without the loss of a single one of his little party.
He remained at home, after this exploit, nearly a year, then
again, but for the last time, sought the distant territories of
the Callagehahs with another band of his warriors; again
fortune smiled upon her seemingly chosen favorite; for he
struck another death-dealing blow, obtaining many scalps,
then bade the unfortunate Callagehahs a final adieu, returned to his native land with his warriors, and annoyed
them no more.

The Choctaws and Muscogees, in years long past, were
proverbial enemies, and hated each other with uncompromising bitterness; therefore, embraced every opportunity to
manifest their hostility the one toward the other. On one
occasion a party of Muscogees secretly entered the Choctaw territories and, among other depredations committed
on their devious route, they burned the house of Pushmataha, who, with his family, was absent from home engaged
in his favorite amusement—a grand ball-play. As soon as

he returned home and found it a heap of smoking ruins, and learned who had committed the mischief, he at once collected a company of warriors and sought the Muscogee Nation with the same determination and resolution that he had previously sought that of the Callagehahs; and when arrived, he repaid them tenfold for the destruction of his home. Many years afterward Pushmataha was the first Choctaw chief who led a war-party of 800 warriors against the Muscogees in what is known as the Creek War of 1812.

Several Choctaw companies joined Washington's army during our Revolutionary war, and served during the entire war; some of them were at the battle of Cowpens, under General Morgan; others, at the battle of Stony Point, under General Wayne, and others, at the battle of Tellico Plains, under General Sullivan, sent by General Green to punish the Tories and northern Cherokees (at that time the only Cherokees hostile to the Americans) for the destruction of Fort Loudon, situated on the Tennessee River in the territories then of North Carolina, whom he overtook at Tellico Plains, engaged and routed, with great loss on the part of the Tories and Cherokees, also securing the women and children whom they had taken prisoners in the fall of Fort Loudon, and devastating the country of the hostile Cherokees as he went, in driving them, (Tories and Cherokees) through Deep Creek Gap, in Cumberland mountains, into the now State of Kentucky; and there ending the pursuit, Sullivan returned to Kentucky; and there ending the pursuit, Sullivan returned and joined his command near Yorktown. It is said, those Cherokees never did return to their former homes, but became incorporated with other Indians in Kentucky; others were under Washington at the capture of Yorktown, and witnessed the surrender of Cornwallis.

An amusing incident was related to me when in the Choctaw Nation in 1888, in which a Choctaw scout, under General Sullivan, previous to the defeat of the Tories and Cherokees at Tellico Plains, was the chief hero. This scout, from his short and thick set form, was given the name

Dutch Johnnie, by the soldiers. Dutch Johnnie was an un-compromising enemy to the hostile Cherokees, for the reason that a scouting party of theirs had killed his wife and only child; and in revenge he had sworn eternal hatred against the Cherokees. Learning this, Gen. Sullivan appointed Dutch Johnnie as one of his chief scouts, much to the joy of Johnnie, as it gave him a broader field in which to seek and obtain the much desired revenge. He soon became noted for his intrepidity, endurance, skill, and valuable reports in regard to the enemy; and by his many noble traits also became the pet of the army. At one time, he was returning to the command from a long scout of several days' absence, and had reached within ten or fifteen miles of the army, when night overtook him at an old and long deserted house. It had been raining all day, so the story goes, and was still raining and growing dark. As any port in a storm had long been Dutch Johnnie's motto, he at once resolved to accept the offered hospitalities of the forsaken mansion; and, without formality, entered the open space, where once had hung the door that then lay upon the ground, a wreck of its former glory, and surveyed its apartments. He found it consisted of but one room, with but one ingress or egress, one chimney of sticks and dirt, and four or five logs extending across the room above, about four feet apart, upon which were loosely laid some boards extending from one to the other.

Being a good retreat from the rain and chill without, Dutch Johnnie soon stretched himself upon the puncheon floor in his wet clothes, too considerate to build a fire in the hearth by which to dry and warm himself, and thus attract the eye of an enemy engaged in the same business as himself, and was just passing into the shadows of the land of dreams when his ears whispered "danger without." He instantly arose to a sitting posture and heard approaching footsteps. Instantly he seized his rifle and quickly and noiselessly climbed up the wall and lay down upon the boards, and there waited future developments. The approaching footsteps grew plainer until they stopped before the house. Then all was hushed for a few moments, and then the intruders entered. Dutch Johnnie from above could see nothing, so intense was the darkness; but soon learned that his visitors were a company of Tories and Cherokee warriors, who, like with him, had sought the hospitality of the deserted house from the inclemency of the night. He understood enough English to learn much of their plans as the Tories conversed with each other. In the course of an hour all had stretched themselves upon the puncheon floor, and were shortly after wrapt in sleep; yet with a sleepless sentinel eight feet above, who could see nothing—not even his hand before him—but hear everything, even to the low breathing of his unwelcome visitors below. Poor, entrapped Johnnie, how was he to safely get out of the dilemma? If he remained until morning some curiosity seeker might climb the wall to see what lay above, and then Dutch Johnnie's doom was inevitable. After cogitating the matter over carefully, he finally concluded he would try and escape by noiselessly descending the wall which he had ascended; but the question arose in his mind—how far from the wall in which the doorway was cut was the first parallel joist over which space he discovered there were no boards when he first entered the house. When he had taken his position above he had stretched himself full length (face downward) upon the boards, with his head toward the wall he desired to descend. He began at once to reach out with his right hand into the darkness for the wall, but his arm was too short. Again and again he stretched it out, but to no avail. Anxiety, at length, overcame his prudence; for, in attempting to extend his body a little over the joist that he might be enabled, perchance, to reach the coveted wall, the boards, which were not nailed to the joist, slipped from their places and fell together with Dutch Johnnie in a promiscuous mass upon the sleepers below.

The sleepers, thus suddenly aroused, were utterly bewildered, and unable to decide whether a cyclone had struck the house, an earthquake was upon them, or the knell of time was at hand. But Dutch Johnnie's presence of mind rendered him equal to the emergency having, however, the advantage of his foes in knowing why he had made such a desperate charge, alone and in utter darkness, upon them; for he seized a board with both hands, sprang to his feet, and began to strike, right and left in the dark, with super-human force, accompanying the act with reiterated Choc-taw warwhoops intermingled with General Sullivan's war-cry in English; which at once caused the Tories and Cher-okee warriors to believe that it was Sullivan and his troop-ers upon them; therefore, each one sought, in frenzied haste, the one, and only egress into the open air, jumping, tumbling, falling, rolling out. Soon the house was left in possession of Dutch Johnnie alone; then to make the victory complete, he sprang to the rifles of his foes stacked in a corner of the room and then to the door where he fired off each one in rapid succession accompanied with reiterated warwhoops, which made each flying Tory and Cherokee believe that himself alone had escaped. As he seized a gun and fired it off, he threw it upon the floor, and sprang for another, and so continued to do until he had fired the last; then, not knowing what might still be in the house, since the pitchy darkness prevented anything being seen, he leaped out, uttered several warwhoops of victory, and sought safety amid the darkness of the forest feeling his way as best he could. When he had gone far enough to feel safe from immediate danger, he sat down and waited for the light of the returning morning; then hastened to the encampment, where he arrived in safety about an hour after sunrise. He soon related his adventure to General Sullivan, who sent a company of troopers back with Dutch Johnnie to prove the statement of his romantic adventure, and night conflict with the enemy, over whose unknown numbers with a post-oak board, he had gained a complete victory. When the company had reached the battle ground and entered the again tenantless and silent fort, they found the fallen boards upon the floor under which lay Johnnie's rifle—sufficient proof of his rapid descent upon the enemy, while the twenty empty rifles that lay upon the floor, gave entire satisfaction, none more so than to Dutch Johnnie himself, that he had defeated his enemies as one to twenty, by his rapid descent upon them with his shower of boards, followed by the vigorous use of one alone in his stalwart hands accompanied with his terrific warwhoops. Of course, he became the hero of the day. The twenty rifles were justly awarded to him as trophies of his victory; which he traded for various articles necessary for his comfort and protection in his anticipated future adventures. He lived through the war as an indispensable scout, proving himself fearless in battle, and oft dazzling his comrades by his daring acts.

THE MEETING IN 1811, OF TECUMSEH, THE MIGHTY SHAWNEE, WITH PUSHMATAHA, THE INTREPID CHOCTAW.

I will here give a true narrative of an incident in the life of the great and noble Choctaw chief, Pushmataha, as related by Colonel John Pitchlynn, a white man of sterling integrity, who acted for many years as interpreter to the Choctaws for the United States Government, and who was an eye-witness to the thrilling scene

Colonel John Pitchlynn was adopted in early manhood by the Choctaws, and marrying among them, he at once became as one of their people; and was named by them "Chahtah It-ti-ka-na," The Choctaws' Friend; and long and well he proved himself worthy the title conferred upon, and the trust confided in him. He had five sons by his Choctaw wife, Peter, Silas, Thomas, Jack and James, all of whom proved to be men of talent, and exerted a moral influence among their people, except Jack, who was ruined by the white man's whiskey and his demoralizing examples and influences. I was personally acquainted with Peter, Silas and Jack. The former held, during a long and useful life, the highest positions in the political history of his Nation, well deserving the title given him by the whites, "The Calhoun of the Choctaws"; but of whom I will speak more particularly elsewhere.

England in her anticipated war with the United States in 1812 early made strenuous efforts to secure the co-operation of all the Indian tribes, both north and south, as allies against the Americans, as she had done against the French previous to supplanting them in 1763; though, not with that success that she did in arraying them in opposition to the Americans; for to the honor and praise of the majority of the early settlers of the French among the North American Indians be it said, that they had won the respect, confidence, and love of the northern Indians especially, by their freedom from all arrogance, abuse and oppression, and by honest dealing with them, comparing well in this particular with the Quakers, and thus seeming to the highly appreciative Indians more as affable companions and genial friends, than insolent and pretended masters, as the English had assumed to be, and afterwards the Americans, who followed in their wake; both of whom, early and late, introduced the traffic in whiskey among them, which had been effectually prohibited by the French down to that time.

Having secured the co-operation, however, of many of the northern tribes to operate under the command of the cruel Proctor, the English then turned their attention to the securing of the southern tribes as allies, especially the five great and most warlike tribes then within the boundaries of the United States, viz: the Choctaws, Chickasaws, Cherokees, Muscogees and Seminoles; and that they might the more effectually and with greater certainty secure the aid of those brave, skilful and daring warriors of the South, the renowned Shawnee chief, Tecumseh, was sent to persuade them by his great influence and unsurpassed native eloquence to unite with them as allies in the expected war. As one of the bravest and most skillful Indian chiefs that ever trod the American soil; as a statesman in the council of his nation; as a foresighted politician; as a man of integrity and humanity, according to the morals of his people; as a man of comprehensive mind, rich in resources for every emergency; as a man of undaunted nature, Tecumseh stands with no superiors and few equals upon the pages of Indian history.

Willingly, therefore, did Tecumseh accept the embassy to the southern tribes in behalf of the English; nor could they have confided their mission with greater hope of success to a more influential chief, or a more bitter enemy to the Americans than to Tecumseh. North and south, far and near, was the name of the great Shawnee chief and warrior known. His mother was a Muscogee and his father a Shawnee; and both were born in Alabama, at a village called Sau-van-o-gee (afterwards known as "Old Augusta") on the Tallapoosa River, though Tecumseh's father and grandparents belonged to the Shawnees of the North. They moved to the then wilds of the now State of Ohio with their family of several children, where, in 1768, Tecumseh was born. He had five brothers, all of whom were noted warriors. He also had one sister named Tecum-a-pease who was highly endowed as a woman of strong character and sound judgment, and a great favorite of her warlike brother, over whom she exercised great influence. At the age of nineteen years Tecumseh visited the South, once the home of his parents, where he spent a few years principally among the Muscogees, the relatives and friends of his mother—engaging with them in their hunts and various amusements, and winning their admiration by a heroism free from temerity, and a friendship free from partiality.

In the spring of 1811, Tecumseh, with thirty congenial spirits all well mounted, again left his northern home and directed his course once more to the South to visit those distant friends, not as before, a pleasure seeker in their hunts, national festivals and social amusements, but as one seeking co-operative vengeance upon a common foe, the pale-face intruders and oppressors of their race. Silently and fearlessly did the little band of resolute men, keep their course until they reached the broad territories of the Chickasaws through which they passed, nor ceased their march, until they entered the Choctaw Nation in the district over which Apukshunnubbee was the ruling chief and there pitched their camp. Soon the tidings were borne throughout the district fanning the hitherto quiet inhabitants into a blaze of the wildest excitement, and many rushed at once to see the great chieftain and his warriors; actuated more however through curiosity than expectation of learning anything concerning the intent or purpose of their coming; for an Indian ambassador is ever silent upon the subject of his mission, and opens not his mouth but in council assembled. In solemn pomp, therefore, Tecumseh and his warriors were escorted to the home of Apukshunnubbee, to whom Tecumseh stated that his business was of a national character. At once Apukshunnubbee summoned the warriors of his district to convene in council, at which a resolution was passed calling the entire Choctaw Nation to assemble in a great council, extending the invitation alike to the Chickasaw Nation, stating as a reason, that it was made through the request of Tecumseh, as an ambassador of the Shawnees; that he, with thirty warriors, was now a guest of Apukshunnubbee, and had a proposition to lay before the council of vital import to both Nations. A day was also appointed and the place designated, in and at which the two Nations should assemble in united council to hear the words of the mighty Shawnee. The place selected at which the council was to convene, was a point on the Tombigbee River, five miles (by land) north of Columbus, Mississippi, and now known by the name of Plymouth.

Immediately runners were sent out to the remotest points of their country, also to the Chickasaws, to notify all of the coming event; and soon they were seen on their fleetest horses speeding in wild haste and in all directions, over their wide extended territory. For many days previous to the convening of the council, hundreds upon hundreds of warriors, in various groups, were seen slowly and silently

wending their way through the forests from every direction
toward the designated place for the meeting of the two
Nations in council with the mighty chief and Shawnee
ambassador; and when the appointed day came, many thousands had presented themselves. Col. John Pitchlynn stated
to the missionaries who established a mission among the
Choctaws several years after, that he never saw so great a
number of Indian warriors gathered together.

But the light of that memorable day seemed to wane
slowly, and its sunset was followed by that seemingly
breathless pause and stupor so oft experienced in a southern
clime. Then a huge pile of logs and chunks, previously prepared, was set on fire—the signal to the waiting multitudes,
who sat in groups of hundreds around chatting in low tones
and smoking their indispensable pipes, constructed in the
heads of their tomahawks. Each group arose without delay
or confusion and in obedience to its mandates, marched up
in solemn and impressive silence, and took their respective
seats upon the ground forming many wide, extended circles
around the blazing heap, but leaving an open space of
twenty or thirty feet in diameter for the occupancy of the
speaker and his attendants.

The chiefs and old warriors always formed the inner
circle; the middle-aged, next, and so on to the outer circle,
which was composed of the young and less experienced
warriors. All being seated, the pipes were lighted, and
commenced their rounds through the vast concourse of
seated men; and each one, as a pipe came to him, drew a
whiff or two, and then, in turn, passed it on to the next,
while profound silence throughout the vast assembly
reigned supreme, disturbed alone by the crackling and
sputtering of the burning logs.

What a beautiful characteristic of the North American
Indians was that of repressing every emotional feeling when
assembled in council or otherwise, and observing the most
profound silence when one of their number was speaking!
Even in the social circle, never but one speaks at a time

while the closest attention is given and the most profound silence observed by the others. This was and is a part of their education, an established rule of their entire race, into the violation of which they were seldom if ever betrayed by any kind of excitement whatsoever; and in visiting the Choctaw and Chickasaw councils in 1885, I found they still adhered to the old established rule with the same rigid tenacity as did their ancestors east of the Mississippi River in the days of the long-ago. For this noble virtue they are termed taciturn and grave, yet their national sensibilities are deep, active and strong.

Soon Tecumseh was dimly seen emerging from the darkness beyond into the far reflected light of the blazing logs, followed by his thirty warriors. With measured steps and grave demeanor they slowly advanced. In silence the circle was opened as Tecumseh and his followers drew near through which they slowly marched, then immediately closed behind them surrounding them by thousands of strangers; but nothing to fear, for the peace pipe was in the left hand of the mighty Shawnee, an emblem rigidly respected by all North American Indians all over the continent. When Tecumseh had reached a point near the fire, he halted and his thirty warriors at once seated themselves on the ground forming a crescent before their adored chieftain, while he, the personification of true dignity and manly beauty, stood erect and momentarily flashed his piercing eyes over the mighty host.

Every eye was now fastened upon him, and though his face wore a calm expression yet there was a nervousness about him withal that plainly indicated one of those sensitive organisms that kindle at the slightest warmth. The scene of this juncture, stated Col. Pitchlynn, was grand and imposing indeed. Every countenance told of suppressed feeling, and every eye sparkled with mental excitement.

He began his speech in a grave and solemn manner, stated Col. Pitchlynn, which I here give in substance, as follows:

"In view of questions of vast importance, have we met together in solemn council to-night. Nor should we here debate whether we have been wronged and injured, but by what measures we should avenge ourselves; for our merciless oppressors, having long since planned out their proceedings, are not about to make, but have and are still making attacks upon those of our race who have as yet come to no resolution. Nor are we ignorant by what steps, and by what gradual advances, the whites break in upon our neighbors. Imagining themselves to be still undiscovered, they show themselves the less audacious because you are insensible. The whites are already nearly a match for us all united, and too strong for any one tribe alone to resist; so that unless we support one another with our collective and united forces; unless every tribe unanimously combines to give a check to the ambition and avarice of the whites, they will soon conquer us apart and disunited, and we will be driven away from our native country and scattered as autumnal leaves before the wind.

"But have we not courage enough remaining to defend our country and maintain our ancient independence? Will we calmly suffer the white intruders and tyrants to enslave us? Shall it be said of our race that we knew not how to extricate ourselves from the three most to be dreaded calamities—folly, inactivity and cowardice? But what need is there to speak of the past? It speaks for itself and asks, 'Where today is the Pequod? Where the Narragansetts, the Mohawks, Pocanokets, and many other once powerful tribes of our race?' They have vanished before the avarice and oppression of the white men, as snow before a summer sun. In the vain hope of alone defending their ancient possessions, they have fallen in the wars with the white men. Look abroad over their once beautiful country, and what see you now? Naught but the ravages of the pale-face destroyers meet your eyes. So it will be with you Choctaws and Chickasaws! Soon your mighty forest trees, under the shade of whose wide spreading branches you have played

in infancy, sported in boyhood, and now rest your wearied
limbs after the fatigue of the chase, will be cut down to
fence in the land which the white intruders dare to call
their own. Soon their broad roads will pass over the graves
of your fathers, and the place of their rest will be blotted
out forever. The annihilation of our race is at hand unless
we unite in one common cause against the common foe.
Think not, brave Choctaws and Chickasaws, that you can
remain passive and indifferent to the common danger, and
thus escape the common fate. Your people too, will soon
be as falling leaves and scattering clouds before their
blighting breath. You too will be driven away from your
native land and ancient domains as leaves are driven before
the wintry storms.

"Sleep not longer, O Choctaws and Chickasaws," continued the indefatigable orator, "in false security and delusive hopes. Our broad domains are fast escaping from our
grasp. Every year our white intruders become more
greedy, exacting, oppressive and overbearing. Every year
contentions spring up between them and our people and
when blood is shed we have to make atonement whether
right or wrong, at the cost of the lives of our greatest chiefs,
and the yielding up of large tracts of our lands. Before the
pale-faces came among us, we enjoyed the happiness of
unbounded freedom, and were acquainted with neither
riches, wants, nor oppression. How is it now? Wants and
oppressions are our lot; for are we not controlled in everything, and dare we move without asking, by your leave?
Are we not being stripped day by day of the little that
remains of our ancient liberty? Do they not even now kick
and strike us as they do their black-faces? How long will it
be before they will tie us to a post and whip us, and make
us work for them in their corn fields as they do them? Shall
we wait for that moment or shall we die fighting before
submitting to such ignominy?"

At this juncture a low, muffled groan of indignation
forced its way through the clinched teeth running through

the entire assembly, and some of the younger warriors, no
longer enabled to restrain themselves, leaped from their
seats upon the ground, and, accompanying the act with the
thrilling warwhoops of defiance, flourished their toma-
hawᶜ⁻⁻ in a frenzy of rage. Tecumseh turned his eyes upon
them with a calm but rebuking look; then with a gentle
wave of the hand he again continued: "Have we not for
years had before our eyes a sample of their designs, and are
they not sufficient harbingers of their future determina-
tions? Will we not soon be driven from our respective
countries and the graves of our ancestors? Will not the
bones of our dead be plowed up, and their graves be turned
into fields? Shall we calmly wait until they become so
numerous that we will no longer be able to resist oppression? Will we wait to be destroyed in our turn, without
making an effort worthy our race? Shall we give up our
homes, our country, bequeathed to us by the Great Spirit,
the graves of our dead, and everything that is dear and sacred to us, without a struggle? I know you will cry with me.
Never! Never! Then let us by unity of action destroy them
all, which we now can do, or drive them back whence they
came. War or extermination is now our only choice. Which
do you choose? I know your answer. Therefore, I now call
on you, brave Choctaws and Chickasaws, to assist in the
just cause of liberating our race from the grasp of our
faithless invaders and heartless oppressors. The white
usurpation in our common country must be stopped, or we,
its rightful owners, be forever destroyed and wiped out as
a race of people. I am now at the head of many warriors
backed by the strong arm of English soldiers. Choctaws
and Chickasaws, you have too long borne with grievous
usurpation inflicted by the arrogant Americans. Be no
longer their dupes. If there be one here tonight who be-
lieves that his rights will not sooner or later, be taken from
him by the avaricious American pale-faces, his ignorance
ought to excite pity, for he knows little of the character of
our common foe. And if there be one among you mad

enough to undervalue the growing power of the white race
among us, let him tremble in considering the fearful woes
he will bring down upon our entire race, if by his criminal
indifference he assists the designs of our common enemy
against our common country. Then listen to the voice of
duty, of honor, of nature and of your endangered country.
Let us form one body, one heart, and defend to the last
warrior our country, our homes, our liberty, and the graves
of our fathers.

"Choctaws and Chickasaws, you are among the few of
our race who sit indolently at ease. You have indeed enjoyed the reputation of being brave, but will you be indebted for it more from report than fact? Will you let the
whites encroach upon your domains even to your very door
before you will assert your rights in resistance? Let no one
in this council imagine that I speak more from malice
against the pale-face Americans than just grounds of complaint. Complaint is just toward friends who have failed in
their duty; accusation is against enemies guilty of injustice.
And surely, if any people ever had, we have good and just
reasons to believe we have ample grounds to accuse the
Americans of injustice; especially when such great acts of
injustice have been committed by them upon our race, of
which they seem to have no manner of regard, or even to
reflect. They are a people fond of innovations, quick to
contrive and quick to put their schemes into effectual execution, no matter how great the wrong and injury to us;
while we are content to preserve what we already have.
Their designs to enlarge their possessions by taking yours in
turn; and will you, can you longer dally, O Choctaws and
Chickasaws? Do you imagine that that people will not
continue longest in the enjoyment of peace who timely
prepare to vindicate themselves, and manifest a determined
resolution to do themselves right whenever they are
wronged? Far otherwise. Then haste to the relief of our
common cause, as by consanguinity of blood you are bound;

lest the day be not far distant when you will be left single-handed and alone to the cruel mercy or our most inveterate foe."

Though the North American Indians never expressed their emotions by any audible signs whatever, yet the frowning brows, and the flashing eyes of that mighty concourse of seated and silent men told Tecumseh, as he closed and took his seat upon the ground among his warriors, that he had touched a thousand chords whose vibrations responded in tones that were in perfect unison and harmony with his own, and he fully believed, and correctly too, that he had accomplished the mission whereunto, he was sent, even beyond his most sanguine hopes and expectations.

A few of the Choctaw and Chickasaw chiefs now arose in succession and, walking to the center, occupied, in turn, the place which Tecumseh had just vacated and expressed their opinions upon the question so new and unexpectedly presented to them for their consideration; the majority leaning to the views advanced by the Shawnee chief, a few doubting their expediency. Tecumseh was now jubilant, for his cause seemed triumphant. But at this crisis of affairs, a sudden and unexpected change came o'er the scene. Another, who, up to this time, had remained a silent but attentive listener, arose and, free of all restraint, marched to the center mid the deep silence that again prevailed. A noble specimen also, was he, of manly beauty, strength, and unlettered eloquence. As he drew himself up to his full height, there was revealed the symmetrical form of the intrepid and the most renowned and influential chief of the Choctaws, a man of great dignity, unyielding firmness, undisputed bravery, undoubted veracity, sound judgment, and the firm and undeviating friend of the American people. He was Pushmataha.

All eyes were at once turned to and riveted upon him, as he momentarily stood in profound silence surveying the faces of his people. Though habitually of a lively and jovial disposition, yet Pushmataha could rival the lynx when he applied his penetrating mind to detect the weak points of his opponent. His long black locks fell back from a broad manly brow, from which shone dark, eloquent eyes full of depth and fire; his face broad and of a clear olive tint, his lips thin and compressed, all united to give an expression of firmness and intellectuality. The solemn manner and long silence that he assumed fell with unmistakable meaning upon the silent throng, upon whose faces still shone the light of the blazing council fire, reflecting no longer conflicting emotions, but one seemingly united all pervading sentiment. War and extermination to the whites. Pushmataha's observant eye read its deep signification. But nothing daunted, he began his speech in the ancient method of opening an address (long since obsolete), thus: "O-mish-ke! A numpa tillofasih ish hakloh." (Attention! Listen you to my brief remarks); and then continued in substance as follows:

"It was not my design in coming here to enter into a disputation with any one. But I appear before you, my warriors and my people not to throw in my plea against the accusations of Tecumseh; but to prevent your forming rash and dangerous resolutions upon things of highest importance, through the instigations of others. I have myself learned by experience, and I also see many of you, O Choctaws and Chickasaws, who have the same experience of years that I have, the injudicious steps of engaging in an enterprise because it is new. Nor do I stand up before you tonight to contradict the many facts alleged against the American people, or to raise my voice against them in useless accusations. The question before us now is not what wrongs they have inflicted upon our race, but what measures are best for us to adopt in regard to them; and though our race may have been unjustly treated and shamefully wronged by them, yet I shall not for that reason alone advise you to destroy them, unless it was just and expedient for you so to do; nor, would I advise you to forgive them, though worthy of your commiseration, unless I believe it would be to the interest of our common good. We should

consult more in regard to our future welfare than our
present. What people, my friends and countrymen, were so
unwise and inconsiderate as to engage in a war of their own
accord, when their own strength, and even with the aid of
others, was judged unequal to the task? I well know causes
often arise which force men to confront extremities, but, my
countrymen, those causes do not now exist. Reflect, therefore, I earnestly beseech you, before you act hastily in this
great matter, and consider with yourselves how greatly you
will err if you injudiciously approve of and inconsiderately
act upon Tecumseh's advice. Remember the American
people are now friendly disposed toward us. Surely you are
convinced that the greatest good will result to us by the
adoption of and adhering to those measures I have before
recommended to you; and, without giving too great a scope
to mercy or forbearance, by which I could never permit
myself to be seduced, I earnestly pray you to follow my
advice in this weighty matter, and in following it resolve to
adopt those expedients for our future welfare. My friends
and fellow countrymen! you now have no just cause to
declare war against the American people, or wreak your
vengeance upon them as enemies, since they have ever
manifested feelings of friendship towards you. It is besides
inconsistent with your national glory and with your honor,
as a people, to violate your solemn treaty; and a disgrace to
the memory of your forefathers, to wage war against the
American people merely to gratify the malice of the
English.

"The war, which you are now contemplating against
the Americans, is a flagrant breach of justice; yea, a fearful
blemish on your honor and also that of your fathers, and
which you will find if you will examine it carefully and
judiciously, forbodes nothing but destruction to our entire
race. It is a war against a people whose territories are now
far greater than our own, and who are far better provided
with all necessary implements of war, with men, guns,
horses, wealth, far beyond that of all our race combined,

and where is the necessity or wisdom to make war upon such a people? Where is our hope of success, if thus weak and unprepared we should declare it against them? Let us not be deluded with the foolish hope that this war, if begun, will soon be over, even if we destroy all the whites within our territories, and lay waste their homes and fields. Far from it. It will be but the beginning of the end that terminates in the total destruction of our race. And though we will not permit ourselves to be made slaves, or, like inexperienced warriors, shudder at the thought of war, yet I am not so insensible and inconsistent as to advise you to cowardly yield to the outrages of the whites, or wilfully to connive at their unjust encroachments; but only not yet to have recourse to war, but to send ambassadors to our Great Father at Washington, and lay before him our grievances, without betraying too great eagerness for war, or manifesting any tokens of pusillanimity. Let us, therefore, my fellow countrymen, form our resolutions with great caution and prudence upon a subject of such vast importance, and in which such fearful consequences may be involved.

"Heed not, O my countrymen, the opinions of others to that extent as to involve your country in a war that destroys its peace and endangers its future safety, prosperity and happiness. Reflect, ere it be too late, on the great uncertainty of war with the American people, and consider well, ere you engage in it, what the consequences will be if you should be disappointed in your calculations and expectations. Be not deceived with illusive hopes. Hear me, O my countrymen, if you begin this war it will end in calamities to us from which we are now free and at a distance; and upon whom of us they will fall, will only be determined by the uncertain and hazardous event. Be not, I pray you, guilty of rashness, which I never as yet have known you to be; therefore, I implore you, while healing measures are in the election of us all, not to break the treaty, nor violate your pledge or honor, but to submit our grievances, whatever they may be, to the Congress of the United States, according to the articles of the treaty existing between us and the American people. If not, I here invoke the **Great Spirit**, who takes cognizance of oaths, to bear me witness, that I shall endeavor to avenge myself upon the authors of this war, by whatever methods you shall set me an example. Remember we are a people who have never grown insolent with success, or become abject in adversity; but let those who invite us to hazardous attempts by uttering our praise, also know that the pleasure of hearing has never elevated our spirits above our judgment, nor an endeavor to exasperate us by a flow of invectives to be provoked the sooner to compliance. From tempers equally balanced let it be known that we are warm in the field of battle, and cool in the hours of debate; the former, because a sense of duty has the greater influence over a sedate disposition, and magnanimity the keenest sense of shame; and though good we are at debate, still our education is not polite enough to teach us a contempt of laws, yet by its severity gives us so much good sense as never to disregard them.

"We are not a people so impertinently wise as to invalidate the preparations of our enemies by a plausible harangue, and then absolutely proceed to a contest; but we reckon the thoughts of the pale-faces to be of a similar cast with our own, and that hazardous contingencies are not to be determined by a speech. We always presume that the projects of our enemies are judiciously planned, and then we seriously prepare to defeat them. Nor do we found our success upon the hope that they will certainly blunder in their conduct, but upon the hope that we have omitted no proper steps for our own security. Such is the discipline which our fathers have handed down to us; and by adhering to it, we have reaped many advantages. Let us, my countrymen, not forget it now, nor in short space of time precipitately determine a question in which so much is involved. It is indeed the duty of the prudent, so long as they are not injured, to delight in peace. But it is the duty of the brave, when injured, to lay peace aside, and to have re-

course to arms; and when successful in these, to then lay
them down again in peaceful quiet; thus never to be elevated above measure by success in war, nor delighted with
the sweets of peace to suffer insults. For he who, apprehensive of losing the delight, sits indolently at ease, will
soon be deprived of the enjoyment of that delight which
interesteth his fears; and he whose passions are inflamed by
military success, elevated too high by a treacherous confidence, hears no longer the dictates of judgment

"Many are the schemes, though unadvisedly planned,
through the more unreasonable conduct of an enemy,
which turn out successfully; but more numerous are those
which, though seemingly founded on mature counsel, draw
after them a disgraceful and opposite result. This proceeds
from that great inequality of spirit with which an exploit is
projected, and with which it is put into actual execution.
For in council we resolve, surrounded with security; in
execution we faint, through the prevalence of fear. Listen
to the voice of prudence, oh, my countrymen, ere you
rashly act. But do as you may, know this truth, enough for
you to know, I shall join our friends, the Americans, in
this war."

The observant eye of Tecumseh saw, ere Pushmataha
had closed, that the tide was turning against him; and,
maddened at the unexpected eloquence, the bold and irresistible arguments of the Choctaw orator, the moment
Pushmataha had taken his seat he sprang to he center of
the circle and, as a last effort to sustain his waning cause,
cried out in a loud, bold and defiant tone of voice, "All who
will follow me in this war throw your tomahawks into the
air above your heads." Instantly the air for many feet
above was filled with the clashing of ascending, revolving
and descending tomahawks, then all was hushed. Tecumseh then turned his piercing eyes upon Pushmataha with a
haughty air of triumph, and again took his seat. All eyes
were instantly turned to where the fearless hero sat. At
once the mighty Choctaw, nothing daunted, sprang to his

feet, gave the Choctaw hoyopatassuha (warwhoop), then, with the nimble bound of an antelope, leaped into the circle, and hurling his tomahawk into the air, shouted in a loud and defiant tone, "All who will follow me to victory and glory in this war let me also see your tomahawks in the air."

Again the air seemed filled with tomahawks. Again silence prevailed. What now was to be done in this dilemma of a dubious issue? If half followed the suggestions of Tecumseh and took sides with the English, and the other, those of Pushmataha declaring for the Americans, it would virtually be civil war, and that should not—must not be. To settle the question, after many conflicting suggestions had been proposed and rejected by first one and then the other of the two opposing parties, it was finally resolved to refer the matter to an aged Choctaw seer, living some distance away, and abide by his decision. The council adjourned to await his coming. A proper deputation was immediately in the evening of the second day accompanied by the old and venerable Choctaw hopaii (seer). As the twilight of the declining day approached, the council fire was replenished, and when night again had thrown o'er all her sable mantle, the council once more convened.

Again Tecumseh made the opening speech, rehearsing his designs and plans before the attentive seer and warrior host in strains of the most fascinating eloquence. Again followed Pushmataha, who fell not behind his worthy competitor in native eloquence and logical argument. No other spoke, for both parties had mutually left the mooted question in the hands of the two great chiefs, statesmen and orators. When the two distinguished disputants had been respectively heard by the aged seer, he arose and slowly walked to the center of the circle, gazed a moment over the silent but solicitous throng, and then said: "Assemble here to-morrow when the sun shall be yonder"—pointing to the zenith—"build a scaffold"—pointing to the spot—"as high as my head; fill up the intervening space beneath with dry wood; bring also a red heifer two years old free of all disease, and tie her near the scaffold; and tomorrow the Great Spirit will decide for you this great question."

On the next day the appointed hour found the multitude assembled; the altar erected; the wood prepared, and the sacrificial offering in waiting. The seer then ordered the heifer to be slain; the skin removed; the entrails taken out and placed some distance away; the carcass cut up into small pieces and laid upon the scaffold; he then applied a brand of fire to the dry wood under the scaffold; then commanded the vast multitude, all, everyone, to stretch themselves upon the ground, faces to the earth, and thus to remain in profound silence until he ordered them to rise, which command was instantly obeyed; then seizing the bloody skin he stretched it upon the ground, hair downward, and quickly rolled himself up in it, and commenced a series of prayers and doleful lamentations, at the same time rolling himself backward and forward before the consuming sacrifice uttering his prayers and lamentations intermingled with dissonant groans fearful to be heard; and thus he continued until the altar and the flesh thereon were entirely consumed. Then freeing himself from the skin, he sprang to his feet and said: "Osh (the) Ho-che-to (Great) Shilup (Spirit) a-num-pul-ih (has spoken). Wak-a-yah (rise) ah-ma (and) Een (His) a-num-pa (message) hak-loh (hear)." All leaped to their feet, and gathered in close circles around their venerated seer, who, pointing to the sky, exclaimed: "The Great Spirit tells me to warn you against the dark and evil designs of Tecumseh, and not to be deceived by his words; that his schemes are unwise; and if entered into by you, will bring you into trouble; that the Americans are our friends, and you must not take up the tomahawk against them; if you do, you will bring sorrow and desolation upon yourselves and nations. Choctaws and Chickasaws, obey the words of the Great Spirit." Enough! As oil upon the storm-agitated waters of the sea, so fell the mandates of the Great Spirit upon the war-agitated hearts of those forest warriors, and all was hushed to quiet; reason assumed again her sway; peace rejoiced triumphant, as all in harmony sought their forest homes; and thus the far scattered white settlers, in Mississippi, Alabama, Georgia and Florida, and the western portion of Tennessee, escaped inevitable destruction; for, had Tecumseh been successful in uniting those five then powerful and warlike tribes into the adoption of his schemes scarcely a white person would have been left in all their broad territories to tell the tale of their complete extermination; since the wily Shawnee had laid off for each tribe its particular field of operation, before he had left his northern home to entice them into daring schemes. The whites were then but few, scattered here and there, and at great distances apart, and could not have competed even with the Choctaws alone, as they, at that time, numbered between thirty and forty thousand warriors, and, besides, the blow would have fallen upon them when least expected and most unprepared.

But the long cherished hopes of Tecumseh were blasted, and Pushmataha erected his trophies upon his defeat. Though greatly disappointed, yet not disheartened, Tecumseh at once set his footsteps toward the Muscogee Nation.

Pushmataha, who then lived near St. Stephens, now in Washington County, Alabama, turned his steps directly for that little town. Rumor of Tecumseh's presence among the Choctaws and Chickasaws, and the council on the Tanapoh Ikbih River, had preceded him; and when he arrived at the little place he found it in a blaze of excitement, for a thousand exaggerated reports had but added to the conjecture as to the convening of the two tribes in com..on council, with the noted Shawnee chief. But their fears were wholly allayed when Pushmataha, whose veracity none questioned, rode into the little town, and gave a short sketch of the proceedings at the council, and also proffered the services of himself and warriors to the Americans, which were cordially accepted by George S. Gaines, then United States agent to the Choctaws, and who, in company with the noble chief, immediately hastened to Mobile, to inform General Flournoy of Pushmataha's proposition. To the astonishment of all, General Flournoy refused to accept the offer of the great Choctaw chief and warriors; while from every mouth loud curses and bitter denunciations were heard against his considered folly and seeming madness. With heavy heart and unpleasant forebodings Gaines returned to St. Stephens with Pushmataha, whose silence but too plainly told the wound inflicted.

Fortunately, however, Flournoy reconsidered his refusal, and at once sent word to Gaines not only to accept the proposal of Pushmataha in the name of the United States, but also to go immediately into the Choctaw Nation and secure the Choctaws as allies in the approaching war. There had been great apprehension lest the Choctaws would unite with the Muscogees and other disaffected tribes, as allies to the English; which they would, perhaps, have done, had Flournoy's rejection of Pushmataha's proposal been given previous to the council. Pushmataha, without delay, returned to his people then in the northern district of his Nation—contiguous to the Chickasaw Nation, and there assembled his warriors in council; while Gaines hastened to Colonel John Pitchlynn's house, near where the council with Tecumseh had but shortly adjourned, and where he was fortunate enough to meet Colonel McKee, United States agent to the Chickasaws. At that time, the Choctaw Nation was divided into three districts, of which Pushmataha was the ruling chief of the eastern, Apukshunnubbee, of the northern, and Moshulatubbee of the southern. Gaines at once left Colonel Pitchlynn's and hastened to the Choctaw council, where he found Pushmataha and several thousand of his warriors already assembled; to whom Pushmataha made a long and eloquent speech denouncing the ambitious views of Tecumseh, and extolling the friendship of the American people; then offered to lead all who would follow him, to victory and glory against the enemies of the Americans. As soon as he had concluded his speech, a warrior sprang from his seat on the ground, and striking his breast repeatedly with the palm of his right hand, shouted: "Choctaw siah! Tushka chitoh siah aiena! Pimmi miko uno iakiyah." (A Choctaw I am. I am also a great warrior. I will follow our chief). To which action and sentiment the whole council at once responded. In the mean time, McKee hastened with Colonel John Pitchlynn to the Chickasaw Nation, and succeeded in assembling them in council, and successfully secured them also as allies to the Americans. Thus, by the firmness, influence and eloquence of the great and good Pushmataha, Tecumseh's plans were thwarted, and those two then powerful tribes, the Choctaws and Chickasaws, secured as allies to the Americans, in the war with England in 1812, and also in that known as the Creek war.

In the council convened, in which the Choctaws declared in favor of the Americans against the English and the Muscogees, Pushmataha publicly announced that, every Choctaw warrior who joined the Muscogees, should be shot, if ever they returned home. Still, there were thirty young warriors under the leadership of a sub-chief named Illi Shuah (Dead Stink), who joined the Muscogees. It was said, five or six lived to return home after the defeat of the Muscogees, all of whom Pushmataha caused to be shot. But an aged Choctaw (long since deceased) whom I interviewed concerning the subject, stated that all the thirty warriors, who joined the Muscogees under Illi Shuah, were slain in battle to a man; but Illi Shuah escaped and finally returned home, but he did not remember whether Pushmataha had him shot or not. In the Creek war, Pushmataha, assisted General Jackson with seven hundred warriors; and in the Battle of New Orleans, with five hundred. In both of which they proved themselves to be worthy allies in bravery and in the use of the deadly rifle.

The noble Pushmataha descended not through a successive line of chiefs, but was of common parentage. Yet of whom it may be truly said: He was one of nature's nobility, and born to command—a man who raised himself from the obscurity of the wilderness unlettered and un- taught; but by his superior native talents, undaunted brav- ery, noble generosity, unimpeachable integrity, unassumed hospitality to the known and unknown, won the admiration, respect, confidence and love of his people; and also, of all the whites— high or low, rich or poor—who were person- ally acquainted with him. He was truly and justly the pride of the Choctaw people when living, and their veneration today though long dead. He acknowledged no paternity. Yet, his own statement in regard to his genealogy, as related to me by the aged Choctaws of the past, is still mentioned by their descendants at the present day, with great pride, as characteristic of the manly independence of their honored chieftain. It is in substance as follows:

On one occasion a deputation was sent by the Choc- taws to Washington City to present the respects of their na- tion to the President of the United States who, at that time, was Andrew Jackson,[23] and to assure him of their abiding friendship toward him as the "Great Chief" of the American people, and to also confer with him relative to the future interests and welfare of their nation. The renowned Push- mataha was one of the deputation. A few days after their arrival in the city a reception was given to them, at which many of the cabinet and representative officers were pres- ent. Among the many and various questions that were asked of the different members of the delegation was the question, How they became so distinguished among their people? To which various answers were given, each telling his own story of the exploits which brought him out of obscurity and placed his name in the temple of human fame. Pushmataha, up to this time, had said nothing. At length President Jackson requested the interpreter to ask him how he became such a great warrior and renowned chief. To which Pushmataha coolly and with unassumed

[23] Andrew Jackson was not yet president at the time of Pushmataha's visit to Washington. It is probable, however, that there was a meeting between the two at the capital.

indifference replied: "Tell the white chief it's none of his business." This unexpected retort attracted the attention of all present and all eyes were at once turned upon the bold chief. Jackson amused at the reply and pleased at the manly independence of the noble chief requested the interpreter to propound the same question again; which was done but to which Pushmataha seemed to give no heed. The curiosity of all being greatly excited, the question was asked still again. To which Pushmataha then replied: "Well, if the white chief must know, tell him that Apushamatahahubih has neither father nor mother, nor kinsman upon the earth. Tell him that once upon a time, far away from here in the great forests of the Choctaw Nation, a dark cloud arose from the western horizon, and with astonishing velocity, traveled up the arched expanse. In silence profound, all animate nature stood apart; soon the fearful cloud reached the zenith, then as quickly spread its dark mantle o'er the sky entire, shutting out the light of the sun, and wrapping earth in midnight gloom. Then burst the cloud and rose the wind; and while falling rains and howling winds, lightnings gleam and thunders roar, in wild confusion blended, a blinding flash blazed athwart the sky, then hurled its strength against a mighty oak and cleft it in equal twain from utmost top to lowest bottom; when, lo! from its riven trunk leaped a mighty man; in stature, perfect; in wisdom, profound; in bravery, unequalled—a full-fledged warrior. 'Twas Apushamatahahubih."

In November, 1812, Pushmataha visited General Claiborne. When he approached the General's tent, he was received by the lieutenant on guard, who invited him to drink. Pushmataha answered only with a look of contempt. He recognized no equal with one epaulette. When Gen. Claiborne walked in, the Choctaw chieftain shook him by the hand and proudly said, as to an equal, "Chief, I will drink with you." He was six feet two inches in height, of powerful frame and Herculean strength, and with features after the finest models of the antique, composed, dignified,

and seductive in his deportment, and was the most remarkable man the Choctaws ever produced since the days of
Chahtah, the Great Miko of their traditional past. He was
sometimes called Koi Hosh, (The Panther); and sometimes,
Ossi Hosh, sometimes, Oka Chilohonfah (Falling Water);
the two first alluding to his quick movements and daring
exploits in war, and the latter, to the sonorous and musical
intonations of his voice.

Sam Dale, the renowned scout of General Andrew
Jackson in the Creek war of 1812, stated that he had heard
Tecumseh and the Prophet of the Shawnees; Bill Weather-
ford of the Muscogees; Big Warrior of the Cherokees, and
Apukshunnubbee of the Choctaws, besides the most distinguished American orators in Congress, but never one who
had such music in his tones, such energy in his manner and
such power over his audience as Pushmataha, the Choctaw
chief, patriot and warrior.

Many characteristic anecdotes are related of him, of
which I will mention a few: A feud once existed between
him and another Choctaw chief of the Yazoo district, and it
was generally believed that when they met their tomahawks
would settle the difference between them. One day his rival
was seen approaching in company with a large party of
warriors; and on a nearer approach, manifested great agitation irresolutely grasping his tomahawk. Pushmataha, as
soon as he discovered him shouted his challenging warwhoop, rushed toward him with his long hunting knife in his
hand, then suddenly stopped, and with a smile of the utmost
contempt, cried out "Hushi osh chishikta! Katihma ish
wun nichih! Hosh mahli Keyumahlih. Ea, ho bak! Ea!"
(Leaf of the red-oak! Why do you tremble? The wind
blows not. Go, coward.) The word hobak is considered
by the Choctaws, as a word of the greatest reproach and
most unpardonable offense that could possibly be applied
to a man, its true signification being an eunuch.

Pushmataha was very sensitive at the appearance of
anything that even bore the appearance of oppression. A

few soldiers, at that day, were stationed at the agency among the Choctaws; and one of the soldiers being addicted to drunkenness, and at one time having become boisterously drunk, was tied to a tree, for the want of that necessary appendage to an Indian agency, as well as to all towns among the whites, a jail or guard house, until he became sober. Pushmataha happening to pass by and seeing the soldier tied asked him of what he was guilty, that he should be placed in so humiliating a condition; being told the cause, he at once released the unfortunate man, exclaiming, "Is that all? many good warriors get drunk."

Pushmataha, in unison with the ancient custom of the Choctaws, had two wives. Being asked if he did not consider it wrong for a man to have more than one living wife, he replied: "Certainly not. Should not every woman be allowed the privilege of having a husband as well as a man a wife? and how can every one have a husband when there are more women than men? Our Great Father had the Choctaws counted last year, and it was ascertained that there were more women than men, and if a man was allowed but one wife many of our women would have no husbands. Surely, the women should have equal chances with the men in that particular."

During the Creek war of 1814, in which Pushmataha was engaged with eight hundred of his warriors as allies of the United States, as before stated, a small company of Choctaw women, among whom was the wife of Pushmataha, visited their husbands and friends then in the American army in the Creek Nation. A white soldier, grossly insulted the wife of the distinguished Choctaw chief, for which the justly indignant chief knocked him down with the hilt of his sword, instead of plunging it through his body, as he should have done. Being arrested for the just and meritorious act, and asked by the commanding general the reasons, he fearlessly answered: "He insulted my wife, and I knocked the insolent dog down; but had you, General, insulted her as that common soldier did, I would have used the point upon you instead of the hilt, in resenting an insult offered to my wife." And he would have been as good as his word; for a Choctaw then, as now, is not slow in resenting any insult offered to the female portion of his family, and his work is quick and sure; and had not the noble Pushmataha regarded the soldier who insulted his wife, as too contemptible a creature for the point of his sword, he would have plunged it through his body without a moment's hesitation; and that he only knocked him down with the hilt, is sufficient evidence that he did not regard him worthy its point.

Pushmataha was exceedingly fond of engaging in that ancient and time-honored amusement, the famous to-lih (ball play); and in which the Choctaws, as well as the southern portion of their race, took great delight.

While battling with his warriors for the interests of the Americans under Andrew Jackson, in 1814, General Jackson presented to Pushmataha a complete military suit and sword, as worn by the American generals; which he wore with manly and becoming dignity until the close of the war; which, after the close, he took off and hung up in his cabin, and never afterwards put on; but donned his native garb and once more became the Pushmataha of his people. Having become wearied, however, in looking upon the white man's insignia—that feeble representation of true greatness in the opinion of the Choctaw hero—he took the suit from its resting place, rolled it up and fastened it to one end of a long rope, then attached the other end to his belt; and then, with quiver full of arrows hung over his left shoulder and bow in hand, marched through various parts of his village, dragging the insignificant badge of meritorious distinction on the ground behind him; at each house he approached, he shot a chicken, if one was found; took it up and inserted its head under his belt; then continued his silent walk, and seeking another house, there shot another chicken, also slipped its head under his belt; and he continued his march from house to house with a solemn and silent gravity, taxing each a chicken until he had shot as many as he could slip heads under the belt. The owners of the chickens said nothing, knowing that some fun was ahead. He then walked to an untaxed house with his load of chickens dangling from his belt, had them nicely dressed and cooked, then invited all from whom he had taken a chicken to come and partake of the feast he had thus unceremoniously prepared for them. They went and had a jolly time, Pushmataha figuring as the gayest among the gay. He left his suit lying upon the ground before the door of the house at which he deposited the chickens, a frail memento of human greatness with its hopes departed.

In 1823, Pushmataha, then about sixty years of age, walked about 80 miles from his home (being too poor to own a horse, and too proud to borrow one) to attend a council of his Nation. Mr. John Pitchlynn, then United States interpreter to the Choctaws and Mr. Ward, United States agent, (with both of whom I was in boyhood personally acquainted), were present at the council. At the adjournment of the council, Mr. Ward suggested to Mr. Pitchlynn that they purchase a horse for the old chief. Mr. Pitchlynn readily acquiesced in the proposition, but with the proviso that Pushmataha must pledge his word that he would not sell the horse for whiskey. Pushmataha cheerfully gave the pledge, received the horse and departed for his distant home highly elated with his unexpected good fortune. A few months after he visited the agency, and Ward discovered that he was again minus a horse, and learned, upon inquiry, that he had lost the presented horse in betting him on a ball-play. Ward at once accused him of violating his pledged word, which Pushmataha as firmly denied. "But you promised," continued Ward, "that you would not sell the horse." "True I did;" retorted the venerable old chief. "But I did not promise you and my good friend, John Pitchlynn, that I would not bet him in a game of ball." Ward conceded the victory to Pushmataha, and chided him no more.

In 1824, this great and good man visited Washington City in company with other Choctaw chiefs, as delegates of their Nation to the Unted States government; at which time he made the following remarks to the Secretary of War, which were written down as he spoke them.

"Father, I have been here many days, but have not talked, have been sick. I belong to another district, different from these my companions and countrymen. You have no doubt heard of me, I am Apushamatahahubih. When in my own country, I often looked towards this Council House, and desired to see it. I have come, but I am in trouble, and would tell my sorrows; for I feel as a little child reclining in the bend of its father's arms, and looks up into his face in childish confidence to tell him of its troubles; and I would now recline in the bend of your arm, and trustingly look in your face, therefore hear my words.

"When at my distant home in my own native land, I heard that men had been appointed to talk to us; I refrained from speaking there, as I preferred to come here and speak; therefore I am here to-day. I can boastingly say, and in so doing speak the truth, that none of my ancestors, nor my present Nation, ever fought against the United States. As a Nation of people, we have always been friendly, and ever listened to the applications of the American people. We have given of our country to them until it has become very small. I came here years ago when a young man to see my Father Jefferson. He then told me if ever we got into trouble we must come and tell him, and he would help us. We are in trouble, and have come; but I will now let another talk."

The above was but a preliminary to a speech he intended to make, and which, had he lived to have delivered, would have proved to his hearers in Washington his great native eloquence, which had been so long and much eulogized by the whites who had often heard him around the council fires of his Nation.

In conversation with the noble General Lafayette during the same visit to Washington City Pushmataha closed with the following: "This is the first time I have seen you, and I feel it will be the last. The earth will separate us forever—farewell!" How prophetic! He died but a few days after. When stretched upon his bed of death, fully conscious of his near approaching end, he calmly turned his eyes upon the faces of the Choctaw delegates standing around him, and said: "I am dying, and will never return again to our native and loved land. But you will go back to our distant homes; and as you journey you will see the wild flowers of the forests and hear the songs of the happy birds of the woods, but Apushamatahahubih will see and hear them no more.

"When you return home you will be asked, 'Apushamatahah katimmaho?' (where is Apushamatahah?)), and you will answer, 'Illitok' (dead to be). And it will fall upon their ears as the sound of a mighty oak falling in the solitude of the woods." His dying words were—"Illi siah makinli sa paknaka tanapoh chitoh tokalichih" (As soon as I am dead shoot off the big guns above). The request of the dying hero was strictly complied with. The minute-guns were fired on Capitol Hill as the solemn and imposing procession of half a mile in length marched to the cemetery.

His surrounding brother chiefs erected a monument over the grave of their distinguished chieftain, with the following epitaph,—"Apushamatahah, a Choctaw Chief; lies here. This monument to his memory is erected by his brother chiefs who were associated with him in a delegation from their nation, in the year 1824, to the government of the United States. Apushamatahah was a warrior of great distinction. He was wise in council, eloquent to an extraordinary degree; and on all occasions, and under all circumstances, the white man's friend. He died in Washington on the 24th day of December, 1824, of the croup, in the 60th year of his age."

Pushmatah had only one son, who was named Johnson. He moved with his people to their present homes, and served them in the capacity of prosecuting attorney for many years, in Pushmataha District. He lived to prove himself worthy of his distinguished father, and in many respects was a true scion of the parent trunk.

Truly, if the adventures through which Pushmataha passed had been preserved, they would have furnished alone abundant material for all the writers of romance in the United States, for years. It is conceded by all who knew him, that he was the most renowned warrior and influential chief of the Choctaw Nation, since their acquaintance with the whites.

But why have not the services of Pushmataha—that remarkable friend of the American people—been written? Alas! he was an Indian. But I mistake! They have been written; and to-day, after the lapse of nearly three-quarters of a century, the aged Choctaws speak his name with loving reverence, while the young listen with wondrous delight to the thrilling stories of his life in many an humble home in their territory.

The death of Pushmataha shrouded the countenances of the bereaved chiefs at Washington in the deepest unaffected gloom during their remaining short stay in the city. One a young warrior of noble mien, whose power of self-command was not equal to his seniors in age and experience betrayed emotions that told of a heart overwhelmed with the keenest and deepest anguish. To offered words of consolation by some of the whites, he replied: "I'm sorry"; and being questioned why he should be more deeply grieved than the others, answered: "I'm sorry it was not I who had died"; signifying that his country would have sustained but little loss in his death, in comparison with the loss sustained by the death of Pushmataha. But the recorders of the incident have greatly misrepresented that young Choctaw by stating that the firing of the minute-guns and the pageantry displayed at the burial of Pushmataha alone produced the deep sorrow manifested, because he himself was not the subject of the honors conferred. That young and sorrowing Choctaw youth was Nitakachieubih (Give us the day to kill), the nephew of Pushmataha, and proved himself to be a worthy scion of the ancestral tree, as a statesman and counselor among his people, sustaining his high honors with dignity through a long and useful life and dying as his noble uncle—lamented by his nation. In traveling through their present country, many of the aged Choctaws (old friends when living east of the Mississippi River) have expressed great indignation that Nitakachie was so unjustly misrepresented.

We, the American people of to-day, still pay (and justly too) the highest honors to the name of General La Fayette, who extended so generously a helping hand to our fathers in their darkest hour of need; remembering him with filial reverence and gratitude unalloyed, but silently bury in oblivion the name of Pushmataha, as unworthy of eulogy or even a place in the annals of history; though he, at the head of his brave warriors, with purity of motives and without expectation of reward, also extended to them a helping hand in a gloomy hour of their history, and saved the primitive white settlers of Mississippi, Alabama and Georgia—then few, far between, and feeble—from actual extermination.

In a letter to me, September 5, 1891, Judge Julius Folsom, son of Rev. Israel Folsom, thus wrote: "In the year 1861, two delegates of the Choctaw Nation, Peter P. Pitchlynn and Israel Folsom, were in the city of Washington, D. C., attending to business in which our Nation was interested, but accomplished nothing, as the prospect of an approaching war between the North and South absorbed every other consideration. The two delegates, as soon as they learned that war had actually commenced between the North and South, hastened home that they might use their influence (which no two men exercised more over their Nation than they) in an effort to keep the Choctaw Nation upon neutral ground. But alas, they were too late! Already had the Confederate troops taken possession of our country, and they found everything in a state of wildest confusion. Up to this time, our protection was in the United States' troops stationed at Fort Washita, under the command of Colonel Emory. But he, as soon as the Confederate troops had entered our country, at once abandoned us and the fort; and, to make his flight more expeditious and his escape more sure, employed Black Beaver, a Shawnee Indian,[24] under a promise to him of five thousand dollars, to pilot him and his troops out of the Indian country safely without a collision with the Texas Confederates; which Black Beaver accomplished. By this act the United States abandoned the Choctaws and Chickasaws.

"Our Indian Agent, Douglas H. Cooper, also betrayed the United States by his acts, for he at once joined the rebellion, and urged the Indians of both the Choctaw and Chickasaw tribes to do the same, backing his arguments with the threat of confiscation of both land and stock if they refused. But under all this pressure, abandoned by the North, and threatened by the South, they stood upon neutral grounds until the middle of June, 1861! Then, there being no other alternative by which to save their country and property, they, as the less of the two evils that confronted them, went with the Southern Confederacy.

Your friend,   Julius Folsom."

Contemporaneous with Pushmataha was the Choctaw chief Apukshunnubbee who was of the Hai-yipa-tuk-lo Clan (meaning Two Lakes.) He also was a Choctaw whose blood was uncontaminated with anything foreign, a man of sterling merits, whose name is held in grateful and proud remembrance by his people to this day. He was also a quiet and unobtrusive man, but faithful in the discharge of his duties as chief; and his seemingly premature death was a national loss to his people, and deeply deplored by them.

[24] The historian will remember that the celebrated guide, Black Beaver, was a Delaware.

He lost his life by accidentally stepping off a balcony at night, at a hotel in Maysville, Kentucky, his neck being dislocated by the fall, while going to Washington City as a delegate with Pushmataha and others of his Nation. Little has been preserved of Apukshunnubbee's life but that he was an honest man. Amosholihubili [25] (To destroy as by fire), was a noted chief of the Oklafalaiah Clan (Long People). It is said the name of this clan had its origin in a Choctaw family who, both parents and children, were uncommonly tall. Moshulatubbee, than whom a more far-sighted man, white or red, is seldom found, was a true patriot; he was calm and dignified in council; possessing a black, keen penetrating eye, and a lowering yet meditative brow on which a thousand emotions of conflicting thoughts and designs seemed to have stamped a portion of their obscurity. Many years prior to the expulsion of his people from their ancient homes, his character was assailed by the white intruders who strolled about over the country, and of whom he had seen and learned enough to convince him, as well as many others, of their utter want of scarcely a redeeming trait of character; therefore, strenuously advocating measures for their expulsion from the Choctaw country and prevention of their return, he was called Hattak-upi-humma okpuloh, (a Bad Red Man).

Moshulatubbee through whose veins unadulterated Choctaw blood alone coursed, and of which he was justly proud, moved with his people to their present homes, where he spent the few remaining years of his life (for he was then an old man) in encouraging their desponding hearts to rise above misfortune and adversity. Though not a fluent speaker, yet he spoke with a dignified but gentle humility; he addressed the reason and good sense of his hearers, and not their passions and prejudices. His untutored delivery was indeed graceful; his argument connected and convincing, and his manners, calculated to attract audiences and hold attention. He lived several years beyond the allotted

---

[25] Elsewhere I have changed the spelling of this chief's name to Moshulatubbee.

life of man, reaching nearly four score years and ten. He died at home among his friends and people, honored, respected and loved by his nation, though age seemed not to have diminished his mental faculties, and but slightly impaired his physical powers; and to the last he continued a grand old man, who, while he was as confiding as a child in those who had won his confidence, was full of fire and vigor when he was convinced that wrong had been done either to himself or his people. Always a hater of shams and deceits, liars and defamers, and being never a dissembler nor a coward, liar or defamer himself, there was no room to doubt the side on which he would be found in any cause where there was a question about its truth or its justice; and withal a kindlier, gentler spirit than Moshulatubbee possessed was seldom found. The years of his aged wife, who survived her venerable husband many years reached within a few years of a century.

Pushmataha, Apukshunnubbee and Moshbulatubbee were the head chiefs of the Choctaw Nation in 1814, the latter being the youngest; but after the demise of the two former, Coleman Cole and Nittakachihubih, the nephew of the renowned Pushmataha were chosen as their successors a few years previous to the treaty of 1830 at Bok Chuckfiluma Hehlah (dancing rabbit creek), Nittakachihubih succeeding his uncle and Coleman Cole, Apukshunnubbee.

Subsequently Greenwood Le Flore superseded Coleman Cole as leading chief of the Apukshunnubbee District, and David Folsom superceded Moshulatubbee in his District; to the proceedings of the latter succession Moshulatubbee taking exceptions, and being strenuously supported by Nittakhachubih, he openly disputed the claims of David Folsom to the chieftaincy over him; while Coleman Cole, who was of Shukchih Humma descent, and proved himself an upright and honest man during his whole public, as well as private life, quietly returned to private life after he was superseded by Le Flore, moved west with his people and spent his remaining days in using his influence by precept

and example, for their welfare and happiness, and died in
the fall of 1884 at the honored age of four score and ten, at
his home near Atoka, Indian Terraitory. But Moshulatubbee, still chafing under his political defeat, and viewing
the appointment of Colonel David Folsom as chief of the
district over which he had so long ruled, as an unjust
encroachment upon his rights, resolved to sustain his claims
at all hazards. At this time there had just been paid to the
Choctaws an annuity, which getting into the hands of
Moshulatubbee, sustained by a strong party of his adherents, and also by Nittakachih and his entire district, he
refused to pay it, or any part of it, into the hands of Colonel
Folsom, the proper person to hold it for distribution. This
seemingly bold step at once threw the entire nation into a
high state of excitement. A council was immediately called,
to be represented by the two districts—the one over which
Nittakachih presided and the one over which Colonel Folsom had just been appointed. The council at once convened
and, as was expected, controversy ran high and the dispute
waxed warmer and warmer, and the breach grew wider and
wider, resulting in the adjournment of the council sine die,
without any definite conclusion being attained; and each
party, with anything but amicable feelings the one toward
the other, returned to their respective homes—Colonel
Folsom and his partisans to their homes in the northern part
of the district, the others to theirs in the southern.

Nittakachih was as true a specimen of the North
American Indian warrior as ever lived. True courage, than
which no other quality commands so great admiration
among men, seemed to have been written in every linea-
ment of his face, and his unflinching eyes convinced at a
glance that no earthly power could intimidate him. Though
small in stature, yet nature had cast his limbs in a mould of
delicate yet manly beauty, and also endowed him with a
constitution which seemed to bid defiance to almost all
changes, as well as to fatigue and privations of every kind.
His disposition seemed, in great degree, to partake of the

qualities of his bodily frame; and as the one possessed
great activity, strength and endurance, the other, under a
calm semblance, had much of the fiery love of glory which
constituted the principal attribute of the Indian character.
But the face of Nittakachih might well be termed a lumin-
ous medium of the passions. The bright or the dark, the
lurid cloud and the calm sunshine, made themselves known
not only in the voice and gesture, but also in the ever-vary-
ing expression of his eloquent countenance. His self-command under any and all circumstances, and his calm and
unassumed fearlessness in the hour that tests the soul of
man, were truly wonderful; and, as an illustration, I will
here relate an incident of his life, in connection with that of
Colonel David Folsom, having its origin in the deposal of
Moshultubbee and the elevation of Colonel David Folsom
to his place as a chief concerning which I have just spoken.

As soon as the council adjourned, Colonel David Folsom, fearing the hot words passed in the council might be
but the preliminaries to something serious, immediately
sent a messenger to Greenwood Le Flore then living in the
extreme western portion of the Nation to inform him of the
unpleasant state of affairs existing in his district, and the
causes; and also the fears he entertained of its resulting in
bloodshed. Le Flore, comprehending the situation at once,
collected a large body of his warriors without delay and
hastened to Colonel Folsom's place of residence, then
known as the Choctaw Agency, twelve or fifteen miles
miles south of the present town of Starkville, Mississippi, on
the road now leading from Columbus to Jackson, then
known as the "Old Robinson Road."

In the meantime rumor was on the wing that Moshulatubbee and Nittakachih had threatened to depose Colonel
Folsom and reinstate Moshulatubbee even if it had to be
done by the tomahawk and rifle. Colonel Folsom at first
regarded the rumor as having no foundation in truth—a
feint on the part of Moshulatubbee and Nittakchih to
bring him to their measures—but soon learned to his sur-

prise and sorrow that they evidently meditated hostilities, as they were actually collecting their warriors at the then trading-house of the Choctaws with the whites, on the Tanapo Ikbi River, now known as Demopolis. Colonel Folsom immediately sent out his runners to call together his warriors; and then were seen these runners, mounted upon their fleetest horses, speeding with the velocity of the wind from village to village and from neighborhood to neighborhood, calling to arms. Truly, it was astonishing in how short a time the Choctaws, at that day and time, could send any intelligence they desired to convey, from any part of their country to another. If anything of importance occurred today in any part of the Nation it was known on the morrow at distances seemingly incredible.

All was now in a blaze of wild excitement. The missionaries in their quiet and peaceful homes did not anticipate anything serious at first, even as was thought by all that the events that foreshadowed our Civil War of 1861, would have its origin in blustering only to terminate in an empty noise; but the thrilling war whoop that now disturbed the hitherto quiet, echoing by day and by night from hill to hill through their then boundless forest; the renewed life and active energy displayed by the warriors, who but the day before reclined in silent reverie before their cabin doors, or in listless indifference smoked their pipes, but too plainly announced to them, that a fearful storm was not only fast gathering, but seemed ready to burst with all its terrific fury upon the Choctaw Nation, and who could tell where or upon whom its fury would be spent! The paleface intruders, loafers, stragglers, and traders, taking the hint, bade the country a hasty adieu; but the missionaries hoping for better, still lingered with their families, but stood in readiness for precipitous flight at a moment's warning should safety absolutely require it. Colonel David Folsom's residence, then known and long after remembered as the old Choctaw Agency, was appointed as the place of rendezvous for his assembling warriors, there to unite with the coming forces of LeFlore. The warriors of Colonel Folsom living in the northern part of his district, passed directly by Hebron, the missionary station and home of Mr. Calvin Cushman, on their way to the point of rendezvous. Many parties stopped in passing and conversed with him concerning the unfortunate state of affairs; and replied to his interrogatories, as to the propriety of his leaving the nation with his family at once, or wait for further developments, by urging him to remain, and assuring him, at the same time, a timely notice of approaching danger, and also a sufficient escort to conduct him and family to a place of safety. Mr. Cushman, having implicit confidence in their plighted word, resolved to remain, though not entirely free of all apprehensions, but stood in readiness to depart with his family at any moment.

For two or three days, and frequently during the night, bands of warriors continued to pass dressed in all the Choctaw paraphernalia of war, and painted as an Indian only can paint—an art known but to him by which the countenance is made to assume a most frightful and awe-creating expression, and the eye that deadly ferocity, which to be comprehended must be seen. Invariably when passing, night or day, as they drew near Mr. Cushman's home the thrilling warwhoop broke the stillness of the forests that stretched around and away from that humble and peaceful missionary habitation, as a signal to its occupants that, though it proclaimed war to others, it was a harbinger of peace to them; but which, after all, was not, to the unaccustomed ear, in strict accordance with the rules of harmony, or to the timid heart very persuasive in its melody.

But this difficulty, the result of which seemed would inevitably terminate in a civil war, was brought to a happy settlement by an incident which I will here relate from memory as I heard it in my boyhood, when narrated to Mr. Cushman by Colonel David Folsom; and which was so impressed upon my youthful mind, that distance nor time has been able to efface it from the pages of memory.

Colonel Folsom stated to Mr. Cushman, in substance, as follows; and which I will place under the caption:

THE MEETING OF FOLSOM AND NITTAKACHIH— THE TWO CHOCTAH CHIEFS.

When the council, convened for the adjustment and final distribution of the annuity, adjourned in such confusion, I feared the consequences that I was apprehensive would follow; but hoped that the conflicting opinions then agitating my people would be harmonized upon calm reflection and the adoption of wise and judicious measures. But when I ascertained that Nittakachih and Moshulatubbee were truly assembling their warriors, I began to view the matter in its true and proper light. I knew those two chiefs too well to longer doubt the full interpretations of their designs as set forth in their actions; for they both were men who indulged not in meaningless parade, or delighted in empty display. Inevitable war—kindred against kindred and brother against brother—with all its horrors and irreparable consequences now seemed to stare me in the face, with no alternative but to speedily prepare to meet it; therefore Le Flore and myself, after due deliberation, resolved, if we must fight, to confine the fighting as much as possible within Moshulatubbee's and Nittakachih's own districts. We at once took up our line of march south toward Demopolis which was in the district of Moshulatubbee, and where they had assembled their warriors.

At the termination of our second day's march, we ascertained through our scouts, that Moshulatubbee and Nittakachih were also advancing with their warriors to meet us. In vain I still sought for some pacific measures that might be advanced to stop further demonstrations of war. To send a flag of truce, requesting a conference with the two disaffected chiefs, would, I felt, prove unavailing, as it would be attributed to fear on the part of myself and Le-Flore, and but render them the more obstinate and unyielding. On the morning of the third day we were informed by our scouts that they were only a few miles distant, slowly but boldly advancing. In a few hours, marching, I looked ahead and dimly saw the outlines of the front warriors here and there visible among the trees, and then the whole army appeared in full view about half a mile distant, all in full war dress and armed complete, advancing slowly and in good order. Even up to this moment I had cherished the fond hope that matters would not be carried to the extreme; but now hope fled, and the speedy destruction of my people and country seemed inevitable. In vain I endeavored to think of some plan that might yet avail and prevent bloodshed. But now the time for futile reflection had passed, and stern determination claimed the hour.

Not a word had been spoken, nor a sound of defiance uttered by either of the still advancing parties; and thus in profound silence each continued to advance until not exceeding two hundred yards intervened, when Nittakachih gave the signal for his warriors to halt, which they instantly obeyed. LeFlore and myself instantly gave the same to our men, which was as quickly obeyed. For several minutes the armies stood and gazed upon each other in profound silence. To me what minutes of indescribable suspense! I speak not boastingly when I affirm that my own safety had not the weight of the sixteenth part of a poor scruple in my reflections. The terrible consequences that would follow the firing of a single gun absorbed my every thought; and how soon that might be done by some inconsiderate and reckless one, no one knew. I still clung to a feeble and lingering hope that the unfortunate affair might yet be amicably adjusted; but what step to take that could lead to that desirable and happy result, at that advanced stage of affairs, I was utterly at a loss.

At this juncture of alternate hope and despair my astonishment was unbounded when I saw Nittakachih leave his men where they were standing and alone advance toward us with slow and measured steps, looking with a calm and steady gaze upon us. Every eye was upon him in a moment, as with firm and dignified steps he continued to advance until he had reached a point half way between the now wondering, but still silent, warriors; then stopped and, slowly raising his arms, he gently folded them across his breast, in calm and dignified silence, looked with fearless eyes upon me, LeFlore, and our astonished men. There he stood in his shining war-dress, the personification of calm courage and heroic daring.

But what his motive in thus presenting himself—deliberate as it was strange—none could comprehend, or even advance a remote conjecture. Yet, all could read that whatever it might be, he meant it; for no one did him the injustice by even supposing that the situation was contrived for dramatic effect. In vain I sought for some token, some sign expressive of his wish. Like a statue he still stood, calm, silent and motionless. It was a bright October morning, clear, sunny and cool, with the bluest of blue skies overhead. In all directions, the forest foliage painted with autumnal hectic, were strewing the bier of the departing year.

Again I looked around for some one from whom I might receive even a conjecture as to the interpretation of the incomprehensible enigma that so mysteriously and unexpectedly had presented itself before us, but none ventured to break the stillness by a word.

I then resolved to go to him alone, be the consequences what they might. With emotions known only to myself, yet with a calm exterior, I started toward him with a slow but firm step, and had walked but a few paces when I observed Nittikachih's warriors silently, but steadily raising their rifles to their shoulders and bringing them to bear directly upon me; and at the same instant heard behind me the ominous click of the rifle-locks of my own men—the signification of which I well understood. With deadly aim Nittakachih's warriors held their rifles upon me, as I drew nearer and nearer to their adored chieftain, who still stood silent and motionless, but with his black, penetrating eyes upon me as if he would read the very thoughts of my heart;

yet without a visible sign of emotion, and utterly unheeding the thousand rifles that also rested upon him, with as many clear and resolute eyes glancing along their dark barrels. The silence was still profound. Not a word, not even the chirping of a bird or rustling of a leaf broke the fearful stillness. I well knew everything was suspended at this juncture upon a pivot which the slightest breath might turn the equally poised scale for the worst, and give a signal for several thousand rifles to begin their work of death, and Nittakachih and myself would be the first to fall riddled with bullets, and our position but made it doubly sure.

With a secret bracing of my nerves I continued to steadily advance, and when within a few paces of him I met his eyes fixed upon mine with that baffling expression, which, I must confess, caused me to feel an inward alarm. But I as quickly subdued my apprehensions, by thinking, with a certain haughty pride which I fear will never be eliminated from my nature, of the dangers I had already met and overcome in my brief but troubled life, and meeting his calm and steady gaze with a smile which I knew to contain a spice of audacity, stopped immediately before and near him, and calmly said, as I noticed the strife of expression between his eye and lip; the one hard, cold and unyielding; the other deprecating in its half smile and falsely gentle, as if the mind that controlled it was even then divided between its wish to subdue and the necessity it felt to win: "Nittakachih, it would be only folly for me to speak as if nothing had occurred to justify your present attitude. It would be doing your good sense and sound judgment but little honor; and putting myself, or rather, ourselves, for we, as chiefs, should be one in the matter of our country's interests, in a position which would make any after explanations exceedingly difficult. For explanations can be given, and in a word, for what has doubtless appeared to you as strange and unwarrantable on our part, explanations which I am sure you will cheerfully accept, as it is not natural for you to nurse suspicions contrary to your

own candid and noble nature." He replied that he was
satisfied with my proffered words of reconciliation, and, as
he spoke his voice assumed its confident tone. Then, looking with his dark and piercing eyes into mine, as if to read
the secret thoughts of my heart, he continued: "I feel that
I can and will again give you the title of friend. Will you
accept it from me, and with it my past confidence and
esteem?" I responded, "I will in behalf of the common
interests of our people"; and then extended my hand to him,
but in a steady mechanical way that I felt committed me to
nothing, for I was fully alive to the possible consequences
of my every act. He took it, though the slight unmistakable
pressure he returned seemed to show that he accepted it for
a true sign of restored friendship, if not of absolute surrender. "You have removed a great weight from my heart," he
again remarked. "Had you been one of the commonplace
type of men, you might have made this a serious matter
for us."

"What have I said and done," I replied, though not so
bitterly, or with as much irony as I might have done, had
that desire to understand the full motive of a condescension
I could but feel was unprecedented in his arrogant nature,
been less keen than it was, "to influence you to suppose that
I will not yet do so?" "Your glance and your honest hand
are your surety," he answered; then with a real smile,
though it was not the reassuring and attractive one he
doubtless meant it to be, we both turned our faces toward
our anxious and waiting warriors, and each gave the signal
of peace and friendship restored. Instantly every rifle was
lowered, and the two armies slowly marched in perfect
order to where we stood, and there shook hands. A council
was then and there convened; satisfactory explanations
made and accepted; peace and friendship restored, and a
terrific civil war averted. And then, as the party turned
their faces homeward, all fired off their guns as an acknowl-

edgment that not a particle of animosity lingered in the heart of a single one of either party, but that entire confidence and friendship was restored.

In more ancient times, when difficulties between two clans or parties had been settled they stacked their arms together, as an evidence that entire confidence, friendship and good will was restored; which ceremony was called "Tanapoh Aiyummih," signifying guns mixed.

Such was the narrative (in substance) related to Mr. Calvin Cushman by Colonel David Folsom sixty years ago, portraying a scene in actual life that stands unequaled in the annals of historic warfare; while also displaying a self-sacrificing and patriotic heroism (especially in Colonel David Folsom) that should put to shame and confusion of tongue those ignorant and senseless babblers who deny to the Indian race the possession of a single virtue.

Nittakachih moved west with his people; remained a few years, and then returned to the home of his nativity in Mississippi to attend to some unfinished business, and while there was taken sick and died; and thus secured for himelf the gratification of dying in his native land, and having his body laid away in peaceful rest among the graves of his ancestors—a privilege so much coveted by the North American Indian.

Had Nittakachih possessed the advantages of a thorough education, he would have placed his name high on the roll of fame among earth's illustrious great as a brave, patriot and honest statesman; yet, without any of those advantages whatever; few, if any, among the whites could equal him in point of true native eloquence, genuine patriotism, self-command, and moral courage, under any and all circumstances. It was my fortune to be personally acquainted with him, and never have I seen, nor do I ever exepct to see, a finer specimen of nature's true man, than was exhibited in Nittakachih. He left one son, who was known as Captain Jackson Nittakachih, and also one son-in-law named Tunapoh Humma, (Red Gum). He was chief at one time of the Kunsha-ache Iksa, which lived on the creek then called Lussah Hocheto, (Big Swamp), now known as Big Black. They both moved with their people to their present place of abode, and died soon after the death of their noble father and father-in-law.

Colonel David Folsom, the first chief of the Choctaws elected by ballot, was a good man in the full sense of that word. Continually filling offices of greater or less importance in his country, still he ever carried the traits of honesty, faithfulness, zeal and energy into every position. He was truly one of those characters that naturally come to the front in all matters, and possessed many of the characteristics of a leader of men. Of his worth as a citizen, public or private, and his Christian faith and life, his people know full well and justly appreciate.

He was elevated to the chieftaincy at a time when his country was agitated by many conflicting emotions; his people were just emerging from the state of nature to that of Christianity and civilization; and the fountains of the great deep of their hearts were being broken up by the new order of things that were being established among them in government and in morals; and in connection with this, the exchange of their homes and country for others remote in the distant and unknown west, by a process of coercion, fraud and tyranny unsurpassed in the annals of man, but justly aroused their fears to the highest pitch, and filled every heart with misgivings and the deepest gloom. I witnessed their indescribable agitation, and heard their wail of woe. Yet, amid the raging storm of conflicting emotions that everywhere prevailed, Colonel David Folsom stood preeminent; the prudent, wise and wholesome counsels he then gave upon all questions to the subordinate chiefs and his agitated people; his calm and noble bearing amid the all-pervading confusion; the firm and undaunted rebuke which his enlightened and enlarged philanthrophy administered to the wrong policy of the uninformed and incon-

siderate, were as oil upon the troubled waters and conspired
to make him the chief influence for good.

But in his home life Colonel Folsom's virtues shone in
all their unvarnished beauty. This was his chosen sphere;
here he delighted to receive and entertain the friends who
were privileged with his intimate acquaintance, official or
private, rich or poor, high or low; and for warmth of affection to his people, kindred and cherished friends; for singu-
lar unselfishness, he had few equals and no superiors anywhere. His sympathies were as prompt and as tender as a
child's, and it was natural and became habitual for his people to go to him when in trouble, to seek council and sympathy which they never sought in vain; nor did he wait to be
sought. He loved outward nature too as the source of conscious pleasurable emotions. He would say, "It rests me to
look upon its varied and lovely scenes, landscapes which
are really a means of education to the susceptible mind,
and which so often have been invested with the charms of
poetry and romance."

During a visit to the Choctaw Nation, in 1884, I unexpectedly came upon a cemetery in my devious wanderings
wherein I found the graves of many Choctaws. Conspicu-
ously among many monuments, stood that of Colonel David
Folsom, whom I had known from youth's early morn. Thus
reads the epitaph:

"To the memory of Colonel David Folsom, the first
Republican Chief of the Chahtah Nation, the promoter of
industry, education, religion, and morality; was born January 25, 1791, and departed this life, September 24, 1847,
aged 56 years and eight months.

"He being dead yet speaketh."

His son, then my companion, and old friend from early
youth, informed me that the above appropriate epitaph was
dictated by Rev. Cyrus Byington, the long known and faithful friend of Colonel David Folsom and his people.

In strolling o'er that silent and lonely habitation of the
dead, I found the graves of many of my old Choctaw and

Chickasaw friends of the long-ago. Close by that of Colonel David Folsom's was the grave of Joel H. Nail, a brother-in-law to Colonel Folsom, and grandfather of Joel H. Nail, now living in Caddo, Indian Territory. He was another true and noble specimen of a Choctaw Christian man. A beautiful marble monument also marked his place of rest, and the following told the curious and inquisitive passer-by who was the occupant:

"Sacred to the memory of J. H. Nail, of the Chahtah Nation, who died at his residence near Fort Towson, August 24, 1846, in the 52nd year of his age.

"Reader prepare to meet thy God."

The present Nail family of the Choctaws are the descendants of Henry Nail, a white man, who came among the Choctaws about the time Nathaniel Folsom, John Pitchlynn and Louis Le Flore came; and as they, so did he, marry among them, was adopted and thus became identified among that people. He rose to the position of chief and exerted, as did the other three above mentioned, a moral influence among that noble and appreciative people with whom he had cast his lot. He had four sons—Joel, Robert, Morris and Joseph. Joel Nail had seven daughters—Harriet, Delilah, Selina, Catherine, Isabelle, Melvina and Emma; and three sons—Jonathan (father of the present J. H. Nail), Adam and Edwin. Robert Nail had one son— the only chief—named Edwin, who was drowned in Blue River; and Jonathan had only one son, the present Joel H. Nail, as above stated, and who is a worthy scion of the old stock and still living; he is a quiet and good man; noble and good in his integrity of character; attractive in the benevolence of his life.

Near to this stood another emblem of frail mortality, which told of one who had lived and died, and upon whose smooth face I read love's tribute of affection. "Sacred to the memory of Major Pitman Colbert, who departed this life February 26, 1853, aged 56 years. He lived an exemplary life. Ever devoted to the welfare of his people (the Chicka-saws), and died respected by all who knew him."

Of Major Colbert may justly be said: He was emi-nently a Christian reformer. His sympathy for his people was intense. He was a true disciple in the temple of knowl-edge; ever devoting his time and labors to those useful pursuits, which alone adorn and embellish the mind, fitting it for the abode of truth. To the light of nature and reason he added the light of the Bible and Revelation; and prompt-ed by a higher and nobler motive, moved and instigated by a Divine impulse, he spent the morn, noon and evening of his life in trying to alleviate the sufferings of others; lived a life of pleasant toil, supporting and elevating his race wherever fallen, curbing the vices of the vicious, correct-ing the waywardness of the dissolute, sustaining the right and condemning the wrong.

But what visions of the long past awoke to memory as I stopped before a monument, whose beautiful symmetry of form had attracted me and read: "In memory of Louis Garland; died August 14, 1853, aged 33 years. Generous, upright and virtuous, he lived an example for all who seek the favor of the good."

More appropriate and truthful words never adorned the tombstone of man. We were fellow students during the years 1839-40-41 and 1842 at Marietta College, Ohio; and both professors and students who may now be living, could they read the epitaph that records Lewis Garland's place of rest, would attest to its truth without a dissenting voice; and I too, though years have intervened with their varied vicissitudes, would here offer some tribute to this my Choc-taw friend. I was born among his people and thus was early initiated into the "mysteries of the Indian character"; and my heart still goes out in fond affection to all those old Choctaw and Chickasaw friends of my youth; in whose honest hearts I have ever found a friendship that never betrayed and a constancy that never wearied.

Continuing my walk through the cemetery, I discovered a grave that had no marble token to tell of its silent occupant. Upon inquiring of my Choctaw companion, he informed me that it was the grave of his brother, Cornelius; another fellow-student of boyhood's merry time. We were chums for two years in college life, and there and then became sincere friends, linked to the recollections of life's early morn, ere sorrow's dark pall had fallen athwart our pathway; but hope with rosy finger still pointed to the flattering possibilities of the promising future. But alas! Consumption claimed him as its own, and he returned to his southern home but to fall into a premature grave. In college he was a diligent student, and stood high in his classes. The high elements of his noble nature were so fully developed that he commanded the respect and admiration of both professors and students. He was consistent in all things and his moral character was blameless.

As a sample of Colonel David Folsom's ability as a letter writer, I will insert a few of his letters written to Rev. Elias Cornelius and others, copied from the original without alteration; and when it is taken into consideration that he never went to school but six months, they may justly cause the blush of shame (if such a thing be within the line of a possibility) to appear upon the cheeks of thousands of white men, who have gone as many years, and yet cannot do half as well.

To Rev. Elias Cornelius:—

Choctaw Nation, Pigeon Roost, July 16, 1818.

My Dear Sir:—

Your letter dated Knoxville, June 2, has come duly to hand, safe this morning, which I am rejoice to learn that you and brother McKee and three other boys are all well and happy. I did learn from you and McKee, when you wrote from Cherokee Nation to me by Mr. Kingsbury, and did write you and direct the letter to City Washington, agreeable to your direction to me. Rev. Mr. Kingsbury was here few days ago from Yellobusher, and he requested that he wanted my brother Israel under his care, and that he was much in need for company in traveling about the nation and which his request was very certainly most pleasing talk to me and Israel. He is under Mr. Kingsbury's care and as he is very industrious boy I make no doubt he will be useful to Mr. K., by the first opportunity that K. may have he will send Israel on to you. My dear friend, I have no means to inform you at present in the regard to my nation as we have had no council since you left here. But I know and all I can say for my nation they are a people much in need for help and instruction, and we look up to the government of the U. S. for instruction, and which I do know the establishment of this school will be the means of the greatest good ever been done for this nation. Our hunting are done for these many years back and for wanting good Father and good Council that the general run of peoples at the Nation have still hunted for game and they have in many become in want. But I know that your wish is pure and love and good for this nation, and therefore I have been talking to my peoples and have advice them for the best during their intention to industrys and farming, and lay our hunting aside, and here is one point of great work is just come to hand before us which is the establishment of a school, and the Choctaws are appear to be well pleased. I thank you for the good and love you have, and what have already done for my nation. Not long since I have heard from Rev. and Mrs. Williams. They are all well. I have not seen them yet. I wish you happiness.

I am your true friend till death,

David Folsom.

N. B. You will excuse my bad writing, as I did inform you that I had only but six months schooling.

Chahtah Nation, Pigeon Roost, Nov. 3, 1818.

To Rev. Elias Cornelius:

My dear sir:—I have just returned from the Chahtah Treaty, and I inform you that Chahtah did not sell or exchange lands with the United States the Chahtah said that it is but two years ago when the Nation sold a large track of country to the United States and therefore they said that they had no more lands to sell, which they cannot think to sell the land which we are living on it and raising our children on it. And I inform you also that the nation a great of friendship to the United States Com. The Nation talk of in Council and mention that it was great benefit for us Chahtah to have school in our Nation, and appear to be well please and rejoiced to have such aids in our Nation. The chiefs wrote a letter to the president of the United States a most friendly talk and I must inform you in one part of the letter to the president, our chief said, Father we are most thankful for your kindly favor that you aided the Society School in our nation. The chiefs are I believe in notion of visiting the father, the president. Give my warm love to my brother McKee and Israel when you shall see them, and tell them we are all well.

I remain your most dutiful friend till death.

David Folsom.

Chahtah Nation, Pigeon Roost, July 6, 1822.

My Dear Friend Rev. Byington:

I was rejoiced to learn from Rev. Kingsbury good news from Elliott, and that health of family was much better. It is indeed good news to me to hear that Mr. Ward has brought the large boys under his Government once more. After all our fuss and talk and grumbling and dissatisfaction on the part of we Chahtahs, I hope good will result from it. I did feel sorry when I was there to witness some bad conduct of the scholars there. But I hope good may overrule for the best—this is my sincere wish. Some days since I was at Mayhew and staid there few days, and I am happy to say to you that family were well, and the scholars are doing well, and all in good health. The children go out to work cheerfully, and come in the school cheerfully, and mine their teacher cheerfully, and on the hole I think they improve most handsomely—and the missionary spirit at Mayhew I think it is good—they all appear to do what they can. We shall have a council 18th inst. at Mayhew—with the chiefs and warriors of this District. I shall want Mr. Kingsbury to give them a straight talk. I have no news to inform you at present that is worth your notice. Give me some news if you have any. Present my best wishes to the Mission family. I am—Dear Sir—your friend,

David Folsom.

Rev. C. Byington.

January 7, 1829.

My Dear Friend Rev. C. Byington:—

I am informed you have gone to Columbus, and I do not know it is best that you were there with the lame hand you had. I did not like the look of your hand other day. I think it would be well for you to be very careful hereafter and endeavor to get your hand well. As to our appoint at Aiikhuna (a school or place of learning), you need not feel any disappointment. I shall try to go over agreeable to promise, it was made to the people, if I should be permitted to go by the almighty hand. I shall try to go and see the people—if I only just go there and shake hands and see the people. Mr. Williams will be there, and he can preach to the people if it be necessary to do so. I trust, if I am not deceived, the Lord has done great things for my soul. Pray for me brother.

I am, dear sir, your friend,

Aiikhuna.   D. Folsom.

I have copied the above four letters of Colonel David Folsom from the original without any alteration whatever. Though there are defects, yet, when we consider the limited opportunity offered in six months' tuition—and only six months—and the writer beginning at the alphabet of a language foreign to his native tongue, and of which he comparatively knew nothing, are they not remarkable productions, especially in that of their orthography? And when we also take into consideration that Colonel David Folsom is but one of hundreds of Choctaws, as well as of other North American Indians all over the continent, as will be successfully established, do not the united voices of truth and justice proclaim the falsity of the assertion, "The Indian could never be educated from his savagery." Here I will introduce to the reader the Rev. Israel Folsom, a younger brother of the great and good Colonel David Folsom, either of whom to know was to love, yet true Choctaw Indians.

His conversion to the Christian religion was somewhat peculiar. After he had become the head of a family, he came in possession of some deistical books handed to him by some of that class of whites who would not only degrade the Indian upon earth but also damn his soul in eternity. For several years he carefully and diligently read the deistical works, to the gradual neglect of the religious books, especially the Bible, all of which, had been furnished him by those devoted missionaries, with their frequent prayers for God's blessing to accompany them. Those prayers of faith followed the Choctaw student from his home east of the Mississippi River to his new home in the west; when he still read his deistical books, and devoted much thought and calm reflection upon their teachings while engaged in the duties of his extensive farm and stock ranch. One beautiful spring morning, having ridden out upon the prairie to look after his cattle, and while reflecting upon what he had read the night before, which denied the existence of a First Great Cause, he asked himself: "Then whence came the green grass that now covers this vast prairie as with a carpet, that stretches away before me on every side? Whence came the innumerable flowers of variegated colors that so delight my eye? Whence came the cattle, the horses, the birds, and all other animals? Ah! Whence came I, myself? There must be a God. There is a God!" Then and there he sprang from his horse, fell upon his knees, and in earnest prayer sought light from Him, who hath said, "In the day that ye seek me with all thy heart, I will be found of thee," and arose a changed man. He at once turned his steps homeward, entered his house, and without speaking a word gathered every deistical and infidel book that had so long contaminated and polluted his house and led him astray, and in one pile threw them into the fire; then went out of the house, took his stand where he could see the top of the chimney, and, as the black smoke, made blacker by the consuming falsehoods of their infamous contents, ascended in dark rolls to the sky, shouted as he waved his hand to its final adieu, "Behold infidelity"! and from that moment gave his life to the ministry.

By precept and example, he endeavored to lead the minds of his people into the paths of virtue and truth. In his nature he was modest and retiring, but his social qualiies were of the highest order; and as husband, father, citizen, friend and preacher of the Gospel, he illustrated in his daily life all those noble attributes which make up and form the highest type of true manhood. Truly, so grand a specimen of the old school of Presbyterianism should not be lost from the view of succeeding generations.

One has spoken of him as "one of the saintliest men with whom he had ever been acquainted"; and all those who knew him will fully acquiesce in the truth of that statement. He was indeed a most sincere Christian; a man of great spirituality; in which there was nothing morbid or sentimental, nor yet bustling and obtrusive; but unaffected and genuine, and at the same time most active and efficient. Though not what the world would call a brilliant preacher, yet he possessed what many brilliant preachers lack—good, common sense; for extravagances or eccentricities never marred his own labors nor were the legitimate effects of his pulpit works cancelled by his errate life.

Rev. Israel Folsom always gave one tenth of his annual income to the church; and in his will, left one tenth of his property to the church to which he was attached. His native strength and force still seemed like the beautiful country in which he lived—once wild and rugged indeed, but now softened and humanized by years of culture. He died April 24, 1870, and was buried at Old Boggy Depot, Choctaw Nation, Indian Territory, aged 67 years, 11 months, and 22 days. Such was Rev. Israel Folsom, of whom it may be said: He was a remarkable illustration of the power of Christianity—a great mind, once entangled in the meshes of error, but broke away, grasped the truth and yielded not with his expiring breath.

I will here give the following account of the Choctaw people, from the pen of their great and good countryman, Rev. Israel Folsom, which I have copied from the original without alteration whatever, furnished me by his daughter Czarena, now Mrs. Rabb, and never before published:

"The history of the aborigines of America has been one of the most prominent and interesting subjects of inquiry and research of the present age. The manners, habits, customs and peculiarities of the different Indian tribes, have, for many years, formed a theme of deep interest and praiseworthy investigation to the philanthropic and scientific world. While their traditions are worthy of being preserved, on account of their similarity to some of the wondrous and attractive events recorded in the Old Testament, various and unsatisfactory are the conjectures set forth regarding their parent root or origin. Some, with a good show of plausibility, have attempted to prove that they are of Jewish extraction and constitute a remnant of the lost ten tribes of Israel; others as earnestly agree, that they are but a branch or off-shoot from the Tartar, Sclavonic or Tyrus race; while, on the other hand, a class of speculative historians make bold to assert that they are not of Asiatic lineage, and do not, therefore, owe in common with mankind their descent from Adam. The first view is supported by the Indians themselves, but gives little strength or additional force to the argument. Whatever value, or otherwise, may be attached to one or all of these theories, which to a large extent they only are, one thing is clear and beyond contradiction, that the white people in general have, comparatively speaking, but a very imperfect knowledge of the Indian race.

"During the earlier period of the history of America, and shortly after its discovery, the monarchs of Europe, fired with the lust of conquest and spoil, attempted, but in vain, to subjugate the Indians and rivet the shackles of slavery upon them. They however, carried this purpose so far into execution, as cruelly to tear them away from their peaceful homes and endeared families, and transported them by thousands into various parts of the world. These unjust proceedings, instead of quenching the indomitable love of liberty, which so strongly and brightly burned in their breasts, served only to arouse the full power of resistance against their oppressors, which ultimately had the effect of freeing them from such bondage.

'They may bury the steel in the Indian's breast;
They may lay him low with his sires to rest,
His scattered race from their heritage push,
But his dauntless spirit they cannot break.'

"From that period up to the present time, the Indians have been and are still receiving everything but justice. In fact ever since the Christian world gained a foot-hold upon the American continent and erected the cross on its shores they have had no rest, but have been defrauded, trodden down, oppressed, scattered, and weakened. Their condition has been one of constant suffering and injustice. Avarice, the demon of civilized man, has worked heavily upon them, the result of which is, that only a sad and melancholy history can be written in regard to their past and present conditions. Yet a people possessed of such rare and remarkable traits, should not be permitted to pass away without some notice and record of their history.

"But how true, when nature is wounded through all her dearest ties, she must and will turn on the hand that stabs and endeavor to wrest the poniard from the grasp that aims at the life, pulse of her breast! And this she will do in obedience to that immutable law, which blends the instinct of self-preservation with every atom of human existence. And for this, in less felicitous times, when oppression and war succeeded alternately to each other, was the name Indian blended with the epithet 'cruel,' therefore, when they (the whites) talk or write about the Indians' wild, savage, and irreclaimable nature, they speak not nor write as they know or feel, but as they hear, by which and through which they have been educated to regard the Indian race as beings forming a lower link than humanity in the chain of nature, and finding only a place for them in the ranks of ferocious beasts of prey; but this, with other innumerable errors of both excusable ignorance, but in most cases, that of inexcusable ignorance and great want of principle, is shamefully unjust; since the Indians' cruelty to the White Race as a whole, has not been greater than that practiced upon them by the White Race, proving that they possess as humane dispositions as any nation of people under the same circumstances and in the same state of moral and intellectual culture.

"As comprising an important chapter of this great subject, I will now proceed to give a brief narrative of the Choctaw tribe of red people—their traditions, government, religious belief, customs and manners, anterior to the introduction of the Gospel among them. To guard against any misconception, however, I deem it proper to state that their traditions and history are so much commingled, it is difficult to separate them without destroying, in a great measure, the interest of the subject, and I have, therefore, to some extent, interwoven them.

Name and Migration from the West.—The Prophet Warrior, and the Enchanted Pole.—"The name Choctaw, or Chahtah, is derived from a prophet warrior who flourished at a time too remote for fixing any date, as it is only handed down by tradition from one generation to another.

"Headed by him, tradition informs us, the people in one grand division migrated to the East from a country far toward the setting sun, following the Cherokees and Muscogees, who had moved on, four years previous, in search of a suitable spot for a permanent location. He is said to have been possessed of all the characteristics essential to the carrying out of such an enterprise to a successful termination. His benevolence and many other virtues are still cherished and held in sacred remembrance by his people. The country whence they migrated, or the causes which induced them to seek another place of habitation, is wrapt in mysterious oblivion, as their tradition begins abruptly with the epoch of migration. In moving from place to place, Chahtah is said to have carried a high staff or pole which, on encamping, was immediately placed in front of his wigwam, where it remained until they broke up encampment. His wigwam is represented to have been placed in the van of all the tribe. When the pole inclined forward—a power which it was believed to possess—the people prepared to march. This is somewhat analogous to the cloud by day and pillar of fire by night, by which the Lord, through His beloved servant, guided the children of Israel from Egypt. After many years of wanderings during which they, in common with those who have ever engaged in similar enterprises, suffered many trials and privations, they at length arrived at a certain place, where the staff stood still and, instead of bending forward, inclined backward, which was regarded as a sign they were at their journey's end. To this place where the staff stood still, Chahtah gave the name of Nun-nih Wai-ya. The exact period of the termination of their wanderings is unknown. So soon as they got in some degree settled, Chahtah called the warriors together for the purpose of organizing a code of laws for their government. At this place of rest, Nunnih Waiya, they built strong fortifications in order to protect themselves from any foe who might conceive hostile intentions against them. Whether or not they were ever assailed is unknown. The remains of the fortress, however, is still to be seen in Mississippi. A long time did not elapse before their newly acquired territory was found to be too limited to hold their rapidly increasing numbers, and they were in consequence compelled to spread themselves over the adjacent country, and form themselves in villages. It is a well authenticated fact that from this out-pouring or scattering, sprung the Indians called Shukchi Hummas and Yazoos.

Domestic Government.—"In the domestic government the oldest brother or uncle was the head; the parents being required merely to assist in the exercise of this duty by their advice and example. This was similar in a great degree to the Patriarchal government in vogue among the Jews.

Tribal Government.—"The tribal or national government was vested in the royal family. Their criminal code was simple in the extreme—life for life. For minor offenses they inflicted punishments or imposed fines suited to the nature of the case. They were under the government of custom or common law of the Nation. All their matters of dispute or difficulty were settled in open council. They had no such officers as constables or sheriffs, but the chief had power at any time to order out any number of warriors to bring offenders to justice. The chief's office was one merely of supremacy or leadership, and consequently there was no pay attached to it as at present.

Idols — Spirits — Sacred Fires. — "They never worshiped idols, or any works of their own hands, as other savage nations. They believed in the existence of a Great Spirit, and that He possessed super-natural power, and was omnipresent, but they did not deem that He expected or required any form of worship of them. They had no idea of God as taught by revealed religion—no conception of His manifold mercies, or the atonement made for sin. All they felt was a dread of His attributes and character, made manifest to them by the phenomena of the heavens. But in common with the believers of the Scriptures, they held the doctrine of future rewards and punishments. They differed from them, however, as to the location of heaven and their views of happiness and misery. Heaven, or the happy hunting grounds, in their imagination, was similar to the Elysian fields of the heathen mythology. There the spirit of those who had been virtuous, honest and truthful, while on earth, enjoyed, in common with youthful angels, all manner of games and voluptuous pleasures, with no care, no sorrow, nothing but one eternal round of enjoyment. They believed that angels or spirits seldom visited the earth, and cared but very little about doing so, as being supplied in heaven with everything suitable to their wants, nothing was required from the earth. According to their notion, heaven was located in the southwestern horizon, and spirits, instead of ascending, according to the Christian idea, sped their last journey in a line directly above the surface of the earth in the direction of the southwest horizon. Previous to a spirit's admission into the happy hunting ground, it was examined by the attendant angel at the gate, who consigned it to heaven or hell according to its deeds on earth. Their hell, or place of punishment, as they termed it, was the reverse of the happy hunting ground—a land full of briers, thorns, and every description of prickly plants, which could inflict deep cuts, causing intense pain from which there was no escape; onward they must go—no healing oil for their wounds—nothing but an eternity of pain—no games—no voluptuous pleasures—nothing save an illimitable land of blasted foliage.

"They also believed in the existence of a devil, whom they designated Na-lusa-chi-to, a great black being, or soul eater, who found full occupation in terrifying and doing all manner of harm to people. He accords well with the one described in the Scriptures; 'who goeth about like a roaring lion seeking whom he may devour.' Previous to a spirit winging its flight to the happy hunting ground, or the land of briers and blasted foliage, it was supposed to hover around the place where its tabernacle lay for several days—four at least. They believed that the happy hunting ground was at a distance of many days' journey. When a person died, provision was prepared for the journey under the supposition that the departed spirit still possessed hunger. Upon the death of a man, his dog was killed, that its spirit might accompany that of its master. Ponies, after they were introduced, were also killed, that the spirit might ride. They believed that all animals had spirits. During four days a fire was kept kindled a few steps in front of the wigwam of the deceased, whether the weather was cold or hot. They imagined, that if the spirit found no fire kindled in that manner for his benefit, it would become exceedingly distressed and angry, especially when the night was cold, dark and stormy. A bereaved mother, on the loss of her child, would kindle up a fire and sit by it all night. The wife on the loss of a husband performed the same vigil. In either case a rest in sleep was denied. For six months or more, in case of the death of a chief, the sorrowing and mourning relations indicated their grief in many ways. The men, in the early part of their time of mourning, remained silent and subdued, ate very sparingly, and abstained from all kinds of amusements, and from decking themselves out in their usual manner; the women did the same, with this difference, that they remained at home prostrated with grief—their hair streaming over their shoulders, unoiled and undressed, being seated on skins close to the place of burial or sacred fire. They not unfrequently broke the silence of sadness by heart piercing exclamations expressive of their grief. For a long time they would continue to visit the grave regularly morning and evening to mourn and weep.

Mode of Burial—Bone-Pickers.—Origin of the Mississippi Mounds.—"The mode of burial practiced by the Choctaws consisted in placing the corpse five or six feet from the ground upon a platform of rough timber made for that purpose, covered with a rough kind of cloth of their own making, or skins of wild animals and bark of trees. After remaining in that condition until the flesh had very nearly or altogether decayed, the bones were then taken down by the bone-pickers (person appointed for that duty) and carefully put in wooden boxes made for that purpose, which were placed in a house built and set apart for them. These were called bone-houses; whenever they became full, the bones were all taken out and carefully arranged to a considerable height somewhat in the form of a pyramid or cone, and a layer of earth put over them. This custom, which prevailed among many different tribes, is, no doubt, the origin of the Indian mounds, as they are generally called, which are found in various parts of the country, particularly in the States of Mississippi and Alabama, formerly the home of the Choctaws. When the custom of placing the dead upon platforms was abandoned, which met with strong opposition, they buried their dead in a sitting position in the grave; around the grave they set half a dozen red poles about eight feet high, and one about fifteen feet high, at the top of which a white flag was fastened. The occupation of the bone-pickers having been abolished, it then became their business to make and set up red poles around the graves, and afterwards to remove them at the expiration of the time of mourning, and hence they were called pole-pullers. They were respected by the people, and for less labor being imposed upon them, they were pleased with the change in the burial of the dead. At the pole-pullings, which as stated, was at the expiration of the time of mourning, a vast collection of people would assemble to join in a general mourning. After much food had been consumed they would disperse to their respective homes, and the mourning relations would oil their hair and dress up as usual.

Tradition of the Flood.—"The tradition, as related by wise men of the Nation, about the flood, is as follows: A long continued night came upon the land, which created no

small degree of fear and uneasiness among the people.
Their fears were increased at seeing the terrible buffaloes,
and the fleet deer making their appearance, and after them
the bears and panthers, wolves, and others approaching
their habitations; suspicious at first of their intentions, they
thought of placing themselves beyond the reach of the
more dangerous animals, but instead of exhibiting any
disposition of ferocity, they seemed rather to claim protection at their hands. This presented an opportunity of having
a jubilee of fasting, and they therefore indulged themselves
to the fullest bent of their propensity and inclinations by an
indiscriminate massacre of the animals. Having thus feasted for some time, they at last saw daylight appearing. But
what surprised them much, was, they saw it coming from
the north. They were at a loss what to think of it. They,
however, supposed that the sun must have missed his path,
and was coming up from another direction, which caused
the unusual long night, or perhaps he had purposely
changed his course, to rise hereafter in the north instead of
the east. While such conjectures were making, some fast
runners arrived as messengers coming from the direction of
the supposed daylight, and announced to them that the
light which they saw was not the daylight, but that it was
a flood slowly approaching, drowning and destroying everything. Upon this report the people fled to the mountains,
and began to construct rafts of sassafras wood, binding
them together with vines, believing this expedient would
save them from a watery grave. But alas, delusive hope!
for the bears were swimming around in countless numbers,
being very fond of vine twigs gnawed them through, thereby setting loose the materials of the raft, and bringing the
people under dark waters. Their cries, wailing and agony,
were unheard and unseen. But there was one man who
prepared and launched a strong peni or boat, into which he
placed his family and provisions and thus floated upon the
deep waters. For days the Penikbi (boat builder) strained

his eyes looking all around for the purpose of discovering the existence of some animal life, and a place at which to anchor his vessel.

"Nothing met his sight save the cheerless waste of waters. The hawks, eagles and other birds of the same class, had all, when they found that the tops of the mountains could not render them a lighting place from the flood, flown to the sky and clung on to it with their talons, and remained until the flood abated, when they returned to their old haunts and resumed their natural propensities and habits. An indication of the disappearing of the flood thus manifested itself. A crow made its appearance and so much delighted to see the boat, that it flew around and around it. The Penikbi, overjoyed beyond measure, addressed the sable bird, wishing to elicit some information from it as to whereabouts, and whether or not the flood was subsiding any, but it heeded him not, seeming to be determined to consult its own safety before that of any one else; but scarcely had the crow winged away from the peni before a dove was described flying towards it and on reaching it, the Penikbi with joy perceived a leaf in its bill. It flew several times around but did not alight; after doing so took its course slowly flying toward the west, but seemingly anxious that Penikbi would steer in the direction it flew, which he did faithfully following the course. In this way many a weary mile was traveled, before seeing a place to land. At length a mountain became visible, and never did a benighted mariner hail the sight of land as Penikbi did, when its summit became visible. When he had safely landed, the dove flew away to return no more. Though this diluvial story is in some respects absurd, still, the intelligible portions of it coincide with those evidences which are embalmed in the convictions and understanding of the Christian world, in the authenticity of the inspired Word. It is strange that the Choctaws should have been in possession of those particulars long before the white man spread before them the pages of life."

Ancient Choctaw tradition affirms that a drouth followed by a famine in corn, peas, beans, etc., prevailed throughout their country far back in the days of their forefathers, which continued over three years; that all the tributaries of the Tanapoh Ikbi (Gun Maker), now known as the Tombigbee River, together with all the lakes and ponds, were completely dried up; that the river ceased to run, the water standing only in holes here and there, that all the larger game left the country, going west; that the buffalo, then inhabiting their country, never returned. Does this tradition point back to those remote ages in which the Prophet of God and king Ahab figured? This traditional drouth of the Choctaws continued over three years, that of the Prophet three and a half years. Did it extend to the western continent, or did the tradition refer back prior to their ancestors' migration from the eastern to the western continent, the Tanapoh Ikbi and the buffalo being additions of a future generation?

Iksa:—"The Choctaws were divided into various clans called Iksa, established and regulated upon principles of unity, fidelity and charity. They held this to be a necessary and important custom to be strictly kept and inviolably observed by them at all times and under all circumstances, and never to be forgotten. If one should be found in a strange place far from home, and should be placed in a situation to need assistance, all he had to do was to give the necessary intimation of his membership of one of those Iksas, and upon the mention of the name of that clan he would never fail to meet one or more, who would immediately extend to him the hand of friendship. Should he be sick, in want or in distress, relief would be immediately administered. The marriage of persons belonging to the same Iksa was forbidden by the common law of the tribe. The brotherly love, so strongly inculcated and highly recommended in the Inspired Volume, was to a great extent practiced under this sort of arrangement. It was considered that the Nation could not exist without the Iksa. One Iksa performed these last offices to any of its own Iksa. Each had their bone-pickers—old men being usually chosen for that purpose and were held in high esteem on account of their age and office.

Doctors:—"I believe it is an acknowledged fact, there is no nation in existenc, or has ever existed, but has had doctors. This shows the importance of the profession. The Choctaws also were not without them. But perhaps with the advantage over all others, of having as many of the female as of the male sex, who were quite as successful in their practice as the latter. The doctors made use of herbs and roots in various forms, applied and given in different modes—for emetics, cathartics, sweats, wounds and sores; they also made use of cold baths, scarification, cupping and blistered by means of burning punk, and practiced suction to draw out pain; some used enchantment, while others practiced by magic, pretending to have learned the art of healing. Mormon-like, by special revelation, communicated to them in some retired and unfrequented forest. It was in this way, also, it was said, that the war-prophets were raised up to lead the people to battle. At a high price and much expense the doctors of both sexes learned the mode and manner of the use of herbs and roots. It is a fact worthy of remark, that even now many of them are in possession of some useful and important means of cure. They have, among other things, an effectual remedy for the bite of the rattle-snake, or of any other venomous reptile, the bite of which they consider very easy of cure.

Mesmerism.—"Mesmerism was known among them, though they regarded it with wonder and dread, and it was looked upon as injurious and hurtful in its results; while those who practiced this curious art had often to pay very dearly for it, for they were frequently put to death. Ventriloquism has also been found among them, and used solely for vain, selfish and evil designs, but to the great danger of life of the person practicing it, for the Choctaws believe that whatever appears supernatural, is suspicious and likely at any time to be turned to evil purposes.

Eclipses.—Black Squirrels Eating up the Sun.—"Before correctly understanding the true causes of the eclipses of the sun, all heathen nations have had their superstitious belief in regard to them. It was so with the Choctaws. Their notions were strange indeed. When the sun began to get less in his brightness, and grow dark and obscure, they believed that some ethereal black squirrels of large size, driven by hunger, had commenced eating him and were going to devour him. With this belief they thought it was their duty to make every exertion they could to save the great luminary of day from being consumed by them. Therefore every person, both men, women and children, who could make a noise, were called upon to join in the effort to drive the squirrels away. To do this they would begin in the same manner as persons generally do in trying to start a squirrel off from a tree. Some would throw sticks towards the declining sun, whooping and yelling, at the same time shooting arrows toward the supposed black squirrels.

Dances.—"They had various kinds of dances as well as other people, many of which were, however, insignificant and do not deserve a notice here; but there were others which were considered important and national, such as the ball-play dance, the war-dance, eagle-dance, and scalp-dance, all of which seem to have been the result of rude and savage ideas. The training of their young men consisted principally in three things; viz.: War, hunting, and ball-playing. The last was a national play with ball-sticks, in which they all took much pride. In that for war, the young men were required to pass through many hard exercises of the body in order to inure them to hardships and suffering. They were required to receive inflictions of tortures on their naked bodies, once a year, and also to plunge into deep water and dive four times in about one minute, during one of the most cold and frosty mornings. Lectures on the subject of bravery and sincerity, truth and justice towards their friends, were often given them by some of the bravest of their head-men. In fact, no other person was allowed to address the young, or the people at any time, but those only whose bravery had been known and acknowledged among them. They were also carefully drilled in the use of the bow, with which they were expert and perfect. They would hardly ever miss a deer or turkey at the distance of fifty yards.

"The girls were trained up to perform various kinds of domestic employments as well as to work in the field which was but little at that time. They took no small degree of pride in the latter, viewing it as a proper sphere for their exertions. The women would ridicule and laugh at the men who would dare to undertake that kind of labor, which was considered as properly belonging to the women. Their maxim was—men for war and hunting; while home is the place for women, and theirs the duty to work.

Ancient Choctaw Courtship:—"When the young Choctaw beau went the first time to see his 'Fair One,' after having resolved upon matrimony, he tested his own standing in the estimation of his anticipated bride by indifferently walking into the room where she is seated with the rest of the famly, and, during the general conversation, he sought and soon found an opportunity to shoot, slyly and unobserved, a little stick or small pebble at her. She soon ascertained the source whence they came, and fully comprehended the signification of those little messengers of love. If approved, she returned them as slyly and silently as they came. If not, she suddenly sprang from her seat, turned a frowning face of disapproval upon him and silently left the room. That ended the matter, though not a word had been spoken between them. But when the little tell-tales skipped back to him from her fingers, followed by a pair of black eyes peeping out from under their long silken eye-lashes, he joyfully comprehended the import and, in a few minutes, arose, as he started toward the door, he repeated his informal 'Ea li' (I go), upon which a response of assent was given by the father or mother in the equally informal 'Omih' (very well).

"He returned in two or three days, however, with a few presents for the parents, and to secure their approval. Which being obtained, a day was appointed for the marriage— a feast prepared and friends invited. When all had assembled, the groom was placed in one room and the bride in another and the doors closed. A distance of two or three hundred yards was then measured off, and at the farther end a little pole, neat and straight was set up. Then, at a given signal, the door of the bride's room was thrown open, and at once she springs out and starts for the pole with the lightness and swiftness of an antelope. As soon as she has gotten a few rods the start, enough for her to keep him from overtaking her if she was so inclined, the door of his room was thrown open, and away he runs with seemingly superhuman speed, much to the amusement of the spectators. Often, as if to try the sincerity of his affection, she did not let him overtake her until within a few feet of the pole; and sometimes, when she had changed her mind in regard to marrying him, she did not let him overtake her, which was public acknowledgment of the fact, and the groom made the race but to be grievously disappointed—but such a result seldom happened. As soon as he caught her, after an exchange of a word or two, he gently led her back by the hand, and were met about half way by the lady friends of the bride, who took her from the hands of the groom yielding to their demands with seeming reluctance, and led her back into the yard to a place in front of the house previously prepared for her, and seated her upon a blanket spread upon the ground. A circle of women immediately formed around her, each holding in their hands the various kinds of presents they intended to bestow upon her as a bridal gift. Then one after another in short intervals began to cast her presents on the head of the seated bride, at which moment a first-class grab-game was introduced. For the moment a present fell upon her waiting head it was snatched therefrom by some one of the party—a dozen or more making a grab for it at the same instant—regardless of the suffering bride, who was often pulled hither and thither by the snatchers' eager fingers becoming entangled in her long, black ringlets. When the presents had all been thus disposed of, the bride not receiving a single article, the twain were pronounced one—man and wife; then the feast was served, after which all returned to their respective homes with merry and happy hearts."

As the land was free to all, the happy groom, a few days after his nuptials, erected with the assistance of his friends, a neat little cabin in some picturesque grove by the side of some bubbling spring or on the banks of some rippling brook. A small iron kettle in which to boil their venison, and a wooden bowl in which to put it when cooked, were sufficient culinary utensils for the young house-keepers. They needed no mahogany tables or carved chairs, for, they sat, as the Orientals, upon the ground. The bowl with its contents was placed in the center of the cabin and the husband and wife sat around it, and with the wooden or horn spoon, helped themselves one after the other. If they had guests the same rule of etiquette was observed—each one being free to make a dip with the spoon into the contents of the bowl, thence to the mouth, in regular turn.

Ta-ful-a, (Tomfuller), was their favorite and hence standing dish, and is to this day. It consists of corn, pounded in a wooden mortar with a wooden pestle to take off the husks, then thoroughly boiled; sometimes peas or beans are mixed and cooked with it, then it is called Tafula tabi ibu-lhto.

Then, again, hickory or walnut kernels or meats are mixed and cooked with it; it is then called Tafula oksak nip▪ibulhto; if walnut kernels, then it is called Tafula ok-sakhahe (walnut) nipi ibulhto.

They used a very pleasant beverage of acidulated fo-i (honey) and o-ka, (water); also they made a very palatable jelly from the pounded roots of the China brier, strained through baskets, and mixing dried farina with honey. They pounded hickory and walnuts together, and having passed them through boiling water, and then through strainers of fine basket work, it produced an inspissated liquor, the color and consistency of cream, and richer and of finer flavor.

Laws—Of the Choctaws regulating the marriage of white men to the Choctaw women:

Whereas, the Choctaw Nation is being filled up with white persons of worthless character by so-called marriages to the great injury of the Choctaw people.

Section 1st.—Be it enacted by the General Council of the Choctaw Nation assembled: That the peace and prosperity of the Choctaw people require that any white man or citizen of the United States, or of any foreign government, desiring to marry a Choctaw woman, citizen of the Choctaw Nation shall be and is hereby required to obtain a license for the same, from any of the Circuit Clerks or Judges of a Court of Record, and make oath, or satisfactory showing to such Clerk or Judge, that he has not a surviving wife from whom he has not been lawfully divorced, and unless such information be freely furnished to the satisfaction of the Clerk or Judge no license shall issue.

Section 2nd.—Be it further enacted: That every white man or person applying for a license as provided in preceding section of this act, shall before obtaining the same, be required to present to the said Clerk or Judge a certificate of good moral character, signed by at least ten respectable Choctaw citizens by blood, who shall have been acquainted with him at least twelve months immediately preceding the signing of such certificate.

3rd. Be it further enacted, before any license as herein provided shall be issued; the person applying shall be, and is hereby required to pay to the Clerk or Judge, the sum of twenty-five dollars, and be also required to take the following oath: I do solemnly swear that I will honor, defend and submit to the Constitution and Laws of the Choctaw Nation, and will neither claim nor seek from the United States Government, or from the Judicial Tribunals thereof any protection, privilege or redress incompatible with the same, as guaranteed to the Choctaw Nation by the treaty stipulations entered between them, so help me God.

Sec. 4th. Marriages contracted under the provisions of this act, shall be solemnized as provided by the laws of this Nation or otherwise null and void.

Sec. 5th. No marriages between a citizen of the United States, or any foreign Nation, and a female citizen of this Nation, entered into within the limits of this Nation, except hereinbefore authorized and provided, shall be legal, and every person who shall engage and assist in solemnizing such marriage, shall upon conviction before the Circuit Court of the District of this Nation, be fined fifty dollars, and it shall be the duty of the prosecuting attorney of the District in which said person resides to prosecute such person before the Circuit Court, and one-half of all fines arising under this act, shall be equally divided between the sheriff and prosecuting attorney.

Sec. 6th. Every person performing the marriage ceremony under the authority of a license provided for herein, shall be required to attach a certificate to the back of the license and return it to the person in whose behalf it was issued, who shall within thirty days therefrom place the same in the hands of the Circuit Clerk, whose duty it shall be to record the same, and return it to the owner.

Section 7th.—Be it further enacted: that should any man or woman, a citizen of the United States, or of any foreign country, become a citizen of the Choctaw Nation by inter-marriage and be left a widow or widower, shall continue to enjoy the rights of citizenship, unless he or she

shall marry a white man or white woman, a citizen of the
United States, or of any foreign government, as the case
may be, having no rights of Choctaw citizenship by blood;
in that case, all his or her rights acquired under the provision of this act shall cease.

Section 8th.—Every person who shall lawfully marry
under the provision of this act, and after abandon his
wife, shall forfeit every right of citizenship and shall be
considered intruders and removed from this Nation by
order of the principal Chief.

Section 9th.—Be it further enacted; that this act take
effect and be in force from and after its passage.

Proposed by Isham Walker.

Passed the House, November 6, 1875, J. White, speaker.

Passed the Senate, November 9, 1875, J. B. Moore,
President Senate.

Approved, November 9, 1875, Coleman Cole, P. C.,[26]
Choctaw Nation.

I hereby certify that the foregoing act in relation to
white men marrying an Indian woman, or white woman
marrying, etc., is a true and correct copy from the Original
Bill now on file in my office. In testimony whereof I have
hereunto set my hand and affixed the seal of the Choctaw
Nation.

This the 9th day of October, 1884.

Thompson McKinney,
National Secretary Choctaw Nation.

It no doubt would have been better for the Choctaws,
if they had strictly adhered to a resolution drawn up and
adopted in an ancient council of their tribe. A white man
at an early day, came into their country, and in the course
of time married a Choctaw girl and as a natural result, a

[26] The abbreviation stands for Principal Chief, the elected chief executive under the
Choctaw constitution. Elsewhere Cushman refers to this official as the "governor," a title
often used informally.

child was born. Soon after the arrival of the little stranger, (the first of its type among them), a council was called to consider the propriety of permitting white men to marry the women of the Choctaws. If it was permitted, they argued, the whites would become more numerous and eventually destroy their national characteristics. Therefore it was determined to stop all future marriages between the Choctaws and the White Race, and at once, ordered the white man to leave their country, and the child killed. A committee was appointed to carry the decision into execution, yet felt reluctant to kill the child. In the meantime, the mother, hearing of the resolution passed by the council, hid the child, and when the committee arrived they failed to find it, and willingly reported that the Great Spirit had taken it away. The mother kept it concealed for several weeks, and then secretly brought it back one night, and told her friends the next morning that the Great Spirit had returned during the night with her child and placed it by her side as she slept. The committee had previously decided, however, that if ever the child returned it might live; but if it never came back, they then would know that the Great Spirit had taken it. The boy was ever afterwards regarded as being under the special care of the Great Spirit, and became a chief of their Nation. The law was repealed; the father recalled and adopted as one of the tribe; and thus continued from that day to this—so affirms one of their ancient traditions, those Indian caskets filled with documents from the remote past, but which have long since passed into the region of accepted fables.

As proof that the North American Indian has love for country and home, I will here insert the following (never before published) taken from the original MS., written by Rev. Israel Folsom, just before his people were driven from their ancient possessions east of the Mississippi River to their present place of abode. Their lands had been promised to the Choctaws "as long as water should run and grass should grow."

THE INDIAN'S SONG.—LO! THE POOR INDIAN'S HOPE

"Land where brightest waters flow,
Land where loveliest forests grow
Where warriors drew the bow—
Native land farewell.

"He who made yon stream and tree,
Made the White, the Red man free,
Gave the Indian's home to be
'Mid the forest's wilds.

"Have the waters ceased to flow?
Have the forests ceased to grow?
Why do our brothers bid us go
From our native home?

"Here in infancy we played,
Here our happy wigwams made,
Here our fathers' bones are laid—
Must we leave them all?

"White men tell us of God on high.
So pure and bright in yonder sky—
Will not then His searching eye
See the Indians' wrong?"

The following is from the pen of a missionary who has long labored among the Choctaws and knew of what he spoke, and is sufficient testimony of the moral worth of him of whom he wrote:

"Choctaw Nation, April 9, 1885.

"Dear Brother Murrow[27]:—

"I write you a sad letter. Our old Brother Peter Folsom is dead. He was taken sick the first day of April, and has been growing worse ever since. He died today. I am writing by his beloved body. His spirit is in heaven. I can write no more. Please publish his death in the Champion,[28] that all friends may know.

'Your brother in Christ,

'Simon Handcock.'

[27] Joseph Samuel Murrow, a Baptist missionary in the Choctaw country.
[28] The Indian Champion was a newspaper publisher at Atoka under tribal auspices.

"Such was the sad news that reached me. I knew Bro. Folsom personally for twenty-seven years. Truly, 'a great man has fallen.' He was great—first and chiefest, because he was good. He was good in a moral and Christian sense. He was the first Choctaw who united with a Baptist church. This was in the year 1829. No charge of unfaithfulness to Christ has ever been made against him for over fifty years. He was an eloquent and active preacher of the Gospel. He established a number of churches, and developed and trained excellent pastors for them all. He might appropriately be termed 'the father of the Baptist mission work in the Choctaw Nation.' His piety was known and read of all men. He enjoyed the confidence and esteem of everybody—red, white and black. He walked with God, and is not, for God has taken him.

"Second.—He was 'great,' because he was useful as a citizen. Uncle Peter was a true Choctaw. He loved his people; he sought their interests. For many years he was a prominent man in the councils and national affairs. He was a safe and wise counselor; was never accused of betraying a party to any crookedness nor a member of any ring. He often represented his Nation at Washington City. While there he always maintained his moral, upright character. His religion and purity were not left at home.

"Third—he was 'great,' because he was charitable; 'But the greatest of these is charity,' or love. I think Uncle Peter loved everybody and everything that was good. His heart, his home, his purse were always open. Indeed, he was, perhaps, too charitable, for he was often imposed upon. The poor, the needy, the distressed, whether red, white or black, were never turned from him without help or comfort. For many years he enjoyed a competency of this world's goods, for he was a good manager. But the war broke him up, and he died in poverty. And yet he held an interest in a large and just claim against the United States

Government.[20] A claim recognized by Congress as just and ordered paid. Technicalities and red-tape delays hindered this payment. O what a shame! A rich and prosperous Government, with millions piled up in the treasury vault, owing money justly to a feeble people who need it, and who die in poverty and suffering for the want of it. But our brother needs it not now. He is free from poverty and injustice. He is rich and happy.

"J. L. [S.] Murrow."

Rev. Peter Folsom had two sons—Jerry and William. He had also three daughters—Susan Francis, Sophia and Kizia—all of the daughters are deceased.

Judge Loring Folsom, now the only surviving child of Colonel David Folsom and his first wife, Rhoda Nail, was long one of the leading men of the Choctaw Nation, but retired from the political arena several years ago, and has ever since been living in peace and quiet on his farm one and a half miles south of the town of Caddo, which took its name from a tribe of Indians whom the Choctaws defeated in battle on a group of high hills at the base of which Judge Loring Folsom now lives. This was the last battle in which the Choctaws were ever engaged as a Nation.

But no study is needed to ascertain that Judge Loring Folsom is also a genuine man. He filled the high and responsible position of Circuit Judge in his district for nearly twenty years, with credit and honor; though retired to private life, like his amiable father, he possesses a strong, clear mind, which he has cultivated with assiduous success, in consequence of which he has obtained a large amount of general information, by extensive reading, close observation and mature reflection. He is well posted in all the political

[20] This was the Net Proceeds, long famous in Choctaw annals. It grew out of the failure of the United States to fulfill the conditions of the Removal Treaty of 1830. It was finally referred for arbitration to the United States Senate, which in 1859 made an award of $2,981,247.30. Two years later the Government paid the Choctaws an installment of $250,000. But the Civil War began just at that time, and the payments stopped. It required litigation in the United States Court of Claims and an appeal to the Supreme Court before the remainder of the award was paid in 1888. During the years that it was pending the Choctaw government appointed delegates on contingent fees to push this claim. All of the original appointees and several of their successors died, like Peter Folsom, before payment was finally made.

affairs of his own nation, and also of the United States. His whole public life, in all the different and responsible fields in which he has been called by his people to labor, attest the purity and loftiness of its tone and purpose.

The Two Friends—The Red and the White.—During my travels in the Choctaw and Chickasaw Nations in 1884, I arrived one evening the 19th of June, at the quiet and unostentatious village of Doaksville—one among the first towns located in their present country when arriving from their ancient domains east of the Mississippi River, in the year 1832. It soon became a place of considerable trade; but ultimately proving to be very sickly it was nearly abandoned; and, at the time I visited it, was but a relic of the past—having only one small dry goods store and eight or ten resident houses. My object in visiting it was to find a Choctaw friend, one among the few then living and known as friend in the broadest sense of the word, in days of the long ago. On entering the little place I found many Choctaws there of both sexes and of all ages, the store full within and its immediate environments covered with diversified groups of men, women and children sitting and standing. I asked a Choctaw man standing near, if he knew Henry Folsom, and if he was in the town? Looking around a moment he pointed to a group of men a short distance away and said: "Yummun-o (that one) chish-no (you) pisah (see) pil-lah (yonder)." Dismounting I slowly walked towards the group with fixed eyes upon him who, I had just been told, was the object of my search. As I approached, all eyes of the little group turned upon me with inquisitive gaze; but, by my steady look at him alone, he seemed intutitively to know that he was the one I sought; acting accordingly, he quietly arose and advanced, with measured steps, to meet me looking straight into my face. As each approached the other, I recognized the features and knew 'twas he—the long lost friend of the far distant past—though now in the dignity and the sadness of his declining years; once more, after so many years, I looked upon him, whom of all others, aside from kindred ties, I loved as one among the best of earthly friends, and knew I was thus to him; and again felt the strange magnetic charm of his noble soul, so well known in days of yore and remembered still; for he had stood to me during all the years for all that was good. As we drew nearer, I saw also, that o'er him hung the shadows of fragile health, and thought 'tis but the old type of receding years.

We met, he paused a moment, surprised and uncertain. I looked upon his wrinkled brow as memories uncalled rushed upon me, and with extended hand, said: "Henry, friend of my youth, have you forgotten me?" Grasping my offered hand he replied: "Forgotten my earliest friend! Never! Wrong me not thus! Much of my life now seems a blank to me, and our reunion in this our decline of life gives me joy."

"Henry, how many joyous reminiscences as well as blighted hopes do thy name and face now arouse from their long sleep amid the scenes and events experienced together in the years now so far behind!"

"Cush, I rejoice for what I bestowed and regret what I took away. But are not what you call blighted hopes oft changed into fruits of good?"

"Even so, Henry. But how the forms and faces of loved ones, long since recorded among the dead, seem to rise up before me now as they have not done for years before."

"Yes, friend Cush, like sprigs cast upon the waters of a turbid stream they have been swept apart to meet on earth no more. But how is it that we've never met upon the highways of life, until in this my home of retirement and solitude?"

"Oft I've heard of you and thus kept upon your trail; have suffered with you and your race in the bitterness of your wrongs; have gloried in your patient endurance though distant away. Yet, you and your people seem to have made a noble use of your adversity."

"Ah, old friend of better days, I'm heart-sick of the eternal babbling of the white people about my race and its so-called worthlessness. It is your race (no reflections upon you) who blinded us but to deceive; yours, who was never satisfied until it had won our confidence only to violate it; yours, who curse us in right and in wrong; yours, who, if you see us at peace, imagine your lives are endangered and drive peace away; yours, who eternally rants at us as savages, yet little know and less care, that their mockery destroys more lives than it has ever saved."

I made no reply. How could I when feeling the truth of his words so deeply? Yet, with the thoughts of other days which my presence had called up so unexpectedly there seemed as suddenly to steal on him one fresh, soft and loving memory—that of our joyous boyhood's days. "Friend of my youth," in calm and gentle tones he said: "Pardon me! I did not wish to speak of those things, but they came up uncalled. In the bliss of my early life, in which you, old friend, was a large sharer, I looked upon the White Race with a wonder, in which mingled much of admiration, but more of veneration, when first presented to me in its representative, the noble self-sacrificing white missionary. But I learned, as I grew on to manhood, that there were few, very few white missionaries among the White Race. But because the White Race has destroyed my own, I would not stoop so low as to deny the power of its cultivated intellect. It is worthy of its fame; but not, that I acknowledge its superiority over that of the red, only in the cultivation. But regard me none the better, friend Cush, that I thus speak; for there are still times in hours of reflection, if a reckoning could come between my race and thine, in which I could resort to deadly weapons, I, with my race entire, would, though few and feeble, deal with the common destroyer hand to hand and blow for blow."

"But, friend Henry, has not the United States Government manifested much lenity towards your race?" Instantly he replied in an excited and high tone of voice. "Lenity! lenity! did you say: Alas! we are but the miserable wards of a tyrannical government."

There was the vibration of deep and intense feeling in his words as he thus continued: "Have not the misguiding influences of the whites hurled down to ruin the manhood of my race, by the mighty arm of superior numbers and implements of war; and then by the taunts, mockery, injury, hate and cruelty with which it has always been requited for nobly resisting aggression, oppression, outrage and extermination? Surely, it would be superhuman if it had not despaired, long since, of all hope or belief in truth and justice earthly or divine."

"I freely, but not without shame, confess, Henry, that all you have stated is but truth and only truth. Yet, I rejoice in also knowing that all the wrongs and sufferings of your race have not been able to wrench from it its better and nobler nature." An involuntary sigh escaped him, as he replied: "That is idle talk. My race is no better nor worse than any other race of mankind; nor are we demi-gods, to rise above all natural passions, and unmoved see evil triumph. Robbed us, you say? 'Tis true! yet, wisely kept to windward of your law, Might is Right, and took our heritance by forcing us to disinherit ourselves, and in lieu thereof bequeathed us a mess of pottage—a combination of whiskey, poverty, degradation, suffering, death—and called it—'Purchase.' "

Thus he swept on. I knew that he had striven to live only the life of a reader and thinker; and to leave behind him all weight of regret and the useless indulgence of vain hopes. But now looking backward to multiplied remembrances, the events of those days rose up and forced themselves upon him; and many things returned to his mind and knocked for admittance which, until now, had passed unheeded by; for he had long striven to hurl from memory the remembrance of his and his peoples wrongs and losses— the former beyond avenging, the latter beyond redemption.

But as they look back to all they have endured, all they have lost, could they but feel the fierce blood of retributive instinct rise and burn in them? They could not be human and feel otherwise.

"But how came you, friend Cush?"

I but pointed to my horse.

" 'Tis well! Go get him. Yonder's my home, amid those trees on the ridge, a quarter of a mile away. Let us seek its quiet."

We reached his house. He paused at the yard gate and said: "What think you, old friend of this my home?"

"It has the appearance of quietness, peacefulness, and happiness unalloyed, and surely must constitute much of pleasure to your declining years." It was indeed a quiet place bordering even on the romantic. But alas, how still! how lonely! We entered the open door. Reader, no gilded ornaments adorned this my Choctaw friend's humble home; no luxurious furnishings attracted the eye as you entered its portals, but a piano and violin, whose appearance bespoke the vicissitudes of many years yet his sweet solaces in hours of despondency and gloom; but here his house stands far back amid broad-armed oaks of centuries' growth. Yet, it still remains with its inmates (father and son and a few Negro servants, slaves of former days) in that same quiet spot with open doors to all.

Dr. Folsom lost his wife (daughter of the great and good Chickasaw John Colbert) and daughter many years ago; but true to his early love, he had remained a widower, living alone with his unmarried son.

I pointed to the full orbed moon that lighted up the eastern sky; then to the earth beneath and sky above blushing in wild and romantic beauty; then to the giant oaks that stood around in silent majesty. He then said in a low tone of voice: "I too love them all."

Reader, 'twas amid such a scene, and at that lovely hour, we sat, a group of three, on the moonlighted piazza in exchange of thoughts. To me his conversation was fascinating—full of grace and originality; brilliant I will not call it, for it was too mellow and restful to be thus character- ized.

> We spoke of many a vanished scene,
> Of what we once had thought and said,
> Of what had been, and might have been;
> And who was changed, and who was dead;
> And all that fills the hearts of friends,
> When first they feel with secret pain,
> Their lives thenceforth have separate ends,
> And can never be one again.

He also spoke of our youth's bright and promising morn— "God's days," as he expressed it. Then he spoke of the silent stealing on of man's days and years, the unseen and unfelt progress of his life from youth to age. Now he speaks of his people, of their vicissitudes and sorrows, their past history, their present condition, their future hopes and prospects; then he spoke of those heart memories that never die, those memories of his early home east of the Mississippi.

He talked too of art, literature and modern science, but in the quiet, unconscious way of one with whom knowledge flows as a full stream, and to whom knowledge and research (for he was a man of fine education and scientific attain- ments attained at school, and had also mingled freely dur- ing a long life with men of learning and culture) have taught that deep yet saddening truth—the limitation of human knowledge.

Picturesque too was he; and though nearly three score and fifteen years had been his earthly pilgrimage, yet he walked with elastic steps, and his form still was finely expressive of sinewy energy. But his regular, clear cut features and dark, piercing eyes still possessed a touch of melancholy in their depths, indicating his slightly mixed blood—the quick intelligence of the white man with the mingled sadness of the red, a sadness impressed as a herit- age by long years of oppression and wrong. I observed it also in the broken but still majestic warriors of his race, as I mingled among them—a buried yet still living resentment—a touch of defiance in the prevailing coldness of their mein, and a gleam of suspicion in the forced smile they still alike bestow on all strange white men.

A few short weeks after I had left him in perfect health, and turned to other duties, a letter from a Choctaw friend informed me of his death. Then and there I felt I had lost a friend of a lifetime—a friend of unconquerable integrity, true and faithful in all things; one whose heart was warm; intelligence strong, and whose devotion to his convictions and his obligations immovable. He lived beyond the allotted years of manhood's three score years and ten of the Psalmist, yet his busy brain and untiring hand wrought on, as if the vigor of a changeless youth.

I found a few others, here and there, in my travels over the country that were familiar figures in my boyhood and manhood days, and of whom I now may say: one look at the honest, good-humored, kind expression of their faces, and intuitively I yet loved them; and again, as oft before, I listened with delight to their ancient legends as their aged eyes brightened and sparkled at the most improbable passage of the narrative, but which I assumed not to doubt for fear of wounding their sensitive hearts; yet fascinating to me since truth and fancy were so intermingled that they rivaled the most extravagant fairy tale; and who, when their heroes' stars had set, turned their faces away from their ancient domains and here in their present homes carved out their own fortunes and handed down their honored names to posterity; but making me admire and love the red race more than ever because of the all-absorbing devotion that made them lose their own identity in that of their ancient great.

I will here present to the reader the memoirs of Nathaniel Folsom, the oldest of the three brothers who cast their lot in their morning of life among the Choctaws, and became the fathers of the Folsom House in the Choctaw Nation, as related by himself to the missionary, Rev. Cyrus Byington, June, 1823, and furnished me by his granddaughter Czarena Folsom, now Mrs. Rabb.

"I was born in North Carolina, Rowan County, May 17, 1756. My father was born in Massachusetts or Connecticut. My mother was born in New Jersey. My parents moved to Georgia, and there my father sent me to school about six months, during which time I learned to read and write. My mother taught me to read and spell at home. My father had a great desire to go to Mississippi to get money; they said money grew on bushes! We got off and came into the Choctaw Nation. The whole family came; we hired an Indian pilot who led us through the Nation to Pearl River, where we met three of our neighbors who were returning on account of sickness. This alarmed my father, who then determined to return to North Carolina. We came back into the Nation to Mr. Welch's, on Bok Tuklo (Two Creeks), the father of Mr. Nail. At this time I was about 19 years of age. At that place we parted. My father knocked me down. I arose and told him I would quit him, and did so by walking stranght off before his face. I do not remember what I did, but I always thought I was not in fault. My parents then moved into the Chickasaw Nation. I entered into partnership with Mr. Welch, and could do many things for him. In the Chickasaw Nation my brother Israel ran away from my father and came to me. He died at the age of 18 near where Mr. Juzon now lives. He was a good young man. My parents moved again to Fort St. Stephens. My brother Ebenezer visited me several times; he also sent me word to come and move him up into the Nation. I did so. He lived with me two years. Still he wanted to go to Mississippi, and wished I would raise a guard and send him there. I did so. Brother Edmond and two sisters went with him, and there my father died, on Cole's Creek, Mississippi. I really believe my mother was a pious woman. I traded a long time in the Nation, sometimes taking up three or four thousand dollars' worth of goods. I followed trading about thirty years. I lived principally at Bok Tuklo, fifteen miles this side of Juzon's (i. e. north). There was a great town of about four hundred Indians. The French King lived there. I learned the Choctaw language very slow. I was never perfect in the language. But after ten years I could do any business with the Choctaws. I bought a Bible of Robert Black about twelve years ago. This is the first Bible I ever owned. Before that I cared nothing about the Bible. I first heard a sermon by Mr. Bell at the Pigeon Roost about twelve years ago. I heard Lorenzo Dow pray once. About this time I began to have serious thoughts. Before this I had none. My mind was affected by what the missionaries said, who came from the North. Soon after my son Edmond died. One Sabbath I had a great conflict in me. I heard a sermon at the Pigeon Roost. My friends thought I felt bad because my son died. But it was something else. At that time there was a great change in me, which has remained ever since. This was in August, 1824. I joined the church at Mayhew, October, 1827, in my 72nd year. I have been the father of twenty-four children, fourteen of whom are living. I have lived to see six of them join the church, and three others sit on the anxious seat." According to an entry in the church record of Mountain Fork church, Nathaniel Folsom died October 9, 1833, in his 78th year.

Mr. Rufus Folsom, great grandson of Nathaniel Folsom, also kindly furnished me with a sketch of his great grandfather, which was nearly the same as the above—closing, however, with the following: "In September, 1830, the government of the United States made a treaty with the Choctaws for their lands east of the Mississippi River, and in October, 1832, our old great grandfather, afflicted with a palsy of the limbs for many years, started from the old Nation to come to this. He reached Mountain Fork, and there resided till the 9th of October, 1833, when he died, aged 77 years, four months, and twenty-seven days."

Signed,   Rufus Folsom,
                          Folsom Station, Indian Territory.

Nathaniel Folsom married Aiahnichih Ohoyoh (A woman to prefer above all others). She was a niece of Miko Puskush, (Infant Chief), who was the father of Moshula-tubhee. She descended from a long ancient line of chiefs, and belonged to the ancient Iksa Hattakiholihta, one of the two great families, the other being Tashapaokla (Part of a People); the laws of which forbid any person, male or female, to marry any one of the same Iksa. Though Mr. Nathaniel Folsom had acquired but a limited education, yet he was a moral man, and the good example he set before the people of his adoption and with whom he had cast his lot, won their respect, confidence and love, which he fully reciprocated to the day of his death. According to the ancient custom of the Choctaws, he had two wives at the same time. Aiahnichih Ohoyoh and her sister, whose name has not been preserved. Colonel David Folsom and Rev. Israel Folsom were sons of Aiahnichih Ohoyoh; and Captain Robert Folsom and Isaac Folsom were sons of her sister; with all the four I was personally acquainted. Robert and Isaac lived near Hebron, and were prominent members in the church at that mission. I will here insert an extract from a letter now before me, written by Mr. Nathaniel Folsom to Rev. Cyrus Byington on the death of his daughter and Lewis Folsom, his grandson, dated March, 1830, which truly manifests the humble and pious heart of the father and grandfather. I copy it from the original with no alteration whatever.

Dear friend Mr. Byington: I desire to let you know my felings at this present time. I feel satisfied it is the Lord's will. God give her to me and he has taken her away and his will is right and good in all things that befalls us wicked mortals here upon earth. I bless God for it all things that befalls me it is the holy will of the blessed God it is rite an good. I hope her soul at rest with the blessed Savior of the world I believe she has gone to Him for ever this turble thing of my grand son at Mayhew thar is no hope. O children take wareng by this I say turn O children and remem-

ber your Creator God on you all will die but wat wil becum
of your little souls if you repent on earth you all are lost ever
I say my dear childun quit your bad ways an turn to Lord
with all your heart and Christ wil reserve you for he loves
little children if you obey his commandments my dear
friend you no my felings about children that blessed Book
the Bible is the gide to larn us all to fit us to the worlds to
come the Lord bless you all."   N. Folsom.

The death of his grandson Lewis Folsom to which the
good old man so pathetically alludes, was indeed a sad
affair. I was acquainted with Lewis, his grandson, whose
father was Capt. Robert Folsom. Lewis and Joel Nail, his
cousin and son of Henry Nail, were driving four horses attached to the end of the two levers of a mill, two horses at
the end of each. The two boys got into a play in which they
soon began to throw corn cobs at each other, while riding
around on the levers and driving the horses. Unfortunately
Lewis jumped upon the big cog wheel and was instantly
killed.

I was personally acquainted with his father's entire
family. His youngest sister, Else, now Mrs. Perkins, is still
living. His father, at the time of the sad occurrence, was in
their present territory, being sent with others by their Nation, to look after the country preparatory to the exchange
which was afterwards made with the United States Government in 1830.

From an old M.S. left by Nathaniel Folsom in his own
hand writing, I here insert the following extracts obtained
through the kindness of his granddaughter Czarina Folsom,
now Mrs. Rabb, living in Atoka.

"The Choctaws were more numerous than now. Thirty
years ago it is probable there were nearly 30,000. Before I
came here the smallpox killed two-thirds of the people. The
measles also destroyed a great many. There was one town
entirely destroyed by the measles.

"They had axes and hoes, but not a plough in the Nation. I gave twenty-two dollars for the first plough I had;

twenty dollars for a bushel of salt; ten dollars for a common blanket. Goods were then brought from St. Augustine, Florida, on pack-horses. I gave once twenty dollars for a half bushel of salt in a time of war (the Revolution).

"The woman's dress was a petticoat that came just below the knees, and a head-gear; and in the winter a tight woolen jacket with bright buttons in front. They had an abundance of blankets by sewing the feathers of turkeys together. They had but few iron pots and kettles, the articles were dear.

"When anyone died a scaffold was made in the yard near the house, put high enough to be safe from the dogs. On the top of this the body was laid on its side; and then a blanket or bear skin was thrown over it; and there it remained until it perished. Then the bone-pickers came and picked the flesh off and put the bones in a box. The head was adorned and put away in a box, and then the boxes were put away in a bone-house—a house set apart to receive them, and placed at the edge of the town. At this time there was a large collection of people. The bone-pickers had some ceremonies, but I do not recollect them. Twice a year—fall and spring—the people assembled, and had a great gathering over the bones of the dead. The two families would meet. One day one family would cry; and on the next day the other would cry, and then the bones would be brought out in the boxes and buried. A little present was made to the bone-pickers.

"Ever since about the time of the Revolutionary War the Choctaws began to leave their towns and settle in the woods for the benefit of their stock. I was the first to settle on the Natchez trace at Pigeon Roost, about twenty-five years since. Still, at the time of the exodus of the Choctaws, in 1832, they had many large and populous towns and villages in their Nation which I personally knew.

"Kings.—Some inherited the office; others were appointed by the French and English. Amosholihubih is the old family (i. e., the old family of kings or chiefs). David's old uncle was of the royal family.

"The Indians spoke in a different style from what they do now. The doctors are great deceivers. One came to me and said he could cure me of my lameness (palsy in the limbs). I told him if he would cure me, I would give him a horse; if he did not cure me, I'd give him nothing. The doctor inquired where the lameness commenced. I told him, in the sole of my feet. He then examined them, got down, spit on them and sucked the place until a long time, as though he'd draw something out. After awhile he got up and then made a great effort to get something out of his mouth; at length he took out a small piece of deer skin, as appeared, and said he had drawn that out of my foot. I asked him where the hole was. He said: 'It never makes a hole.' I took the bit of leather and talked to him, and told him that doctors were the greatest liars in the world. 'You never pulled that out of my foot. You cut it off from some deer skin and put it in your mouth. Now stop telling such lies, or somebody will injure you.' He looked very much ashamed and walked off. Before the doctors begin to doctor, they sing a long song, whisper a prayer, and then commence.

"At that time there were several white men among the Choctaws, all of whom married Choctaw wives, and thus became identified with that people. The descendants of nearly all of whom are still among the Choctaws to this day.

"Hardy Perry," continued Nathaniel Folsom, "brought the first neat cattle into the Nation."

The old gentleman evidently refers to the eastern part of the Nation, where he lived; since it was well known that either about the same time or a short time before Perry's drove were first introduced into the eastern part of the Nation, and the waters of the Tombigbee River, Louis and Michael LeFlore and Louis Durant introduced a small

herd into the western part of the Nation, and located it on
the waters of the Yazoo River. But thus continues Mr.
Folsom.

"He bought them of the French at Mobile. Twenty-five
dollars for a cow and calf. This was soon after I came into
the country. Benj. James then bought one. I was the third
man. From these the stocks of cattle have sprung. There
was abundance of horses. There were many hogs in the
Nation when I first came. I have seen nearly thirty dogs at
an Indians house. They resembled the wolf.

"David Folsom went to school on Elk River, Tennessee.
Started off alone at sixteen years of age, at least 250 miles
from home, and was there six months. That was the end of
his schooling there. I employed another man a month to
teach him figures. That was seven months' education.

"About this time (he seemed to forget to mention dates)
he was married to Rhoda Nail. He took her out of the
Indian Territory to a magistrate and married her lawfully.
She is his wife, and this is the first instance I know of,
where an Indian was married according to our laws."

John Pitchlynn, the name of another white man who at
an early day cast his lot among the Choctaws, not to be a
curse but a true benefactor. He was contemporaneous with
the three Folsoms, Nathaniel, Ebenezer and Edmond; the
three Nails, Henry, Adam and Edwin; the two Le Flores,
Louis and Mitchel, and Louis Durant. John Pitchlynn, as
the others, married a Choctaw girl and thus become a bona
fide citizen of the Choctaw Nation. He was commissioned
by Washington, as United States interpreter for the Choctaws in 1786, in which capacity he served them long and
faithfully. Whether he ever attained to the position of chief
of the Choctaws is not now known. He, however, secured
and held to the day of his death not only the respect, esteem
and confidence of the Choctaws as a moral and good citizen,
but also that of the missionaries who regarded him as one
among their best friends and assistants in their arduous
labors for the moral and religious elevation of the people of

his adoption. He married Sophia Folsom, the daughter and only child of Ebenezer Folsom. They had five sons, Peter P., James, Thomas, Silas and Jack, all of whom were men of fine talents and high position, reflecting credit on their ancient and honorable name, except Jack, who was led astray and finally killed.

How many strange little incidents oft happen to various persons the cause of which none can satisfactorily explain; many of which are similar to the following that Major John Pitchlynn once experienced in early life! He stated to the missionaries that he, in company with sixty Choctaw warriors, was once returning home from a trading expedition to Mobile—then, a small town and trading point of the Choctaws. One night they all had lain down upon their blankets side by side, and all soon fell asleep but himself, who, by a strange and unusual restlessness, was unable to sleep. For a long time he rolled this way and that upon his blanket, but all to no purpose; he could not sleep. Finally he arose, took up his blanket and laid down on the opposite side of the fire which had been made for the common benefit of the camp. Scarcely had he adjusted himself upon his new bed when a large tree suddenly fell to the ground and exactly across the bodies of his six sleeping comrades, killing every one of them, and leaving him a lone survivor of the camp. Major Pitchlynn often afterwards spoke of this incident as a manifestation of a special Providence; his unaccountable sleeplessness on that night, and his getting up and going to the other side of the fire to sleep, as a divine interposition in his special behalf. Peter was born January 30, 1806, in a little village called Shik-o-poh (The Plume), which was then in what is now Noxubee County. In early youth young Peter manifested a disposition for intellectual attainments; he attended the great councils of his Nation as an attentive hearer but silent spectator, and sought every opportunity to inform himself of all that was transpiring around him. As he grew up his desire to obtain an education increased, and he was finally sent to a school in Tennessee.

He returned home at a time his people were negotiating a treaty with the United States Government; when and where he made himself the object of much conversation, in the way of reproof by some, and commendation by others, in refusing to shake hands with Andrew Jackson, the negotiator of a treaty, which, in his youthful judgment, he regarded as an imposition upon his misled and deluded people and an insult to his Nation; this opinion was never changed to the hour of his death years after. After remaining at home awhile, he went to school at Columbia Academy, Tennessee; thence to the Nashville University, where he graduated; and afterwards became, as the sequel will show, a great and useful man to his Nation.

During his scholastic days at the Nashville University, General Jackson visited there officially as a trustee, and on seeing young Peter, at once recognized him as the Choctaw boy who had some years before refused to receive him as an acquaintance, or recognized in him a friend. Jackson, than whom few were better judges of human nature and moral worth, determined to win the friendship and confidence of the proud and manly young Choctaw, and succeeded finally in changing the old feeling of dislike to one of warm personal friendship, which sacred ties were never broken. After he graduated he returned home and settled, as a farmer, upon the outskirts of a beautiful prairie to which his name was given, and down to the war of 1861 it still bore, and perhaps does yet, the name. "The Pitchlynn Prairie."

His remarkably manly form and bearing; his. beautifully shaped head covered with long, black, shining hair and possessed with as black, piercing eyes as ever penetrated to the secret thoughts of the heart; his broad cheek-bones and brown complexion together with his natural and unaffected courteousness, affability and generous disposition, all served to contitute Peter P. Pitchlynn as stately and complete gentleman of nature's handiwork as I ever beheld. He erected a comfortable house upon the spot selected for

his home, and won the heart of the youngest daughter of
Nathaniel Folsom, (Rhoda) to whom he was soon married
accordingly to the usages of the whites, by the missionary,
Rev. Cyrus Kingsbury.

In 1824 a law was passed by the council of the Nation
organizing a corps of Light-Horse, who were clothed with
the authority and also made as their imperative duty to
close all the dram-shops that were dealing in the miserable
traffic in opposition to law and treaty stipulations. The
command of this band was given to young Peter P. Pitchlynn, and in one year, from the time he undertook to erase
the foul blotch (traffic in whiskey) from the face of the
country, he had successfully acomplished it.

From his soon known abilities he was early elected a
member of the National Council, an honor never before
conferred upon one so young. Pitchlynn at once brought
before the council the necessity of educating their children,
and argued the great advantages that would accrue therefrom; and, that the students might more readily become
accustomed to the usages of the whites, he suggested the
propriety of establishing a school for Choctaw youths in
some one of the states. It was decided, therefore, by the
council in accordance with his proposition, and a Choctaw
Aademy was established near Georgetown, Kentucky sustained by the funds of the Nation, and stood, until driven
from their ancient domains, a proud monument of the Choctaws' advancing civilization under the fostering care of
God's missionaries sent to them.

In the year 1828 he, with another Choctaw, two Chickasaw and two Muskogee warriors, constituted a delegation
appointed and sent by, and at the expense of, the United
States Government, to go upon a peace-making expedition
into the Osage country west of the Mississippi River, now
the State of Kansas, as the Osages and Choctaws were and
had been uncompromising enemies for years untold; and if
peace could be established between them, it was believed
that the Choctaws would the more readily consent to the

exchange of lands, as was afterwards made. The little band of six, few but resolute and fearless, with Pitchlynn as their chief, went first to Memphis, then a little village; thence to St. Louis, where they received necessary supplies from the Indian superintendent; thence to Independence, consisting then of only a few log cabins, where they were received and hospitably entertained by a son of the renowned Daniel Boone. At Independence they were joined by an Indian agent; thence they started and made their first camp on a broad prairie near Shawnee village. The Shawnees had never before seen a Choctaw, Chickasaw or Muskogee; nor had they ever seen a Shawnee, except in the person of Tecumseh and his thirty warriors, in their memorable visit to their three nations in 1812, while each knew of the existence of the other. On the following morning Pitchlynn and his little band directed their footsteps toward the Shawnee village, with the decorations of the pipe of peace gaily fluttering to the prairie breeze above their heads. Upon seeing the peace-pipe extended, the Shawnees at once came out to meet them, and escorted them in much pomp and ceremony into their village, where a council was soon convened to learn the object of the strangers' visit; which soon being explained, pledges of friendship were exchanged and speeches made, and the strangers earnestly solicited to remain the next day to attend a grand feast that would be given to them in honor of their visit, which was duly accepted; and then the little band again took up its line of travel toward the territories of the Osages. For several days they traveled along the famous Santa Fe trail, then turned in a southeast direction, traveling over beautiful prairies skirted here and there with timber.

One day, about the middle of the afternoon, a few deer were seen on a prairie a half mile distant, and Pitchlynn left his company to continue their course, while he would try to procure some venison for their supper. He had approached nearly near enough to risk a shot, when he was discovered by the deer, who scampered off across the prairie. At that moment he discovered a small herd of buffalo, at one of which he tried to get a shot; but they, too discovered him and took to flight. He pursued them a mile or two, but finding he was getting too far away he stopped his pursuit and turned to overtake his companions by traveling at an angle that would enable him to overtake or strike their trail several miles south of where he had left them. But after riding a few miles he saw about half a mile before him a ridge of undulating prairie, on the opposite side of which he felt sure his company must have passed. As the sun was now nearing the western horizon, and he knew not how far his companions were ahead of him, he started for the top of the ridge in a brisk gallop until he reached the base of the hill, then reined in his horse to a steady walk as he ascended the ridge, ever keeping in practice the safe motto, "Caution is the mother of safety." And well he did, for he was then in the country of Osages, who, not knowing his mission, would have made short work of him, had they met him. As he drew nearer the top the slower he rode, and thus cautiously moved until he could see the valley beyond, and there he saw a company of Osage warriors but a short distance ahead. Some were riding slowly along intently looking on the ground, while others had dismounted and were leading their horses, now stooping with eager look and then pushing the grass this way and that, as if to find something lost. Pitchlynn at once comprehended the whole. They had found the trail of his companions and were using their woodcraft to read the signs indicated, and learn whether friends or foes had passed, and also their number.

Pitchlynn at once reined his horse backward until he was below the brow of the hill, then turned and rode slowly down until he had reached its base lest the sound of his horse's feet should betray him; then struck off at full gallop in a south direction and continued it until night called a halt. He then dismounted roped his horse upon the grass, and lay down to sleep. In the morning he arose and was soon again on his dubious way, making a wide circuit to avoid running again upon his unwelcome neighbors. Again night overtook him a lone wanderer in a pathless wilderness, without having made any discoveries as to the whereabouts of his companions, or his enemies, the Osages. Again he stretched himself upon the grass and found forgetfulness in sleep. Again he started and was rejoiced, after an hour's ride, to strike the trail of his friends whom he overtook in the evening of the same day. Not knowing what had become of him, or where to look for him in the endless wilderness, they had traveled slowly, hoping that he would yet come up; but when the second night came without his return, they had given him up as lost.

The Osages, for unknown reasons, did not pursue them. If they had, there would have been a final separation as the Osages so outnumbered them, that not one of the little company would have been left to tell the tale. The unexpected return of their chief gave new life to all, and they pursued their journey with renewed vigor. In a few days they came to a large Osage village situated on a high bluff on the Osage River, and camped near the same, where they remained several days safe under the pipe of peace, whose decorations of ribbons fluttered above their camps; the Osages refusing, however, to meet them in council, since but a short time previous a war party of Choctaws had invaded their country, and in a battle had slain several of their warriors. Still Pitchlynn proposed a treaty of peace and after much equivocation and delay the Osages consented to meet Pitchlynn and his little band in council; but nothing definite was done on the first day, though Pitchlynn told them that he and his party, the first Choctaws that had ever proposed peace to the Osages, had traveled over two thousand miles through the request of the United States Government, to propose a treaty of perpetual peace and friendship. To which an Osage chief made a haughty and defiant reply. The next day in council assembled, Pitchlynn also assumed an air more of haughty defiance than that of a suppliant for peace, and in his speech, in reply to the

Osage chief's speech made the day before, boldly said:
"After what the Osage warrior said to us in his talk yesterday, we find it difficult to restrain our old animosity. You
tell us that by your laws it is your duty to strike down all
who are not Osage Indians. The Choctaws have no such
laws. But we have a law which tells us that we must always
strike down an Osage warrior whenever we meet him. I
know not what warpaths you may have followed west of
the Great River but I know very well that the smoke of our
council fires you have never seen as we live on the other
side of the Great River. Our soil has never been tracked by
an Osage only when he was a prisoner. I will not, as you
have done, boast of the many warpaths we have followed.
I am in earnest and speak the truth, when I now tell you
that our last warpath, since you will have it so, has brought
us to the Osage country, and to this village. The Choctaw
warriors now at home would be rejoiced to get a few hundred of your scalps, for it is thus that they get their reputation as warriors. I tell you this to remind you that we also
have some ancient laws as well as the Osages, and that the
Choctaws know too how to fight. Stand by the laws of your
fathers, and refuse the offer of peace that we have now
extended to you, and bear the consequences that will
follow.

"We are now a little band in your midst, but we do not
fear to speak openly to you and tell you the truth. We expect to move soon from our ancient country east of the
Great River to the sources of the Arkansas and Red Rivers,
which will bring us within two hundred miles of your country; and then you shall hear the defiant warwhoops of the
Choctaws in good earnest and the crack of their death-dealing rifles from one end of your country to the other; nor
will they cease to be heard until the last Osage warrior has
fallen; your wives and children carried into captivity, and
the name of the Osages blotted out. You may regard this as
vain boasting, but our numbers so much exceed that of your
own that I am justified, as you well know, in my assertion.

You say you will not accept the white paper of the Great Father at Washington; therefore, we now tell you that we take back all we said yesterday about a treaty of peace. If we are to have peace between the Choctaws and Osages, the proposition must now come from the Osages. I have told you all I have to say, and shall speak no more."

This bold speech of Pitchlynn's had the desired effect, causing a great change to come suddenly over the spirit of the Osages' dreams; therefore, on the next day the council was again convened and the Osages, without further solicitation, negotiated for peace, which was soon declared, and followed by a universal shaking of hands and great demonstrations of friendship, intermixed with unassumed joy in the happy result. A grand feast was at once prepared, at which everything presented a joyous appearance, while peace-speeches furnished the greater part of the entertainment; the honor of delivering the closing speech was awarded to Pitchlynn, in which, with his usual eloquence, he portrayed before the eyes of the attentive Osages the benefit that would accrue to them as a Nation to lay aside their old manner of living and begin a new kind of life—that of adopting the customs of civilization. He spoke of his own people, the Choctaws, who had conformed to the customs of civilization, by encouraging white missionaries to come among them and teach their children, and by turning the attention of the men to the cultivation of the soil; and had given up war as a source of amusement, and hunting as their sole dependence for food, and how much benefit they had already derived in so doing, and he would advise the Osages, as well as all Indians, to do the same; as it was the only means of preserving themselves from the grasping habit and power of the white men. If they would make an effort to elevate themselves in the scale of civilization, the American government would treat them with greater respect, and they thus would preserve their nativity.

At the close of the peace ceremonies and festivities a a party of Osage warriors, with the Osage speaker of the council, were appointed to escort, as token of peace and friendship between the Osages and Choctaws, Pitchlynn and his little company to the borders of the Osage territories, a distance of one hundred and fifty miles. There the Osage escort bade their old enemies, but now newly-made friends, a formal adieu, and returned to their villages, while Pitchlynn and his five companions, after an absence of nearly six months, turned their faces homeward with light hearts, pursuing a southern direction down the Canadian River, and continuing along the Red River valley, and finally reached home in safety.

Peter P. Pitchlynn, while upon this adventurous journey, picked up a little Indian boy belonging to no particular tribe, whom he adopted and carried home with him, had him educated at the Choctaw academy in Kentucky; and that homeless boy of the western prairies became one of the most eloquent and faithful preachers that ever preached the "glad tidings of great joy" among the Choctaw people.

Peter P. Pitchlynn first formed an acquaintance with the great American statesman, Henry Clay, in 1840, when traveling on a steamboat. While on board, he one day heard two apparently old farmers discussing the subject of agriculture, to whose conversation he was attracted, and soon became a silent but deeply interested listener for more than an hour; then going to his stateroom he told his traveling companion what a treat he had enjoyed in the discussion between "two old farmers" upon the subject of farming, and added: "If that old farmer with an ugly face had only been educated for the law, he would have been one of the greatest men in this country." That "old farmer with an ugly face" was Henry Clay, who was delighted at the compliment paid to him by the appreciative Choctaw.

The noble Peter P. Pitchlynn was in Washington City at the time of the commencement of the civil war in 1861, attending to the national affairs of his people, but at once hastened home, hoping that they would escape the evils of the expected strife, and returned to his home to pursue the

the quiet life of a farmer among his own people. But the Choctaws, as well as the Chickasaws, Cherokees, Creeks and Seminoles, from their position between the contending parties, were not permitted to occupy neutral grounds, but were forced into the fratricidal strife, some on the one side and some the other, but to the inconceivable injury of all.

Of Peter P. Pitchlynn it can be said, he was teacher, philosopher and friend among the Choctaws, cherishing with great pride the history and romantic traditions of his people. As a private citizen, he was a good man; as an official and public servant, he was a pure man. As a high official in his country, he too was a pious man; nor thought the religion of Jesus Christ derogatory to the position of a public official. He possessed such sweetness of spirit, such gentleness of manner, such manly frankness, such thorough self-respect on one hand, and on the other, such perfect regard for the judgment of others, that one could not help loving him, however conscience might compel conclusions on matters of mutual consequence unlike those he had reached. Often indeed, one was even more drawn to him when in opposition, because he was so true and just that his respect carried with it all the refreshment of variety with none of the friction of hostility. And with all he was a spirited citizen of his country, who lived and labored, not for selfish gain and self-emolument, but for the good of his people.

The Cravat family of Choctaws are the descendants of John Cravat, a Frenchman, who came among the Choctaws at an early day, and was adopted among them by marriage. He had two daughters by his Choctaw wife. Nancy and Rebecca, both of whom became the wives of Louis LeFlore. His Choctaw wife dying he married a Chickasaw woman, by whom he had four sons, Thomas, Jefferson, William and Charles, and one daughter, Elsie, who married a white man by the name of Daniel Harris, and who became the parents of Col. J. D. Harris, whose first wife was Catherine Nail, the fourth daughter of Joel H. Nail. The descendants of John

Cravat are still among the Choctaws and Chickasaws, and known as prominent and useful citizens in the two nations.

The LeFlore family of Choctaws are the descendants of Major Louis LeFlore, and his brother, Michael LeFlore, Canadian Frenchmen, who, after the expulsion of the French from the territories of Mississippi by the English, first settled in Mobile, Alabama, then a small trading post. After remaining there a few years, Louis moved to the now state of Mississippi and settled on Pearl River, in the county of Nashoba (Wolf). Thence he moved to the Yazoo Valley, where he lived until he died. As before stated, he married the two daughters of John Cravat, Nancy and Rebecca. By the former he had four sons in the following order of their names: Greenwood, William (who was drowned in Bok Iskitini), Benjamin and Basil; and five daughters, viz: Clarissa, Emilee—the names of the others not remembered. After the death of Nancy he married Rebecca, by whom he had two sons, viz: Forbis and Jackson. Clarissa married a white man by the name of Wilson, and living, at the time of the exodus of her people, in what is now known as Winston County, Mississippi, east of the town of Louisville. Wilson having died she married a man by the name of Alfred Leach and moved with him to the western part of Winston County, and settled on the banks of a creek called Lobucha (corrupted from Lah-buch-ih, to make warm). She there died. Her children, by her first husband, moved with their people to the west. Emilee married A. H. Carpenter, a Frenchman of high family. He practiced law in Jackson, Mississippi, and rose to an eminence that caused him to be regarded as a lawyer having few equals and no superiors. Mr. Carpenter died in 1852, followed by his wife in 1860. They left two sons, Jerome and Surry. Jerome at the age of fifteen entered the Confederate army as a private, serving under General Robert E. Lee in Virginia. He was wounded July, 1862, at the battle of Malvern. After he had recovered he served as one of General Joe Johnston's body guards, and acted in the capacity of dispatch bearer. Soon after the war he went to Mexico and received a commission as Colonel in Maximilian's army.

At the defeat of Maximilian, the youthful Jerome was condemned to be executed with the unfortunate prince; but was saved by the timely intervention of Secretary Seward. As an acknowledgment of Jerome's services and devotion to Maximilian, the emperor, Francis Joseph, conferred the title of baron upon him, and also offered him a position in the Austrian army, which he declined to accept. He returned to the United States, and was shortly afterwards killed in a duel with Amos Price, leaving a wife to mourn his untimely death. He had no children. The other three daughters married as follows: One married John Harkins, who became the grandfather of Colonel G. W. Harkins of the Chickasaw Nation; another married a man by the name of Traydu or Traydew; and the other married a man by the name of Harris.

The LeFlores have always held a prominent place in the annals of Choctaw history. Basil and Forbis were the only sons who followed the fortunes of their banished people to the west. William, as before stated, was accidentally drowned in Bok Iskitini; Benjamin lived and died at his old home on the banks of a stream where he kept a ferry, called Yockanookany, a corruption from Yakniokhina, (the land of streams).

Major Louis LeFlore was adopted by the Choctaws, and gradually rose to great distinction as a chief among that appreciative people. He with his brother Michael, who came to Mississippi and also settled in the Yazoo Valley, and Louis Durant, also a Frenchman, and the progenitor of the Durant family of Choctaws, first introduced cattle into the western part of the Choctaw Nation from Mobile, about the year 1770, the first animal of the bovine species ever seen by the Choctaws in that part of the Nation. They drove their little herd to the waters of Pearl River in now, Nashoba County, and placed them upon the range, then seemingly unlimited in its wide extended forests and impenetrable canebrakes. As a matter of course the cattle were a great curiosity to the Choctaws. The LeFlores and Durant told an amusing incident that took place a short time after their arrival at their ranch with the cattle. A little yearling had strayed from the herd. It so happened that three Choctaw hunters soon after pitched their camp a few miles from the newly established cattle ranch being entirely ignorant of its near proximity, and also of the new animals just introduced into their hunting grounds. One day, as usual, the three hunters left their camps for a hunt, each taking his course yet keeping near each other. During the day one of them discovered the yearling slowly emerging from a little plat of cane. Unseen by the lonely calf, he stood, gazed, and wondered. Naught like that had ever been seen upon his hunting path before. What it was, whence it came and how, baffled the wildest flights of even conjecture. 'Twas not a deer, nor a panther, nor yellow wolf! Must he signal for his companions? It might flee, must he shoot? He might only wound and cause it to attack, and then what! But he raised his trusty rifle and brought it to bear upon the unsuspecting calf; at that moment he discovered that it was eating the grass similar to his native deer; at once his fears were allayed and he concluded not to kill but to capture the prodigy, and take it alive to his camp as a living wonder.

Setting his gun against a tree, he bolted for the calf; which hearing the approaching footsteps, raised its head, gazed a moment, and seeing the fast approaching and equally strange object, at once gave the signal for a test of speed by elevating its rear appendage to an angle of forty-five degrees, and the race began. Finally the physical endurance of a Choctaw hunter proved superior to that of a city calf; for he ran but a few feet behind his coveted prize. But alas for human hopes! With a desperate spring in which were centered all his hopes, he made a grab at the tail of the despairing calf which then drooped at twenty-two and a half; when, seemingly to comprehend his design, the calf gave it a vigorous twitch as it leaped a treacherous log that lay concealed in the grass over which he tumbled headlong to the ground. The lucky calf, comprehending the advantage offered, again raised its flag to forty-five, and with invigorated strength increased its speed, and was soon out of sight.

With hopes blighted, the unfortunate hunter crawled up to a sitting posture and commenced rubbing his bruised and painful knee, when he discovered that the whole top of the knee moved hither and thither at his slightest push, a thing untaught in his book of anatomy, and at once concluded that his leg was fearfully shattered. He whooped to his comrades, who, happening to be near and hearing his call, hastened to his side. They also, upon close examination of the wounded limb, arrived at the same conclusion with the supposed injured man, when the two LeFlores and Durant, searching for the strayed yearling, rode up; and taking in the situation at a glance, after a few words of inquiry, they soon explained the anatomy of the human knee to the three hunters by showing them that the moving of the knee-cap was common to all, and did not denote a broken bone. Being thoroughly convinced of its truth, the fallen man arose to his feet, gave a brief account of his adventure, pointed the direction in which the strange beast had disappeared; and the three Choctaw deer hunters, and the three white calf hunters, soon found the wanderer and safely placed it again within the fold; then the three Choctaws returned to their forest camp to talk over the adventures of the day, as well as the knowledge gained regarding the new animal introduced, whose flesh was equal, if not superior, to that of their famous deer, and also of the addition to their knowledge in osteology.

Major Louis LeFlore resided for many years on the waters of the Pearl River raising cattle, and early became a wealthy man; from his stock, which increased rapidly in their abundant range and genial climate, the surrounding

Choctaws supplied themselves with cattle. He then moved to the Yazoo Valley where he spent the remainder of his days respected and loved. As colonel, he commanded a battalion of Choctaw warriors under Jackson at the taking of Pensacola in the Creek war of 1812.

Greenwood, after his father's death, succeeded him as one of the chiefs of the Choctaw Nation, which he retained until the exodus. He was a man of great energy, to whom nature had given force of character; and had he also had the advantages of high mental culture, he would have been a leader of men. He did not move west with his people, but remained at his old home in a little town called Greenwood, situated on a tributary of the Yazoo River, where he lived to an advanced age, died and was buried there. He was married twice. His wives were sisters, the daughters of John Dunley of Alabama. The old chief was highly respected by the whites, and was elected to the state legislature as a member from Yazoo County; and afterwards was elected to the state senate from Yazoo and Carrol Counties.

William lived near the Yelobusha River (corrupted from Yaloba-aia-sha—where tadpoles abound). He, too, was a respected and useful man. He was unfortunately drowned in Bok Iskitini (as before stated) in the pride and manhood of his life, regretted and mourned by all his numerous acquaintances and friends. His body was recovered and buried at his home.

Forbis and Basil were the only two sons who moved west with their people, both lived to an advanced age; the former died in 1883, the latter in 1886. Both were pious men and died in strong faith of a blissful immortality. Forbis, in relating his Christian experience, once said: "I was once a very wicked man. God gave me a long rope—a mighty long rope—but I cut it right short off." And his Christian life after he embraced the religion of the Son of God, proved that he did cut "right short off" from his wickedness. Forbis LeFlore was indeed a man of stern merits, and blended with his force of character were gentleness of spirit and entire conscienciousness, by which he obtained the confidence of his people; and while he merited all their esteem by his virtues, he also secured their affections by them.

Basil LeFlore was a man than whom a purer one is seldom found in this age of the world. He filled the highest public offices of his Nation with honor to himself and his country. Kind words and pleasant smiles spread sunshine throughout his whole actions; his home was a model home, where all the virtues known to man seem to congregate and delight to dwell. I speak from personal knowledge. But his crowning virtue was his earnest piety, his simple, trusting faith. He carried his religion with him everywhere, which burned with a steady beautiful light, making its influence felt far and wide. His public services were not less patriotic than his private virtues were conspicuous. The former are monuments to his wisdom and honest statesmanship, and will ever be viewed by his admiring people as stars in the firmament of their Nation.

He died full of years (well spent) at the home of a friend, October, 1886, living a few miles from his own, whom he was visiting. His death was sudden and unexpected—falling dead from his chair while at the supper table. A Choctaw friend informed me of his death, by letter in the following truthful and memorable words: "Gov. Basil LeFlore is dead. He is the last of the family. It is a national loss to the Choctaw and Chickasaw people. Our best old men are fast disappearing."

Michael LeFlore, the brother and only relative of Major Louis LeFlore among the Choctaws, the people of their adoption, had five sons, viz: Thomas, Michael, Joel, Ward and Johnson, and two daughters, Mary and Sophia. Thomas was chief in their present Nation for several years. When I last heard of his widow she was still living near Wheelock, Choctaw Nation, and is said to be bordering on a hundred years of age. Young Michael served as major in the Confederate army through the Civil War.

Louis Durant, a Canadian Frenchman, was the progenitor of the Durant family among the Choctaws, who came, as before stated, to the Choctaw Nation with the two brothers, Louis and Michael LeFlore, about the year 1770. He, like his friends and contemporaries, the two LeFlore brothers, also selected a wife among the Choctaw forest flowers, but whose name has been lost amid the vicissitudes through which her people have passed. They had three sons, Pierre, Charles and Lewis; and two daughters, Margaret and Syllan. The father and three sons served under their renowned chief, Pushmataha, as allies of the Americans in the Creek war of 1812.

Pierre had seven sons, viz: Fisher, George, Jefferson, Sylvester, Isham, Ellis and Joseph. Ellis and Sylvester served in the Confederate army during the Civil War of 1861, the former in the rank of major. Alexander Durant, one of the Supreme Judges of the Choctaw Nation, (with whom I am personally acquainted) is a son of George Durant. Fisher Durant had three sons, Bissant, Dixon and Jesse. Dixon is a minister of the Gospel. He is a poor man in a pecuniary sense, but rich in a spiritual sense. He seems to live alone for the cause of his Divine Master and the salvation of his fellow men.

Margaret Durant married a man by the name of Eli Crowder; and Syllan, a William Taylor. The two husbands were with their father-in-law and their three brothers-in-law in the Creek war of 1812 as allies of the Americans.

Eli Crowder secured for himself, in the Creek war of 1812, the name Muscokubi (Muscogee or Creek-Killer), which he ever afterwards bore; being called by the Choctaws, Muscokubi, and by the whites, Creek-Killer. The following are the circumstances by which he gained the name:

At one time, during the campaign, a company of Choctaw warriors, of which he was a member, was encamped on the outskirts of the main body of General Jackson's army, then in the Muscogee or Creek Nation. Crowder at that

time, possessed a little pony which had served him faithfully in more than one trouble, and to which he was greatly
attached. He frequently would attach a little bell to the
neck of the pony and turn him out at night upon the range
to graze, and go early the next morning and drive him back
to camp. Frequently the pony would wander a mile or
more from the camp during the night, and Crowder had
been warned of the danger of his morning walk after the
pony, since a scouting Muscogee might be attracted some
night by the bell, and finding it upon the horse, naturally
conclude that the owner would be out after him in the
morning, and would lie in ambush for him, and, ten to one,
would lift his scalp. But Crowder seemed to have no fears,
One morning, however, in going after his pony, he heard
the little bell at rather an unusual distance away, which
aroused his suspicions a little that perhaps the pony had
been driven there by a Muscogee scout in order to draw the
anticipated owner as far into the solitudes of the forest and
away from the Choctaw camp, whose location he perhaps
well knew, that he might the safer shoot him; therefore, he
kept a vigilant outlook. He had approached within two
hundred yards of his pony when his watchful eye detected
the quick movements, as he thought, of an object four or
five feet above the base of a large tree a few rods to the left
of the still quietly feeding pony.

Crowder made no halt, but while he guarded with
eagle eyes the suspected tree, he placed double duty upon
his ears and also glanced everywhere around. He had
walked but a few paces farther when he noticed a seemingly unnatural protuberance, scarcely visible, on one side
of the now truly suspected tree. As he steadily continued,
he noticed the protuberance slowly, but surely enlarging.
Little by little it grew in size until the outlines of half the
size of a man's head was discernible—then instantly disappeared. That told the tale. In a twinkling he formed his
resolution. It was to continue walking towards the pony
until within sure range of his rifle, and then risk the chance

of securing the first shot. As he expected, again he saw the unnatural protuberance slowly forming on the side of the tree at the very spot where it had twice formed before; slowly, but steadily, inch by inch, it grew until it was in size as before, then as instantly disappeared. Muscokubi ran as nimbly and lightly as a cat towards the tree, which brought him in easy range, and stopped, raised his rifle and held it with unerring aim upon the very spot where the apparition had so oft appeared and disappeared.

Soon he saw the dark barrel of a rifle becoming slowly visible and becoming plainer and plainer to view as it extended out along the side of the tree and pointing toward him, then was motionless; then as before, the apparition slowly began to form; inch by inch it enlarged, but just as it reached its former size the sharp crack of Muscokubi's rifle, followed by a dull, heavy thud, united with the tinkling pony bell to break the forest silence. He then re-loaded his rifle, and again slowly advanced to the (to him) so nearly fatal tree to learn the extent of his morning adventure, and there saw a Muscogee warrior stretched full length in death, as he had expected, with the right side of his head torn off. For a moment he gazed upon his fallen foe; then severed the scalp from the head, attached it to his belt, and with it and the rifle of the outwitted warrior as proofs of his adventure, returned to the camp slowly driving the truant pony before him.

Eli Crowder, alias Muscokubi, lived, as would seem at the present day, to the extrordinary age of 102 years, 2 months and 11 days; but longevity among the Choctaws at that time, as well as among other southern tribes, was of very common occurrence. His first wife was a white woman by whom he had two sons. From her he separated—cause unknown. He then married a Choctaw woman by whom he had nine sons and two daughters: Harris, Jackson, Phebe, James, Catherine, Solomon, David, Louis, Washington, Martin, and one who died in infancy.

His Choctaw wife dying, he married a Chickasaw woman, by whom he had nine sons, Francis, Marion (known as Dick), Eli, Van (known as Bob); the fourth died in infancy; then followed Thomas, William, Joshua, George and John. Louis Crowder, (or Louie, as he is called, and to whom I am indebted for all the above concerning the Crowder family, the sixth son of Muscokubi by his Choctaw wife, is acknowledged throughout the Choctaw Nation as the best interpreter in it. He has been acting in the capacity of general interpreter for the Choctaws and missionaries during the last forty-five years. He is a consistent member of the Old School Presbyterian Church (South). His grandfather, James Crowder, was an ordained Methodist minister of the Gospel; and two of his uncles, Jeptha and Levi, were class leaders in the Methodist church. He has been greatly afflicted with rheumatism for many years, yet has born his affliction with becoming Christian fortitude, ever wearing a smiling face and a cheerful countenance.

John Harkins, a white man, is the father of the Harkins family of Choctaws. His advent to the Choctaw Nation was, as near as can be ascertained, about the year 1800 or soon afterwards. He was a man of high-toned principles, and contemporary with the Folsoms, Nails, Pitchlynns, Le-Flores, Durants, Cravats, Crowders, and others of the long ago, who married among the Choctaws; all men, who, having cast their lot among that people made their interests their own, and sought, by every means in their power to elevate them in the scale of morality and virtue.

John Harkins married a daughter of Major Louis LeFlore, by whom he had four sons—Willis, George, Richard and James. Willis married Salina Folsom, oldest daughter of Col. David Folsom. They had two sons, George W. and Crittendon, and one daughter, Salina.

Col. George W. Harkins was a graduate of Danville College, Kentucky. He was a man of acknowledged abilities; a lawyer by profession, and a fine jurist and wise counsellor. He for many years acted in the capacity of delegate to Washington in attending to the national affairs of the Chickasaw Nation, with which people, though a Choctaw by consanguinity, he cast his lot. He was a bold, vigorous and able defender of the rights of his people in the Congress of the United States; and by energetic and fervent perseverance, with solid learning, he rose to eminence in the spheres of an active life, as well as in his profession. He died in August, 1891.

Salina, the only daughter, is a lady of fine literary attainments, and high cultivation of both mind and heart. She has never married, but seems to prefer fighting the battles of life single-handed; though many a young swain has taken issue with her in regard to her convictions. She graduated in one of the female colleges of Tennessee, after which she engaged, for a while, in teaching, but for several years was engaged as telegraph operator at Talbott Station, Tennessee. She at different intervals visits her relatives and friends in the Choctaw Nation, then returns to her duties in Tennessee.

George, of the four sons of John Harkins, was one of the chiefs of the Choctaw Nation in 1852, in conjunction with Cornelius McCurtain and George Folsom.

But it would not be practicable, were it even possible, to give a sketch, though short, of the lives of all the Choctaws who became conspicuous by their virtues and noble deeds, both of unmixed and mixed blood, being wise in counsel, brave in the field of battle, judicious in peace, orators by nature, and who eloquently and courageously presented the wrongs and sustained the rights of their people.

It has been my good fortune, as well as pride and pleasure, to be personally acquainted from youth to old age with the majority of those Choctaws whose characteristics I have thus delineated; and with the ancient and present habits, manners and customs, of whose people I have made myself fully acquainted by the diligent study, the long and free association and close observation of over three score and ten years; and it has ever been, and will ever continue to be, my sunniest memories to know that I have ever stood as the friend of the Red Man, as my parents before me who severed the ties of all that makes life most dear, leaving all behind, to go to the rescue of the Choctaw people in obedience to their Divine Master's injunction—"Go ye into all the the world and preach my Gospel"—and also that I have been blest with such noble friends as I have found, secured and still possess in them.

And though I freely and proudly acknowledge my prejudice in their favor, if love and friendship without alloy, based upon true merit, are worthy that title, yet I have endeavored to give a truthful sketch of those noble and as worthy men as ever blest a Nation, though much more might be said of their virtues; and with equal truth of hundreds of others of that noble people, both men and women, who have lived and died, and others who still live, but occupied a less public, yet none the less useful and glorious sphere in life, since they did their duty and thus filled it nobly.

It is the first time their names have been presented to the world; and I have ventured this just and true sketch for the consideration of those of my own race who have heretofore seemingly felt, and therefore evidently exercised but little interest in the North American Indians, beyond that found in reading the falsehoods and vituperations published against them in the sensational articles of the day by many of the newspaper men.

What more could be expected but that the Indian Race should be regarded, root and branch, as being incapable of possessing or exercising any of those virtues whose tendencies are to elevate and adorn the human race? To the refutation of this false charge, have I given to the world the characteristics of the Indian, hoping that it might serve, to some extent at least, to remove from the minds of those open to conviction, the gross errors under which they have been living in regard to that unfortunate but noble race.

Still I know the sketch given of those noble Choctaws may be, and will be cast aside by those over whom long established prejudice still sways her merciless sceptre, with the interrogatory, "Can anything good come out of Nazareth?" To which I respond: There did. A glorious light which exposed to view a world that lay in moral and intellectual darkness. What next? This much. What I have written, I have written; and with a full knowledge of its truth, sustained by over three quarters of a century's personal acquaintance and experience with the Choctaw and Chickasaw Indians, and confirmed by hundreds of others whose acquaintance and experience are greater than my own, and bidding defiance to successful contradiction.

But it will not trouble me, as far as my own individual interests are concerned, if the facts presented are rejected as the wild and absurd hallucinations of a disordered brain; but only in behalf of the down-trodden Indian I would that they might be otherwise accepted; as I am well aware that a brief period will place me beyond all anxiety in their behalf, and I shall leave them to the humanity, or inhumanity, of another generation; but in which, God grant, others, more able and worthy than myself, shall rise up as their true friends and successful protectors against any future generation whose humanity may not exceed that of the present. Old and worthy friends they are, long tried and ever true, therefore doubly dear in their misfortunes. I still delight to take them by the hand as of old and listen to their voices, and though but few remain with whom I trod life's flowery paths, scattered here and there at their humble homes and around their peaceful firesides; yet the names of those whose places in the old family circle are vacant now still live in tender recollection; and my sojourns among them have been to me like rambling amid pleasant scenes of the remembered past; and bringing long hidden beauties again to light by the fresh cementing of that friendship has existed untarnished through the vicissitudes of nearly eighty years.

The government of the Choctaws is modeled after that of the state of Mississippi, and was adopted before they were exiled from their ancient domains to their present places of abode. The executive power is lodged in a governor. Each county in the Nation chooses a sheriff and other officers by ballot. The legislative department consists of a general council, comprising a senate and house of representatives. The Nation is divided into three districts, from each of which four senators are sent. The members of the house of representatives are chosen by ballot from the various counties. The judiciary consists in a supreme court of three judges, one from each district. The names of three judicial districts are Push-ma-ta-ha, A-puk-shun-u-nubbee, and Moshulatubbee, the names of three of their former and famous chiefs. The senior judge is the Chief Justice. This court has only appellate jurisdiction. A prosecuting attorney is elected in each district, whose duty it is to represent the Nation in all civil and criminal cases. The national capital is Tush-ka Hum-ma, (red warrior) where a National Council and Supreme Court are annually held, convening on the first Monday in October of each year.

In the First District, the court [30] holds its session during the entire session of their courts; and my informer remarked: "It is beautiful to see how harmoniously and Christian-like they engage in these religious exercises and devotions."

I was informed by the Choctaws, when visiting Tushka Humma in October, 1884, during the session of their council, that during the session of their district courts as well as that of the national council, which are invariably opened by prayer, they have preaching every night in the week; and that many of the district judges, attorneys and jurymen, are ministers of the Gospel of all denominations, preaching alternately at night.

[30] A typographical error is apparent here. Evidently Cushman meant to say that one of their church gatherings was regularly held at the time of the court sessions.

THE CHICKASAWS

Conquest or Progress! It is the same, since it is with blood that the book of humanity is written. The pages here devoted to the narrative of the Chickasaw Indians are not an exception. To some it may seem useless and even wrong to recall these pages of history so distant in the past, which began in wrong, continued in wrong and will end, so far as human observation can judge, in wrong, and then ask nothing better than to be forgotten. Alas, experience has shown that to change the mode of life of a primitive race is to condemn it to death; since always regarded as an inferior race by their conquerors, they have been swept away without justice or mercy, a people who had existed in an unbroken line of descent from prehistoric ages unknown.

East of the Mississippi River was also the Chickasaws' hereditary domain, who, like the Choctaws, were first made known to the Eastern world by Hernando de Soto who invaded their country in the month of November, 1540. View again the heroism of those ancient Choctaws in the patriotic defense of their city, Moma-Binah. Take also a retrospective view of those foreign marauders afterwards quartered for the winter in Chikasahha, November, 1540, the most ancient city of the Chickasaws, whose king (the Chickasaw rulers were anciently called kings instead of chiefs) had received De Soto and his followers (though uninvited) with the greatest kindness, and extended to them the hospitality of his town and people; but who, preparatory to the renewal of his journey in the following spring, manifested his gratitude to the Chickasaw king by haughtily demanding two hundred of his warriors to accompany him as burden bearers and servants of the camp. To which demand the Chickasaw king evaded a direct answer by requesting a few days in which to lay the matter before his people in council assembled, but during which interval prepared for a bold resistance; and, ere the invaders were aware, gave his reply to De Soto's demand in the defiant warwhoop; then setting fire to their town in which the perfidious Spaniards were sleeping, the Chickasaws rushed upon their invaders.

They bravely fought until hundreds of their warriors were slain and longer fighting was vain; not without, however, making it a deadly fought victory to the Spaniards, by burning Chikasahha, in which De Soto had quartered his soldiers for the approaching winter, and killed many of his men and horses, destroying the greater part of his baggage, throwing his entire army into confusion; and though the Chickasaws were finally defeated by superior arms, yet De Soto was glad to bid them an eternal adieu without any further demonstration of their prowess.

No history records the Chickasaws' past prior to their acquaintance with the White Race. Like their entire race, it is hidden amid the mysteries of the unknown. But from the legends handed down through the long and bewildering tracts cf time by their "wise old men," those Chroniclers of the North American Indians' long ago, as related to the missionaries seventy-five years in the past, their tradition in regard to ancestry, migration, etc., are the same as the Choctaws, being one tribe and people until the division made by their two chiefs Chikasah and Chahtah many years after their arrival and location east of the Mississippi River.

In the year 1819 the Synod of South Carolina resolved to establish a mission among the Southern Indians east of the Mississippi River. The Cherokees, Muscogees, Seminoles, Choctaws and Chickasaws then occupied Georgia, Florida, Alabama and Mississippi. Rev. David Humphries offered to take charge of the intended mission. He was directed to visit the Indians, obtain their consent and select a suitable location. Rev. T. C. Stewart, then a young licentiate, offered himself as a companion to Mr. Humphries. They first visited the Muscogees (Creeks), who, in council of the Nation, declined their proposition. They then traveled through Alabama into Mississippi, and proposed to establish a mission among the Chickasaws. They found them on the eve of holding a council of the Nation to elect a king. In that council, held in 1820, permission was granted the missionaries to establish missions in their Nation, and a charter was signed by the newly-chosen king. The two missionaries then returned to South Carolina. During the return Mr. Humphries concluded that he was not called to preach to the Indians. But the Rev. T. C. Stewart, during the same journey, firmly resolved to undertake the self-denying work, and offered to take charge of the contemplated mission. The Synod gladly accepted, and at once commenced making preparations to enter upon the life of a missionary to the Chickasaws. In January, 1821, he reached the place chosen for a station, and named it Monroe Station, in honor of James Monroe, the then president of the United States. Mr. Stewart was the only missionary. Two men, however, accompanied him with their families—one named Vernon, a mechanic, the other named Pickens, a farmer. Houses were erected, a farm opened, a school established, and preaching through an interpreter.

Rev. T. C. Stewart was born in the year 1793, and died in Tupelo, Mississippi, October 9, 1882.

In early youth I was personally acquainted with that great philanthropist, sincere and self sacrificing Christian, T. C. Stewart; and in recalling the reminiscences of those years of the long ago, I can but regard them as treasures from the memory of those who were indeed honest and sincere friends of the entire North American Indian Race. Yet those memories are freighted with sadness, when reflecting that all those hallowed relics have passed away leaving the poor Indians, for whom they so long and faithfully labored, to struggle among wolves (many in sheeps' clothing) with few such shepherds to counsel and lead them as those old missionary heroes of eighty years ago; while those years with their vicissitudes have silvered the heads of the only two remaining children now living of those bearers of the glad tidings of great joy to the descendants of two traditional brother-chiefs Chahtah and Chikasah; the one a daughter living in Belpry, Ohio; the other a son living in Greenville, Texas. Both were born among the Choctaws at the Missionary Station Mayhew.

The little colony soon became a centre of Gospel light and civilizing influences to the Nation. Other missionaries came at different times to aid the one man, who began the good work: Rev. Hugh Wilson, in 1821, from North Carolina; Rev. W. C. Blair, from Ohio, in 1822; James Holmes, of Pennsylvania, in 1824. The first two named, after the removal of the Indians, went to Texas, where their bodies now sleep. Mr. Holmes was licensed to preach after he came to the mission as teacher. He became a doctor of divinity and taught a classical school of high reputation at Covington, Tennessee, for many years, and died at an advanced age. But it is unnecessary to enter into a detail of the fruits of this mission. It will suffice to say that many Indian youths who have become prominent in their tribe as legislators, preachers of the Gospel and influential citizens, received their education, in part or in full, at Monroe. The foundation of a Christian civilization, to which the Chickasaws have years ago reached and still firmly maintain, may be safely said, was laid in the mission of which the noble T. C. Stewart was founder.

About the year 1822 Rev. Haynes opened a school in the Chickasaw Nation, near the southern line of the Cherokee Nation, under the Presbyterian Board of Foreign Missions, for the benefit of which George Colbert established a boarding house. This school and the one established at Monroe by Rev. T. C. Stewart, January, 1821, soon became flourishing institutions of learning. In the course of years a son of Rev. Haynes married a Chickasaw girl who formerly had been a pupil at his father's school. He (the son) labored among both the Chickasaws and the Choctaws as a missionary until they emigrated west. He lived with his Chickasaw wife nearly forty years, when she died. He then (1884) went west to live with his daughter, Mrs. Eads, who lives in Lone Oak, Denton County, Texas. At that time he was 88 years of age, still in his mental vigor and attending to his ministerial duties.

In 1821 the Methodist church sent out Rev. Alex Deavers as a missionary to the Chickasaws, who remained among them until they moved west. He had two sons, one of whom married a Chickasaw girl and the other a Choctaw.

De Soto and his band gave to the Choctaws at Moma Binah and the Chickasaws at Chikasahha their first lesson in the white man's modus operandi to civilize and Christianize North American Indians; so has the same lesson been continued to be given to that unfortunate people by his white successors from that day to this, all over this continent, but which to them, was as the tones of an alarm-bell at midnight. And one hundred and twenty-three years have passed since our forefathers declared all men of every nationality to be free and equal on the soil of the North American continent then under their jurisdiction, except the Africans whom they held in slavery, and the Native Americans against whom they decreed absolute extermination because they could not also enslave them; to prove which, they at once began to hold out flattering inducements to the so-called oppressed people of all climes under the sun, to come to free America and assist them to oppress and kill off the Native Americans and in partnership take their lands and country, as this was more in accordance with their lust of wealth and speedy self-aggrandizement than the imagined slow process of educating, civilizing and Christianizing them; and to demonstrate that it has been a grand and glorious success, we now point with pride to our broad and far-extended landed possessions; and to the little remnant of hapless, helpless and hopeless Indians who calmly wait their turn to be wiped out as tribes and nationalities[1] that they also, as all their race before, may give place to our glorious institutions of civilization.

[1] Cushman refers to the liquidation of the Five Civilized Tribes, which was then in process. Their land was broken up into individual allotments, their invested funds were divided per capita, and their governments were abolished. They became citizens of the United States, and subsequently of the State of Oklahoma.

Justly have the ancient Chickasaws been regarded as the bravest and most skillful warriors among all the North American Indians; and it has been affirmed that they never were conquered, though fighting oft under adverse circumstances; and also, had they maintained the fight with De Soto but a few hours longer, they would have defeated him and utterly destroyed his army. The surrounding tribes recognized and acknowledged them as justly the lords and masters of the vast territory they claimed extending from the Yalobaaiasha (Tadpole Habitation—corrupted to Yalobusha), Mississippi, north to the Ohio River, and from the Mississippi to the Muscle Shoals in the Tennessee River; and oft the Indian hunters from the prairies of Illinois and the lakes of the North, in pursuing the deer and buffalo in the then wide extended and magnificent forests south of the Ohio River, trespassed upon those of the Chickasaws and fierce and bloody battles ensued. As it is the Choctaws boast—"they never in war shed an American's blood"— so it is the Chickasaws' boast—"they never in war shed a white man's blood of English descent."

Neither the Choctaws nor Chickasaws ever engaged in war against the American people, but always stood as their faithful allies. It has been published that, after the destruction of Fort Mims by the Creeks, in 1812, "the Chickasaw towns began to paint and sing their war songs; and the Choctaws had snuffed the scent of blood and were panting for war, and ready to draw the scalping knife against the Americans." This was founded alone on rumor promulgated for sensational purposes. True, had the Choctaws, Chickasaws and Cherokees united with the Muscogees and Seminoles in 1812, depopulation of all the white settlements within their territories would have been the inevitable result. The Chickasaws and Choctaws, though distinct nations, yet speaking nearly the same language, were generally animated by the same views and motives; had nearly the same customs and habits; were governed by the same principles, and followed by the same fortunes.

[Cushman then leaves the Choctaws and Chickasaws to devote many pages to general Indian history. He begins with the exploration and settlement of eastern North America by Europeans; describes the conflicts and rivalries between imperial powers and the involvement of the Indians; and traces the westward movement and the resulting Indian wars. After relating the grand design and defeat of Pontiac, he comes back briefly to a contemporary Indian Territory parallel—]

Military land-warrants of incredible numbers had been issued, and a frenzied mania for western lands seemingly absorbed every other desire in the hearts of the people of that period; and which has not abated from that day to this, but rather increased, as was practically illustrated in the Oklahoma craze that added so much "glory" to these United States, but to the pecuniary loss of the defrauded Creeks.[2]

[Then follow details of American encroachment in the Ohio country after the French and Indian War. The Chickasaws are brought briefly into the story by one incident of the Revolution—]

In 1780 Colonel George Clark erected Fort Jefferson on the Mississippi River, in the territories of the Chickasaws, a few miles below the mouth of the Ohio. In the year following the Chickasaws, justly indignant at the erection of Fort Jefferson upon their soil, besieged it under the command of the great Colbert; therefore, General Clark hastened from Kaskaskia with re-inforcements, upon the arrival of which the Chickasaws drew off a little distance. Soon after, however, Clark dismantled the fort, returned to his own, and the Chickasaws quietly returned to their homes.

[More pages are then devoted to Indian affairs in the Old Northwest in the years following the Revolution. Here in the enforced land cessions Cushman again points out a contemporary parallel—]

[2] This small tract in the center of the Indian Territory which gave its name to the present state, had been "purchased" by forced sale from the Creeks and Seminoles (Cushman apparently overlooked the Seminole interest) and opened to white settlement in 1889. This broke the barrier that had set the Indian Territory apart as a home for Indians, and other land openings quickly followed.

How clearly this old precedent, handed down from that day to this, was illustrated in the securing of the Oklahoma Territory,[3] and also that from the Sioux, in which fraud, falsehood, hypocrisy and rascality are the only characteristics that are visible in the whole.

[Closing his account with the crushing defeat of the Indians in the Ohio country by General Anthony Wayne in 1794, Cushman finally returns to the Chickasaws—]

But here I will close this cursory review of the fearful sufferings and cruel destruction of that portion of the human family, who formerly possessed and inhabited the northern and western part of this continent as a free and happy people; then fell into the hands of France, and subsequently into those of England, to be finally handed over to the United States as old and useless goods and chattels. And though I have but exhibited the mere skeleton of their wrongs and woes inflicted by the hands of white civilization and professed Christianity, yet I will return to my subject, the Chickasaws, from which I have so long and far wandered; not to repose in hope of fairer morn in tracing the line of their history, since there can be no hope expected in this age abounding, as all heretofore have, more with vice than with virtue.

While the English east of the Alleghany mountains were adopting active, but secret measures, to stop the progress of French colonization on the banks of the Mississippi River, their traders were meeting the French traders everywhere among the southern Indians, and their mutual animosity and competition causing frequent quarrels, oft terminating in collisions, in which the unfortunate Indians always became involved on the one or the other side. But the French, at an early day had excited the animosity of the Chickasaws by failing to protect a band of their warriors who had solicited an escort from Mobile to their homes

[3] By the time of Cushman's writing the original "Oklahoma" had expanded into an "Oklahoma Territory" comprising the western half of the present state. The Liquidation of the Five Civilized Tribes, then in process in the eastern half, was designed to prepare the whole area for statehood.

through the Choctaw Nation, with whom they were then at war; but in passing through the Choctaw Nation, though under a French escort, they were slain to a man by the Choctaws. The Chickasaws, believing it was done through the connivance of the French, never forgave them; and in all the quarrels between the French and English traders they took sides with the latter, and finally became the firm and undeviating friends and allies of the English, and the most bitter enemies of the French, giving them more trouble than all the other southern tribes, and whom they regarded as the most dreaded enemies among all the Indians in the Mississippi valley.

Their territory lay exactly between the French settlements in Louisiana and Illinois and thus made all intercourse extremely dangerous. The high point upon which Memphis, Tennessee, is located, then known as the Chickasaw Bluffs, was a favorite spot selected by the shrewd and wily Chickasaw warriors from which to make their attacks upon the French boats ascending and descending the river. Bienville, then governor and commander of the French colonies in the Mississippi valley, adopted every possible method to retaliate upon that brave Nation, and too often succeeded in arraigning the Choctaws, his allies, against the Chickasaws—greatly to the injury of the two injudicious and misguided tribes. In 1719 he succeeded in influencing the Choctaws to declare war against them, in which they, by the assistance of Bienville in the way of arms and ammunition, defeated the Chickasaws in several hard contested battles, and so weakened them that they for awhile ceased their attacks upon the French, though retaining, to the fullest extent, their hatred and animosity toward them. Bienville, in one of his letters regarding this fratricidal war exultingly said: "The Choctaws, whom I have set in motion against the Chickasaws, have destroyed entirely three villages of this ferocious Nation, which disturbed our commerce on the river. They have raised about four hundred scalps, and made one hundred prisoners. Considering this

state of things, it is a most important advantage which we
have obtained, the more so, that it has not cost one drop of
French blood, through the care I took of opposing those
barbarians to one another. Their self-destruction operated
in this manner is the sole efficacious means of insuring
tranquility to the colony."

It now seems almost incredible that such a crazed infatuation should possess the Choctaws as to so utterly blind
them from comprehending the dark designs of Bienville
when arraigning them against their own race, and especially
against their kindred Chickasaw brethren.

In July, 1720, the English traders among the Chickasaws involved them in turn in a war with the French, by
influencing them to kill Serigney, a French officer, whom
Bienville had sent among them to induce them to withdraw
from the English and give their trade to the French.

In 1731, after the destruction of the Natchez as a Nation, a few of whom had fled to the brave and generous
Chickasaws for protection, Governor Perier, who had been
appointed commander of the colony in the place of Bienville, then deposed and recalled to France, sent orders to
the Chickasaws to drive the Natchez fugitives out of their
territories, if they did not wish to secure his animosity; to
this insolent command, they replied: "We neither respect
you as a friend, nor fear you as an enemy. We have extended the hand of friendship and safety to the unfortunate
Natchez, and vow to protect them." This defiant message
caused the French governor to foam with rage; and he at
once resolved upon immediate war upon "those insolent
savages," and, as an introductory to his designs, adopted
measures to again array the Choctaws in hostilities against
them, but evidently not without just apprehensions of success; for in a letter written at this time to his government
Beauchamp, the commander at Mobile, said: "The Choctaws are not friendly disposed towards us, which is greatly
to be regretted; for should this tribe declare against us, we
should be compelled to abandon the colony. The Natchez

war principally endangered the traders on the Mississippi River, but a Chickasaw war would cause apprehension throughout the whole colony. They have already sent three emissaries to seek the alliance of the Illinois Indians against us, who, however fell into our hands, and Governor Perier intends ordering them burnt."

But Perier was disappointed in carrying out his warlike designs against the Chickasaws, and thus avenging the imagined insult offered to the governor of an obscure little French colony somewhere in the wilds of America for in 1733, Bienville after an absence of eight years, was reinstated as governor in the place of Perier. It was at this time the king of France fully determined to firmly establish his supreme authority throughout the entire valley of the Mississippi, then called Louisiana. But that little, yet seemingly indomitable, Chickasaw Nation, stood in the path; and though the French openly derided the Chickasaws, yet they secretly dreaded them, and not without just cause. It was they, who had influenced and encouraged the Natchez to attack and destroy the French at Fort Rosalie, November 28, 1729, which however, ultimately resulted in the overthrow and annihilation of the unfortunate Natchez themselves. It was they who had successfully debarred all communication between the French colonies at Kaskaskia and New Orleans, by sustaining their independence, thus weakening the French upon the continent by a division of their possessions; while the English traders from Virginia and the Carolinas—the uncompromising rivals and inveterate enemies of the French in securing a foothold by which to establish their permanency upon the territories of the southern Indians—were welcomed by the Chickasaws in all their towns and villages and throughout their entire territory. Therefore to speedily secure and successfully retain the eastern valley of the Mississippi for the French, it was necessary to first overthrow the Chickasaws. "They must be wiped out" was the fiat of the French; yet they successfully and gloriously triumphed, after a long and fearful struggle of eighteen years, alone and unaided except by a few Natchez refugees.

After Bienville was reinstated, he spent the whole year (1734) in futile attempts to induce the Choctaws to make war upon that still resolute and defiant people; but at this juncture of affairs, a Choctaw chief by the name of Shulush Humma (shoes red) appeared upon the stage, who proved to be as shrewd a diplomatist as he was a brave and consummate warrior, and well understood how to shuffle his cards to the best advantage, as he oscillated between the solicitations of the English and the French for the favor of his alliance. But the French proved unsuccessful; for Bienville induced Shulush Humma to undertake a war expedition with a thousand warriors against the Chickasaws, with whom Bienville also sent Lesuer, a French officer, with thirty soldiers. But the ever vigilant Chickasaws had learned of the whole proceedings, and at once sent a delegation under a white flag to meet them and buy them off with English goods of which they had a large amount; in this they succeeded, and the war party returned home, without attempting any further demonstrations of hostilities, except Shulush Humma, who, for no other apparent reason than that of shame to return to Bienville without having made some demonstration, attacked a little Chickasaw village with a few of his warriors as he was on his way home; but was at once repulsed with a loss of four of the attacking party.

Bienville, though greatly disconcerted, appeared indifferent so far as to renew the former treaties of alliance with the Choctaws, as he well knew the salvation of the French colony depended wholly upon the friendship and the aid of that powerful tribe. But during the interval of those protracted negotiations, the Choctaws, through some unknown cause, became divided into two parties, or factions, one in favor of the English, the other of the French.

But the ever watchful Chickasaws, aided alone by the avenging Natchez refugees, were not idle during the slow and dubious negotiations of the French with the Choctaws, but boldly attacked the French whenever and wherever an opportunity presented itself; and especially the Natchez, enraged with a burning sense of their long series of wrongs, outrages and misfortunes at the hands of the French, sought everywhere to avenge their nation's destruction.

But the Chickasaws evidently cherished a desire for peace for having captured three Frenchmen, an officer named DuCader, a sergeant, and a private soldier, they requested DuCader to write to Bienville and inform him that they desired peace; and as a manifestation of their sincerity, they made the soldier the bearer of the letter to Bienville, requesting him to also confirm the statements set forth therein. The soldier arrived safely in New Orleans, and delivered the letter to Bienville, informing him also of the desires of the Chickasaws. But Bienville at once wrote back to DuCader, that he would not make peace with the Chickasaws; nor would he sacrifice the interests of the French Nation to the safety of two men; therefore he and the sergeant must make the best of their misfortune by escaping, otherwise suffer the consequences. DuCader and the sergeant, under the guise of securing peace, did eventually outwit the Chickasaws and made their escape, returning safely to New Orleans.

Bienville immediately wrote to the French Minister of Marine earnestly asking for four additional companies of troops to be added to his forces, then amounting to only two hundred men; and with which he did not feel justified in risking the "glory and honor of the French arms" in a battle with the Chickasaws, "who could call into the field four hundred and fifty warriors." His appeal was acknowledged by the arrival, soon after, of more troops; and Bienville commenced his preparations for an expedition against the Chickasaws, with an avowed determination to wipe them out as a Nation and take possession of their territory.

He organized two armies, one in Mobile, then in the Choctaw Nation; the other in Illinois; the former to be commanded by himself, the latter by D'Artaguette, then governor of the Illinois district. The two were to form a junction by the 31st of March, 1736, in the Chickasaw territory
at the village, where, 196 years before, DeSoto had wintered. Bienville had instructed D'Artaguette to meet him
with all the French troops he could possibly collect, and
also with as many warriors of his Indian allies as he could
get. This invasion, with the avowed purpose of exterminating the Chickasaws was planned and undertaken by the
direction of the French government, "whose solicitude was
anxiously turned to it with high anticipations of a successful
result."

But Bienville was unable to leave Mobile with his army
until the 4th of April; and slowly ascending the devious
windings of the Tombigbee River, the troops reached Fort
Tombigbee on the 23rd, which had been built 250 miles
above Mobile on the western bank of the river by a party
sent forward for that purpose. At this fort Bienville secured
the aid of six hundred Choctaw warriors by presents and
promised rewards for every Chickasaw scalp, which increased his force to twelve hundred men. Thus prepared to
wreak his long cherished vengeance, Bienville again began
his tedious way up the windings of that crooked stream to
a point then called "Tunmuntucche (Where the bow was
strung)"—corruption of the Choctaw word Tumuhushi, signifying village—and afterwards known as Cotton Gin Port,
twenty-one miles southeast of the famous great village of
the Chickasaws then called Chikasahha, but afterwards
the "Chickasaw Old Fields," which he reached on the 22nd
of May, and there landing his army, he threw up a temporary fortification, in which he placed his artillery, and sent
out Choctaw scouts to obtain information of D'Artaguette.
On the 25th of May, Bienville, leaving a strong guard to
protect his boats, took up his line of march toward Chickasahha, and arrived within three miles of it the same day,

and there encamped for the night, during which the Choctaw scouts returned, but without having ascertained anything concerning D'Artaguette. Bienville at once despairing
of all hopes of D'Artaguette's co-operation, resolved to risk
an attack alone, being numerically as three to one of the
Chickasaws; therefore, before daylight on the morning of
the 26th, he stealthily marched upon what he expected to
find a village of unsuspecting and sleeping inhabitants; a
plan so judiciously adopted and successfully executed by
the modern Sherman and Sheridan style of "military heroes"
whose military fame rested alone upon their skill in pounc-
ing upon sleeping Indians and butchering them regardless
of age or sex.

But Bienville's disappointment in not finding D'Artaguette in waiting was only suppressed by finding the ever
vigilant Chickasaw warriors calmly waiting for him from
behind the strong fortifications with which they had encir-
cled their ancient city over which the British flag also waved
in flaunting defiance, while here and there within the fortifications were seen a few prodigal sons of Old England, as
they flitted with hurried steps from side to side.

The Chickasaws had protected their favorite city with
five forts, each well provided with loop-holes; also a larger
one constructed of logs placed upright and firmly in the
ground in near and convenient proximity to the five smaller
parts, and in addition to this they had strongly fortified
houses. During the first day Bienville made two unsuccessful efforts to storm this Chickasaw log and dirt citadel, but
was quickly driven back, with great loss; for upon both
charges the innumerable loop-holes that studded the fortifications seemed a zone of fire and a hail-storm of leaden
bullets swept the ranks of the besiegers. For three successive days did the French attempt to scale the walls of that
little fort, but to meet with defeat, for the Chickasaw warriors met them at every point and heroically disputed every
inch of ground. It is stated, the French soldiers had provided themselves with wooden breast-plates, as a protection

from the Chickasaw arrows, which it was believed would be the only weapon with which they would have to contend. No wonder their astonishment was great, when, instead of a shower of arrows to rebound from their breast-plates, a hailstorm of leaden bullets greeted them, against which their wooden shields were as gossamer.

But the six hundred Choctaw warriors regarding the French as nothing short of idiots to thus charge upon and shoot at logs instead of a visible enemy, remained at a commendable distance during the three days' fight, and easily discerning the inevitable result of such a mode of proceeding, they at once bade the French and Chickasaws an informal adieu, and sought their distant homes. The morning of the 29th of May, 1735, found Bienville badly whipped and in inglorious retreat with his army for his boats, vigorously pursued by the exulting Chickasaws, who followed closely upon the heels of the disorganized soldiers, pouring into their unpadded backs volley after volley of leaden messengers of death; and thus terminated Bienville's exterminating invasion of the Chickasaw country, a disastrous defeat with the loss of many men killed, wounded and captured.

On May 30, Bienville, throwing his few pieces of light artillery into the river, hastily embarked with his army, and greatly humiliated and despondent in regard to the "honor of the French arms" entrusted to his care, paddled down the river, leaving the brave Chickasaws in quiet possession of their homes and country, and, on the last of June, landed his crestfallen troops on the banks of the Bayou St. John.

The cannon thrown into the river were found in its bed near Cotton Gin Port, during a low stage of the water, by the early settlers of the state of Mississippi, and were believed by the uninformed and credulous, to have belonged to DeSoto, and thus marked the spot where he crossed the Tombigbee River in his memorable raid through the Chickasaw territories in 1540 and 1541.

But what of D'Artaguette and his invading army from the Illinois district? Alas! Bienville learned the sad intelligence after he returned to New Orleans that D'Artaguette had arrived in the Chickasaw territory according to the time designated, hence many days in the advance of him, and when he had advanced close to Chikasahha he also, as Bienville afterwards did, sent out Indian scouts to obtain tidings of him, who soon returned without gaining any information. But the next day a courier brought a letter to D'Artaguette informing him that Bienville would not be able to reach Chikasahha before the first of May, and also instructed him to govern his movements in accordance thereto, upon which D'Artaguette immediately called a council of his officers and Indian chiefs who at once, and unanimously, advised an immediate attack; to which D'Artaguette yielded, and forthwith marched on with his army numbering 130 French soldiers and 360 Indian warriors, and made a bold and fierce attack upon Chikasahha. But equal was their astonishment, with that of Bienville afterwards, when five hundred Chickasaw warriors and thirty Englishmen suddenly made a furious charge upon them from behind a hill, near the mouth of a creek called Nita Bok (Bear Creek) and with such fearless impetuosity accompanied with the terrible Chickasaw hoyopatassuha (war whoop) that the Indian allies fled in wild dismay, though the French soldiers stood their ground and bravely fought until forty-five of their number were killed, then began a slow and orderly retreat, which was soon discovered by the Chickasaws who made a fearless charge upon them which at once destroyed all order among the soldiers and caused them to fly panic-stricken, terminating in a complete and disastrous rout. Shouting their wild and exulting warcry, the victorious Chickasaws pursued the fugitives, killing fifty and wounding many others. At this juncture a storm suddenly arose and raged with such terrific fury that further pursuit was stopped, or scarcely one would have survived. The victory of the Chickasaws was complete, and the booty secured in the camp outfit of the French was highly prized, especially the guns and ammunition which amounted to 450 pounds of powder and 12,000 bullets, which they soon after brought into requisition in defeating Bienville. Also a large amount of provisions were taken and many horses captured. But D'Artaguette was not as fortunate as Bienville. He and Vincennes, the second in command, and a Jesuit priest were taken prisoners and all were burned at the stake according to the North American Indian mode of revenge, and also in strict accordance with the example set before them in 1731 by Governor Perier, who had burned the three Chickasaw warriors sent by their Nation to seek the alliance of the Illinois Indians, but unfortunately fell into his hands while on their mission.

A youth sixteen years of age, it is stated, led the survivors of that unfortunate battle back to their homes in Illinois; and thus terminated the expedition of D'Artaguette to assist Bienville in the utter extermination of the Chickasaws. Many prisoners were also taken by the Chickasaws in the defeat and retreat of Bienville to his boats, all of whom perished at the stake. During the fearful tragedy, a Jesuit priest, also a prisoner, proposed to his fellow prisoners, as they waited their inevitable doom, that they all march together into the fire and thus exhibit to the Chickasaws how Frenchmen could die; to which all consented, provided he would lead the way. Then commending their souls to God, they together chanted the miserere as the signal for starting, and all calmly and resolutely marched up and threw themselves into the flames and perished together. The Chickasaws were so astonished that they looked on the scene in silence and made no opposition whatever; and such was the finale of Bienville's hopes to destroy the peace-seeking Chickasaws root and branch. Had he been taken prisoner by the Chickasaws and suffered death at the stake, instead of his soldiers, even mercy might have exclaimed: "He merited his fate."

Years afterward, the old Chickasaws oft rehearsed to the missionaries the traditional account of their two great victories over the French, and proudly displayed to their view, as trophies, many relics of the two battles which commemorated the defeat of D'Artaguette and Bienville.

There is a little incident connected with the battle in which D'Artaguette and his army were destroyed that merits a place in memory. In the pursuit of the fugitives a young Chickasaw warrior named Hlikukhto hosh, (the humbing bird) captured a little French girl five years of age, named Nancy. The chivalric young warrior spared the child, and, captivated by her wonderful beauty, there and then resolved, in the coming future, to make the pale-face maiden his wife. In accordance therewith The Humming Bird watched over his little captive protege and prospective wife from innocent childhood to beautiful womanhood with zealous care, having her trained and educated in strict accordance with the most approved Chickasaw style of etiquette, while he ever manifested to her a proper reserve, attended with the greatest respect and devotion as she grew to womanhood. In the course of years his devotion was reciprocated by French Nancy, as she was called. In due time the nuptial ceremony was performed in accordance to Chickasaw custom and usage. French Nancy raised a family and lived to a great age. Rev. T. C. Stuart, the missionary, stated he saw her and made her acquaintance in 1821, at which time she was 91 years of age, according to the year she was captured (1735) by Hlikukhlo, at the age she was said to be at the time of her captivity. She remembered some of the circumstances of her capture and seemed to delight in narrating them. She still retained her European features, said Rev. T. C. Stuart, but in every other respect was Chickasaw. She was respected, honored and loved by the entire Chickasaw Nation, and regarded as a living monument of their victory over their inveterate enemies, the French. She died and was buried at Monroe, the old missionary station.

Through the instigation of the French the war was continued between the seemingly infatuated and blinded Choctaws and Chickasaws during the entire year 1737, yet without any perceptibly advantageous results to either. But Bienville devoted the year 1739 to preparation for another invasion of the country of that indomitable people; and, as an introductory step he sent an embassy, in March, 1739, to the Choctaws to conciliate their good will and obtain their aid. And strange as it may appear, Bienville secured thirty-two villages out of forty-two to the interests of the French, while, through the instigation and influence of Shulush Humma, the remaining ten decided in favor of the English.

And now, for the first time in their history, the Choctaws were divided into two parties. Shulush Humma, elated with his success in securing to himself even ten villages, made a clandestine visit, with about a hundred of his warriors, to the English settlements in now the State of Georgia, but for what purpose, it was never satisfactorily ascertained. By some, it was thought, he desired to adopt measures of mutual action between the English and his party against the French; by others, that he was influenced alone by the hope of reward. Be it as it may, he, through the influence of some unknown cause, suddenly changed his course of action, and, returning home, at once declared himself in favor of the French; soon after which he burned three English warehouses and then started, without delay, with a band of his warriors, on a war expedition, against the Chickasaws.

Bienville was greatly pleased at the turn Shulush Humfa had taken, as with the assistance of the entire Choctaw Nation, his hopes of exterminating the Chickasaws would now be fully realized. But to make his second attack upon them a sure and complete success, he adopted every measure possible that might strengthen his plans; therefore called into requisition all the available troops he could command not only in Illinois and Canada, but even obtained troops from France; and still to be more sure, he chose a different route from that by the way of the Tombigbee River. He now determined to ascend the Mississippi River to a point on its banks, to be previously ascertained, nearest to Chikasahha; this point was found to be near the mouth of a little creek called Margot, a few miles below the present city of Memphis, Tennessee, and about 120 miles from Chikasahha.

The forces to be drawn from Illinois and Canada were to assemble on a river then St. John in now the state of Arkansas, with their headquarters on the bluff then called Chickasaw Bluff, on which is now located Memphis, Tennessee. By the last of June, 1739 twelve hundred French soldiers and twenty-four hundred Indian warriors (allies of the French) had congregated, and the doom of the Chickasaw patriots seemed inevitably sealed. But inexplicable causes delayed the French army at the place of rendezvous during the whole summer; in the intervening time, many soldiers, especially those from France and Canada, fell victims to the diseases peculiar to that malarial climate; in addition to this, their supply of provisions failed, as fully half, which had been forwarded from Fort St. Francis failed to reach their place of destination; and also two hundred and fifty horses and fifty beeves, sent from Natchitoches, were lost enroute; nor was the marching route to Chikasahha fully established until nearly two months of exploration had been spent, by which time (January, 1740) their provisions were exhausted.

But Bienville obstinately refused to accede to any measures that tended to giving up the expedition, until coerced by a council of war convened in February, which declared a retreat absolutely indispensable. Immediately the main body of the army began its retreat down the Mississippi River, March, 1740. But Celeron, the commander of the Canadian troops, with one hundred Canadian soldiers and five hundred Indian warriors, determined, upon his own responsibility, to go on to Chikasahha, and at once took up his line of march. But the Chickasaws, fully aware of the great army organized to invade their country, and also of the approach of Celeron, whom they believed was but the van of the French army, sent an embassy to him to treat on measures of peace. Celeron at once accepted their proposition, nd told them to report to Bienville, whom they soon overtook on his retreat to New Orleans. The Chickasaws evidently did not comprehend the true state of affairs, for, had they truly known the demoralized state of the French, the peace embassy, instead of following after Bienville, would have hastened home, and at once prepared to receive Celeron, whom they could easily have defeated, as they had D'Artaguette and afterwards Bienville.

But Bienville gladly accepted the propositions of peace, yet stated to them that the terms agreed upon would not include the Choctaws in the stipulations, and, therefore, they would still continue the war against them, and he would also continue to pay to the Choctaws the promised reward for every Chickasaw scalp taken by them until they should satisfactorily remunerate them for the many injuries they had done them. Celeron at once returned to Fort Assumption, on the bluffs, which he destroyed and then started with his soldiers for their distant Canadian homes; while Bienville, with his troops, sought his southern post at New Orleans.

Peace was then proclaimed to have been established between the Chickasaw Nation and the Kingdom of France; but it was a peace that left the Chickasaws the undaunted and unconquerable lords of their own country. To the honor and praise of the Chickasaw people, it may truly be said: They fought single handed and alone for eighteen years against the French and their numerous Indian allies, kept them out of their country and maintained their independence to the last. They defeated D'Artaguette and Bienville in 1736; Marquis of Vaudreuil in 1752, and Regio in 1753; and in 1771 sustained their authority over an extensive country, embracing the territory from middle Mississippi north to the mouth of the Ohio River, and from the Tombigbee River west to the Yazoo.

The French regarded the treaty of peace which Bienville had made with the Chickasaws as of no weight or importance, since the Choctaws still maintained that they had not as yet (1741) received any compensation for the injuries inflicted upon them by the Chickasaws. Consequently, these two nations were still at war, greatly to the satisfaction of the wily French, who, with all their boasted friendship for the Choctaws, secretly rejoiced equally at the weakening and destruction of the one or the other of those two war-like nations, while an incomprehensible infatuation seemed to effectually close their eyes, especially the Choctaws', against seeing the dark designs and artful hypocrisy of the French.

But in their fratricidal conflicts the Choctaws, being fully supplied with guns and ammunition by the French, often got the advantage of the Chickasaws, who, at various times, seemed to be threatened with the fate of the Natchez—utter destruction and extinction—as their numbers were fast being thinned and their strength ebbing away. At this crisis of affairs the different little bands of Natchez, who had found a temporary asylum among the Chickasaws from their inveterate enemies, the French, and who had bravely assisted them in defense of their country, now, having learned that their presence but entailed additional trouble upon their protectors, withdrew from them and sought safety among the Cherokees, who openly extended to them the hand of pitying charity.

The closing of the year 1742 still found the misguided Chickasaws and Choctaws engaged in war, as the Choctaws had now declared through the influence of the French, that they would continue the war until the Chickasaws were driven from their ancient domains, or entirely exterminated; and the first clause, at least, of their fratricidal threat seemed about to be verified, for many of the Chickasaws were then seeking an asylum among the English in the Carolinas.

About two miles south of West Point, Mississippi, there are, or were many years ago, two mounds standing in a line of north and south, about 140 yards from each other. The tradition of both the old-time Chickasaws and Choctaws states that, in the years of the long past, a great battle was fought near where the two mounds now stand, between a company of Chickasaw and Choctaw warriors. The battle proved to be a drawn one, and both parties agreed to bury their dead without molestation, the one by the other. A large hole was excavated by each party in which they placed their respective dead, and filled up the grave, and then erected the mounds over their dead and buried warriors. The Chickasaws' dead occupied the northern and the Choctaws' the southern. This battle, no doubt, was one among the many they fought in their conflicts with each other in behalf of the English and French, and today stand as living monuments of those fratricidal wars that so weakened both nations, to the secret joy of both the English and the French.

At this juncture of affairs, May 10, 1743, the marquis of Vaureuil arrived at New Orleans, and assumed command of the colonies, Bienville having been again deposed. As soon as the Chickasaws learned that Bienville had been superceded by a new governor, they sent four of their chiefs, at the close of the year 1743, to sue for peace; but Vaudreuil informed them he would enter into no treaty with them, unless they would drive all English traders from their territories; and not even then would he treat with them unless in concert with the Choctaws. The four chiefs then requested time to lay his terms of peace before their people.

Early in the following year, the Chickasaws again sent an embassy to Vaudreuil and informed him they would accept his first proposition, if he would supply them with goods and ammunition as the English had done, but still Vaudreuil would take no action in the matter without first obtaining the sanction of the Choctaws. Great indeed was his surprise in learning that the Chickasaws and Choctaws were at that very time endeavoring to establish peace between themselves, without his knowledge. Vaudreuil determined at once to defeat the object of all such negotiations, and immediately went to work for the accomplishment of that end; first, by postponing the making of a treaty himself with the Chickasaws; second, by using every means to again devise the animosity so long existing between the two Nations. Alas! he succeeded but too well in his nefarious designs.

But down to the year 1746, the Chickasaws were still maintaining their ground against fearful odds; while the Choctaws, now becoming weary with their long protracted wars against them, many of them became their friends and even allies; among the most prominent of whom stood the renowned Shulush Humma, who by his daring deeds had become a terror to the Chickasaws, and also Alabaman Mingo (a corruption of Ullabanoh Miko, the only child of a chief), who had long been considered as a firm friend of the French; still, the French retained many friends among the Choctaws, who were now called "the French party"; and those who were disposed to be lenient to the Chickasaws and had extended to them the hand of peace and friendship were called "the English party."

But now the judgments of God seemed about to be visited upon the Choctaws, by sending upon them an infatuation more fatal to themselves than were the hostilities to the Chickasaws, for early in the year 1748 the animosity of the two parties arose to that degree that a civil war, fierce and bloody, was the actual result, to the infinite delight of both the French and English. Each party formed themselves into small bands and made hostile excursions, the one against the other. Also, the English faction made excursions against the French, and the French faction against the

English. A band of the English party made an attack upon a German settlement under the jurisdiction of the French, killed a German, wounded his wife and took captive their daughter. And the leader of the band was in turn killed by his own brother, who was also a leader of one of the bands of the French party; also a brother of Shulush Humma, who had been sent on an embassy to the Carolinas with a small party to solicit aid from the English settlements, was attacked by a company of the French party and had eight warriors slain. On July 14 a French party rushed upon a village of an English party and slew thirteen, among whom were two noted chiefs, upon which the English party, maddened with the desire of retaliation, rushed upon a village of the French party, and there a fierce and desperate hand-to-hand fight with tomahawk and knife ensued, in which both sides lost grievously, but resulting in the defeat of the English party with a loss of eighty killed and an equal number wounded, whom they carried off in the retreat, but many of whom afterwards died. Many such fratricidal battles followed in quick succession, the English party always sustaining the greater loss. Such an insane warfare and foolish destruction of life, sapping the very foundation of their national existence, finally put the Choctaws to thinking, which soon brought them to their senses. Both parties began to see that they were cutting each others' throats for the sole benefit of the English and French pale-faces.

At once a council of the old and wise men of the Nation was convened to devise measures to bring about a cessation of hostilities. After a few days of calm and solemn deliberation, the chief cause of the unfortunate state of affairs was traced to Shulush Humma, and the immediate verdict of the council was death to him; and in accordance thereto, that noted chief and consummate warrior was slain by a deputation, appointed for that purpose, while returning one day to his home with a company loaded with English goods. It was hoped that the death of Shulush Humma would be effective in restoring peace and harmony to the Nation, and it would have been had not the English, still desiring to weaken as much as possible their old enemies, the Choctaws, determined that peace should not be made between the two contending factions if it was possible to prevent it; therefore they clandestinely secured the appointment of a brother of Shulush Humma to the chieftaincy of that renowned chief's party, and thus thwarted the good designs of the council and prolonged the fratricidal war, to the serious injury of the contending Choctaws, who continued the devastating strife until 1750, when it terminated with the advantage on the part of the French faction, at which time only two of the thirty-two villages still adhered to the interests of the English; who, having lost 130 of their warriors in a terrible battle that shortly afterwards ensued, now sought peace of the French, who granted it with this humiliating proviso: "That the punishment of death should be inflicted on any and every Choctaw who should kill a Frenchman, be he chief or common warrior; and if any one or more Choctaws should attempt to rescue the guilty party, or parties, from the punishment of this sentence, then the entire Choctaw Nation should unite, assist and inflict death also on all those who attempted to rescue the guilty party, or parties; and also that death should be inflcted upon any Choctaw who should lead an Englishmen into his village; nor in such a case, should retaliation for his death be sought by any one of his Nation; and also they should put to death the Englishman thus introduced; and also the Choctaws should continue hostilities against the Chickasaws so long as they existed as a Nation."

The Chickasaws, now also reduced to the verge of destruction by their long struggle with the combined forces of the French and Choctaws, once more sued for peace with the French; but to their solicitation, Vaudreuil coolly replied, "That he would consider the matter." But the truth is, he did not want to treat with the Chickasaws upon any terms of peace whatever. In a letter written shortly after to his government, he stated: "With regard to the Chickasaws, we must postpone all action, and patiently wait until we can organize and make another expedition against them"; and assigns his reasons that, "By the failure of the expedition, undertaken against them between the years 1735 and 1740, the Indians have arrived at the conclusion that we cannot conquer or destroy them; and until we erase from their minds the impression of our inability to subdue them, by giving full retaliation for our unsuccessful operations against them, the honor of our arms will remain tarnished."

After two years of consideration on the solicitation of the Chickasaws for peace, Vaudreuil, instead of giving them a reply pro or con, spent the intervening time in the organization of another war expedition against them; and, in 1752, he started with seven hundred French soldiers and a large body of Indian warriors to exterminate that brave nation. But his expedition proved as complete a failure as the previous three, for the Chickasaw heroes, at Chikasahha, where they had repulsed D'Artaguette and Bienville seventeen years before, also, whipped Vaudreuil, and he, too, sought safety in an inglorious retreat, without erasing from the minds of those indomitable Chickasaw warriors "the impression of our inability to subdue them." Yet he was blest with the consoling reflection that he had done something, at least, in the way of "giving full retaliation for our unsuccessful operations against them"; since he could state in his report that he had been enabled, though in full retreat, "to burn a few deserted Chickasaw villages, destroy a few fields of corn, and kill a few cattle of the enemy"—neither Bienville nor D'Artaguette could say as much—and "the honor of our arms will" not now "remain tarnished."

In 1753 Vaudreuil was appointed Governor of Canada, and Kerlerec took the place of Vaudreuil as Governor of the Louisiana Colony; and shortly after, in a letter to his government, August 20, 1753, he said: "I am satisfied with the Choctaws. I believe them true to their plighted word, and it is necessary that we should be the same to them. They are a people who reflect and reason more logically than it is generally supposed."

After the appointment of Vaudreuil as Governor of Canada the French made no more "exterminating expeditions" against the Chickasaws. But Kerlerec, shortly after he had taken the place of Vaudreuil, had an interview with several chiefs of the Arkansas tribes at New Orleans whose good will he won by his affected generosity and seemingly great friendship and hospitality; nor was he unmindful of the "failure of the expeditions undertaken against the Chickasaws"; therefore, lest the "honor of our arms remain tarnished," he embraced the opportunity offered to induce the chiefs of the Arkansas tribes to make war upon the Chickasaws. Kerlerec also made strenuous efforts to induce those chiefs to make war upon the Cherokees, who had entailed the hatred and animosity of the French, because they had extended the hand of pity and protection, in connection with the Chickasaws, to the homeless and forlorn little band of Natchez, who had escaped the wholesale slaughter of their people by the hands of their unrelenting enemy, the French.

That the Chickasaws were once a numerous and powerful people, even at the beginning of their hostilities with the French; and that their warriors were among the most sagacious and fearless men that ever went into battle, no stronger evidence is necessary than the fact, they stood alone and maintained their independence against the combined forces of the Canadian, Illinois and Loiusiana colonies, together with the soldiers sent from France and their numerous Northern Indian allies, also the Choctaws, then the most dreaded nation of warriors, except the Chickasaws, among the North American Indians, from 1716 down to the time France ceded her North American possessions to England in 1763; defeating four French armies, well organized and equipped, and their Indian allies, sent against them, each of which, in numbers and munitions of war, was superior to them as the ratio of three to one, and driving them from their territories; and though Roman states, in his "Barnard Roman's Florida,"page 571, "In 1771, this once powerful and warlike tribe could not number over three hundred warriors," yet the combined forces of their white and red enemies failed to conquer them.

The following letter written by Governor Claiborne of Mississippi, in 1802, to Samuel Mitchell, United States agent to the Chickasaws, expresses much truth in regard to the Indians:

"I am well pleased with your efforts to advance the happiness of our Chickasaw brethren. I hope, under your tutorage, that they will soon acquire the habits of civilization. Exert all your influence to induce the men to have fixed abodes, culitvate the soil, and encourage the women to habits of domestic life. Continue to supply them with wheels and cards, scissors, thimbles, needles and thread. Retain a competent weaver constantly in your employ and persuade a few young girls to learn the art from him. A competent man of undoubted morals must be procured who must take the necessary pains to teach them, and I will see him liberally compensated. It is desirable to place a few intelligent Indian lads with your wheelwright and blacksmith. In all cases it is my express injunction that the white mechanics, you are authorized to employ, shall be men of sober habits and of good character. They are to be there not only as artisans, but as teachers, to set an example to an untutored people, entrusted to my guardianship by their great Father, the President, and he demands that they shall be treated as his children, and not, in any instance, be exposed to the evil example of bad white men. Say to my old friend, Major Colbert, his wish to have his son educated in and by the United States shall be promptly recommended by me; and, I doubt not, will be so directed by the President. A trading house for the accommodation of the Chickasaws has been established at the Bluffs, and the factor has been instructed to sell at prices merely to cover cost and charges. Complaint of undue charges must be made through you to me. You did right to exert your influence for peace between the Chickasaws, Choctaws and Osages. The United States is bound by treaty to restrain the tribes within their limits from warring against tribes in the Spanish dominion."

What if the noble, humane and Christian sentiments expressed in the above letter by Governor Claiborne had been adopted and truly carried out by the Government and people of the United States from the date of the above letter to the present, who now could justly describe the happy and prosperous condition of every Indian tribe within the jurisdiction of the United States?

In 1792, in a council held at Chickasaw Bluffs, where Memphis, Tennessee, is now located, a treaty was made with the Chickasaws, in which they granted the United States the right of way through their territory for a public road to be opened from Nashville, Tennessee, to Natchez, Mississippi. This road was long known, and no doubt, remembered by many at the present time by the name "Natchez Trace." It crossed the Tennessee River at a point then known as "Colbert's Ferry," and passed through the present counties of Tishomingo, Ittiwamba, Lee, Pontotoc, Chickasaw, Choctaw, thence on to Natchez, and soon became the great and only thoroughfare for emigrants passing from the older states to Mississippi, Louisiana and South Arkansas. Soon after its opening, it was crowded by fortune seekers and adventurers of all descriptions and characters, some as bad as it was possible for them to be, and none a good as they might be.

One of the most noted desperadoes in those early days of Mississippi's history was a man named Mason, who, with his gang of thieves and cut-throats, established himself at a point on the Ohio River then called "The Cave in the Rock," and about one hundred miles above its junction with the Mississippi River. There, under the disguise of keeping a store for the accommodation of emigrants, keel and flat boatmen passing up and down the river, he enticed them into his power, murdered and robbed them; then sent their boats and contents to New Orleans, through the hands of his accomplices to be sold. He, at length, left "The Cave in the Rock," and sought a new location on the Natchez Trace, where he established himself, and soon attained to such a power, that he and his well organized band of out- laws became a terror to all from the banks of the Mississippi River to the hills of Alabama and Tennessee. Over this wide extended territory he was "monarch of all he sur- veyed" for several years; and though many efforts were made by the law abiding citizens to kill or capture him and break up this nest of land pirates, yet he always managed to outwit his pursuers. Ultimately a strong party organized themselves at Natchez and went in pursuit of the daring robber. The company having arrived on the banks of the Pearl River, soon learned that the object of their search was in the vicinity, but before making an attack upon him, they concluded to dine, feed and rest their horses. During this, two of the company, allured by the anticipated delight of a swim, plunged into the cool and clear waters of the river and swam to the opposite bank, but to give themselves into the hands of the vigilant Mason, who had closely watched their maneuvers.

Having secured the two thoughtless bathers, Mason at once assumed a bold and defiant attitude, and called out to his would-be capturers on the opposite bank and informed them that all further demonstration of hostilities on their part would be followed by the instant death of their two captive friends; and also stated if they wished to save the lives of their companions to stack their guns and ammunition at once on the banks of the river at a designated place and he would send for them; if they punctually and obediently complied with his demand he would return their two friends, unharmed. The demands of Mason were duly obeyed and several of his party swam across the river and took possession of the guns, while the two captives were placed in full view with rifles pointing in unpleasant proximity to their heads. Then Mason released his prisoners and bade them return in the way they came; to which they gladly and without hesitation complied. He then sternly ordered the crestfallen company to mount their horses and return to Natchez, adding that it would not be healthy for them to indulge in a hunt again for him, as he would not let them off so gently if they should again fall into his hands.

Treachery finally effected what all other means failed to accomplish. Shortly after, a man of high standing and his two sons were robbed by a party of Mason's band, as they were passing along the Natchez Trace, though they received no bodily injury. After their return home, Governor Claiborne, of the Mississippi Territory, offered a large reward for Mason, dead or alive, a copy of which soon found its way to the notorious bandit, over which, it is said, he manifested much merriment. But the reward proved too great a temptation for two of his band, and they treacherously slew Mason and carried his head in secret triumph to Governor Claiborne. It was at once recognized by many of the citizens. But the joy of the two traitors in anticipation of the reward was of short duration, since among the many spectators were the two sons, who, with their father, had been robbed shortly before, and who at once recognized the two scoundrels as being of the party who had robbed them. At once they were arrested, tried, convicted, and paid the penalty of their crimes upon the gallows. And thus was broken up one among the most notorious gangs of robbers that infested the Natchez Trace.

However, another daring gang sprang up a few years after the death of Mason, under the leadership of one John A. Murrell, who also sought upon the Natchez Trace their victims to murder and plunder during the years 1830 and 1840. And numerous were the bloody deeds and daring robberies committed by those bold free-booters upon the lonely traveler who had the nerve to venture through that long stretch of wilderness and solitude alone; and the thefts of horses and Negroes from the planters, especially the Negroes, whom they enticed away under the promise of taking them north to a free state; then, after selling and stealing them a few times under the pretense to the deluded Negroes of getting money to defray their expenses to a free state, they would kill them and sink their bodies in a river or lake. Murrell was finally captured, tried and condemned to life imprisonment in the penitentiary at Nashville, Tennessee. After a few years of confinement he professed religion (it was said), and his health failing, he was eventually pardoned, then became a preacher of the Gospel, and shortly afterwards died.

General Andrew Jackson led his victorious army along this road (the Natchez Trace) on his return from New Orleans in 1815. Before steamboats began to plough the waters of the Mississippi River, all kinds of produce were transported to New Orleans in keel and flat boats from the upper countries. When arriving there both boat and cargo were sold, and the owners with their employes returned home, some on horseback and more on foot, by the way of the "Natchez Trace." Bands of these rough and fearless boatmen flocked along on the old trace to their distant homes in north Mississippi, Tennessee and southern Kentucky. The intervening wilderness of forests were illuminated with the camp-fires, and the midnight silence of the then vast solitudes broken by their bacchanalian revelries. All characters blended together in those straggling bands of wild and reckless humanity; the jolly boatmen whose lives were spent on the bosom of the majestic "Misha Sipokni" and in the romantic and fascinating jolifications of the camp; men of education and refinement; adventurous youth, who never before was out of sight of the smoke of his native village or humble home; the sturdy farmer; the shrewd trader; the calculating merchant; the wily gambler, and the daring robber, were, to a greater or less extent, represented.

But the "Old Trace" has long since been effaced by the ploughshare and buried in the field of forgetfulness amid the corn and cotton plantations, together with the throbbing hearts, then buoyant with hope and elated with joy, distracted with fear or burdened with care that followed its windings and dubious ways through the Chickasaw and Choctaw Nations nearly a century ago.

In 1794 the United States Government secured the aid of several companies of Chickasaw warriors to co-operate with its troops against some of the northwestern tribes of Indians with whom it had become involved in war. The following is a war commission given by George Washington, then President of the United States, to a Chickasaw chief called Mucklesha Mingo (corrupted from Mokulichih Miko—to outdo or excel—chief. The chief who excels):

George Washington, President of the United States of America. To all who shall see these presents, greeting:

"Whereas, I am authorized by law to employ such a number of Indians and for such compensation as I shall think proper, within certain limitations, to act against the hostile tribes northwest of the Ohio.

"And, whereas, it is expedient that in case of such an event certain chiefs should be previously designated; and having full confidence in the well tried friendship of Muckleshamingo, a chief of the Chickasaw Nation, I do hereby appoint him to rank and to receive pay as Captain of Militia while he shall actually be in the service of the United States and co-operating with the troops thereunto belonging. And I do hereby direct that on such occasions he be respected accordingly.

"Given under my hand at Philadelphia, this the 20th of July, in the year of our Lord 1794, and in the 19th year of the Independence of the United States.

"G. Washington.
"By command of the President, J. Knox."

After the French lost their claimed possessions upon the North American continent and were driven therefrom, the Chickasaws, from that time to the present, have been at peace with the world of mankind; and though they never wholly recovered from the long devastating wars with the French, yet they fully maintained their independence to the last.

Their country lay adjoining the Choctaws on the north; and, like that of the Choctaws, was as fertile and beautiful a country as the eyes of man ever looked upon. With no undergrowth whatever the great variety of majestic trees of centuries' growth covered the hills and valleys; yet with the ground everywhere concealed under a thick carpet of grass one to two feet high, intermixed, especially on the prairies, with wild flowers of every shade of color. In the months of April and May strawberries were found profusely scattered amid the grass of the undulating prairies that lay along the banks of their rivers and creeks, and here and there scattered amid the hills and valleys of their forests; then summer too yielded her immense store of blackberries on every side; in turn, followed autumn with prodigal abundance of hickory nuts of several varieties, walnuts, pecan, huckleberries, wild plums, persimmons, wild grapes, muscadines, all of excellent flavor; while from early spring to late autumn, among the wide extended branches of the forest trees their forest orchestra filled the groves with melody.

There amid those magnificent parks of primitive nature, deer in great numbers, grazed with their cattle and horses, while everywhere could be seen flocks of wild turkeys feeding under the forest trees whose tops seemed alive with jolly squirrels, all undisturbed only as the swift arrow from the noiseless bow or the deadly bullet from the unerring rifle demanded food for the Chickasaw; while the vast canebrakes along all the water courses abounded with carnivorous animals of various kinds in great numbers, furnishing skins and furs to supply the necessities of the lords who justly claimed dominion over those vast solitudes.

But to one who has witnessed all the changes which have taken place in the native characteristics of the southern Indians in their former independence and happiness, as also in the appearance of their ancient domains since their first settlement by the White Race, all seem as a dream of the night or romance of the imagination; and he finds it difficult to realize the features of that forest wilderness which was the home of his boyhood days, alike with that of the red man. The humble little cabins of the generous and hospitable Indians, their little fields of corn, pumpkins, potatoes and beans that furnished their supplies of bread, etc., have long since been swallowed up in the wide-extended cotton fields of civilization, and the vast forests have disappeared and when he reflects on their original aspect, his thoughts seem to revert to a period of time greatly more remote than it really is.

A few years after the exodus of the Chickasaws and Choctaws, and before the tide of white emigration had set in the most prominent feature of their forsaken country was its profound solitude; and he who roamed through the forests, as bequeathed to the White Race by the Chickasaws and the Choctaws, was truly alone.

Though such a hunter's paradise will never be found again upon the North American continent; yet hunting alone was not wholly free of danger, though the hunter was seldom without his dog, whose native sagacity taught him to be as watchful as Argus. Under his footsteps the sluggish, yet spiteful, rattlesnake might be coiled in watchfulness; or the wily panther stretched upon the limbs of a tree might suddenly drop from his perch upon him, as also his cousin, the catamount, which, in those early days, not unfrequently tried his physical strength with man.

When watching at a deer lick at night by the light of the full moon, in which the writer has indulged years ago in the Mississippi forests, the hunter found as his rival in the same sport, the panther or the catamount, sometimes both. An incident of this kind happened to a hunter in Oktibbihaw County, Mississippi, shortly after the exodus of the Choctaws. He had found a deer lick in Catarpo (corruption of the Choctaw word Katapah, stopped, referring to the obstructions in the creek by drifts) swamps, which was much frequented by the deer. He built a scaffold fifteen or twenty feet high on the edge of a lick, and on a beautiful night of the full moon, shortly after sundown, took his seat thereon. About ten o'clock at night a deer noiselessly entered the lick a few rods distant from his place of concealment, and, began licking the salty earth; he was just in the act of shooting it, when his attention was attracted from the deer to a moving shadow upon the ground between him and the deer, he at once looked up to ascertain who his neighbor was, and was not a little surprised to see a huge panther standing on a projecting limb of a tree, that reached nearly over and just behind him, and preparing to spring upon the unsuspecting deer. Not being very fastidious just then, he quietly yielded the right of precedence to his fellow hunter. For several minutes he gazed upon the huge beast as it maneuvered upon the limb seemingly doubtful as to making a successful spring. Finally the panther made a tremendous leap, passing almost directly over the hunter's head, and lit directly upon the deer's back. The bleating of the helpless deer momentarily broke the stillness of the forest, and then all was hushed. The panther pulled his victim to the outer edge of the lick, stood a moment and then with mighty bounds disappeared in the surrounding forests. During all this the hunter sat quietly upon his perch cogitating over the novel scene. But his reveries were suddenly interrupted by a wild and terrible yell, seemingly half human and half beast; then came an immediate response from a distant point in the swamp. That was enough to bring the hunter's cogitations to a fixed determination, manifested by the agility displayed in descending the scaffold, and the schedule time on which he ran towards home, leaving the two panthers to enjoy their supper of venison in their native woods.

The Chickasaws, at the time the missionaries were established among them, like the Choctaws and other southern tribes, lived in rude log houses provided with a few culinary articles, and with skins and furs, elaborately dressed and finished, for their bedding; of which were principally made by the women, who were equally skilled in the art of making earthenware for all domestic purposes, as they were proficient in the art of preparing the skins and furs of various animals for domestic use. Their shoes, called moccasins, were principally made of the skins of deer thoroughly dressed by a process, unequalled by the art of the whites, and beautifully ornamented with little beads of various colors.

As ornaments, the men wore four or five broad crescents of tin highly polished, or of silver when to be obtained, suspended upon the breast, one above the other, and one around the head. They also used little beads in ornamenting their leather garments, intermingled with fancy embroidery. Their favorite embellishment, as with all North American Indians, was the vermillion paint with which they decorated their faces. This mode of decoration was confined to the men.

The women, like their white sisters, wore ornaments suspended from their ears, bracelets around their necks, and also strings of various kinds of gaudy beads.

The ancient Chickasaws were deservedly celebrated for their handsome young women; and seldom have I looked upon such specimens of female grace and loveliness as I have seen among the Chickasaws three quarters of a century ago in their former homes east of the Mississippi River, nor do they fall much below at the present day. They were truly beautiful and, best of all, unconsciously so. Oft was I at a loss which most to admire—the graceful and seemingly perfect forms, finely chiseled features, lustrous eyes and flowing hair, or that soft, winning artlessness which was so pre-eminently theirs.

The greatest care was bestowed upon their children by the Chickasaw mothers, whom they never allowed to be placed upon their feet before the strength of their limbs would safely permit; and the child had free access to the maternal breast as long as desired, unless the mother's health forbade its continuance. Children were never whipped by the parents, but, if guilty of any misdemeanor, were sent to their uncle for punishment (the same as the Choctaws), who only inflicted a severe rebuke or imposed upon them some little penance, or, what was more frequent, made appeals to their feelings of honor or shame. When the boys arrived at the age of proper discrimination—so considered at the age of twelve or fifteen years—they were committed to the instructions of the old and wise men of the village, who instructed them in all the necessary knowledge and desired qualifications to constitute them successful hunters and accomplished warriors. As introductory lessons, they were instructed in the arts of swimming, running, jumping, wrestling, using the bow and arrow; also, receiving from those venerable tutors those precepts of morality which should regulate their conduct when arrived at manhood. The most profound respect was paid everywhere to the oldest person in every family, whether male or female, whose decisions upon all disputed points were received with cheerful and implicit obedience. No matter how distant their blood relations might be, all the members of a family addressed its head as father or mother, as the case might be; and whenever they meant to speak of their natural father, they said, "My real father," in contradistinction to that of father applied to the chief or head of the family.

The itinerant white trader, with his smuggled whiskey, was, and will ever be, the patent instrument in the hands of the devil of demoralization among all Indians, and counteracted the moral and religious influence of the missionaries of the long ago, as well as of the present day. Still those devoted teachers of righteousness of the long past succeeded in removing many of their ancient superstitious customs and beliefs in an almost incredible short space of time. The power and influence of the medicine man, the magic power of their personal totems, and alike that of the rain maker, the prophet, soon vanished before the light of the Gospel of the Son of God; and it was truly affecting to witness with what deep and unfeigned interest they listened to the history of the Cross, as narrated by those true and devoted servants of God, seventy-five years ago; and how soon, under the Divine guidance, they seemed to comprehend and feel the regenerating influence of revealed religion. With unfeigned astonishment they heard the story of the atonement. For a man to yield his life to the demands of a violated law for the life he had taken, or that a friend might die for a friend, was their own law and creed; but for one to voluntarily die for a known and inveterate enemy—yea, for the Son of the Great Spirit to willingly die for those who despised and reviled him required more than the logic and eloquence of the missionaries could accomplish; but it pleased the Divine Spirit to enlighten their understandings, and they soon manifested an earnest faith clearly visible in their prayers, daily walk and conversation and in their lives and deaths.

As the art of writing was unknown to the Chickasaws, before the advent of the missionaries among them, their history rested alone upon tradition; and that a correct, truthful and enduring knowledge of their traditional lore might be imparted to each generation, the young men were, at various intervals, summoned before the aged patriarchs of the Nation to have rehearsed to them the sacred things in which they had been previously instructed, and which were soon to be wholly entrusted to their care, that it might be ascertained whether there would be found any omissions from forgetfulness, or additions proceeding from flights of youthful fancy, or the pruriency of invention.

It was a general custom among all the southern Indians, when they believed a just cause of war against another tribe had presented itself, to pursue a certain preliminary course, though similar to a great extent, yet must be regarded as having its origin in a custom which became the law of Nations. In all such cases the old men of the Nation constituted the council of war, who deliberated with great gravity and solemnity upon a question involving such momentous and dubious results. But in all their deliberations, whether issues of the highest or lowest importance were at stake, the one speaking was never interrupted under any circumstances; and even in social conversation but one talked while the others listened in profound silence and with strict attention. This was a universal characteristic among all southern Indians, which I have learned by personal observation among the Chickasaws and Choctaws during a life of over seventy-five years, and also by reliable information from others who lived for many years among other tribes; and it was difficult for them to reconcile the chattering of the whites in their social gatherings with their ideas of propriety and good sense, when hearing them all talking at the same time, to them apparently without a listener.

But to return to the council of war. If, after due deliberation, they concluded that their Nation had been wronged to such a degree as to justify their action, an embassy was immediately sent to seek redress! If granted, the "Pipe of Peace" was then smoked and a renewal of friendship established.

The "Pipe of Peace," which was tastefully decorated with a profusion of fanciful ornaments, the white feathers of the eagle being the most conspicuous, was respected everywhere by the North American Indians, and the bearers of that sacred emblem were always safe in going and returning under any and all circumstances.

But if satisfactory explanation was refused, the embassy hastily returned home, and the warriors of the Nation at once summoned in council, in which war measures were discussed and adopted during which the "Pipe of War" was smoked; this pipe was similar in shape to the peace-pipe, with the exception that the colors of its ornaments were different, red being the most prominent.

During these preliminaries, the opening tribe not unmindful of the gathering storm, were also performing their war ceremonies. With some tribes, a declaration of war was made by leaving a hieroglyphic picture near a principal village of the Nation against which war was declared, and executed in such a manner as to be fully comprehended by the challenged who the challengers were. If the challenged did not desire war, an embassy bearing the pipe of peace was immediately sent to the offended Nation with full powers of negotiating for peaceful relations between the two nations, which most always terminated successfully.

When preparing for war, the Chickasaws, like their entire race, of whom I have read or personally known, painted their faces in such a manner (known only to the North American Indians) as to give the face an expression of fierceness that must be seen to be justly comprehended. A few days before going upon the warpath a day was solemnly appointed for a great feast, consisting of all the varieties of food that could be obtained; but every night previous to the day of the feast those contemplating going upon the war-path engaged in the war-dance during the greater part of the nights dressed in all the paraphernalia of Indian warfare. The warriors also came to the prepared feast fully equipped with every necessary appertaining to the warpath, but with no superfluous articles whatever that might have a tendency to impede their actions. Before they partook of the waiting repast some celebrated old chief or noted old warrior, with the war-pipe in his hand, who, from the decreptitude of age, had been placed upon the "retired list" among the seers and prophets of the Nation, delivered a speech to the war-going company, in which he rehearsed his own exploits, not in the spirit of self-adulation, but as an honest exhortation to them to emulate his deeds of heroic valor; then encouraged them to go in trusting confidence; to be great in manly courage and strong in heart; to be watchful, keen in sight and fleet in foot; to be attentive in ear and unfailing in endurance; to be cunning as the fox, sleepless as the wolf and agile as the panther; not to be eager beyond prudence; and when wisdom so dictates, to flee as the swift antelope, as your lives are of great worth to your Nation, and even one life necessarily or unnecessarily sacrificed, will bring sorrow to the hearts of your people. But to the appreciation of which no outward manifestation whatever was made, as an Indian warrior is ever silent upon any and all emotions of his heart, yet the aged orator plainly read its significance in each silent and attentive face, and was satisfied. Then he filled the war-pipe with prepared sumac leaves and tobacco; lighted it; drew a few whiffs, then passed it to the war-chief, the leader of the forth-going war-party, who also drew a few puffs, and from him it went the rounds of the entire party, each in profound silence drawing a whiff or two and then passing it to the next in turn. After this impressive ceremony they turned to the prepared feast and did ample justice thereto; after which, the "war-post," painted red, was set up, at which the chief of the war-party rushed and struck with his tomahawk with all his strength, as if one of the enemy. Then followed his warriors in regular order, each doing the same.

Then followed again the war-dance, the finale of the war ceremonies, which continued two or three consecutive nights during the intervening days of which their relatives and friends observed a strict fast and engaged in solemn and supplicating prayer to the Great Spirit for their success against their enemies, and their safe return.

The Chickasaws were addicted to one vice, the vice of gambling. They bet on the proper handling and the skillful shuffling of his ball-sticks, the fleetness of his feet, and his power of endurance; while his white brother risked his money on the proper handling and skillful shuffling of his paper cards.

Among the many redeeming traits of the Chickasaws was their care for and protection of their orphans. Never have there been found among the Chickasaws or Choctaws homeless and friendless orphan children, thrown out to shift for themselves, and left "to root pig or die." I have seen, time and again, in many families among the Chickasaws and Choctaws from one to four adopted orphan children; and they were adopted, not through mercenary motives, but to be protected, cared for and loved, not to be enslaved for the few dollars and cents that anticipation whispered would be made out of them by adoption.[4] And one might live a lifetime in a family of adopted orphans, and, unless told, he would not even suspect but that all the children were of the same parentage.

The ancient Chickasaw divisions of the tribe were called yakissah, (here stops). In reference to family connections in marrying they were the same as the Choctaws. No persons of the sama yakissah were allowed to marry. Also they have been called in chukka holhtenah hochifo, most frequently abbreviated to Inchukka holhte chifo, (his house or clan is numbered and named); and with the same reference as yakissah, and also iksa of the Choctaws. If a man violated the law by marrying a woman of his own yakissah, he forfeited his own rights and privileges, and also his children of the same; but the wife forfeited nothing.

The Chickasaws, like their brethren, the Choctaws, never betrayed any trust reposed in them. No matter what, whether of great value or of little consequence, was left in their charge to be taken care of, that confidence was never betrayed. They were true to their friendship, never being the first to violate its sacred ties. But like all their race of the long ago, they possessed but little idea of compensation; therefore were easily made the victims of unprincipled white traders. But, beginning to realize that they received very little in return for a very large amount given, they adopted a very proper plan, as they thought, to test the honesty of white traders, but which gave them completely into their hands. It was this: they first offered for sale the most indifferent article they had in whatever the line of barter consisted, and asked a higher price for it than its intrinsic value; and if the white man accepted it without dispute, it was sufficient evidence to them that he did not

---

[4] Cushman here refers to the once widespread custom among the whites of "binding out" orphan or otherwise dependent children to work in the family until they should attain their majority. As he implies, these "bound" children were in a state of virtual slavery.

design to wrong them, and their confidence in his integrity
was firmly established. But if the trader refused to make
the purchase in harmony with the Chickasaw offer, the
bargain was at once closed by the suspicion that the white
man intended to defraud them. But the Whites soon learning the Chickasaws' method of testing their honesty, at once
bought the first article offered at the full price set upon it
by the owner without a whimper, and thus gained their
confidence; and without hesitation, entered the door of
trade thus opened and continued to defraud the misguided
Chickasaws.

The ancient Chickasaws had four laws only; all of
which were strictly adhered to and rigidly enforced
throughout the entire Yakissahs of the Nation. First, the
law of murder, which placed the slayer wholly and exclusively in the hands of the oldest brother of the slain, who
never failed to execute the law, the standing verdict of
which was "An eye for an eye and a tooth for a tooth"—
death. In case the deceased had no brother or brothers,
then the next nearest and oldest male relative became the
self-appointed executioner. Nor did anyone, not even the
nearest relations of the slayer, interfere in the matter in any
way whatever—either to assist or oppose. If the slayer fled,
which was very seldom if ever the case, his oldest brother,
and if he had no brother, then the next nearest and oldest
relative in the male line was slain in his place; after which
he could return in safety and without the fear of molestation, but to be ostracised and forever stigmatized as a coward. In all such cases a woman was never slain in the place
of a man. On account of this rigid and inexorable custom
of dealing with him who had slain his fellowman, murders
were very few and far between, as the slayer well knew the
inevitable consequence that would follow unless he fled to
parts unknown, which would be attended with eternal disgrace to himself, family and kindred, at the sacrifice also of
his brother's life, or next nearest male relative.

Second, whipping for minor offenses; after which the culprit was reinstated to favor without any disgrace being attached to his name for his offense or punishment. He had violated the law, but had paid the penalty thereunto attached. The claims of the law were satisfied and therefore it was a thing of the past, to be mentioned no more, and it never was.

Fourth. The property of deceased parents descended to the brothers and sisters of the deceased, and not to their own children.

To us a strange, unjust and inconsistent law; but of which I was informed, as above recorded, by Governor Cyrus Harris, in 1886, who was regarded as among the best posted of the Chickasaws in regard to their laws and customs when living in their ancient domains.

Up to the time the Chickasaws moved west (1836-'38), their country was divided into three districts, viz: Tishomingo, Sealy and McGilvery. At the time of their exodus west to their present places of abode, Tishomingo (properly Tishu Miko, chief officer or guard of the king) was the chief of the Tishu Miko District; Samuel Sealy, of the Sealy District, and William McGilvery, of the McGilvery District.

The Chickasaw ruler was styled king instead of chief; and his chief officer was called Tishu Miko.

Ishtehotohpih was the reigning king at the time they left their ancient places of abode east of the Mississippi River for those west. He died in 1840. He was the last of the Chickasaw rulers who bore the title, king. After his death the monarchical form of government, which was hereditary, as I was informed by Governor Cyrus Harris, was abolished, and the form of republicanism adopted. The power of their kings was very circumscribed, being only about equal to that of their present governor. The king's wife was called queen, but clothed with no authority whatever, and regarded only as other Chickasaw women.

That Tishu Miko was a wise counselor and brave warrior among the Chickasaws is about all that has escaped oblivion, as little has been preserved of his life by tradition or otherwise. He was the acting Tishu Miko of Ishtehotohpih at the time of the removal of his people to the west. He died in 1839, the year before his royal master. He was appointed during life as one of the chief counselors to Ishtehotohpih; and when he advised the king upon any mooted question, so great was his influence over the other counselors, as Governor Harris stated, that they at once unanimously acquiesced to his propositions, but invariably with the reiterated exclamation, "That's just what I thought! That's just what I thought!" while the king said but little, but generally adopted the suggestions of Tishu Miko.

Tushkaapela (Warrior-Helper) was a former Chickasaw king, but was made an invalid for life by an accident which rendered him unable to walk in an upright position, but slowly crawled about by means of a buck's horn in each hand extended behind him, and his feet thrust forward, presenting an object of great compassion. His wife was named Pakarli (blossom), corrupted by the whites Puc-caun-la.

The ancient Chickasaws, unlike the Choctaws, buried their dead soon after life became extinct, placing in the grave with the corpse, if a man, his clothes, war and hunting implements, pipe and tobacco, and a few provisions; if a woman or child, the clothes, and other little articles the deceased may have prized in life, and a few provisions. A Chickasaw widow mourned twelve full moons for her deceased husband, while the other relatives prolonged their mourning only three; at the close of which a Special Cry was appointed at night, which was kept up until the break of day; then the end of the hair of the mourners was clipped and a string handed to them with which they tied up their hair, which had been permitted to hang loose over their shoulders from the death of their kindred to the end of the three moons, the appointed time for mourning.

Suicide was sometimes committed by the ancient Chickasaws, but very seldom. When it was, it was invariably done with their favorite instrument of death, the rifle.

Many of their doctors were well informed in the medicinal properties of various herbs and roots found in nature's pharmacopoeia, and were remarkably successful in their practice, especially in cases of common fevers, the bite of snakes, and many other ills to which frail humanity is so subject everywhere; they were more skilful years ago than at the present day, relying principally upon the white doctors located among them.

But much practical sense would the best white physicians of the long ago have displayed, and much useful information obtained concerning the medicinal virtues of many herbs which Nature then presented in her wild botanical garden (now forever lost) if they had humbled their foolish pride of imagined superiority over the Indian enough to have studied his pharmacy a little more attentively.

When living in the ancient domains of their fathers the Chickasaws had many native women among them who practiced the healing art; and not a few of them became quite adepts in their profession. A few female physicians are still found among them.

Some of the most skillful doctors were regarded by their people as being not only wise in the knowledge of the medicinal properties of various herbs and roots which their boundless forests furnished so abundantly, but also gifted with the power of making it rain when so inclined; but they did not make as frequent illustrations of that power by actual experiment, as did some of the Choctaws.

As among all North American Indians, as far as I have been able to ascertain, so too had the Chickasaws those privileged personages, the rain maker, medicine man and the prophet or seer. The first, in seasons of protracted drouth, was invoked to exert his mysterious power to bring about an abundant shower; the second to interpret dreams and charm away spells, and the third to lift the veil from the dim and mystic future.

The ancient manner of Chickasaw courtship was not very taxing upon the sensitiveness of the bashful prospective groom; since he had but to send a small bundle of clothing carefully tied up in a large cotton handkerchief by his mother or sister to the girl he desired to make his wife. This was immediately taken possession of by the mother of the wished-for bride and kept for a few days before presenting it to her daughter; and when presented, if accepted, it was a bona fide acknowledgment on her part of her willingness to accept him as her husband, of which confession he was at once duly notified; if otherwise, the subject was there and then forever dropped, and the disappointed swain found consolation in the privilege of presenting another bundle of clothes to some other forest beauty. But best of all, the swain, whether bold or timid, was always spared that dreadful ordeal of soliciting the "yes" of the "old folks," as his mother took that duty upon herself, and was almost always successful. The coast being clear of all breakers, the elated lover painted his face in the most approved style, donned his best suit, and sought the home of his betrothed with fluttering heart, who, strictly on the lookout, met him a few rods from the door, and proudly escorted him into the house where they, themselves, in the presence of friends and relatives, performed the marriage ceremony by the man presenting the woman with a ham of venison; or a part of some other eatable animal of the chase; she at the same time presenting him with an ear of corn, or sack of potatoes; all of which betokened the man should provide the household with meat, and the woman with bread. Thus they were made man and wife, and so considered by all.

The Chickasaws, like all the human race in all ages past, indulged in that time honored amusement, the dance. Their ancient national dances were the same as the Choctaws; Hoyopa-hihla (war-dance); Hakshup-hihla, (scalp-dance); Tolih-hihla, (ball-play dance); Tanschusi-hihla (green corn dance); Yunnushhihla, (buffalo dance). Then followed the

social or fun-making dances, such as Akanka-hihla, (chicken
dance); Issuba-hihla, (horse dance); Shut-tun-nih-hih-la
(tick dance); all of which excelled, in purity of sentiment,
many of the civilized exotics, adopted by us, in this refined
age of Christian progress, such as the 'round-dance," etc., if
all be true that is stated about them by those who still
retain some idea of decency and respect for its just claims.
But I judge only from hear-say, never having witnessed the
performances.

In a few only of their social dances, all of which were
performed in the open air, men and women participated
together. Rarely more than one musician at a time engaged
in that department of the entertainment; he sat sometimes
on a block of wood, and sometimes on his mother earth, as
he unyieldingly beat a little drum, accompanied its monotonous tones with his voice in a chanting kind of soothing
lullaby.

The Chickasaws had two dances sacred to the women
alone, in which they only engaged. One was called Itilusa-
hihla (blackwood dance); the other, Itakhalusahihla (black-
mouth dance). They also had a dance called Tanspichifah
(crushed or pounded corn), in which various meats were
mixed and cooked, now called Tarns-pe-sho-fah. This dance
was only performed before the door of a house in which lay
the sick and only indulged in at the injunction of the alikchi
(doctor) who was attending the sick; this ancient dance of
the years of the long past is still kept up among the Chickasaws by some of the full-bloods.

When a doctor was called in to see a patient if after ex-
erting his skill in the knowledge of the medicinal virtues
known in nature's pharmacy, he found his patient gradually
growing worse, he ordered a Tanspichifah hihla. At once
it was announced by sending messengers throughout the
neighborhood, and the appointed day found the friends
assembled. Then a straight line was drawn from the centre
of the doorway of the house in which the sick was confined,
to a smooth and straight pole fifteen or twenty feet in

length, gaily decorated, that had been firmly set up eight or
ten rods from the door. Two guards called Tishu, each
armed with a long stout switch, were each stationed at the
opposite end of the line, whose duty was to prevent anything, man or beast, from crossing the mystic line either
way. In the meantime a fire was kindled a short distance to
one side over which was suspended a large iron vessel filled
with pounded corn and meats. The ground having been
previously and cleanly swept for a little distance each side
of the line from the door to the erected pole, and all things
being ready for the dance, the bed upon which the patient
rested was drawn into a position in the room fronting the
door, to give the patient full view of the merry dancers, see
the gaily decorated pole, and hear the tones of the little
drum as it responded to the quick and vigorous strokes of
the musician; that thus the thoughts of the sick might be
diverted from the depressing influences of the mind dwelling too long upon the malady with which he or she was
afflicted. Then the alikchi brought out two women from
the house gaily decorated with ribbons and beads of various
colors, and also having thimbles or rattles made of dry luksi
hakshup (terrapin shell) attached to their moccasins or the
skirts of their dresses, and placed them together on one side
of the line, while several men stationed themselves on the
opposite side of the line; then the alikchi returned to his
duties in the sick room, the musician started his favorite
tune, and the dancing commenced; the men confining their
exercises strictly to one side of the line, and the two women
to that of the other, each being extremely cautious not to
step over its magic bounds. From one to two women only
danced at the same time; when wearied they gave place to
others to whom were handed the little bells or luksi hak-
shups taken from their ankles and dresses, which the fresh
dancers attached to their persons in like manner as the
others had done.

The leader or director of the Tanspichifah was called
Tikbahika (going first). The above generally commenced an

hour or two before sun down and continued until the shades
of twilight began to appear, then gave place to the partaking of refreshments found previously prepared in the iron
vessel around which both dancers and spectators gathered
in happy merriment. During the hours devoted to the
dance, the doctor, true to his trust, had been attentive to the
fluctuating symptoms of his patient; administering at one
time a decoction of different herbs; at another, performing
his mystic ceremonies, among which was the vigorous rattling of a dry gourd, into which had been placed some peb-
bles, over the head and around the body of his confiding
patient, and squirting from his mouth, at different intervals,
a quantity of the decoction upon the exposed breast of his
patient. After the refreshments the dancing was resumed,
but in the house instead of the yard, where it was kept up
until a late hour of the night, all spectators being without;
during which the monotonous tinkling and rattling of the
thimble bells and terrapin shells, in discordant harmony
with the little drum, all mingling with the voices of the
dancers chanting, E-yih-hah-heh! E-yih-hah-heh! was
enough, it did seem, to kill or cure; or, at least, to forever
put to flight the "Evil Spirit" which the worthy disciple of
Esculapius had declared to be present, and baffled his
healing skill by counteracting the efficacy of his medicines
and mystic ceremonies.

However, if the patient recovered, in spite of all the din
produced by the contest between the doctor and the "Evil
Spirit" for the victory, the doctor bore off the palm; and his
skill was deservedly undisputed. But if the "Evil Spirit"
won the victory by counteracting the virtues of his medicines and mystic ceremonies, causing the death of his patient, the doctor, unwilling still to yield the palm of victory
to the "Evil Spirit," found a more honorable cause for his
defeat; therefore, he solemnly and with great gravity announced that his patient had been shot by an Isht-ul-bih
(Witch-ball) from an invisible rifle in the hands of an invisible witch which left no visible signs of its mysterious power;

but the secret effects of which were beyond the skill of any and all human doctors, to which his dupes gave ready assent; and thus the reputation of the invisible and indefeasible power of the hattakyushpakummi (witch) was confirmed, and the alikchi was enabled to come out of the contest with a reputation unimpared.

The ancient Chickasaws, like the Choctaws, had their specified cries over the graves of their dead. At the day appointed, the relatives, friends and neighbors assembled and one little group after another took their seats on the ground in a circle around the grave, then drew their shawls and blankets over their heads and commenced their doleful lamentations, which must be seen and heard to form any just idea of the scene. The "cry" continued for several days and nights, then terminated with a feast; after which the name of the deceased was pronounced no more. The dead are with the past; for them how fruitless our despair, was their final and just conclusion.

The Chickasaw mother, like her Choctaw sister, was blessed in one particular amid all her trials. She, too, was exempt from the curse which the Sacred Writings declare was imposed upon parturition; and the necessity of a doctor or midwife on such occasion was unknown. A woman, about to become a mother, retired to some private place alone, and in a few hours returned with her child, and quietly resumed her occupations.

The ancient Chickasaws, unlike their kindred, the Choctaws, entertained no superstitious views in regard to the eclipse of the sun or moon; regarding it as a phenomenon inexplicable, and to be the height of folly to be alarmed and worried over that which they had no control. They called an eclipse, either of sun or moon, hushi luma (sun hidden). Sometimes a total eclipse of the sun was termed hushi illi (dead sun), and sometimes hushi kunia (lost sun). They called the moon hushi ninak aya (the sun of the night).

The traditions of the Chickasaws are silent in regard to the flood; at least nothing has been preserved upon that subject. Rather strange! since the Choctaws, to whom they were so closely allied by consanguinity, and the Cherokees, Muscogees, Shawnees and many other tribes spoke of it in their traditions.

Pakitakohlih (hanging grapes), from which the present town Pontotoc, Mississippi, derived its name, was a town known to the French, in the days of Bienville, by the name Chickasahha; and afterwards to the English as "Chickasaw Old Town"; then to the Americans as "The Chickasaw Old Fields"; and was, according to Chickasaw tradition (no doubt correct) the same "Old Town" in which De Soto wintered with his army in 1540, and over whose heads the Chickasaws burned to expel him from their territories; but which they afterwards rebuilt. The venerable "Old Town" was known to the Spaniards at an early day by the name Chicaco; and truly no spot of ground in the Southern States has deservingly greater military fame than "Old Chicaco." This ancient town of the Chickasaws was located upon the banks of a little stream to which they also gave the name Pakitakohlih, on account of the profusion of wild grapes that hung upon its shady banks; and though nothing now remains to tell where the ancient "Chicaco" once stood, still Pakitakohlih continues its gentle meanderings by the perished city of the dead.

But where are they, the once numerous, free and happy Chickasaws, who, in the years gone by, stood alone and maintained their independence against the combined efforts of the French and their Indian allies? They too, with their chivalry and glory, have passed away leaving no trace behind them, except in the little handful that still survives.

As to the Choctaws two years before, so to the Chickasaws, places of rendezvous were appointed in different localities at which they were commanded to congregate, preparatory to their being driven off; and they were herded together in little groups under the guidance of their respective chiefs, who, one after another, moved off with his little band towards the setting sun. Here was seen a mother

calling her unconscious children from their gambols beneath the forest oaks to fall into ranks with a starting group;
then, as she took her place in file, turned her face again and
again to take one more long lingering look upon the loved
scenes of her youth and advanced years; while the loud
laugh of the white teamsters, who accompanied them, at
some rough remark made by some one of their number,
jarred like a discord in some mournful tune upon that
mother's heart.

There, too, was seen the brave warrior and fearless
hunter, as he turned away from his hunting grounds with
its many objects sacred to memory, taking his place in front
of his family circle; and as they bade their final adieu to the
graves of their ancestors, their homes and native land, they
moved off in silence.

But did they leave behind them the religion of the
World's Redeemer as taught them by the faithful missionaries? Not at all. They took it with them as their most
sacred treasure, and worshipped the God of their salvation
under the canopies of the forest oaks in the wilderness of
their new homes for a few years. Then arose, here and
there, amid the forests a log cabin church and a school-
house. Next, in regular succession, comes a sufficiency of
commodious and comfortable churches and school-houses;
and 1861 found them a thoroughly civilized, Christianized,
prosperous, contented and happy people. Then came our
Civil War, into which we dragged them, and out of which
we sent them stripped of everything. Yet, Phoenix-like,
again they arose from the ashes of desolation and stood
once more as a people whose indomitable resolution is unsurpassed in the annals of mankind.

But still not satisfied, we again have entered their little
garden of contentment, with the determination, this time, to
divide their lands in severalty as the introductory wedge to
the destruction of their nationality and our immediate possession of their country, hurling them headlong, without
chart or compass, sail or rudder, to shift for themselves

among a race who possess but one characteristic, "get money," and but one belief, "no good Indian but a dead Indian."

But, as that of the Choctaw country, so it may equally and truly be said that a more beautiful and richer country could not be portrayed on the canvass of nature than was also that of the Chickasaws now forming the north half of the State of Mississippi. They, like the Choctaws, annually burned the grass of their forests throughout their entire country; and thus the landscape was unobscured by any wood undergrowth whatever, while the tall forest trees, standing so thick as to shade the entire ground, spread their giant arms over the thick carpet of grass beneath, variegated with innumerable flowers of all colors.

For several years after the departure of the Chickasaws not a vestige of change was seen; no sound of the woodman's ax, or even the distant crowing of the domestic cock announcing the approach of white civilization, broke the profound silence of the vast forests, undisturbed by man, yet swarming with animal life. Travel where you would, though no sign indicating the presence of man was seen, yet you felt not alone; above you countless warblers rendered the air resonant with the wild but sweet music of nature's harmony; before you the wild turkey flapped his broad wings carelessly and seemed only to change his position that he might the better observe the actions and ascertain the intentions of the new and white-faced intruders upon his ancient heritage; while here and there droves of deer crossed and re-crossed your path at different intervals, sometimes running with fleetest feet, at others quietly grazing, then gaily gamboling in the tall, waving grass.

Who that beheld that lovely land and enjoyed its romantic scenes, but still delights to dwell in memory upon its former charms, as it then lay in all its primitive loveliness and glory, fitted up and bequeathed by the Great Spirit to his Chickasaw children for their abode; but out of which they were cruelly and shamefully defrauded by the United

States in a treaty concluded October 20, 1832, at the Council House on Pakitakalih Creek and ratified March 1, 1833, by the United States Senate.

This treaty having the same designs against the Chickasaws, and as effectually accomplished as that against the Choctaws two years before on the banks of Bok Clukfi Luma Hihlah, September 28, 1830, was made and entered into by John Eaton and John Coffee, on the part of the United States, and seventy-three members of the Council, on the part of the Chickasaw Nation.

There were four Chickasaw families at that day, as I was informed by Governor Cyrus Harris, who kept their houses so neat, and their yards so free of all grass, weeds and rubbish of all kinds, that they were called by the whites, "The clean house Indians." Three of the heads of the four families were brothers, and the other a brother-in-law to the three. The chief or the head man of the four families was named Chikasah nana ubih (pro. Chik-a-sah nar-nar-ub-ih, and sig. A Chickasaw who kills anything), and his two brothers, the one Ishkitahah (pro. Ish-ke-tar-hah and sig. No mother or mother gone), the other, Innihtowa (pro. In-nih-to-wah, sig. Warm the ball). The brother-in-law was named Aiyuka ubih (pro. Ai-yu-kah ubih and sig. Each one kill, or to kill each one).

At an early day a few white men of culture and of good morals, fascinated with the wild and romantic freedom and simplicity of the Chickasaw life, cast their lot among that brave and patriotic nation of people. These white men were James Gunn, Logan Colbert, John Gilchrist, Malcomb McGee, James Allen and John Bynum, and their descendants are still among the Chickasaws. An aged daughter of John Bynum, with whom I am personally acquainted, as also with her children, was, in 1890, still hovering upon the stage of human life.

At the time of the establishment of the Christian mission under the jurisdiction of Rev. T. C. Stuart, Malcomb McGee was a venerable and highly venerated character among the Chickasaws. He was born, according to his own statements, of Scotch parents in the city of New York about the year 1757. Shortly after his parents arrived in America, his father enlisted in the colonial army in an expedition against the French, and was killed at the storming of Ticonderoga, only a few months before young Malcomb was born.

About this time marvelous rumors of the vast and magnificent plains of Illinois, covered by innumerable herds of buffalo, wild horses, deer and great varieties of other wild animals, excited the cupidity of the adventurous, and a company of enthusiasts resolved to go to that imagined earthly paradise, among whom was the young widow McGee. In those days to reach that point from New York, New Orleans had first to be reached by sea; thence up the Mississippi River by a keel-boat worked by hand, which took months of arduous toil and great privation to make a voyage from New Orleans to St. Louis. The journey, however, was undertaken and successfully accomplished. But in that then world of wilderness the young widow McGee soon found herself reduced to extreme poverty, with none near who were able to assist her. At this time a man by the name of McIntosh visited the distant little colony on the Illinois River; learning her distressful situation, he advised her to let him adopt young Malcomb as his own son under the promise of being a father to the boy in raising and educating him. She finally consented, but with great reluctance, and gave Malcomb, then about ten years of age, to the care and guardianship of McIntosh. But what an ordeal for that mother's heart and that orphan boy, the one to remain in the wilderness of the west; the other to go with a stranger to a wilderness far in the east, to the land of the Muscogees, among whom McIntosh had selected his future home; and afterwards marrying among them was adopted and became one of that war-like people, whose descendants from that day to this have been a prominent family among the Muscogees, now known as the Creeks.

But true to his trust, the generous McIntosh proved a father and faithful friend to the homeless orphan Malcomb, and, a few years after his return to the Muscogees, took him to Mobile, then occupied by the French, and placed him in a school under the jurisdiction of a French family, who, shortly after his guardian had left became so tyrannical, that young Malcomb resolved to free himself from their cruelty by bidding them an informal adieu; and soon he embraced the opportunity presented by some Indian traders visiting Mobile, to whom he attached himself on their return. He did not, however, return to his former home under the roof of his benefactor, McIntosh, but stopped among the Choctaws with whom he remained several years, during which he married a Choctaw maiden by the name of Kanah hoyo (a seeker for somebody). He lived happily with Kanahhoyo for several years, who then dying, he returned to the Chickasaws, his old friends, and solicited citizenship which was readily and cheerfully granted. After living with them a few years, he married a Chickasaw widow, Mrs. Elizabeth Harris, who was the oldest daughter of Molly Oxberry, and the mother of Governor Cyrus Harris, of the Chickasaw Nation.

Malcomb McGee acted as interpreter to the Chickasaws in all their negotiations with the United States for nearly forty years. He was greatly attached to the Rev. T. C. Stuart, and when the Chickasaws were driven from their homes to their present ones Malcomb McGee resolved to remain with Mr. Stuart; and in his yard he lived nearly twelve years in a neat little log house erected by his noble missionary friend for his special use and benefit. But about the year 1848 his daughter and her husband paid him a visit from their western home, and persuaded him to return with them, but he survived only a year after his arrival. He died in the ninety-second year of his age and was buried at Old Boggy Depot, in the land of the Choctaws, also his long and faithful friends.

James Gunn, whose name is commemorated in that of a town called Gunntown, situated in Lee County, Mississippi, was one among the six white men previously mentioned, who at an early day cast their lot of life among the Chickasaw people. He was a native Virginian, and also a fearless and indomitable loyalist, who stood for the crown in the troubled days of Charles the First and the Roundheads; and when the Revolution proved triumphant, and the rising glory of these United States had been announced, the old royalist, disdaining the society of successful rebels, bade an adieu forever to the home of his youth, and sought a more congenial one among the true native sons and freemen of North America. He secured a wife named Okashuah (Stinking Water); a name, though not of classic fame or enviable signification, it is reasonable to presume, yet did not detract from her merits as an amiable and devoted wife and mother. They had only one daughter, named Molly, who married a Cherokee warrior named Oxberry, and her oldest daughter by this marriage was named Elizabeth, who became the mother of Governor Cyrus Harris; and another of her daughters, by the same marriage, was, in 1890, living near Colbert Station, Chickasaw Nation, I. T., at the advanced age of ninety-six, and is known as Grandma Alberson. Molly was also the mother of the celebrated Chickasaw beauty named Rhoda. James Gunn died in 1826; his age has not been preserved; but, it is said, he was a very old man at the time of his death.[5]

Many young white sprigs who visited the Chickasaw Nation, when they saw Rhoda, the Chickasaw belle, the fairest rose that bloomed in the forests, solicited her heart and hand, but 'twas all in vain. Rhoda gave her youthful heart to one of her own race, Samuel Colbert, a son of Major James Colbert; the exodus of her people soon following her nuptial day. She became the mother of one daugh-

[5] Indeed he must have been old, for Charles I was beheaded in 1649. Apparently Cushman has telescoped several generations of family history into the life of one individual. Probably James Gunn's ancestors were among the Cavaliers who took refuge in Virginia after the defeat of Charles I, and he himself followed the family tradition by adhering to the Tory cause during the American Revolution.

ter, but after living several years with her husband a final separation, from some unknown cause, took place between her and her husband. Several years after which she married a man by the name of Joseph Potts, who took a dose of strychnine through mistake for quinine, in 1862, while at the house of Governor Cyrus Harris, and died from its effects in a half an hour. A son of Governor Harris had found the vial of strychnine in the road a few rods from the house and brought it in, believing it to be a vial of quinine someone had accidentally dropped, and hence the fatal result.

BIOGRAPHICAL SKETCH OF CYRUS HARRIS, EX-GOVERNOR OF THE CHICKASAW NATION

Cyrus Harris, who was of the House Emisha taluyah (pro. E, we, mish-ar, beyond, ta-larn-yah, putting it down) was born, as he stated to me, three miles south of Pontotoc, Mississippi, on the 22nd day of August, 1817. He died at his home on Mill Creek, Chickasaw Nation. He lived with his mother until the year 1827, when he was sent to school at the Monroe Missionary Station, at the time that Rev. Thomas C. Stuart, that noble Christian missionary and Presbyterian minister, had charge of the school, and in which many Chickasaw youths, both male and female, were being educated. In 1828, he was taken to the state of Tennessee by Mr. Hugh Wilson, a minister also of the Old School Presbyterian faith and order, and placed in an Indian school located on a small stream called Roberson Fork, in the county of Giles. This humble little Indian school was taught by a man named William R. McNight. Cyrus, at the close of the year 1829, had only been taught the rudiments of an English education, to spell in the spelling-book and read in the New Testament. In the early part of the year 1830, he took up the study of geography and reading in the first and second readers, which terminated his school-boy days, as he returned home that year and never attended school again. When he returned to his home he found it vacated; but learned that his mother had moved to a place near a little lake then known as Ishtpufahaiyip (pro. Isht-poon-fah,

Horn, haiyip, lake), eighteen miles southwest of the present city of Memphis, Tennessee. Thither he at once turned his steps, and soon found his mother in her new home, where he remained but a short time (then thirteen years of age) as he was soon sent to stay a while with an old lady as company for her, whose husband a short time before, had been killed by a Choctaw who had been adopted by the Chickasaws.

Cyrus remained a few months with the bereaved widow, but he became so lonely, there being no neighbors nearer than three miles, that his boyish heart could endure it no longer; though he amused himself the best he could by hunting and shooting rabbits, squirrels and birds with his bow and arrows, often visiting his mother living a few miles distant. He again returned to his mother but to remain a short time as before; as his uncle by marriage, Martin Colbert, a most excellent man, employed him to come and assist him with his stock.

Cyrus Harris who spoke both the Chickasaw and English languages, having learned from a friend that there was a demand for interpreters, sought at once the land office established at Pontotoc, three miles from the home of his birth, and fortunately succeeded in securing a position as clerk in a dry goods store, and also to interpret for one John Bell, who was then Surveyor General, but kept a trading house. He remained only a short time as clerk, for he soon obtained a more lucrative position in acting as interpreter for the deputies of John Bell and one Robert Gordon who were partners in buying lands. At this time the United States agent and the Chickasaw commissioners were busy in locating lands. Land speculators followed up the agent and commissioners, that no opportunity might be lost in which a profitable speculation might be made.

Cyrus Harris now became an indispensable personage in the firm of Bell & Gordon. In 1839 the land sales were brought to a close and the Chickasaws were then informed, without equivocation, that their room was more desired than their presence; and as nothing more could be made out of them, they could now go West or to the devil, it made no difference which, so they were expeditious in the matter. Cyrus Harris was appointed as one of the interpreters to inform the Chickasaws to meet at once in council and appoint the day in which they would depart from their ancient heritage.

The Chickasaws at once took up their line of march westward, feeling that rather than abide such a tempest of rascality as was daily exhibited before their eyes in the wild and crazy scuffle for a few acres of earth by which to quench their raging thirst for gain, they would flee even from heaven did such a stream of strife and corruption threaten an entrance there.

On the first of November, 1837, Cyrus Harris, with his mother and a family of friends, left to join the emigration, then awaiting transportation at Memphis, Tennessee, which soon arrived, and the greater part of the Chickasaws, under the jurisdiction of one A. Upshaw, the emigration agent, left for Fort Coffee, Choctaw Nation, Indian Territory, by way of steamboats. Cyrus Harris and mother, with a few other families, went through by land to Fort Coffee. When they had arrived there they learned that their friends were encamped near Sullyville (Skully, a corruption of the word Tuli—the full word being Tuliholisso—money paper, or paper money; a place where the Government paid them their annuities), but the "ville" part of it is unquestionably English.

Harris remained in camp at Sullyville about two weeks; then, with several families, started to find a desirable place for settling, and finally located on Blue River. This was in 1838. While living there he was induced to enter the political arena of his country. In 1850 a council was convened at Boiling Springs, in Ponola (Cotton) County, in which he was appointed to accompany Edmond Pickens to Washington City to arrange some national business, which proved ineffectual from some injudicious recommendation.

On returning home Mr. Harris sold his place on Blue River and settled at Boggy Depot. He resided there a year, and again sold out and moved to a point on Pennington Creek, about a mile west of Tishomingo, where he remained until November, 1855. Not satisfied there, he once more sold and moved to a place on Mill Creek, where he still lived in 1884. In 1854 he was again appointed a delegate, with several others, to Washington City. In 1856, after the adoption of the Chickasaw constitution, he was elected governor of the Chickasaw Nation. Having served two years, with commendable discretion and sound judgment, he was re-elected, and filled the gubernatorial chair for two more years, after which he was elected two more terms, serving his people with the same integrity. During his four terms of eight years, peace, harmony and prosperity prevailed throughout the Chickasaw Nation.

In 1876, ex-Governor Cyrus Harris was again brought before the Chickasaw people as a candidate for the office of governor, but was defeated by his opponent, B. F. Overton, who served his people faithfully and satisfactorily through his first term, and at the next election was re-elected. In 1880 Cyrus Harris was again brought out by his friends, contrary to his wishes, and was pronounced elected by the legislature, but, it was said, votes were counted out just enough to illegally elect his friend, B. C. Burney, a man highly esteemed by the people. Ex-Governor Harris then and there announced that he had forever withdrawn from the political field, and he has strictly adhered to his determination.

Since writing the above the sad tidings of the death of ex-Governor Cyrus Harris was announced in the following obituary:

"Died at his residence, Mill Creek, Chickasaw Nation, Friday, the 6th, Cyrus Harris, ex-governor of the Chicka-

saws. He was buried on the 7th inst. at the family cemetery in Mill Creek.

"To record the passage from life to eternity is the sad-
dest and gravest duty that falls to the lot of the journalist.
The more so, when he announces the death of one whose
loss will be deeply and widely regretted; one beloved of all
men, whose place can never be filled in the homes and
hearts of his people. In recording the death of ex-Governor
Harris, we are fully aware of this fact; for not within the
range of man's recollection has any member of the Chickasaw tribe impressed himself so favorably, so deeply and
effectually upon his generation.

"His public and private characters wrought in the
same mould; both equally incorruptible. The low, the base,
the avaricious, were elements foreign to his existence, while
the chambers of his heart were ever lighted for the reception of such warm impulses and philanthropic ideas as are
rarely met with, save in natures of the noblest type. Despite
his progressive ideas, Cyrus Harris was an Indian in the
truest sense, a patriot and a leader of his people. His country was his greatest care; so whether engaged in legislature,
in administration, or dwelling peaceably in his humble
cottage, his heart and brain were alike harnessed to his
country's welfare. His generosity and his self-sacrifice were
finely displayed in his last executive act. His election by the
people being disputed by the House, in order to avoid
political trouble, he withdrew and retired into private life.

"There is no reward in this world for that which is
incorruptible; naught have the approbation of the good and
the wise. But how meager that reward, after a lifetime of
unselfish labor. Therefore, may the wish grow spontane-
ously in every sorrowing heart, that a new and everlasting
recompense lies within reach of the departed chief.

"To the grief-stricken relatives of Governor Harris, and
to the Nation that mourns a true friend and a wise counselor, the Independent offers its most sincere and lasting
sympathy."

Logan Colbert married a native Chickasaw woman by whom he had four sons, George, John, William and Levi; all of whom arose to prominence and exerted a salutary influence among their people, and became men of authority and distinction. He also had another son by a second marriage, named James, who fell not behind his distinguished brothers.

Why Logan Colbert came to cast his lot at so early an age and so far from the land of his nativity, among the people so remote from all the English settlements, are problems that never will be solved, though it may be conjectured that he came with some of the early English traders and adventurers who assisted the Chickasaws in their wars against the French. At an early day he was a renowned leader among them, and to that degree of celebrity, that one of the names given to the Mississippi River by the early French writers, during the days of their wars with that people with whom he had identified himself, was Rivere de Colbert sustaining the conjecture,[6] that Logan Colbert was the name of the most famous chief among the Chickasaws; who at that time swayed the sceptre of absolute authority over the country along the east banks of Mississippi River to the great annoyance and danger of the French in ascending and descending that mighty stream. Though little else of the life of Logan Colbert has escaped oblivion, except he lived, he died; yet his name has been handed down to posterity in that of his noble line of descendants, who figure upon the pages of Chickasaw history as being among the influential families of that Nation.

Colonel George Colbert, in the prosperous days of the Chickasaw people, lived three or four miles west of what is now known as the town of Tupelo, Mississippi, (Tupelo is a corruption of Tuhpulah—To call or shout). George Colbert became the most wealthy of the four brothers and was, in his personal appearance and manners, very prepossessing.

[6] His "conjecture" is far off the mark. This name was given to the Mississippi River in honor of Jean Baptiste Colbert, great minister of Louis XIV.

He did not act in any public capacity, yet he exerted a great personal influence as a private citizen. He was a true conservative in sentiment and in spirit. He regarded his people, the Chickasaws, uninfluenced by the Whites and uncontaminated by their vices, as having reached the point of national progress most favorable to virtue and earthly happiness; therefore, he opposed all innovations as an evil which wisdom, virtue and patriotism loudly disapproved; and seemingly with much justice, since the Chickasaws (like the Choctaws) were a virtuous people before the Whites came and introduced their vices among them; therefore, he was an outspoken enemy to missions, to schools, to whiskey, in short, to all the good as well as the evils that were being imported into his then happy country, having learned by experience and observation that the evil introduced by the Whites counterbalanced the good in point of amount as five to one; yet he failed to shape the policy of his Nation in accordance with his views, for the missionaries came and introduced Christianity and established it upon a firm basis in spite of the whiskey-traders and others who followed closely in their wake, with all their concomitant vices, who seemed to delight in thwarting the noble efforts of those devoted and self-sacrificing men of God (even as they do at the present day), that they might the more easily drag the Indians down to their own degraded level.

To escape the demoralizing influences of such degraded characters, and not the missionaries, did George Colbert advocate the emigration of his people to the remote wilds of the west, where he hoped and believed the evil tide of innovation would be arrested. In that distant land, he fondly cherished the belief that his nation would throw off the manners and customs of the whites which they had already adopted, and return to the old paths of that simplicity of life in which their progenitors had walked for ages unknown. But he was doomed to disappointment, for not only the missionaries went with his people to their new homes, but the whiskey peddler and his congenial spirits soon followed on their track with the zeal of their master, the devil, where they have been hovering around the outskirts of the Chickasaw Nation, and often sneaking within, from that day to this; and though the Chickasaw people, alike with all their race, have had to fight the devil and his imps in an unequal contest, being hampered by the government of the United States in its laws regarding its worthy sons of freedom, whose proclivities lead them to indulge their "glorious independence" regardless of all laws and every principle of truth, justice and honor, in regard to whiskey in particular; yet the Chickasaws and Choctaws have made that wilderness, to which they were banished, blossom as the rose, while George Colbert sleeps beneath the soil under the shades of the forest trees in the present country of the Chickasaws. He lived and died firmly adhering to the principles which he believed to be the greatest interest to his country. He was a true patriot, and loved the simple manners of the olden times, and could not yield them to give place to modern customs with their accompanying vices; and who can blame him? Alas! the Indians, everywhere on this North American continent, have been compelled to pay a higher price for the few crumbs of Christianity that they have been allowed to pick up and convert to the use of their starving souls than any race of people that ever lived.

General William Colbert was a man of a military turn of character, and in that capacity rose to considerable distinction in the Creek War of 1814. He won the confidence of General Andrew Jackson in that war, and was presented by Jackson with a fine military coat made after the American style, which Colbert carefully kept to the close of his life as one among the most highly treasured relics of the past, and only wore it on important national occasions. He lived a few miles south of a little place then known as Tokshish, a corruption of the word Takshi, (bashful). He died in 1826.

Major Levi Colbert resided near a place then known as Cotton Gin. In early manhood, or rather in boyhood, he was elevated by an act of gallantry to the high position of "Itta wamba micco," as has been so oft published by different writers, and meaning, as given in the wisdom of their interpretation, "Bench Chief, or King of the Wooden Bench." There is no such word in the Chickasaw language as "Itta wamba micco," and it can be but the fabrication of imaginative ignorance. The Chickasaw words for Bench Chief (if there ever was such a personage among them) would be, Aiobinili (a seat) falaia (long) Miko (chief) pro. Ai-ome-bih-ne-lih-far-li-yah Meenkoh, The Chief on the long seat or bench—in our phraseology, The Chief in the Chair of State.

Major Levi Colbert's act of gallantry, by which he was at once elevated to the high position of chief, consisted in having defeated, when but a youth, a war party of Muscogees who had invaded the Chickasaw Nation, at a time when all the warriors of the invaded district were away from home on a hunting excursion. Young Levi at once collected the old men and boys and formed them into a war company and started for the depredating Creeks, whom he successfully drew into an artfully planned ambuscade, by which all the Muscogees were slain, not one being left to return to his own country and tell of their complete destruction. The little stream upon whose banks the battle took place was afterwards called (so says a writer in one of his published articles) "Yahnubly," and gives its signification as "All killed"; but unfortunately for his erudition, no such word is known in the Chickasaw language. There is, however, the word yanubih (pro. yarn-ub-ih) in their language but its signification is iron-wood. While the Chickasaw words for "All killed" (same as the Choctaw) are moma-ubih; the land or place where all were killed.

When the warriors returned from their hunt and learned of the battle and to whom the safety of their families was due, and also the honor of the victory, a council was immediately called and the young hero summoned to attend; when he appeared and the statement of facts had been laid before them, they, without a dissenting voice elevated him to the responsible position of a chief in their Nation.

The following publication appeared a few years ago as a valuable piece of Chickasaw history: "Ittawamba was the name of an office. The word signifies King of the Wooden Bench. The individual who held the high title was elected by the national council. A part of the imposing ceremony by which the officer elected was initiated was as follows: 'At a given signal he jumped from a wooden bench to the floor in the hall of state where the magnates of the Nation sat in conclave. At the moment his feet touched the earth the whole of the assembly exclaimed Ittawamba! The honored individual who heard this voice became the second magistrate of the Nation. Thus he received the orders of Chickasaw Knighthood, Ittawamba micco, or Bench Chief."

But the whole article is such an exhibition of pitiable nonsense, that in reading it to some Chickasaw friends, they all exclaimed: "What a fool!"

But be what "Ittawamba" may, nevertheless Levi Colbert, after his initiation into its wonderful mysteries, proved himself worthy to be not only a "king of the wooden bench," but also, by his talents, purity of principles, energy and force of character, a king upon a regal throne to bear rule over a nation. For several years he shaped the policy, and presided over the destinies of the Chickasaw people with wisdom and discretion.

On the 27th and 28th of September, 1830, the Choctaws, by a treaty with John Coffee and John Eaton, United States commissioners, ceded their lands east of the Mississippi River to the United States. Major Levi Colbert, having heard what they had done, immediately called upon his friend, Mr. Stephen Daggette, and asked him to calculate the interest for him of four hundred thousand dollars at five, six, seven and eight per cent. The Choctaws had taken government bonds at five per cent; Major Colbert at once seeing that they had been badly and most outrageously swindled, exclaimed in a loud and highly excited tone of voice, "God! I thought so." He then informed Mr. Daggette that he was anxious to obtain the calculation, that he might be enabled to explain it to his people in their own language. He also stated to Mr. Daggette that "the United States would soon make an effort to buy the lands of the Chickasaws also, and I want to be ready for them."

This conversation between Levi Colbert and Mr. Daggette took place two years before the treaty with the Chickasaws, which was made on the 20th of October, 1832, at the house of a Chickasaw called Topulka—a corruption of Tahpulah (to halloo or make a noise), but was known, says a writer of the yahnubbih and Ittawamba order of expounders, in his publication, as "Pontaontac," which he also interprets as signifying "Cat Tail Prairie"; but unfortunately for him also, the Chickasaw words for his classic name "Cat Tail Prairie" are Kutus Hasimbish Oktak (pro. Kot-oos (cat) Har-sim-bish (tail) Oke-tark (prairie); therefore, he also must seek elsewhere than in the Chickasaw language for his "Pontaontac" and its signification "Cat Tail Prairie," as there is no such word in the Chickasaw language, nor in any other North American Indian language, it is reasonable to suppose. Pontotoc, the name of a town in north Mississippi, is a corruption, as has been before stated, of the words Paki Tukohli—grapes hung up; hanging grapes.

But such are the gross and ridiculous errors made by those of the present age who not only prove their terrible ignorance by their unmerciful butchery of the Indian languages, but equally so in the exhibition of their shameful prejudice against that persecuted people.

When the United States had resolved to gobble up the Chickasaw country also, as they had the Choctaws' two years before, John Coffee was sent to the Chickasaw Nation to order Ben Reynolds (the Chickasaw agent) to immediately assemble the chiefs and warriors in council to effect a treaty with them.

Three treaties (or rather articles) were drawn up, but were promptly rejected by the watchful and discerning Chickasaws. Then the fourth was written by the persistent Coffee; but with the following clause inserted to catch the noble and influential chief, Yakni Moma Ubih, the incorruptible Levi Colbert, which reads as follows: "We hereby agree to give our beloved chief, Levi Colbert, in consideration of his services and expense of entertaining the guests of the Nation, fifteen sections of land in any part of the country he may select." "Stop! Stop! John Coffee!" shouted the justly indignant chief in a voice of thunder. "I am no more entitled to those fifteen sections of land than the poorest Chickasaw in the Nation. I scorn your infamous offer, clothed under the falsehood of 'our beloved chief,' and will not accept it, sir."

Then a fifth treaty was written out by Coffee, and the council again called together to consider upon its merits; and which, after due deliberation, was finally accepted. The Chickasaws agreed to take United States bonds, but were unable to satisfactorily comprehend the six per cent promised them, until their interpreter, Ben Love, illustrated it as a hen laying eggs. That one hundred dollars would lay six dollars in twelve months, which they at once fully understood.

Ishtehotopa, the king, first walked up with a countenance that betokened the emotions of one about to sign his country's death warrant, and with a sad heart and trembling hand made his mark. Then Tishu Miko advanced with solemn mein and did likewise; then the other chiefs with countenance sad and forlorn; and last of all, the pure, the noble Levi Colbert.

Soon after the treaty had been signed, Major Levi Colbert stated to Mr. Daggette he was not satisfied with some clauses in the treaty which he did not at first correctly understand. Mr. Daggette advised him to go immediately to Washington and get it changed to his satisfaction before it was confirmed by the Senate. Colbert, with other delegates, started immediately to Washington City, but only got as far as his son-in-law, Kilpatrick Carter's, in Alabama, where he was taken sick and died. The other delegates continued their journey to Washington, and secured the desired alteration in the treaty.

What attractive pictures for an art gallery would the scenes presented at that treaty between the Chickasaw Nation and the United States in 1832, at the humble home of Tahpulah, and the one two years before between the Choctaws and the United States. The United States, a great and powerful nation, professing to be governed in all its actions by the principles alone of Christianity. The Chicksaw and Choctaw nations, weak, poor and unlettered, making no professions to intellectual attainments whatever. The former using its skilled ingenuity in deception, misrepresentation and falsehood to defraud; the latter, sustained by truth and honor, watching and deliberating how best to come out of the unequal contest with that alone that justice awards.

But, in justice, it must and shall be said of the Chickasaw agent of 1832, Benj. Reynolds, that he was an honest man. As agent to the Chickasaw people for the United States Mr. Reynolds annually paid them twenty thousand dollars for several consecutive years as annuity. Previous to the treaty Mr. Daggette affirms he assisted Mr. Reynolds in paying to the Chickasaws their annuities, and that Mr. Reynolds distributed the last cent among them, giving to each his or her dues honestly and justly, though every opportunity was offered to defraud them.

James Colbert, the youngest of Logan Colbert's sons, was also a man of great integrity and firmness of character. He acted, for many years, in the capacity of the national secretary. The archives of the Chickasaw Nation were placed in his hands for safe keeping, the majority of which being in his own hand writing; and truly it may be said, antiquaries, in coming years of the far future, may decipher with much interest and profit, the documents written by James Colbert.

Thomas Love, who, at an early day, also identified himself, with the Chickasaw people by marriage, had six sons, viz: Henry, Benjamin (who acted in the capacity of interpreter for the Chickasaws for many years), Isaac, Slone, William and Robert. All of whom have died, except Robert, who was known as Bob Love.

The Chickasaws, in common with all the Indians of the South, possessed many fine orators whose orations were eloquent, persuasive and full of animation. As a race of people the Chickasaws were tall, elegantly proportioned, erect and muscular, with a square forehead, high cheek bones, compressed lips and dark penetrating eyes. In their councils (like all other Indians) grave and dignified, and never indulged, under any circumstances, in noisy harangues; they spoke slowly, distinctly and to the point. It is, and has always been, the universal declaration and belief of the Whites that the North American Indians are taciturn, grave, and never smiled or indulged in merriment or laughter under any circumstances. This is a great error, and but a repetition of the same old edition of the same old story, which, like all else said and written and published about the North American Indians, was begotten by ignorance, conceived in duplicity and brought forth in prejudice—to say the least of it. Never did a more jovial, good natured and light hearted race of people exist upon earth than the North American Indians. True, they were grave and taciturn in the presence of strangers, and the reason is obvious. The white people (excepting the old missionaries of the long ago), in all their actions among them, and in all their conduct toward them, have ever and everywhere assumed an air of superiority over them, which the Indians have ever justly denied; and which justly created in their minds pity for the foolish self-conceit and egotism of the Whites, which seemed to them a lamentable weakness unknown and un-

seen before in the human race; and also created equal contempt for such a display of presumption and evident want
of sound judgment, or rather of common sense; the natural
consequences of which were taciturnity and gravity when in
the presence of such self-imagined august specimens of
humanity.

Even many ministers of the Gospel, sent among the
Indians by the various denominations of the states to preach
to them, preach themselves instead of Christ, by indulging
in unmistakable bantam rooster airs of the superiority of
the whites over the red, detailing their opinions concerning
the progressive renovation that would have certainly ensued
in every department of their national and social affairs had
the Indians, from their first acquaintance with the White
Race, had the good fortune to have enjoyed the advantages
of their ethical wisdom and profound theological erudition.
Often have I been an eye witness to many such exhibitions
of clerical imbecility during my frequent sojourns among
the Chickasaws and Choctaws within the last ten years; and
though as loquacious as Brazilian parrots, yet "Pretty Poll
wants a cracker" was in substance, the climax of their sermons, as Self was so highly esteemed a personage that they
were oblivious to all else.

But such was not the style of men, who in 1815-20 proclaimed the glad tidings of great joy to the Southern Indians. Far from it. They were men of deep piety; of indefatigable energy to lead the Red Race into the fold of Christ;
of unassumed sympathy for them as human beings.
Therefore, they visited them at their homes in their humble
log cabins; sat down among them in the family circle upon
the bear skins spread upon the cleanly swept dirt floor; slept
upon their bear and panther skins in humble gratitude for
as much, when remembering their Savior had not where to
lay his head; ate of their venison, tafulatobi ibulhto (hominy
mixed with beans), and botahkapussa (cold flour). They
sang and prayed with them in the morning; then went with
them to their little fields of growing corn and instructed

them in the art of agriculture and imparted to them new ideas of home comforts. Thus they taught them everywhere and on all occasions, both by precept and example.

The ancient Chickasaws were the most famous trailers of all the southern Indians. Their skill in this art seemed almost superhuman. I call it an art; and it is as much so as is painting or sculpture, while almost as few become proficient in it as in the handling of brush or chisel. It requires constant practice and much knowledge of nature, in all its variations, to learn it thoroughly; and I believe it more natural for an Indian to become a trailer of man or beast than a white man, as they seemed to acquire by intuition what the white has to learn from a lifetime of study. Here and there, I'll admit, a white man may be found who becomes an expert, yet the boasted leaders of civilization fall far behind the natural-born trailers, the North American Indians. Who could learn, through the medium of books or any other way of instruction, but that of a lifetime experience, to determine the age of a trail of man or beast correctly, or tell the number of an enemy and how long since they had passed the spot which you may be examining? Yet the ancient Chickasaw warrior, in his palmy days seventy-five years ago, could do it, and even what tribe of Indians had made a given trail, its age, and all the particulars as correctly as though he had seen them pass. Truthfully did an Indian once exclaim:

"White man travel with his eyes shut and mouth open," alluding to his propensity to talk. "Indian travel all day; say nothing, but see everything." How true! Nothing escaped his observation, whether alone or with others; while the white man talks incessantly and sees nothing but the general features of the things he is passing; therefore, can scarcely retrace his steps for any great distance in a country he has never traveled before; while it is impossible to lose an Indian in any country, no matter how strange or new. When asked how he did it he may reply, Siah (I am) a chuffa (one) kutah (who) ikhanah (remembers); though aften he would make no reply. No matter how loquacious he may have been at home or elsewhere, when upon the warpath or the chase he was silent. The North American Indian was nearly as certain in predicting the weather as a barometer, and his knowledge of the characteristics of the wild animals of his ancient forests would be a prize indeed to the naturalist.

As warriors and hunters the Chickasaws of seventy-five years ago had few equals, but no superiors, among the North American Indians. They were unerring marksmen with the rifle and capable of enduring seemingly incredible fatigue. They would follow the tracks of their game and the signs left by their human enemies for hours, where the eyes of the white man would not detect any sign of a footprint whatever. When hunting or upon the warpath, if they came upon deserted campfires or human footprints they could tell to what tribe they belonged and whether friends or foes.

As an illustration of their skill in discerning and interpreting landmarks and signs, I will here relate a little incident.

In the years of long ago, a Chickasaw had a ham of venison taken from his little log house in which he kept his stock of provisions during the absence of himself and family. He described the thief as being a white man, low stature, lame in one leg, having a short gun, and accompanied by a short-tailed dog. When requested to explain how he could be so positive, he answered: "His track informed me he was a white man by his shoes, Indians wear moccasins; he stood on the toes of his shoes to reach the venison ham, which told me he was a low man; one foot made a deeper and plainer impress upon the ground than the other as he walked, which told me he was a lame man; the mark made by the breech of a gun upon the ground and the one made by its muzzle upon the bark of the tree against which it had leaned, told me he had a gun and it was a short gun; the tracks made by a dog told me of his presence; and the impress he made where he sat upon the ground to the end of that made by his tail, as he wagged it, was but a finger's length which told me the dog's tail was short."

Among the ancient Chickasaws, descent was established in the female line; thus the ties of kinship converged upon each other until they all met in the granddaughter; and thus every grandson and granddaughter became the grandson and granddaughter of the whole tribe, since all the uncles of a given person were considered as his fathers also; and all the mothers' sisters were mothers; the cousins, as brothers and sisters; the nieces, as daughters; and the nephews as sons. They believed in the existence of one great, everywhere-present and overruling spirit, whom they held in the highest reverence, and devoutly worshipped; as to him were attributed the gifts of peace, prosperity and happiness, abundant harvests of corn, beans, pumpkins and success in war and the chase. They also equally believed in the existence of an evil spirit, to whom they attributed the cause of all misfortunes; and here came in the power and influence of the wonder-working medicine man, or prophet, who professed to have attained to a thorough knowledge of both good and evil spirits, and also the ability to command their influence for good or evil, by fasting and prayer and mystic ceremonies.

However, the usages, manners, customs, beliefs and habits of life, national and social amusements of the Chickasaws were, in many respects the same as the Choctaws, and what may be said of the one, may with equal truth be said of the other.

Among ancient Chickasaws and Choctaws there was a tradition concerning the origin of a little lake in Tibih swamp. Oktibihha County, Mississippi. This isolated lake which I have oft visited on fishing excursions, has long been known as Greer's Lake, and is about half a mile long and one hundred feet or more wide. The tradition is as follows: In the years of the long past, many generations before the advent of the White Race, a Chickasaw hunter and his wife, with two little children, (a boy and girl) were camped in

the Tibih swamp near a little hole of water formed by the
roots of a fallen tree. One morning the hunter and his wife
went out in pursuit of game, leaving their children, as usual,
in camp. On their return late in the evening, they were
stupefied with horror and amazement to find that their
camp was swallowed up by the earth, and this lake lay
stretched over the spot. But while gazing upon the scene
perplexed and terrified, they beheld two enormous snakes
swimming upon the newly formed lake and coming directly
towards them, which caused them to flee from the spot in
great consternation. The sudden formation of the lake was
ascribed by them to some miraculous agent, and by the
same power, their children had been transformed into the
two great water snakes; and such was the credulity of the
Chickasaws and Choctaws in the account given by the
Chickasaw hunter and his wife, that down through all subsequent years, even to the time of their emigration west,
the lake and its immediate surroundings were held in superstitious awe. Nor would they live nor approach anywhere
near it. Varied and many were the views concerning its
strange and sudden formation; all, however, agreeing that it
was brought into existence by the wrath of the Great Spirit,
and became the abode of evil spirits ever afterwards.

The ancient Chickasaws once practised the custom of
extingushing the fire in every house in their Nation at the
close of every year, and let them so remain during three
successive days and nights, while the occupants retired to
the woods where they remained. By this means they believed they would rid themselves of all witches and evil
spirits; since, when they came three successive nights and
found no fire they would conclude the family had left their
former place of abode to return no more; therefore, they
also would depart to never return. Then all the Chickasaws
returned to their homes, built new fires and were happy,
being freed from the fear of witches.

THE NATCHEZ

On February 11, 1700, De Iberville, Bienville, Perricaul and Tonti ascended the Mississippi River as far west as the present city of Natchez. They were kindly received (so states the journalist) by the great chief, or Sun, as he was termed, surrounded by six hundred of his warriors, who, according to their own account, had formerly been a great nation. On the 13th the party left Natchez and visited the villages of the Taensas, the customs and habits of whom were the same as the Natchez, being evidently a branch of the latter. During their stay the sacred temple of these Indians was struck by lightning and burned to ashes. To appease the Sun God, the poor, infatuated women threw themselves, and parents, their children, into the consuming flames of the burning temple. Perricaul, who was one of the witnesses of the fearful scene, thus wrote of it: "We left the Natchez and coasted along to the right, where the river is bordered with high, gravelly banks for a distance of twelve leagues. At the extremity of these bluffs is a place called Petit Gulf, on account of the whirlpool formed by the river for the distance of a quarter league. Eight leagues higher up we came to Grand Gulf, which we passed a short distance above, on the right hand side. We landed to visit ⸱ village four leagues in the interior. These Indians are called Taensas. We were well received, but I never saw a more sad sight, frightful and revolting spectacle than that which happened the second day, 16th of April, after our arrival in the village. A sudden storm burst upon us. The lightning struck the temple, burned all their idols and reduced the whole to ashes. Quickly the Indians assembled around, making horrible cries, tearing out their hair, elevating their hands to heaven, their tawny visages turned toward the burning temple, invoking their Great Spirit to come down and extinguish the flames. The fathers and mothers then brought their children, and after having strangled them, threw them into the flames. M. De Iberville was horrified at seeing such a cruel spectacle, and gave orders to stop it and forcibly taking from them the little innocents; but with all our efforts seventeen perished in this manner, and had we not restrained them, the number would have been over two hundred."

Father Le Petit, Superior of the Jesuits, in speaking of the Natchez Indians, whom he had visited at an early day, says: "They inhabited a beautiful country, and were the only tribe that seemed to have an established worship. This temple resembled an earthen oven, of the back of a tortoise, and was one hundred feet in circumference. They entered it by one small door, and there was no window. Above, on the outside of the roof, were three wooden eagles painted red, yellow and white. In front of the door was a shed where the guardian of the temple kept watch. All around was a circle of painted pickets, capped with the skulls of their enemies who had fallen in battle. The interior was lined with shelves on which were baskets holding the bones of their favorite followers, who had been strangled, to attend their masters in the spirit world, made of bark, provided by the patriarchs of the tribe. No woman, except the mother and sisters of the Great Sun, was allowed to enter the sacred edifice. The common people dared only to approach the threshold. The sun was their diety; their great chief was called by the same name, and he, in turn, called the sun his brother. Every morning at dawn, attended by his retinue, the chief ascended a mound to converse with his celestial brother. As soon as the sun appeared in the heavens, the chief saluted with a long howl, and then waved his hand from east to west, and directed what course he should travel! When this personage dies, they demolish his house and throw up a mound, and on that they build a dwelling for the brother of the sun."

Pericault, who was at Natchez in 1703, and at which time the Great Female Sun died, says: "She was really the Great Sun in her own right. Her husband, who was not of the blood royal, was strangled by their eldest son, so that in death, as in life, he might be her submissive attendant and howl to her ghost! On the outside of her house they placed all her effects on a scaffold and on these they deposited the two corpses. They likewise put there the bodies of twelve children whom they had just strangled. These children had been brought by their parents, by order of the eldest son of the deceased, who had the right, as her successor, to put to death as many as he thought necessary to wait on her in the land of spirits. Fourteen other scaffolds were erected, decorated with vines and rude paintings. These were intended for the bodies of the victims, whose nearest relatives, dressed in festive robes, surrounded them with looks and gestures expressive of satisfaction. They then in procession marched to the great square in front of the temple and began to dance. Four days thereafter they again formed in procession and began what is called the 'March of Death' from the square to the house of the deceased. The fathers and mothers of the strangled children held the bodies in their arms. The oldest of these did not appear to be over three years. The relatives of these infants, with their hair closely shaven, began to howl in the most frightful manner. But the adults who were about to die danced around the house of the dead princess, until finally it was set on fire by her eldest son and successor. All then marched to the great temple. The parents who carried their strangled infants then threw them on the ground and began to dance. When the body of the deceased princess was deposited in the temple, the intended victims were undressed and seated on the ground. A cord with a noose was passed around each of their necks and deer skins thrown over their heads. The relatives, who were the executioners, then stood to the right and left of each victim and, at a given signal, all were strangled. The bodies were placed on scaffolds and the bones, when dry, were deposited in baskets in the temple, and constituted a sort of patent nobility. It was a privilege and an honor to die with the Sun."

Even as late as 1730 the Natchez had their temple in which were kept their sacred fire continually burning. According to their traditions, Du Pratz says: "Their territories extended to the River Manchos, or Iberville, which is about 50 leagues from the sea, to the River Wabash, which is distant from the sea about 450 leagues, and that they had about 800 Suns, or princes."

The Natchez, if tradition may be believed, also came from Mexico where they had lived for centuries; alike, with the Choctaw, Chickasaw and Muscogee. They, too, followed the rising sun from west to east, continuing a wandering life for many years, and finally reached the Mississippi River, which they crossed, and settled at a point on the river where the city of Natchez now stands, which was named for them. At that time they were a numerous people, occupying a territory extending from Natchez to Wabash, and claiming many hundred Suns, or members of the royal family. In 1716, the French built Fort Rosalie upon the bluff upon which Natchez now stands, in which they quartered a company of soldiers. In 1720, DePratz vi•ited the Great Sun of the Natchez, and was informed by him, that the Natchez were once a great people extending over a vast region of country, and ruled by many Suns; that one of the keepers of the Temple let the holy fire go out, and in his fright substituted profane fire, thus endeavoring to conceal his negligence; but which caused them to be visited by a dreadful disease which ravaged their country for many years, sweeping thousands of their people into an untimely grave. The Natchez kept a perpetual fire burning in their temples, which was never permitted for a moment to become extinguished. It is stated by some of the early writers, that the Taensas and Mobelians, who were eventually merged into the Choctaw and Chickasaw nations, also kept a perpetual fire burning in their temples, when known by the Europeans in 1721. It is said of the Natchez, "that the sight was never shocked by the appearance of deformity," such as are so frequently observed among the White Race; and with equal truth, the same may be said of all the North American Indians. As all their race, so the Natchez used the bow and arrow as their instrument of offense and defense, which they used effectively against their enemies in war, and supplying themselves with the flesh of the great variety of wild animals in which their endless forests then abounded. They were also skilled in the art of dressing the skins of animals, and thus provided themselves with comfortable clothing, suitable for both summer and winter, using as needles for sewing purposes, the sharp bones of birds, and for thread the sinews of small animals. Their houses, as those of all their race were made of rude materials, with one door for ingress and egress, without floor or chimney, but a little hole left in the roof about the centre of the room, through which the smoke might pass out. The Natchez women are said to have been very proficient in making earthen ware for their domestic purposes, such as pots, cups, bowls, etc.; and also very skillful in the art of dying the skins of animals, their favorite colors being red, yellow, white and black, used in alternate stripes. The men were skilled in managing their canoes, some of which measuring from twenty to thirty feet in length, by two or three in width. In short, what has been said in regard to the ancient manners and customs of the Choctaw and Chickasaw, Cherokee, Muscogee and Seminole Indians is equally applicable to the Natchez, differing only (as all others, however) in their traditions of the origin of man, the flood, funeral ceremonies and burial of the dead.

In regard to the origin of man, the tradition of the Natchez affirms that the Great Spirit molded the first man out of clay, similar to that out of which they made their earthen ware, and being pleased with his work, breathed life into it. After the first man was created, he (the man) suddenly was taken with a violent paroxysm or fit of sneezing when suddenly a strange something jumped from his nose to the ground, where it commenced to hop and dance about, growing larger and larger, until it soon assumed the form of a woman and finally grew to be a perfect woman.

They also had another tradition in substance as follows: In ancient times a man and woman appear among them who descended from the sun. They were so dazzlingly bright that human eyes could not look upon them. The man inform~ l them that he had seen their wretchedness and inability to properly govern themselves, and had been influenced through compassion to leave his bright abode in the sun and descend to earth that he might instruct them how they might live happily. He therefore gave them some moral precepts, among the most important were, first—not to kill man but in self-defense; second—to have but one living wife; third—to be truthful; fourth—to be strictly honest; fifth—to be temperate; sixth—to be generous; seventh—to be charitable; eighth—to help the poor in their distress.

The stranger's appearance and moral precepts inculcated greatly impressed the Natchez, and they at once convened in solemn council during the quiet hours of the night and resolved, upon due deliberation, to request the man to be their chief; and the next morning, with much pomp and ceremony, proceeded to the house to which the stranger and his wife had been consigned for the night and earnestly solicited him to become their chief. He at first declined their intended honor, assigning as his reason that he knew they would not conform to his teachings, and in so doing, he was grieved to state to them, the Natchez would work their own destruction, terminating in utter extermination. But the Natchez, earnestly pressing their request, the stranger finally yielded to their solicitations, but with the following proviso: That they would emigrate to a country to which he would also lead them, where they would be more prosperous and happy; and that they would strictly yield obedience to the laws and regulations he would establish for them, and that their future chiefs should be chosen from his descendants. To all of which they acceded. He then commanded fire from the sun which he gave them with positive instructions to keep it burning in two temples by the use of

walnut wood stripped of its bark as fuel, which temples
were to be built at the two extreme boundaries of the territory, to be inhabited by them. Eight men were selected by
his instruction to serve as priests for each temple, whose
imperative duty was to guard the sacred fire by regular
turns, and death was to be the punishment of him who
should, upon his watch, let the fire go out; since their mysterious lawgiver and chosen chief predicted to them the
most dreadful calamities if the fire ever was extinguished in
both temples at the same time. And more, if by accident or
otherwise, the fire should become extinguished in one of the
temples the keepers were to quickly relight it by obtaining
fire from the other temple, and from nowhere else; still the
guardians of the temple in which the fire had been suffered
to go out should not be permitted to obtain it from the other
temple peacefully, since blood must be spilt on the floor of
the temple, as an atoning sacrifice to the offended spirits;
therefore, the one should resist the other in obtaining the
desired fire, and the other should obtain it, even at the cost
of shedding blood. Implicit obedience was ever given to
their foreign chief who lived to an unusual old age, and
made, and was ever regarded as the founder of their laws
and institutions. After his death they gave his descendants
the title of Suns, from their supposed origin, who ever afterwards ruled, without opposition, in the inherited and promised right of their great progenitor—the mysterious lawgiver from the sun.

Their tradition of the flood was: In ages past a mighty
flood of waters destroyed mankind, but a few who escaped
to a very high mountain, and by them the earth was again
repeopled. They believed in a Great Spirit, the creator and
ruler of the world, whom they regarded as being so good,
kind and benevolent, that it was impossible for him to do
wrong or to harm anything, even if he desired to do so.
They believed, however, in a multiplicity of evil spirits, by
whom all evil in the world was produced; that once a
mighty chief ruled over these spirits, and he committed so

much mischief in the world among mankind that the Great
Spirit chained him in a dark prison; and the evil spirits, his
subjects, have not, since the loss of their chief, manifested
so great desire to do mischief in the world, especially when
humbly petitioned by respectful prayers.

They had many great national festivals, partaking
much of religious character, since they were instituted and
observed with a special view of returning thanks to the
Great Spirit for his continued care and protection.

They reckoned time by moons. Their year began in
March and was divided into thirteen moons; this being done
that the course of that planet might correspond with that
of the sun, thus completing the year. At each new moon a
great feast was celebrated, which was named from the
fruits peculiar to that season, or the particular game that
was hunted during that moon. They celebrated the beginning of the new year (March) with the moon festival, called
the deer, to them one of their greatest and most important
festivals, as resting upon an ancient tradition which was: In
the far distant past, a great Sun, hearing an unusual tumult
in a distant part of his village, hastened to the spot to learn
its cause, and was taken prisoner by the warriors of a hostile nation who had made an unexpected attack upon his
village, having taken it completely by surprise. His people
soon recovering, however, from their momentary confusion
arising from the unexpected attack, and frantic by the wild
cry that was heard throughout the village that their chief
had fallen into the hands of their enemies, rushed in a solid
body to his rescue, and soon routed them with fearful
slaughter, and rescued their chief. In commemoration of
this great achievement, the warriors, at the new moon of
the deer, engaged in a sham battle, in which the Great Sun
took an active part. Dividing themselves into two companies, the one representing the warriors of the Great Sun,
and the other that of the enemy, the former designated by a
white feather in the head-dress, the latter by a red. They
concealed themselves in ambush in close proximity to the

house of the Great Sun. The warriors of the red feathers, under the leadership of a chief renowned for deeds of daring, first crept from their place of ambush and stealthily advanced toward the house of the Great Sun. As soon as they came in view, they rushed upon it with fearful yells. Then the Great Sun rushed from his house, assuming great bewilderment, as if suddenly awakened from sleep; shouting their fearful warwhoop, the assumed enemies rushed upon the bewildered chieftain, and trumphantly carried him off. At this juncture the warriors of the white feathers rushed from their place of concealment with deafening yells to the rescue of their chief, and threw themselves with terrific desperation upon the warriors of the red feather, and then and there was exhibited a wild scene of mimic warfare indescribable by words; and in which even the Great Sun himself was not an idle spectator, for his voice arose above the fearful din in words of cheer to his warriors, while his wooden tomahawk was seen gleaming in ascending and descending mimic strokes amid the struggling throng, apparently performing deeds of valor worthy the Great Sun. Finally, the warriors of the red feather seemingly began to waver, then fled in wild confusion, hotly pursued by those of the white feather many miles; then they of the white feather returned to the village, bearing their chief amid shouts of victory and gladness. In speaking of these mimic battles, the French writers, who were eye witnesses of the novel scene, state that they were true to nature in all their particulars, producing a complete illusion.

The second (April) was called the moon of strawberries, in which the women and children gathered this delicious fruit. The third (May) was called the moon of old corn, in which they feasted upon the corn made the year before, cooked in many different ways. The fourth (June) was called the moon of watermelons, the fifth (July) was called the moon of peaches. The sixth (August) was called the moon of blackberries. The seventh (September) was called the moon of new corn. The eighth (October) was called the moon of the turkey. The ninth (November) was called the moon of the buffaloes. The tenth (December) was called the moon of the bears. The eleventh (January) was called the moon of the geese; then followed February the moon of the walnuts, chestnuts and other nuts. At each return of these moons they indulged in festivals of feasting and dancing, contributing, at the same time, a full share of all the delicacies to their honored chief, the Great Sun.

That they might perpetuate the blood of the Great Suns in all its purity, as given to them by the mysterious stranger of traditional lore, the Natchez established as the fundamental law of their nation, that the right of succession to the exalted position of Great Sun must descend to the men through the female line alone. Thus the female descendants of the Great Sun held the title of nobility, and the honor of giving birth to the chief; and the grandson of Great Sun held a medium place in rank, and his great-grandson ranked with the common people.

But alas for the poor Natchez! An evil day brought the pale-faces among them in the year 1716, who built the fort Rosalie among them and in it garrisoned, as a matter of course, a body of soldiers as a protection in their intended aggression upon and usurpations of the Indians' rights; and from that day the sun of the Natchez's happiness began to wane, but to speedily set forever in the oblivion of utter extermination. As an introduction, Cadillac, on his way up the Mississippi River to search for gold and silver, stopped at Natchez. As soon as the Indian chiefs learned of his approach they marched out in state to meet him, and according to their custom, presented the calumet of peace to him in token of their desired friendship with him. Cadillac became greatly offended at what he regarded as presumption of the Indians in supposing that he would contaminate his pure patrician lips with the touch of their vile pipe. He accordingly treated the peace-desiring Indians as uncouth animals thrusting themselves into his august presence; and unceremoniously departing without having consented to smoke with them, he impressed the Natchez who could not comprehend his rough manners toward them, or understand the nature of his pride, with the belief that he meditated war upon their tribe and was secretly preparing to make an attack upon them; and finding a few French strolling about in their village after the departing of Cadillac, and regarding them as spies, they killed them. Hence the origin of the first misunderstanding between the Natchez and the French.

Then following in the wake of Cadillac, came Bienville on the 24th of April, with a company of soldiers and encamped on an island, situated in the Mississippi River, opposite a village of the Tunica Indians, fifty miles from the Natchez. Without delay he sent a Tunica warrior to the Natchez with the information that he was coming to establish a trading post among them, to exchange with them French goods for their furs. Bienville had been informed that the Natchez were ignorant of the fact, that he knew of their killing the Frenchmen a short time before, therefore he assumed to have come to them as a friend and would-be benefactor, that he might the better accomplish his preconcerted, nefarious designs against them. Gayarre, in his history of Louisiana, Vol. I, p. 140, says: "Three Natchez, as delegates representing their tribe, came to Bienville on the 27th of April 1716, and tendered to him the calumet, as the ensign of peace." But Bienville refused to smoke with them, and pretended to consider himself as not being treated with that respect to which he was entitled, since their great chief had not come in person to welcome him, the chief of the French. "I see," said he, "that your people are not pleased with the idea of my forming a settlement in their territory, for the purpose of trading with them. Otherwise they would have expressed their satisfaction in a more becoming manner. Be it so. If the Natchez are so thankless for what I meant to be a favor, I will alter my determination, and give my preference to the Tunicas, who have always shown themselves such great friends to the French."

After this speech, to hide his treachery the more suc-

cessfully, Bienville caused the three envoys to be feasted
and treated with the greatest hospitality and respect; and on
their return to their villages sent a Frenchman with them
with instructions to extend an invitation to the Natchez
chiefs to a conference on the island on which he was encamped. This greatly embarrassed the Natchez since they
were at a loss as to the best course to be pursued. Some
were of the opinion that it would be imprudent for their
chiefs to thus place themselves in the hands of the French,
who might have heard of the killing of the Frenchmen, and
had now come under the assumed garb of peace and friendship to entrap their chiefs and wreak vengeance upon them.
Others on the other hand argued that from the fact of the
French having come in such a small number, was sufficient
proof that they were still ignorant of the death of their
countrymen, and did not intend to act as enemies. Furthermore, that the chiefs, by refusing to accept Bienville's invitation, would incur his displeasure, and he would establish
a trading post among the Tunicas, and thus enrich their
rivals, to the great injury of the Natchez. This argument
prevailed, and in an evil hour for the Natchez chiefs, their
visit to Bienville's camp was resolved upon, and too late
they learned, even as all their race have learned from that
day to this, that for hypocrisy and treachery the pale-faces
cannot be surpassed, and from that hour a system of oppression was inaugurated by the French against the Natchez to
exterminate them.

In 1725 a son of one of the Natchez chiefs was murdered by a French sergeant, which caused the Indians to kill
a Frenchman named M. Guenot, in retaliation, a reconcilia-
tiontion, however, was soon made, but was not satisfactory
to Bienville. He therefore hastened from New Orleans with
500 men, attacked the Natchez wherever met, burned their
towns and destroyed their fields, upon which a war was
inaugurated, resulting in the defeat of the Indians, who
sued for peace. This was granted on their giving up one of
their chiefs to be executed, who was accused by the French

of being the chief instigator of the war. He was at once slain, and thus closed the second war of the French with the Natchez. In 1726 Bienville returned to France, and Perier succeeded him as governor in 1727. Bienville, by his cruelty and oppression, had entailed the hatred of the Natchez upon all Frenchmen; in this they were encouraged by the Chickasaws who, it has been said, had also projected a general confederation of all Indian tribes to drive the French from their territories.

In 1729 an officer by the name of Chopart was commander of the French settlement. Chopart was naturally of a haughty and tyrannical disposition—a fit subject to lord it over a helpless people. But his oppressive tyranny became so great that it could not be longer endured with any degree of patience by the colony; therefore, complaint was made to Governor Perier at New Orleans who summoned Chopart into his presence. He was tried and found guilty of great abuse of power, and would have been justly punished but for the interference of influential friends who secured his pardon from the governor. The pardoned tyrant returned, of course, to his colony, and inasmuch as he then acted with justice and humanity toward the French who had recourse to a higher authority, the more did he oppress and abuse the Indians who had no higher power to which they could appeal. At this time the Indian company gave instructions to Governor Perier to induce the Indians to remove to a greater distance from the French colony, assigning as a reason, that further collisions with the Whites might thus be obviated. But why not induce the intruding French to remove to a greater distance to obviate further collisions with the Indians?

Chopart, exulting in the prospects of being able to avenge his wounded pride upon someone, now emptied the bottles of his long smothered wrath upon the devoted heads of the unfortunate Natchez, treating them with every insolence he could devise, hoping thus to force them to leave their country and homes to the quiet possession of the

French, a successful plan of robbery adopted to get possession of the Indians' lands. One day he summoned the Great Sun to his presence, and, with a haughty contemptuous demeanor, informed him that he had been instructed by Governor Perier to take possession of the White Apple, one of their most beautiful towns, situated five or six miles from Fort Rosalie; and for them to remove somewhere else out of the way of the plans of the French. The chief turned his eyes full upon Chopart with a calm but inquisitive gaze of astonishment, and said: "My white brother cannot be in earnest, but only desires to try the temper of the Indians. Is my white brother ignorant of the fact that the Natchez built that village many thousand moons ago, and have lived there ever since?" "Insolent barbarian!" exclaimed Chopart. "Call me not brother. Between thy race and mine are no kindred ties; nor do I parley with any of your race. Let it suffice you, that when I command, you must obey." The noble chief, concealing his emotions, with a calm and manly voice, replied: "Brother, such language was never before addressed to me; nor have your people ever before taken our property from us by force. What they wished of ours, we freely gave or they purchased. We prefer peace to war with your nation. There are other lands of ours which we can spare to your people; take them! What more can we do? In the centre of the White Apple is our temple, in which the bones of our ancestors have reposed since we came from the far west to live on the banks of the Great River, and it is dear to our hearts."

"No more of your foolish talk to me," replied the insolent Chopart. "Soon a vessel," he continued, "from our great town down the river will arrive, and if the village of the White Apple is not given into my possession by the time the vessel arrives, I will send you bound in chains to our great chief. I have no more to say. Go." "'Tis well," responded the Indian; "and I go to my people and speak the words before their old and wise men in council." The command of their mighty chief to convene in council was hastily obeyed; and when he laid before them the insolent and outrageous demands of Chopart, the greatest indignation was manifest upon every face. A resolution was unanimously passed to invite the Yazoos, Choctaws, Chickasaws and other contiguous tribes, who had also experienced the insolence and oppression of the palefaces, to bury their former animosities for the sake of the common good, and unite in one grand alliance and great brotherhood against their common foe.

Without delay ambassadors were sent to all the surrounding tribes to lay their proposition before their wise men convened in solemn council. The ambassadors carried little bundles of an equal number of sticks, and to each tribe, who should adopt the resolution, a bundle of the sticks was given with instructions to withdraw a stick from the bundle daily, and the last stick was to designate the day that the combined attack upon the French was to be made throughout their entire country. This manner of keeping any appointed day was anciently practiced by all the southern Indians. In a few days the ambassadors returned with the information that not a single tribe to which they had been sent had refused to accept the proposition, and all would make the attack on the day appointed. Unfortunately for the Natchez, the uncommon movements and unusual activity of their warriors aroused the curiosity of the women. Unfortunately, also, for the Natchez, the mother of the then ruling Great Sun cherished an uncommon friendship for the French, and her curiosity had become greatly excited by the frequent secret meetings of all the wise men of the Nation and also by the going and coming of the embassies who had departed in and returned from all directions, and she had determined to solve the mystery. Alas, who can outwit a woman's excited curiosity? for this Indian queen mother so artfully wrought upon her kingly son that he disclosed the whole plot, even the most important secret for the successful accomplishment of her treasonable designs, where, in the Great Temple was concealed the chron-

ometer of the Natchez, the bundle of sticks, her knowledge
of which proved the successful overthrow of her chieftain
son.

To conceal her feelings from her unsuspecting son, she,
of cour~o, readily and easily assumed to enter heartily into
the plot, though she had determined to warn the French of
their impending danger, if it could be done without the
betrayal of herself. More than once she shrewdly managed
to get word to Chopart of the threatened storm, but he regarded the admonitions as idle stories purposely circulated
by the Indians to drive them from the resolution of seizing
their village, the White Apple. The French manifested by
their conduct no knowledge of their fast approaching doom,
notwithstanding her warnings sent them, the queen-mother,
unrelenting in her efforts to save them, secretly entered the
temple and withdrew several of the sticks from the bundle,
and thus destroyed the concert of action agreed upon
among the tribes, by bringing on the attack of the Natchez
at an earlier day. The traitoress hoped by this means that a
few French might escape and warn the rest of the colony.
But in spite of all the warnings received by Chopart, he still
adhered to the same fatal incredulity, applying the insulting
epithet of cowardice to those who spoke to him of the
rumors that were afloat.

The next day after the convening of the grand council
of the Natchez, the Great Sun presented himself at Fort
Rosalie, and expressed a willingness to Chopart to comply
with his order to evacuate the village of the white people;
but humbly requesting a little more time to select a place to
which they might transport their effects; to which Chopart
acceded, allowing him until the latter part of December,
but with this proviso, that the Natchez should pay to him
(Chopart), during the interval, one barrel of corn, a certain
number of fowls, a certain quantity of furs and bear's oil,
for each cabin of the White Apple village. The Great Sun
and Chopart then parted; the one elated with his prospect
of gain, the other with his prospect of revenge. But the

fatal day, the 29th of November, 1729, came, and ere the sun had reached the meridian, the French were involved in one common destruction; in one short hour the work was complete; and with the loss of only twelve warriors, the Natchez slew two hundred and fifty of their merciless French intruders and haughty oppressors. Chopart, the last to receive his just reward, fled to his garden hoping there to conceal himself; but he was found, dragged forth and handed over to the lowest class of the Natchez warriors, who beat him to death with their war clubs, the highest taking no part in his death, as they considered it dishonorable to imbue their hands in the blood of so contemptible a wretch. Two men only were spared, one a tailor, and the other a wagoner, and three hundred women and children. The Natchez, still ignorant of the queen-mother's theft of the sticks, and that their attack was premature, and believing that the other tribes had acted in concert with them, consequently the French throughout their entire country were cut off, gave themselves up to feasting and dancing.

In the wide extended arrangement of the plot to destroy the French, the destruction of New Orlenas had been assigned to the Choctaws, and the destruction of the little French forts, scattered here and there over the country, had been assigned to the weaker tribes. Thus the extermination of the French would have been complete but for the concert of action being destroyed by the stolen sticks from the chronometer of the Natchez.

A few days after the destruction of the French at White Apple the Choctaws sent an embassy to the Natchez to learn the cause of the premature attack upon the French, thus causing a failure of concerted action against their common foe. When they arrived at the White Apple they angrily demanded of the Natchez an explanation of their strange and incomprehensible conduct and breach of faith. To which the Natchez replied that they had made the attack on the very day indicated by the last stick, and that if any one had violated their word it was the Choctaws in not making the attack also at the time they themselves had made it; at the same time intimating cowardice on the part of the Choctaws as a reason for their failure. To which insinuation the Choctaw deputation took great offense, and at once departed, telling the Natchez that henceforward and forever they would have no further alliance with them, but ever consider them as unworthy of trust, while the Natchez hurled back upon them the accusations of perfidy and cowardice.

In a few days after the departure of the first embassy another one came from a different district of the Choctaw Nation, and were as much dissatisfied in their interview with the Natchez, regarding the explanation of their premature attack upon the French as the former. But learning that the Natchez contemplated killing the two men and the three hundred women and children whom they still held as prisoners, the Choctaw embassy boldly marched in a body to the public square and struck the red post—a challenge of defiance among all Indians—boldly declaring that the Choctaws would no longer be the allies of the Natchez, but would henceforward be the allies of the French, and if they dared kill a single one of the French prisoners then in their hands, every warrior of their great Nation would come in a body against them. This defiant threat brought the Natchez to due reflection and the two men and three hundred women and children were saved. Having given this salutary advice to the Natchez, the Choctaws departed, leaving the seemingly unfortunate Natchez in a state of great perplexity as to the proper step they should take in so dubious a state of affairs.

When Governor Perier learned of the destruction of the French at Fort Rosalie he immediately sent a courier to the Choctaws with instructions to inform them that Governor Perier desired to have a talk with them. The Choctaws at that time were the most powerful of all the tribes, and great doubts were entertained by them in their then critical state of affairs, as to the course the Choctaws would pursue, and it was highly important that their friendship should be secured. The destruction of Fort Rosalie by the Natchez had thrown the French into great excitement, consternation and dread, filling their minds with fear as rumor whispered to their excited imaginations the uprising of the Indians in one grand concert of action against them. And Governor Perier states: "So great was the fear that the Chauaches, a little tribe of only thirty warriors, dwelling a few miles above New Orleans, were even a subject of dread to the French. This induced me to have them destroyed by our Negroes, who executed the mission with great promptness and secrecy, setting an example before the small tribes higher up the river that held them in check. If I had been so disposed I could have destroyed all those nations, which are no service to us, by the Negroes; but who, on the other hand, may influence our blacks to revolt." But he might the more truthfully have said that he caused the innocent and harmless Chauaches to be murdered by the Negroes, that he might create an enmity between the Negro and Indian race, as he no doubt had misapprehensions as to the Negroes remaining quiet in the then excited state of affairs, and not attempt, by joining the Indians, to assert their rights to freedom. What a volume of oppression, wrong and cruelty towards the North American, from first to last, might be written from the sentiment expressed in Governor Perier's, "which are no service to us!"

On the 16th of January, 1730, Perier's fears and anxieties were greatly quieted when he was informed that Le Sueur, a French officer, with seven hundred Choctaw warriors, was on his march against the Natchez. Alas, for the Natchez! They seemed unable to resist the temptation of enjoying the rich booty taken from the French. On the 27th of January, 1730, while indulging in feasting and dancing on the banks of a small creek, in thoughtless security, Le Sueur with his seven hundred Choctaws broke suddenly and unexpectedly upon them and turned their merriment into wailing by killing sixty, taking captive twenty and rescuing fifty-four French women and children ere they could rally and retreat to two forts they had erected. But this was only the prelude.

On the 8th of February, part of the French forces, rendezvousing among the Tunicas, arrived at Natchez under the command of Loubois and united with the Choctaw under LeSueur, followed by the remainder on the next day. On the 14th, the united forces of the Choctaws and French made an assault upon the two forts, which were bravely defended by the Natchez. The French brought four pieces of artillery to bear upon the two little forts, which they had succeeded in planting on an eminence five hundred yards distant, and for six consecutive hours hurled their balls against the two forts with no effect whatever, the Natchez responding with two pieces of artillery, taken in the capture of Fort Rosalie, with like effect. The total failure of the French to produce any effect upon the forts, was humiliating to the French commander, but a source of amusement to the Choctaws; as he had promised them that he would knock down the two forts over the heads of the Natchez in two hours. The ineffectual cannonading was kept up seven days; the Choctaws, in the meantime, laughing and deriding the incompetency of the tanapoh chitoh (big guns); becoming wearied at noise without effect, the Choctaws threatened, on the morning of the 23rd, to return home if the affairs of the siege were not prosecuted in a better manner. This threat of the Choctaws had the desired effect; and on the 24th, the four pieces of artillery were brought to bear upon the two little forts at a distance of three hundred yards, and then the Natchez were told that it was determined to blow them up, even at the sacrifice of the French captives in their possession.

The near proximity of the artillery, together with that of the threat, so intimidated the Natchez that they sent a female captive to make propositions of peace, who remained, without any response being returned to the Natchez. On the 25th a flag was hoisted by the Natchez as a token of peace. Upon seeing this, a Choctaw chief went near to one of the forts, and cried out to the Natchez, "Who ever knew before that the Choctaws encamped around the fort of an enemy for many weeks? Learn from this how great is the friendship of the Choctaws for the French. It is folly for you who are so much less in numbers than the Choctaws to still refuse to give up to the French their women and children. I and my warriors have determined to stay here and keep you in those two forts until you perish by hunger." Upon hearing this the Natchez promised to deliver all their French prisoners to the Choctaws, on the condition that the French would remove to the bank of the river with their artillery. The French assenting to this proposition, the following stipulations were agreed upon by the two belligerent parties: That the French were to withdraw to the banks of the river; the Natchez to deliver their French captives to the Choctaws, and be allowed to remain in quiet and peaceable possession of their country and homes. All of which was agreed upon on the 26th, and thus terminated the siege, the French having lost fifteen men in the affair.

Still the French commander, not regarding himself in honor bound to the adherence of his word, like thousands at the present day, when given to an Indian, had determined, as soon as he had released the French captives in the hands of the Natchez, to recommence hostilities against the Natchez to their utter extermination.

But the Natchez, having learned by sad experience to rely no more upon the promises of the French, had determined to retreat. On the morning of the 27th they handed over all the French women and children to the Choctaws, who, in turn, delivered them to the French, and on the same day the Choctaws departed for their homes. But on the 29th, when the French commander again appeared before the two forts to execute his infamous determination against the Natchez, he found them empty, and their former occupants flown.

Thus was finished this expedition against the unfortunate Natchez, for the successful and speedy termination of which the honor (if honor there be) is due to the Choctaws; for they alone influenced the Natchez to yield; and to the Choctaws only would the Natchez consent to deliver their French prisoners, and then made good their retreat with honor to themseves and without loss; bidding an eternal adieu to their native hills and ancient possessions to seek a place of rest they knew not where, and leaving their abandoned homes to the possession of the French.

The different tribes, acting in the beginning of the war as allies to the Natchez, returned to their former allegiance with the French, and assisted them in destroying the Natchez wherever found. "Since their flight," said Perier, "I have had fifty of them killed or taken prisoners. I buried here six of them, four men and two women."

Soon after this act of the French, a band of Tunica warriors brought to New Orleans a poor Natchez woman whom they had captured while lingering amid the scenes of her youth, and Governor Perier had her burned to death on a high platform erected especially for the ceremony, and to witness which all New Orleans again turned out in state. While slowly being consumed that forlorn Natchez woman far away from kindred and friends, shed not a tear nor uttered a groan, but bore her tortures with Indian fortitude; yet reproached her captors, the Tunicas, who stood around, in bitter epithets declaring the speedy destruction of their people. The dying woman's prediction proved true; for the Tunicas returned home but to be surprised by a band of the homeless Natchez and their nation in turn nearly exterminated.

The Tunicas were destroyed by a brave and resolute band of the Natchez, who had found a temporary asylum among the generous Chickasaws, though the French believed that all the Natchez had sought refuge west of the Mississippi River. But this heroic and indomitable people, scattered in detached bands here and there, did not fail to continuously give satisfactory notice to the French that they were not all exterminated. Therefore, Governor Perier resolved that they should be; and in accordance with that resolution he, on the 4th of January, 1731, personally took command of his army, which had been instructed to rendezvous at the mouth of Red River. But where to find the place where the Natchez had concealed themselves was a problem which presented itself before him not easy of solution. He immediately ascended the Red River; thence into Black River; thence into a stream then known as Silver River; thence into a small lake, near which he had heard the Natchez were concealed, where he arrived on January 19th. Again, fortune frowned upon the poor persecuted Natchez, for on the next day a Natchez boy, wandering too far in his eager pursuit of the chase, fell into the hands of his merciless foes, and, under the fear of terrible threats, betrayed the retreat of his people; and on the 21st the unfortunate Natchez found themselves completely surrounded; and on the 24th, fearing the little fort which they had constructed, and in which their women and children were placed would be stormed, and in that case they would be left to the mercies of a brutal soldiery, made overtures of peace, to which Perier replied, "That he would hold no parley with them, unless they would first give up the Negro slaves they had in their possession, and their chiefs would then come out half way between the fort and the French to have an interview with him."

Twenty Negroes were at once given up. After much hesitation, and how well founded the sequel will show, the Great Sun, the Little Sun, and a subordinate chief came out of their little fort, at 4 p.m. and advanced to the half-way ground and there met Perier with whom to have a consultation. After a few words had been exchanged, a rain commenced falling; upon which the perfidious Perier suggested the propriety of entering a vacant cabin near by, to which they readily consented, but the moment they entered they were made prisoners by a company of soldiers concealed therein. As night came on the rain increased, and during the night became a fearful tempest; during which the subordinate made good his escape. On the next day (25th) forty-five men and four hundred and fifty women and children surrendered to the mercies of their foes during the day. But the night following being again dark and rainy, the rest, about two hundred, fortunately made their escape. Perier began his return on the 28th; and in his dispatches, like our great Indian butchering generals, the "heroic" Sheridan and Sherman, did not forget the indispensable "Too much praise cannot be awarded the officers and men for their gallant conduct against fearful odds and under adverse circumstances"; but forgot to mention, even as his "gallant" counterparts of the present era, the base treachery he adopted to get the Indian chiefs into his hands. When he returned to New Orleans, he took his Natchez prisoners with him, numbering forty-five men and four hundred and fifty women and children, besides the Great Sun and Little Sun, and then sent every one of them to St. Domingo, and there sold them as slaves.

The little remnant of Natchez left, though in the last stage of hopeless despair, instead of yielding, nobly and bravely nerved themselves to desperate deeds of revenge, for they still could call into the field about three hundred warriors. But they were at last defeated, then all hope fled, and the few scattered remnants, in three different bands, sought safety where best they could find it; one sought refuge among the Christian-hearted Chickasaws, who generously gave them a home and protection. But even there they were not idle, for they sought every opportunity to avenge the destruction of their Nation and people, by attacking the French whenever and wherever found.

In 1733 a few still survived and still fought; for Bienville, being at that time reappointed to the governorship in the place of Perier, said, in a dispatch written on the 15th of May, 1733, "That the Tunicas had assured him that the Natchez were not destroyed, but were composed of three bands; the smallest had fled north some distance from their ancient villages; the next was on the banks of the Mississippi River, opposite the Yazoo River, and the third and largest had been received among the Chickasaws who had given them land on which to live." He closed by saying: "I shall use every effort to constantly harass them."

The two bands that still clung near their old homes, and seemed so reluctant to leave forever the banks of that noble river, the Mississippi, became so constantly harassed by the French that they were finally driven to seek a safer place of refuge; therefore, they also retreated to the Chickasaws and joined the band that had preceded them and found shelter and protection among that magnanimous people. Their nation had perished; the remaining little remnant of survivors went west, and were dispersed among the various Indian tribes of that then little known country to the white race, and were lost as a distinct people.

Noble race! Unaccustomed to crouch under oppression, and when the evils of submission became greater than those of resistance, how could it but beget a convulsive burst of indignation and courage, supported by the hope of successfully driving back the merciless invaders of their country and homes! But how vain the struggle against the irresistible power of superior intelligence, crazed to become rich, and the strength of civilization without mercy, honor or truth, a power without morality, unscrupulous and unprincipled, which came among them to wring from them their country, upon which to build its own greatness. The historic Indian is with the past, and his bones are resting in the grave with his pre-historic ancestry; while his surviving descendant, shorn of all his former chivalry and independence, is left alone to battle with the prejudice of the exterminators of his race, who for two hundred years have been pressing it toward that period of evolution we call civilization, but in reality extermination.

But alas, as a falling star tumbling from its primitive place near the gates of heaven, bathed in primitive glory, so has been the falling of the North American Red Race, that noble, brave and wonderful people, into the dark clouds of misfortune and woe, tracking their lone and sorrowful course down through the deep midnight of despair to hopeless oblivion; and though their spring freshness and summer bloom have forever faded away, leaving no hope of a returning morn, still their silent, yet dignified despair, impresses an involuntary respect and admiration. But will that time never come when that spirit of love that seeks the good of the poor, unfortunate Indian will be truly felt and acted upon, and that spirit shall speak in the actions of our congress, sounded in sermons from our pulpits and pleaded in our prayers at the throne of grace.

It is attested by thousands of Christian witnesses now living who personally know, and thousands of Christian witnesses long since dead, who left their testimony behind them in their writings down the revolving years back to over two centuries ago, that the North American Indians everywhere welcomed the religion of Jesus Christ; that they admired the civilization of the White Race, and delighted to be taught in the useful arts and sciences, while they abhorred and dreaded the accompanying vices attending that civilization, as exhibited before them by the lawless, who ever followed close on the heels of the servants of God.

It is a truth, though known to few, that the problems which the North American Indians have presented, ever since their first introduction to the White Race, and still present to this generation in the little remnant, still surviving, are worthy the consideration and study of even the most learned; and that the events which have formed their known history during the last two centuries are worthy to take rank among the marvels of history. May a just and merciful God grant that others shall rise up in the defense of this part of His fearfully persecuted race of mankind, whose pens more efficient than mine shall relate to future generations its wrongs and sufferings; its love of country and freedom; its heroic defense of both; its patience and

silence in misfortunes unparalleled in the history of mankind; its calm resignation in humiliation, after prodigies of
justifiable resistance against overwhelming numbers, while
laboring under the most adverse surroundings ever known
in the history of man fighting for country, freedom, justice
and truth.

And though here, as in the middle watches of the night,
I close my labors, yet I must leave the reader in great doubt
of a fairer morn ever dawning upon the Red Race of the
United States, as such a morn can scarcely be expected, or
even hoped for, in an age abounding more with vice than
virtue, as this hitherto has abounded and still abounds, with
fair prospects of indefinite continuance; since the manifested desire and unyielding determination of the government and people of the whole country have long been, still
are and will ever be, to exterminate their Indian wards—
forever blot out their institutions and every vestige of their
entire race; but hoping and believing that in its oblivion
would also be forgotten the means adopted for the accomplishment of the result; therefore, thousands still mock at
and deride this people, while others oppress, persecute and
slander.

But in this account of the true Native Americans, this
peculiar and, in many respects, wonderful part of God's
created races of man, I regret not that I have wandered far
from the old and beaten track in which former writers have
walked in their accounts given of that people known as the
Red Race of North America; and truly believe that I have
thereby escaped many of the ruts into which they have,
with here and there an exception, alike and invariably
fallen; though in passing through the shadowy lands of
legend and myth, where many of the pen pictures are, to an
unjustifiable and inexcusable extent, imaginary, I deny not
but here and there a slender web of fiction, but free of intended or known falsehood, may be found upon its pages;
as I have sought from many sources, whatever hues and
colors which were considered best adapted to and interest

and variety to its pages; and if it only tends to bring others into sympathy for the Indian race of this continent, one of its principal missions will be accomplished.

True, I have rejected much which might have been written, for which, perhaps, many may think that fact deserves more praise than to be pardoned for that which has been published. Be it as it may; I murmur not at the verdict of the reader; nor make any appeal to posterity. I sought not for human adulation, that ephemeral thing so difficult to obtain and so worthless when obtained; therefore, if it quickly dies, amen! as, in so doing, it will save trouble for those who are inclined to injure from any attempt to kill that which will inevitably soon perish of its own self.

But let this be added, the subject matter of this narrative was begun and ended with a full knowledge of the task that lay before me; and so involved was it in uncertainty, and so tinged with romance and fiction, that had not the interest of and justice to the North American Indians, demanded, at least, that an attempt should be made to shed a ray of true light upon their history, I would not indeed have ventured to attempt to lift the veil and bid a thoughtless world look in again upon that mystic people, and thereby expose them once more to its idle and heartless gaze, chilled with the frosts of incredulity.

I have endeavored to draw a true picture of the representative type of southern Indians and their wrongs, as found in the Choctaw, Chickasaw, Cherokee, Muscogee (now Creek) and Seminole, as they appeared in the four epochs of their known history; from the time of De Soto's invasion into their territories; during the period of the establishment of the French colonies among them; during the transition period following the advent of the Protestant missionaries to them, and their final banishment to the then inhospitable and little known "Wild West," and as they appear, and are to-day, as a civilized and Christian people.

Hoping my labors will not be viewed in a wrong light, yet ready at all times to defend my position as the abiding

friend of the true native North American race, I here bid
the reader a kind adieu, as my narrative is finished; my
manhood's years far behind, with life's declining sun lingering upon its western sky; the years of the past hold the
native Americans' wrongs, and time will tell the rest in the
years to come.

Noble race! I honor you and I love you. We've been
friends together through the years of the Long Ago, enough
for us to know. We'll be so still in all our years to come; nor
time nor distance, though our paths of life diverge, shall
ever efface from our memory's page those words of truth![1]

<hr>

[1] It is evident that Cushman ended his book here, but it proved impossible for him
to stop writing. He appended as a sort of postscript a section of thirty-six pages on the
Mound Builders.

NORTH AMERICA'S MOUNDS AND MOUND
BUILDERS—THEIR ORIGIN
AND DESIGN.

[According to popular belief at the time of Cushman's writing a mysterious race called Mound Builders had inhabited the Western World long prior to the Indians. Cushman set out to refute this theory and to prove that the Mound Builders and the Indians were one and the same race; and he ranges across the entire archeology of North America with stray references to Egypt. All of this material is outdated and valueless except for a few facts about the Choctaws, Chickasaws, and Natchez—]

On the 18th of May, 1838, a party of literary and scientific gentlemen from Natchez, Mississippi, examined two square mounds three and a half miles below the city, between the bluff and the river, about a mile from the river and one-eighth of a mile from the bluff, rising from eleven to sixteen feet above the level upon which they are based. The two mounds stood about five hundred feet apart, ranging north and south of each other, the larger being sixty-six feet square, and sixteen feet high, and the other thirty-three feet square and eleven feet high. An excavation was made in the latter clear to the bottom and, as usual, human bones and numerous and various pieces of Indian pottery and trinkets were found at different depths; as both structures were similar, no excavation was made in the larger one. On the 20th of May, 1838, a party of twenty-five men from Natchez visited a large mound standing about ten miles east of that city. On approaching the mound from the west, states the writer, it presents the appearance of a long, straight battery of earth, with a sloping, regular front and platform at the top, with a few moderate elevations or towers upon the terrace, the whole being overlooked by an abrupt tower at the eastern end towards Natchez; which rises nearly as high above the terrace or platform as that does above the circumjacent plain. In approaching the mound on the southern side, it presents a most imposing and martial character, and the traces of design are so apparent that the observer cannot but ascribe it to the work of man, and involuntarily feels that so enormous a pile must have been the creation of heads that planned, and hands that labored through long periods of time. Its magnitude, however, did not impress the beholder at first with its full proportions; but after ascending its steep face to the broad terrace, which is itself the base of the great western tower and also of four other smaller ones, and glancing at the general outline of the foundation mound, which has the appearance of a parallelogram, with a regular southern side and an irregular front on the north, then walking over the terrace which includes an area of nearly five acres, and looking up at the western tower, itself a parallelogram (perhaps once a perfect one) of eighty or more feet in length and fifty in breadth, the mind fully comprehends the vastness of the structure, and allows due honor to the prehistoric ancestors of the North American Indian race. The height of the great terrace, from its base, was, in 1838, forty-five feet by measurement, and of the great tower above the terrace, thirty-eight feet, making eighty-three feet in all above the plain.

The human skeletons, from the great length of time they had been immured, prevented the examining party from obtaining but few perfect specimens of craniology. At the depth of about two feet from the surface they found the skeleton of a full sized man from which, no doubt, much earth must have washed away during the long years that had passed since there entombed. The skull was indisputably a compressed one of a Flat Head Indian, or one whose head in infancy had undergone the compressing process, a custom, it is said by the early writers, practiced by the ancient ancestors of the present Choctaws.

The sides of the larger mounds are nearly wholly encased about one foot beneath the surface of the earth with a kind of rubbish resembling slack baked bricks, regardless of regularity of form, as if laid upon the original steep faces of the mound to prevent the washing away of the soil. This rude roofing, formed of a clay base, mixed with hair or moss, like modern mortar, may once have been continuous, or it may not have been otherwise than it was when discovered; in either case, it was a sufficient security against the action of rain water. The soil above the rubbish was filled with fragments of pottery, pieces of human and animal bones, charcoal and the debris of the top of the mound and of the smaller towers which seem to have been almost entirely washed away. The pottery found was made of different colors; some pieces were brick colored; others slate colored; others white. The pieces were large enough to show the shape and curve of the circumference of the vessels of which the pieces were a part. Some of the pieces proved the original to have been of beautiful structure.

Garcellasso de la Vega says, in laying off the ground for a town, the first thing that the Indians did, was the erection of a mound, upon the top of which the houses of the chief and his family and attendants were built; and at the base a large square was laid off, around which the principal warriors built their houses, while the common people placed theirs on the opposite side of the mound from the square.

All the early explorers repeatedly state that they saw the mounds in all parts of the country through which they passed. Here then we learn of Mound Builders (Indians) nearly three and a half centuries ago. They were also thrown up as a means of defense. When the French under Bienville defeated the Natchez Indians in 1730, and drove them from their country, where the city of Natchez, Mississippi, now stands, and for whom the city was named, they established themselves upon the Lower Washita, Louisiana. Two years after they were again attacked and defeated by the French, yet they had in those two years constructed mounds and embankments covering an area of four hundred acres, which they used as means of defense against the French in their second attack upon them. This is attested by several authors, some of whom were eye witnesses. This was done nearly two hundred years after De Soto's invasion. Some of these mounds were very large, and were still to be seen forty years ago; and no doubt still stand as monuments of the thrilling scenes which once were enacted there, during which a once pround, prosperous, and happy people were blotted out as a nation.

The Choctaws, who lived in large villages before their exodus from Mississippi to the west, first placed their dead upon scaffolds, near the villages; and those living in the country near their homes, where they were carefully guarded from the beasts and birds of prey, until decomposition had thoroughly accomplished its work. Afterwards on a previously appointed day, the remaining flesh was picked from the bones by officials called bone-pickers, many of whom I have seen in the days of my boyhood. When their duty had been performed, the bones were deposited in a box and carried away and placed in the common bone-house, and there sacredly kept until the appointed day rolled around for a general bone-burying; which was once a year. Then all from neighboring villages and country brought, in solemn and imposing ceremony, the boxes containing the bones of their dead to the place of interment where they were laid away in one common grave, into which were cast as memorial tokens various articles, such as earthen pots, bows and arrows, tomahawks, ornaments, etc.; all of which were first covered with ashes and charred coals, then filled up with earth; then over all was erected a mound. The same cemetery or mound was used as a place of deposit for the bones of their dead for a long series of years, until it became in size and height inconvenient, and then another spot was chosen, upon which, in like manner, another mound gradually arose. That the custom of the ancient Choctaws in disposing of their dead was also practiced by many of the North American Indians, is evident from the fact that, in digging into these mounds, wherever found, after passing through a stratum of earth about two feet in

thickness a bed of ashes and charcoal is first met, then a bed
of human bones together with fragments of pottery, arrow
heads, and Indian ornaments; then follows another stratum
of earth, which is succeeded by a stratum of ashes and charcoal, then of human bones, pottery, ornaments and arrow
points, thus on to the bottom.

I read the following in the American Antiquarian over
the signature of H. F. Buckner:

"Mr. Maxwell, in a historical address, says: 'My conviction is that the high grade of military skill displayed by the
Mound Builders at Carthage, Alabama, attests a knowledge
of the necessities of attack and defense unknown to the
mode of warfare practiced by the tribes found here by
De Soto.' "

I will here state that the old Shakchih Humma fort,
within the enclosure of which was established the missionary station among the Choctaws, called Hebron, of which I
have already spoken, and where I spent many years of my
life, displayed as "high grade of military engineering skill"
and attested a "knowledge of the necessities of attack and
defense" equal to our high grade military engineering skill
displayed in the military forts erected throughout the present Indian Territory, of which I have had an occular demonstration.

"Who the Mound Builders were it is impossible to
determine," continues Mr. Maxwell. "They were not built
by the ancestors of the tribes found here by De Soto, as
they pretended no knowledge of their construction, traditional or otherwise.

"The only tradition they had or have is, that their forefathers found the mounds when they emigrated from the
Mexican Empire to the east of the Mississippi River, exterminated the ancient inhabitants and appropriated the
country."

The above is an egregious error, as far as the Choctaws
and Chickasaws are concerned, for their traditions were
utterly silent in regard to the mounds, except that of Nunih

Waiyah (of which I have already spoken), which is one among the largest, if not the largest, ever found in the now state of Mississippi.

Buckner, quoting from Maxwell's address, continues:

"Prescott says (vol. 2, pp 368 and 391) that the ancient Aztecs, long before the days of Montezuma, had a tradition that when they entered the Mexican valley they found similar mounds, and that two of the largest had been dedicated to the worship of the sun and moon (another proof that they were built by the ancestors of our Indians, among whom the Natchez Indians were worshippers of the sun even after they had settled upon the banks of the Mississippi River), and that two of the largest were dedicated to the worship of the stars, and served as sepulchers for the great men of the Nation besides."

Exactly. They served as sepulchers for the great men of the Nation, for which the ancient Natchez of Mississippi erected the mounds, as well as other North American tribes. "That the plane on which they stood was called Micoati, or The Path of the Dead." Another proof that they were the ancestors of the North American Indians, for the word Micoati is a corruption of the Choctaw words, Miko, king or chief, and aiantah, to occupy; i. e., occupied by the king or chief.

Continuing, Mr. Buckner says: "Of one thing we are sure, the Choctaws loved the bones of their ancestors and of their people. This unlocks the mystery of their funeral rites. They believed in immortality and eternal life; and such was their veneration for their dead that they picked the flesh from their bones. Knowing that they could not carry all their remains, and when forced to remove from one place to another, it was the business of certain appointed persons to carry these bones with them until they could be again deposited in a place of rest and safety."

The last clause above is but one of the thousand errors published about the Indians. The Choctaws never carried the bones of their dead from one place to another, but buried them, and woe to him who desecrated the mound cemetery by digging into it, or in any way disturbed its sacred contents.

But who has ever found the line between the so-called Mound Builders and the North American Indians? No one. Nor will it ever be found. The Indians not only erected mounds for various specific purposes, but fortified their villages with walls, and ditches filled with water; also with rows of palisades interwoven with branches of trees.

At Tampa Bay, where De Soto is said to have landed in his wild search for gold, his chroniclers state "That the house of the chief was erected near the shore on a very high mound made by hand."

And Garcillasso says: "The town and the house of the Cazique (chief) Ossachile" (Choctaw words corrupted from Ossi, eagle, chahlib, swift) are like those of the other caziques."

Biedman says: "The caziques of this country, (supposed to be now Arkansas) make a custom of raising, near their dwellings, very high hills, on which they sometimes build their huts."

La Harpe, in visiting the Indians on the lower Mississippi in 1720, says: "They are dispersed over the country upon mounds of earth made with their own hands."

The Natchez, who were exterminated by the French in 1739, were also Mound Builders. DuPratz, who had lived among them in 1718, says of their customs, "Their temple was about thirty feet square, and erected on a mound eight feet high; that the house of the chief was built on a mound of the same height and sixty feet over the surface. (Father Le Petit, Note, page 142.)

Charlevoix, a Jesuit priest, describes the mounds erected to a considerable extent in his writings, he says: "When a chief died, the mound upon which his house was erected, was abandoned, and a new one thrown up for his successor."

It was the custom of the ancient Choctaws to gather the bones of all who had died during several years, which had been safely kept in their bone-houses in boxes, bury them all together in a common grave and then erect a mound over them. And it is a conceded fact that all Indians ever found in North and South America possess many common features. I have seen the native Indians of Mexico, Arizona and California, and recognized them at once to be of the North American Indian race. I have seen them singly and in groups; given special attention to their features, the expression of their eyes, their walk and manner of sitting, their manner of carrying their babes and heavy burdens, and found them all to be exactly the same as the southern Indians over seventy years ago.

The Indians were also skilled in the art of pottery, as is fully proven by the numerous examples of their work seen by the early explorers. DuPratz spoke particularly of the skill of the Natchez Indians in the art of pottery. Others, after careful examination of the contents and remains of the mounds excavated in different and various states, claimed to be the work of a prehistoric race wholly different from our Indian Race, whom they named "The Moundbuilders," have found them to be, in all respects, exactly like those found in the mounds, known to have been built by the Indians, and also in and around old Indian villages. The Southern Indians had spades and shovels made of cedar, picks, axes and hoes of stone, and spoons of horn; together with the mortar and pestle, with which they prepared their corn for bread, and the Choctaws and Chickasaws use them to this day.

It has been reiterated time and again that the Indians had no traditions concerning the origin and design of the mounds, and for this reason it had been asserted that the mounds are the work of an extinct race of such antiquity as to precede the ancient traditions of the Indians. But in this, as in the majority that has been written about that people, "zeal without knowledge" is more manifest than truth. The traditions of the Indians, until within the past ten years have always and everywhere, been pronounced as myths, absurdities unworthy of credence, though in every instance where they have been put to the test by discovery, they have invariably been confirmed by truth. Besides the Indians everywhere were utterly silent before the whites in regard to the manners, customs and traditions of their tribes, and would only converse upon these subjects with those whites in whom they had the most implicit confidence; therefore, though they possessed many traditions in regard to the memorial mounds, effigy mounds and others, they have been silent, ever silent, upon the subject; and thus have we forever closed the doors of knowledge against ourselves in regard to the history of that past, which we now would gladly read. And it may be truthfully affirmed that, few ever reached that high place in the Indian's heart except the faithful and loving missionaries; they, and they only, ever penetrated beneath the surface into the inner life and secrets of the North American Indians.

But they, being more intent upon the moral and intellectual improvement of the living Indians, gave little care concerning the dead. And those sentimental writers of the present day who claim the Mound Builders to be a race of people far antecedent to the Red, from the fact that the Indians gave a negative reply to all interrogations made to them concerning the mounds, are but the willing dupts of the Indians who keep, as much as possible, from the Whites all things relating to their past. I speak from seventy-five years experience. In 1884 I was in the Choctaw Nation and, upon being introduced to an aged Choctaw, born in his native domains, east of the Mississippi River, I commenced interrogating him in his own language when, after replying to a few questions, he suddenly fixed his keen, black eyes upon me and said: "For what purpose do you ask me such questions?" The Choctaw friend who had introduced me to the old veteran came to my relief most fortunately by telling him who I was; that I was the true friend of all Indians and could be trusted. The old man again turned his eyes upon me, but with a confiding smile which I fully comprehended, and I found no trouble in obtaining a cheerful reply to any and all my questions.

In my travels in the Choctaw and Chickasaw Nations, during the last ten years, I have frequently met aged persons of both tribes with whom I had the pleasure and honor (yes, honor, and of which I am not ashamed even in these my declining years) of being schoolmates, whose confidence in me is still as firm and unshaken as mine in them, and whose assistance in gathering material for this book has been great, for which I here acknowledge my deep and sincere gratitude. God bless my Indian friends everywhere!

Yes, the mounds were tangible signs used to express truths known only to their builders—the Indians; symbols thrown together in that peculiar connection which the white man is left to interpret the best he can, all to end only in wild conjecture and romantic speculation; while the builders, now deprived of all originality and of nearly all remembrance of their former selves, still survive. North America may be truly regarded as an olden land with a modern history.

The Indians, having no written language, preserved and handed down their history to future generations through tradition, much of which could have been obtained a century and a half ago, and even a century ago, which was authentic and would have added much to the interest of the history of the continent of which we boast as our inheritance. The ancient Choctaws selected about twenty young men in the jurisdiction of each chief, who were taught the traditions of the tribe, and were required to rehearse them three or four times a year before the aged men of the nation, who were thoroughly posted, that nothing might be added to or taken from the original as given to them.

And now, as to the odium and even defamation that may be attached to or hurled against me on account of my manifested love for and admiration of the North American Indian Race, I here submit to it all without a murmur or complaint. I will remain silent and passive, and still continue to be their devoted, admiring and loving friend; while I continue through life to rehearse to myself the words of the noble Catlin, that true friend of the North American Indians in toto because he knew them as they ought to be known.

"Have I any apology to make for loving the Indians?
The Indians have always loved me, and why should I not love the Indians?
I love the people who have always made me welcome to the best they had.
I love the people who are honest without law, who have no jails and no poor-houses.
I love the people who keep the commandments without ever having read them or heard them preached from the pulpit.
I love a people who never swear; who never take the name of God in vain.
I love a people who love their neighbors as themselves.
I love a people who worship God without a Bible, for I believe that God loves them too.
I love a people whose religion is all the same, and who are free from religious rows.
I love a people who have never raised a hand against me or stolen my property, where there was no law to punish for either.
I love a people who never have fought a battle with white men except on their own ground.
I love and don't fear mankind where God has made and left them, for they are children.
I love people who live and keep what is their own without locks and keys.
I love all people who do the best they can, and, Oh! how I love a people who don't live for the love of money."

NORTH AMERICAN INDIAN NAMES.[1]

Even as various nations of antiquity of the eastern continent have left the evidences of their former occupation by the geographical names that still exist, so too have the North American Indians left their evidences upon the western (independent of all written history) that they have likewise possessed this continent during unknown ages of the past. The artificial mounds, fortifications, lakes and ponds with their original names and those of rivers, creeks, mountains, bluffs and hills, remain to this day; and here they will remain long after the lips that spoke the language are hushed in death, even continuing to repeat the voices of that prematurely and mercilessly exterminated people.

But alas, how mutilated the orthography and how erroneous the translation of the original Indian names! What a manifestation of the utter want of even the most remote idea of anything constituting their language!

As an illustration I will here insert a few examples taken from a publication bearing date February 2, 1898, and to which is the signature, "John Hawkins in Philadelphia Times," with the caption "Names from Indinas" and also the important announcement, "Some Interesting Information Concerning Their Origin. They Contain Curious Bits of Nature, Thought or Fancy, History or Tradition."

From among the names mentioned I have selected a few which Mr. Hawkins says are "Choctaw names," giving also his orthography and translation:

First.—"Chitimacha (La.)—They possess cooking vessels." Original, Chi-im-ai-ya-chih, Thine to conquer. But the Choctaw words for "They possess cooking vessels" are: Original, Ah-la-bush-li ha-lul-li in, Cooking vessels possess they.

---

[1] It will be apparent to anyone familiar with the Southern Indians that some of the names in this glossary are not Choctaw, and that consequently Cushman's Choctaw interpretations do not apply. For example, Tallase (Talasi, Talise) was a Creek town, and the meaning of the name in the *Creek* language is "Old Town." But I have not attempted to correct Cushman's linguistics. He had given much thought to the meaning of Choctaw names, and even where he has erroneously included names not Choctaw he may occasionally throw light on obscure tribal relationships before the historic period.

Second.—"Owatomy, Straight." Original, Owa-to-my, Hunting in the sunshine.

Third.—"Oklahoma (Beautiful land)." Original, Ok-la-hum-ma, Red people.

It is published in our school histories of the United States that Oklahoma is a Chickasaw word meaning "Beautiful Country." The Chickasaw words for beautiful country are yakni iukli.

Fourth.—"Chicola, The place of foxes." Original, Chu-la ai-an-tah; Fox there.

Fifth.—"Arkansas (Bow on the smoky water). In the Choctaw language, Sho-bo-ta oka chas-sa-la, means smoking water bow, i. e. Bow on a foggy lake.

Sixth.—"Tennessee, River of the great bend." The name given by the ancient Choctaws is Ta-nak-bi chi-toh bok, Big Bend river.

Seventh.—"Missouri, Great muddy river." But the Choctaw words for great muddy river are, Huch-cha hla-chi-ko chitoh. Missouri, if a Choctaw word, is a corruption of Mish-o-hof-fih, Continually rubbing off.

Eighth.—"Alabama, here we rest." Original. Ul-la ba-noh hosh, The only child. The Choctaw words for "Here we rest" are Fohah hup-ish-no yak.

Ninth.—"Mississippi River, the great river." Original. Mish-a-si-pok-ni, Aged beyond. The Choctaw words for great river are bok chi-toh, or Huch-cha chit-oh. Original, Misha-sipokni Huchcha.—A river whose age is beyond computation.

Tenth.—Mr. Hawkins says: "A South Carolina river which now bears the prosaic name of Broad, was known to the Indians (Choctaws) as Eswawpuddenah, the dividing river, after a bloody battle between the Catawbas and Cherokees. The name Piscataway has much the same meaning." But the Choctaw words for "the dividing river" are, Hush-koli bok, and Piscataway is a corruption of the Choctaw words, Pus-ka ta-hah, Bread all gone, or Without bread.

In the Fort Smith (Arkansas) Elevator, February 4, 1887, the following appeared:

"Among the Choctaws—An interesting article from the Cincinnati Graphic, by John R. Music:

"The Choctaw tradition states that they traveled east, until from the summit of a mountain range they beheld a well watered and beautiful land. In rapture they exclaimed: Tsi-gar-ma-kee (Chickamauga) good." But the Choctaw word for good is A-chuk-ma, and Chickamauga is a corruption of the Choctaw words Chik-emai-ah, (may, can, or must, shall or will go in). There is no such word as Tsi-gar-makee in their language, and, it is reasonable to believe, in no other Indian language. Mr. Music thus continues: "The largest town in this region shows the contact of the Choctaws with the Cherokees, Tsatak (Choctaw) and nu-ger (taken out of the water). Here they drew a dead Choctaw out of the water." Truly the "Choctaws" of Mr. Music must be a tribe of Indians known only to himself. The words of the North American Choctaw Indians for "dead Choctaw taken out of the water" are (in our phraseology) Il-li (dead) Chah-tah (Choctaw) shu-e-kuch-ih (pulled out) hosh (the) o-ka (water). He also asserts that one of the ancient clans of the Choctaws was named "Hottah Inholata" signifying "beloved of the people." But the Choctaw words for "beloved of the people," are Ih-o-lih-to-pah (beloved) okla (people) ho (the), the Prep. of is understood before okla, Beloved of the people.

Another, under the signature of Henry Inman, asserts, through the columns of the Greenville (Texas) Banner, October 9, 1889, that the signification of Pushmataha, the name of the renowned Choctaw Chief, is "The Warrior's Seat is Finished."

But the Choctaw words for "the warrior's seat is finished," are Tush-ka ai-ome-bin-i-li ak-oke-ta-hah. Pushmataha is a corruption of the noted chief's true name. Original, A-num-pa-ish-ta-ya-u-bi, a messenger who kills.

Literally, a messenger of death, i. e., one whose rifle, bow, or tomahawk, was alike fatal on the war path or in the chase.

By request of friends I have here given a few Choctaw and Chickasaw ancient names of places, towns, villages, rivers, creeks, lakes, mounds, bluffs, etc., in the now States of Mississippi, Alabama, Georgia, Florida, Louisiana, and others, with the derivations, corruptions, originals, orthography and significations. I first give the corruption, followed by the original and signification:

Appalachee. Original, Ap-ah-li-chih, (an ancient Choctaw clan), To whoop at.

Apalachicola, a town and river in Florida. Original, Ap-e-lu-chih kolih, Help to break.

Apookta. Original, A-yuk-pa (an ancient Choctaw village in Mississippi). A place of happiness.

In a late publication it is stated that Alabama is a corruption of the Choctaw words, "Alba, vegetation," and "amo, gather."

But the Choctaw words for "vegetation gather" are Hush-uk (herbage, grass, etc.,) It-tun-a-hah (gathered). I know of no such word as "Alba" in the Choctaw language. It has the word "amba," signifying However, and the word "amo," signifiying The.

Alabama is a corruption of the Choctaw words Ul-la-ba-noh hosh, The only child, and was the name of a noted Choctaw chief who figured in 1746, contemporary with Shulush Humma, another noted Choctaw chief, during the wars of the French against the Chickasaws.

The old interpretation of the word Alabama as being a Choctaw word signifying, "Here we rest, or rested," is a myth. The Choctaw words for "Here we rest, or rested," are yak (here) hup-ish-no (we—all of us) fo-hah (to rest, or rested).

A-bo-ha kub-lo humma, Strong Red House. The name of an ancient and noted Choctaw chief of the Ok-la hun-na-li iksa, Six People, Iksa, Clan.

Allamucha. Original, A-lum-a-ka, A hiding place. The name of an ancient Choctaw town situated near the Alabama line in Lauderdale County, Mississippi.

Ai-ik-hun-a, A place of learning, a school. The name of a Choctaw village in which was established a missionary station in 1821.

Iuka. Original, Ai-yu-pi, A place of bathing. The name of a town in north Mississippi.

Boguefaliah. Original, Bok-fa-lai-yah, Long creek, in Mississippi.

Buckatunnee. Original, Bok-it-tun-a-hah, collected together. A large creek in Mississippi. The junction of several creeks which, uniting, formed Bokittunahah.

Betapinbogue. Original, Ni-ta-pin-bok, One Bear creek. A large creek in Mississippi.

Buttihatche. Original, But-ih huch-cha, White Sumac river. The name of a creek in Mississippi.

Biwier. Original, Bai-yi-wai-yah, Leaning white oak. A creek in Mississippi .

Bok-sha-ha, Pearl River. The ancient Choctaw name of Pearl River.

Biahela. Original, Bai-yi-il-ah, White oak by itself, lone white oak. The name of a place in Mississippi.

Bulookta. Original, Bo-luk-ta, Square. A place in Mississippi.

Bok-ta-nak-bi chi-toh, Big Bend river. The ancient Choctaw name of the Tennessee River.

Boque Hooma. Original, Bok-hum-ma. Red creek in Mississippi.

Conehatta. Original, Ko-nih-hut-a, whitish pole cat. The name of a creek in Mississippi.

Caila. Original, Co-i-il-li, dead panther. The name of a creek in Mississippi.

Chicopah. Originnal, Shik-o-pah, a plume. The name of a missionary society in Alabama.

Culleoka. Original, Kul-ih-o-ka, water spring, or spring water. The name of a town in Tennessee.

Chickahominy. Original, Che-kiho-mai-yih, to become red quickly. A creek in Virginia. A stream of water which, acording to an ancient Choctaw tradition, suddenly changed its natural color to that of a coffee color, or brown.

Chuk-fi-lum-a hih-lah bok, Dancing rabbit creek. The name of a small creek in Mississippi, upon whose banks the Choctaws, in 1830, ceded the last acre of their ancient possessions east of the Mississippi river to the United States.

Chaffelia. Original, Sa-fa-la-yah, I am long. The name of a creek in Mississippi.

Copiah. Original, Ho-pai-i, War Chief. The name of a county in Mississippi.

Chulahoma. Original, Chu-la-hum-ma, Red Fox. The name of a creek in Mississippi.

Chulatchee. Original, Chu-la-huch-cha, Fox River. Name of a stream in Mississippi.

Chinchehoma. Original, Chish-a-hum-ma, Red Post Oak. The name of an aged Choctaw, whom I personally knew in my youth, and for whom a little stream took its name.

Chattanooga. Original, Cha-hah-nu-chi, Tall wild flax.

Chitimacha. Orinigal, Chi-un-ai-ya-chih,, Thine to conquer. A place in Louisiana.

Calolarchi. Original, Ko-loh-lich-ih, To cut in many pieces. The ancient name of a Choctaw village.

Chickasawha. Original, Chik-a-sah-si-ah, I am a Choctaw. The name of an ancient Chickasaw town in which De Soto and his army wintered in 1541.

Chunkey. Original, Chuki. A martin—the name of a small stream in Mississippi.

Chualley. Original, Chu-ah-la bok, Cedar creek.—The name of a creek in Mississippi.

Catahoula. Original, Ka-wah-chu-la, barking fox.—The ancient Choctaw name of a lake in Louisiana, and now the name of a Parish in Louisiana.

It is published that the word "Catahoula" is a Choctaw word derived from "Okatahulo" and meaning "Beloved lake." But the Choctaw words for Beloved Lake are Ok-hut-ah Ho-li-to-pa. There is no such word in the Choctaw language as "Okatahulo."

Chickamauga—A tributary of the Tennessee River. Original, Chik-emai-ah, may, can or must, shall or will go in.

Caloosahatchee. Original, Chas-su-lah huch-cha, crooked river. The ancient Choctaw name of a river in southwest Florida.

Chauaches. Original, Chah-a-chih, to ennoble. The name of an ancient Choctaw Iksa (clan), which dwelt a few miles north of New Orleans and consisted of only thirty warriors with their families whom Governor Perier caused to be wholly exterminated, in January, 1717, by Negroes—the slaves of the French colony; the particulars of which are given in "History of the Natchez."

Coashatta. Original, Ko-i-sak-tih, panther bluff. The ancient Choctaw name of a bluff on the Bigbee River in Mississippi.

Coahoma. Original, Co-i humma, red panther. The name of a county in Mississippi.

Coosa. Original, Chu-sah, tapering. The name of an ancient Choctaw family who were remarkable for their slenderness.

Etowah. Original, He-to-ka, ball ground. The ancient Choctaw name of a river in Georgia upon whose banks was a noted ball ground.

Eastabutchie. Original, I-ah-ta-ba-shih, to go mourning. The ancient name of a creek in Mississippi, famous for its fatal sickness; therefore, whoever lived upon its banks would have cause to mourn.

Faket chee poonta. Original, Fa-kit-chi-pin-ta, very small turkey. The name of an ancient Choctaw village situated on the Bigbee River in Mississippi.

Falukta bunnee. Original, Fa-lak-na-bun-ah, fox squirrel doubled up. The name of an ancient Choctaw village on the banks of the Bigbee river in Mississippi.

Hatche camesa. Original, Huch-cha chu-lo-sah, quiet river. A river with a quiet current.

Hatchatigbee. Original, Ha-cho-tuk-ni, loggerhead turtle. The ancient Choctaw name of a bluff on the Bigbee River in Mississippi.

I read the following in The Globe Democrat, July 18, 1896: "Habalo chitto, the name of a river in Mississippi, which means big fight." But the Choctaw words for "big fight" are it-tib-ih chi-toh.

Habalo chitto. Original, Ha-bo-lih chi-to-lit, greatly diminished. The ancient Choctaw name of a large stream which had diminshed in depth, owing to the washing from the hills.

Hobakin loopa. Original, Ho-ba-chi yuk-pa, laughing echo. The ancient Choctaw name of a shoal in the Bigbee River in Mississippi.

Hiyoowunnie. Original, Hi-oh-lih un-i, standing berries. The name of an ancient Choctaw town situated on Chick-a-sah-hah creek, a tributary of Pearl River in Mississippi.

Hushookwa. Original, Hash-o-kak, something superior which cannot be treated with impunity. The name of an ancient Choctaw town in which Peter P. Pitchlynn was born. Truly an appropriate name for the birthplace of that renowned Choctaw orator and fearless statesman, once known among the whites in Washington City as the Calhoun of the Choctaw.

Humecheto. Original, Hum-ma-chi-toh, Big Red. The ancient Choctaw name of a creek in Choctaw county, Mississippi.

Ittibano. Original, It-ti-ba-no-wah, walking together. The name of an ancient Choctaw village in Mississippi.

Issaquena. Original, Issiok-hina, Deer Branch. The name of a town in Mississippi.

Koonowa. Original, Ka-no-wa, the walker. The name of an ancient Choctaw hunter.

From the "Globe Democrat, July 18, 1896," from the New Orleans Picayune, the following derivation and interpretation given by one I. H. Watkins, of the Chickasaw word Itawamba, the name of a county in north Mississippi. He gives the original as "Ita-taka-lombi," with the interpretation thereof, "Go and kill." Now the words in the Chickasaw language for go and kill are, mi-ah mich-a-ub-ih. The Choctaws have identically the same words, nor have either any other words for "go and kill." The word "Ita-taka-lombi is utterly foreign to both languages.

Itawamba. Original, It-i-ai-o-bin-i-li, Wooden seat. That is, the seat occupied by the ancient Chickasaw chief in council assembled. Sometimes it was called Ai-o-bin-i-li, bench or seat; fa-lai-a, (long) mi-ko (chicf), i. c., Long Bench Chief; or Chief of the Long Bench. In our phraseology, The Chair of State.

Loosascoona. Original, Lusa-ko-nih, black pole cat, the name of a creek in Mississippi. The ancient Choctaws had four different names for that odoriferous little animal.

Ko-nih, the general name.

Ko-nih chuk-cho, a large striped species.

Ko-nih lu-sa, small, black species.

Ko-nih shup-ik, a peculiar kind having snouts like pigs, and feeding by rooting, according to the Choctaw tradition. But had become extinct long before the advent of the missionaries in 1818. Evidently the ant-eater of Mexico.

Lobutchy. Original, Lah-buch-ih, to make warm. The name of a creek in Mississippi.

Looxapalia. Original, Luk-si-oh-pul-a-lih, Swimming terrapin, a town and creek in Lamar county, Mississippi.

Lucarnatchie. Original, Lus-sah lucha, wet swamp.

Lapantie bogue. Original, La-pit-tah bok, buck creek. The ancient Choctaw name of a creek in Mississippi.

Meshoba. Original, Mi-ah-shoh-bih, go in advance until evening. The ancient Choctaw name of a place in Mississippi.

Mouma. Original, Mo-yum-a, every one. The name of an ancient Choctaw Iksa (clan) in Louisiana. Now the name of a town in the same state, but changed to the name Homer.

Mishawaka. Original, Mish-a-wa-yah, raised in abundance beyond. The name of a town in Indiana.

Mokea lusha. Original, Bok-lus-a, black creek. An ancient Choctaw village in Mississippi.

Mingo ho ma. Original, Mi-ko hum-ma, red chief. A place in Mississippi.

The Choctaws and Chickasaws had two traditional names for the Mississippi River, as follows:

Occochappo. Original, O-ka-chash-po-hosh, the ancient waters.

Father Allouez, a Jesuit priest, when exploring the country from Quebec to Lake Superior, in 1669, first heard of a great river (which proved to be the Mississippi River) called—

Mecassheba. Original, Mi-ko Si-ah, King I am.

Neshoba. Original. Na-sho-ba, Wolf. A county in Mississippi.

Nittayuma. Original, Nit-a-yum-ma, Bear yonder. The name of a creek in Mississippi.

Natchez. Original, Na-chuf-fih, to break off from. A town in Mississippi named after an ancient tribe of Indians that formerly inhabited the country on the Mississippi River; exterminated January 25, 1733, by the French under Bienville.

Noxubee. Original, Nak-sho-bih, offensive odor. The name of a creek and also a county in Mississippi. It took its name, according to Choctaw tradition, from a great battle fought upon its banks in the remote past, between the Choctaws and Muscogees. The Muscogees were defeated and left their slain upon the battle field which were thrown into the creek by the Choctaws; and such were the number that the decomposing mass polluted the air for miles around. It was fought in 1790, according to Choctaw tradition, with 500 warriors slain.

I read the following in the St. Louis Globe Democrat, of July 18, 1896: "There is in the same state (Mississippi) a creek called Noxubee. The change from the original in this word has also been very striking. The Indian form of the word was Ok-a-mak-shobi." There is no such word in the Choctaw or Chickasaw languages.

Nanna Wayah. Original, Nunih Waiyah, leaning mound. The name of a mound in Mississippi, previously mentioned.

Ok-la-ta-ba-shih (the people's mourner) was the Noah of the Choctaws, in their tradition of the flood, who made a boat into which he placed his family and provisions and thus saved them—truly an appropriate name.

Oksa loosa. Original, Os-si lu-sa, black eagle. A town in Illinois.

Opelousas. Original, O-pah lus-sah, swamp owl. The name of a place in Alabama.

Oaktoma. Original, Ok-toh-bi, to be foggy. The name of a creek in Mississippi.

Okefinokee. Original, O-ka-hi-o-lih, waters standing. A swamp in Georgia.

Ossachile. Original, Os-si-chah-li, swift eagle. The name of an ancient Choctaw chief whom De Soto visited in 1540.

Omaha. Original, O-mi-ha (if a Choctaw word), it must be. Said to mean "To go against the current."

Osceola. Original, Os-si-o-lachih, Singing Eagle. The renowned Seminole chief and patriot.

Okolona. Original, Ok-la-lok-on-lih, People gathered together. A town in Chickasaw county, Mississippi.

Os-ki-fa-kop-lih, Stripped Cane. A large and lengthy creek in Mississippi known as Trimcane.

Ocklawaha. Original, Ok-la-yan-ha, People subject to fever. The name of a river in Florida.

Okeion. Original, Oka-i-ah, Moving water. The name of a little place in Mississippi.

The beginning of the creek Oka ittibihha (by abbreviation Oktibihha) was known to the Choctaws as O-ka-ai-it-tu-fa-ma (the coming together of the waters), and refers to the junction of the seven large creeks which form it, viz:

First.—Catarper. Original, Ka-ta-pah, checked or pushed back; i. e., water retarded by drifts.

Second.—Os-ki Fa-kop-lih, cane stripped of its leaves; so called by the Choctaws from the abundance of switch cane growing upon its banks, with which, when stripped of its leaves, they made their beautiful baskets—literally the place where the cane is trimmed.

Third.—Bai-yih (white oak) Wai-yih (leaning over).

Fourth.—Bok (creek) Fa-lai-ah (long).

Fifth.—Hush-ih (sun) Bok (creek).

Sixth.—Ba-cha-ya Bok (line creek), which divided the Choctaw and Chickasaw nations on the north, when living east of the Mississippi river.

Seventh.—Sukatanchi. Original, Shuk-ha Ni-a-chih, hogs fattened. The place where hogs are fattened.

Okahola. Original, O-ka-ho-yah, Filtered water. The name of a town in Marion county, Mississippi.

Oktibbehaw. Original, O-ka-it-tib-ih-ka, the water fight. A county in Mississippi. The name given by the ancient Choctaws to a large creek flowing into the Bigbee river above the town of Columbus, Mississippi, now known as Tibi, (corruption of Ittibih, having fought). It took its name, according to Choctaw tradition, from a great battle fought between the Choctaws and Muscogees years before the advent of the whites, in which the Muscogees occupied the north side of the creek and the Choctaws the south, shooting their arrows across the creek. The Choctaws were defeated, but soon reinforcements returned and drove the Muscogees out of their country.

Opelika. Original, Ok-pul-ila-ka, the lily by itself—the lone lily. The name of a missionary society in Alabama.

Oktarkthalapulla. Original, Ok-tark-toh-boko-lih, bluish white prairie. A beautiful prairie in the southwestern part of Oktibbehaw county, Mississippi, six miles southwest of Starkville, known, before brought into cultivation, as "The Blue Prairie." It was a peculiar looking prairie, presenting a lonely and melancholy appearance, nearly round, perfectly level and extending nearly two miles each way without a tree or shrub upon it, but covered with a carpet of grass standing (in the summer season) from two to three feet in height. It was the last prairie between Starkville and the Mississippi River, surrounded by magnificent forests of oak and pine, in which were found wild game in sufficient quantities to gladden the heart of the most fastidious lover of the chase; in which I, with other congenial spirits, fully shared and enjoyed many years ere progress blotted it out.

Okahatchee. Original, Ok-la-huch-cha, river people. An ancient Choctaw village whose people used river water.

Oaklehy. Original, Ok-la-le-lih, People who plow. The name of an ancient Choctaw village in which several white families lived.

Otocklawfa. Original, Ok-tah-lau-a, Many prairies. A town in Mississippi.

Oaktewally. Original, O-ti-wa-lih, exhibiting chestnuts. The name of a little town in Mississippi.

Okatomie. Original, Ok-a-to-mih, Sunshine in water. The name of an ancient Choctaw village in Mississippi.

Okenachitto. Original, Ok-hin-a-chi-toh, Big stream. The Choctaw name of a large creek in Mississippi.

Okshawali. Original, Ok-shau-a-lih. Light complexion. The name of an ancient Choctaw town, among whose people were many of fair complexions.

Osyka. Original, Os-si-ka, the Eagle. A town in Pike county, Mississippi.

Ofahoma. Original, O-fi-hum-ma, Red dog. Town in Leake county, Mississippi.

Okachickama. Original, O-ka-chukma, Good water. The capital of Yalobusha county, Mississippi.

Yalobusha.   Original,   Ya-lo-ba-ai-a-sha,   Tadpoles abound.

Onalaska. Original, O-na-lu-chah, to arrive being wet. A town in Arkansas.

Okatibbee. Original, O-ka-it-tib-ih, Water fight, i. e., a battle across the water. A town in Lauderdale county, Mississippi.

Oktoc. Original, Ok-tak, prairie. A town in Oktibbeha county, Mississippi.

Pillahatchee. Original, Pil-lah-huch-cha, far off river. A river in Rankin county, Mississippi.

"Ponchatoula, a Choctaw word," says the St. Louis Globe Democrat of July 18, 1896, "is a corruption of Panchagoula, which, according to the declaration of the well informed superintendent of the Choctaw schools in Mississippi, a gentleman who speaks the Choctaw language fluently, means pond lily." The Choctaw words for "pond lily" are Haiyip (pond) Okpul (lily).

Pasgagoula. Original, Pas-ka-ok-la, people having bread. A town in Jackson county, Mississippi.

Solgohachia, a town in Arkansas. Original, Sok-ko-huch-cha, Muscadine River.

Panola. Original, Po-no-la, cotton; the name of a county in north Mississippi.

Pachuta. Original, Pa-sho-hah, to handle, a town in Perry county, Mississippi.

Piache. Original, Pi-e-shih, to care for us, the name of an ancient Choctaw town which De Soto passed through in October, 1540.

Puchcheyanshoba. Original, Pu-chi-yo-shu-bah, pigeon to be lost—Strayed Pigeon, ancient Choctaw village.

Pantotoc. Original, Pa-ki-tak-oh-lih, grapes hung up— Hanging Grapes, the name of a town in north Mississippi.

Seneasha. Original, Si-nih-ai-an-ta, sycamore abound, the name of a little branch in Mississippi.

Shetimasha. Original, Shit-til-e-mah-ai-a-shah, Habitation of the disdainful. The Shittilemahaiashah Indians of

St. Mary's Parish, Louisiana, are evidently a remnant of an ancient Choctaw Iksa (clan), a few feeble sparks still lingering in the ashes of their exterminated Iksa.

Senatobia. Original, Sin-ih-toh-bih-a, My white sycamore. The name of a town in Tate county, Mississippi.

Shubuta. Original Sho-bo-tah, Smoking. A little town in Clarke county, Mississippi.

Siboglahatcha. Original, Is-su-ba-ok-la-hu-cha, Horse River people, i. e., People living on horse river. A creek and town in Calhoun county, Mississippi.

Suqualak. Original, Shau-wa-lah, widely branching. A town in Noxubee county, Mississippi. The name also of a small creek emptying into Noxubee near the great ball play ground, upon which, in 1790, was fought the great battle before mentioned.

Sukatanche. Original, Shuk-ha ne-a-chih, fattened hogs; i. e., the place where hogs fatten. A large creek in north Mississipip and town in Kemper county, Mississippi.

Tangipahoa. Original, Tun-chi-pa-sho-hah, corn handled—where corn was bought and sold.

Tallula. Original, To-lo-ho ah, continually singing. The name of the falls of a river in Georgia, said to be 536 feet.

Talluhah. Original, Tal-lu-hah, a bell. A town in Louisiana.

Tuskogee. Original, Tush-ka-ko-cha, weather warrior, i. e., a warrior who foretells the weather.

Tallasha. Original, Ta-la-ai-ar-sha, Palmetto abound. The place of palmettoes.

Toonisuba. Original, To-no-lishis-su-ba, rolling horse. A place in Mississippi.

Talletuluck. Original, Ta-le-tul-i, Palmetto rock, Palmetto by a rock. A town in Kemper county, Mississippi.

Tacaleeche. Original, Tak-a-li-chih, to put down, town in Benton county, Mississippi. Town and river in Panola county, Mississippi.

Tullahoma. Original, Tul-i-hum-ma, red stone, rock or iron. Town in Jones county, Mississippi.

Wantubbee. Original, Ai-an-ta-ub-ih, to be at and kill. A little place in Mississippi.

Winona. Original, Wa-ton-la, a crane. A town in Mississippi.

Yakanookane. Original, Yak-ni-nak-ish-wa-na, Cat fish land. A creek in Oktibbehaw county, Mississippi.

Yoconapatawfa. Original, Yak-ni-pa-tuf-fih, Land ploughed.

Waupanuckee. Original, Wak-chah-nu-sih, to sleep wide a part. A town in the present Chickasaw Nation.

Tallula. Original, Til-oh-lih, to break off. A town in Issaquena county, Mississippi.

Issaquena. Original, Is-si-ok-hena, deer branch. A town in Mississippi.

Tillitoba. Original, Tul-i-toh-bi, gray rock. A town in Yalobusha county, Mississippi.

Taloeah. Original, Ta lo ah-i-ah, to go singing. A town in Marion county, Mississippi.

Tamolah. Original, Ta mo-ah, lost. A town in Kemper county, Mississippi.

Tallase. Original, Tul-li-ai-sha, rocks abound. An ancient Choctaw village which De Soto visited in 1540.

Toccopola. Original, Tosh-bo-ko-li, mouse colored. A town in LaFayette county, Mississippi.

Toomsuba. Original, Ta-is-su-ba, because or in as much as a horse. A town in Lauderdale county, Mississippi.

Topisaw. Original, Tah-pi-sah, to see now. A town in Pike county, Mississippi.

Talawah. Original, Ta-lo ah, singing. A town in Marion county, Mississippi.

Tubby. Original, Ub-ih, to kill. A town in Itawamba county, Mississippi.

Tooanoowe. Original, To-mih-no-wa, walking in the sunshine. The nephew of Tumoachi.

Tamoachih. Original, Tum o a-chi, you lost. Chief of the Yamacaws, with whom Oglethorpe established a never violated treaty.

Yamacaw. Original Yum-mak-ka-sha-pah, That one to be a part. The name of an ancient clan of Choctows at the time Oglethorpe founded Savannah, Georgia, February 1, 1733.

Tuscola. Original, Tah-ok-la, Now a people. A town in Leake county, Mississippi.

Chickasaw bogue. Original, Chik-a-sah-bok, Chickasaw creek. Town in Mobile county, Alabama.

Choccolocco. Original, Chuk-cho-sok-koh, Thick maple or maple grove. Town in Calhoun county, Alabama.

Choctawhatchie. Original, Chah-tah-huch-cha, Choctaw river. Town in Henry county, Alabama.

Senauki. Original, Kin-nak-li, Limping. The wife of Tumoachi.

Clayhatchie. Original, Chash-ah-huch-cha, Rattling or rippling river. Town in Dale county, Alabama.

Enitachopco. Original, E-nit-tak ok chah, we awaken at day. A town in Clay county, Alabama.

Looxapalia. Original, Luk-si-ok pul-a lih, swimming terrapin. A town and creek in Lamar county, Alabama.

Loachapoha. Original, Lau-a-chih-fo-hah, making many to rest. Town in Lee county, Alabama.

Talladega. Original, Tal-a-ti-hah, pulled up palmetto. Town and county in Alabama.

Tallahatta. Original, Tal-a-hut-a, standing palmetto. A town in Clark county, Alabama.

Tallassahatchee. Original, Tal-a-sa-huch-cha, I am the palmetto river. A town in Calhoun county, Alabama.

Tallula. Original, Tul-u-la, a bell. A town in Fayette county, Alabama.

Talucah. Original, Ta-lo-ah, singing. A town in Morgan county, Alabama.

Tallapoosa. Original, Tul-i-po-shi, Iron dust. A county in Alabama.

Tuscahoma. Original, Tush-ka-hum-ma, red warrier. A town in Choctaw county, Alabama.

Tuscumbia. Original, Tush-ka-um-ba chi, rainmaker

warrior, A town in Colbert county, Alabama. Name of an ancient Chickasaw chief renowned as a medicine war chief and contemporary with the famous Chickasaw chief, John Colbert.

Tuscaloosa. Original, Tush-ka-lu-sa, black warrior. A town and county in Alabama.

Wauhula. Original, Lau-a-chu-la, many foxes. A town in De Soto county, Florida.

Chuluota. Original, Chu-la-an-tah, a fox stays—where foxes abound. A town in Orange county, Florida.

Oktahatchee. Original, Ok-tak-huch-cha, Prairie river. A town in Hamilton county, Florida.

Oclawaha. Original O-ka-lau-a-ha, Many times water. Town in Lake county, Florida. That is, in riding over the country your way is obstructed by lakes, lagoons and ponds.

Chattahoochee. Original, Chuk-lih-huch-cha, Rapid river. A town in Fulton county, Georgia, and river in Georgia.

Chenubee. Original, Chi-a-ub-ih, You kill. Town in Webster county, Georgia.

Chokee. Original, Cho-ki, a martin. Town in Lee county, Georgia.

Ossahutchee. Original, Os-si-huch-cha, Eagle river. A town in Harris county, Georgia. A river upon which eagles abound.

Sallacoa. Original, Sa-la-ko-fah, I made a notch. A town in Cherokee county, Georgia.

Chinchuba. Original, Chin is-su-ba, thy horse. Town in St. Tammany Parish, Louisiana.

Chepola. Original, Che-pu-li, Town in St. Helena Parish, Louisiana. The name given by the ancient Choctaws to a favorite dance, the termination of a protracted feast and general good time.

Chacahoula. Original, Chit-oh-hul-wa, large soft shell turtle. A town in Terre Bonne, Louisiana.

Coushatta. Original, Kau-ah-shak-ba, broken arm. A town in Red River Parish, Louisiana.

INDEX

War, 238-42; gave asylum to Natchez, 379, 385.

Cheyennes: 40.

Chickasah, legendary chief, 18-22.

Chickasahha, Chickasaw town: 357-58, 361, 370-71, 373, 377, 384, 411, 482.

Chickasaw Bluff: 377.

Chickasaw Old Fields: see Chickasahha.

Childbirh: 175, 410.

Children: hardihood, 121, 154-56; training of, 130, 308-9, 396; concern for, 137-38; property of, 169, 403; care of, 175-76, 395-96. See also Family life, Orphans, Women.

Choctaw Academy: 335.

Choctaw Agency: in Mississippi, 277.

Choctaw-Chickasaw relations: one people originally, 18-21, 358, 362; separation, 21; wars between, 29, 31-33, 365-66, 368, 370-72, 376-81; agreement about school, 74; allied against the Shakchi Hummas, 186-90; united peace mission to Osages, 335-41.

Chopart, French officer: 449-53.

Christianity: Choctaw acceptance of, 58, 101-8, 136-37, 202-3, 356; Chickasaw acceptance of, 396-97, 412. See also Baptists, Jesuits, Methodists, Missionaries, Missions, Presbyterians.

Citizenship, United States: anticipated by Choctaws, 58, 67-68.

Civilization: training in, 386. See also Agriculture, Livestock.

Civil War, American: Choctaws in, 272-73, 341-42; Chickasaws in, 412.

Civil War, Choctaw: 34-35, 376-78, 381-83.

Claiborne, William Charles Coles: 386-87, 389.

Clans: Choctaw, 17n, 235, 306-7.

Clark, George Rogers: 363.

Clay, Henry: 341.

Cleveland, Grover: 43n, 44.

Clothing: see Dress.

Coffee, John: 414, 427-29.

Colbert, George: 360, 423-25.

Colbert, James: 417, 423-25, 430-31.

Colbert, John: 323, 423.

Colbert, Levi: 423, 428-30.

Colbert, Logan: 414, 423.

Colbert, Martin: 419.

Colbert, Pitman: 288-89.

Colbert, Rhoda: 417-18.

Colbert, Samuel: 417-18.

Colbert, William: 423, 425.

Colbert family: 386, 423.

Colbert's Ferry: on Tennessee River, 387.

Cole, Coleman: 85, 190, 235, 275-76, 314.

Cole, Robert: 70.

Comanches: 64, 147.

Cooper, Douglas H.: 273.

Corn: origin of, Choctaw myth: 214-16. See also Agriculture, Food.

Cornelius, Elias: 290-92.

Cotton picking: by Choctaws, 105.

Councils: conduct in, by Choctaws, 61-62, 112, 147-48, 197, 246-58, 261-62, 276, 397-98; by Chickasaws, 397-98, 431.

Courts: Choctaw, 356.

Courtship: Choctaw, 309-10; Chickasaw, 406. See also Marriage.

Cravat, John: 342-43.

Cravat family: 342-43.

Creation myths: Choctaw, 199; Natchez, 441.

Creeks: 34, 147, 171; relationship to Choctaws and Chickasaws, 13; Choctaw wars with, 36, 131-35, 180, 237-38, 486-87, 488; treaties with Spain, 41, 45; in War of 1812, 63, 238, 262, 266, 349-52, 362, 425; aboriginal domain, 192-93; Mexican origin, 299-440; peace mission to Osages, 335-41; refused missionaries, 358; Chickasaw war with, 426-27.

Creek War: see War of 1812.

Crimes: between whites and Choctaws, 49-50; among Choctaws, see Laws, Punishments.

Crowder, Eli: 349-52.

Cushman, Calvin: 3, 82, 107, 114,

182-83, 187, 190, 202-3, 210-14, 278-79, 359-60.

Cushman, Horatio Bardwell: early life, 7, 8, 15, 182-85, 210-14; college, 7, 289-90; in Texas, 7, 150-51, 359-60; travels among Choctaws and Chickasaws, 7-8, 121, 137, 174, 191, 208-9, 238, 247, 287, 319-25, 474-75; aims in writing, 8, 233-34, 463-64.

Cushman, Laura: 5, 82, 114, 202-3, 211.

Custer, George Armstrong: 40.

Daggette, Stephen: 427-30.

Dancing: Choctaw, 81, 124, 156-57, 169, 218-19, 308; Chickasaw, 399-400, 406-9; Natchez, 439, 446, 453, 455.

D'Artaguette, Diron: 370-71, 373-75, 378.

Dawes, Henry L.: 43n, 44 and note.

Dawes, Act: 43-44. See also Land, in severalty.

Death penalty: Choctaw, 158-63, 203-8. See also Murder.

Death songs: Choctaw, 207-8, 222.

Deavers, Alex: 361.

Deer: burial of horns, 139.

Deformity: absence of, 440.

Delawares: 152.

De Soto, Hernando: landing in Florida, 472; battle with Choctaws, 22-27, 228, 233; with Chcikasaws, 357-58, 362, 411; towns visited, 482, 487, 490, 492.

Despondency: of Indians, 114, 176.

Diseases: 78, 169-72, 329, 440.

Districts: Choctaw, 27-28, 37-38, 68, 77-78, 261, 356, 479; Chickasaw, 403. See also Okla Falaiah, Okla Hunnali.

Dixon, Chester: 160-62.

Doak's Stand; 57, 60.

Doaksville: 319.

Doctors: Choctaw, 74-75, 92, 171-73, 199-201, 307, 331; Chickasaw, 405, 407-10. See also Prophets.

Domestic manufactures: Choctaw, 105, 330, 488; Chickasaw, 395; Natchez, 441.

Dreams: Choctaw, 173.

Dress: Choctaw, 330; Chickasaw, 395; Natchez, 441.

Drought: Choctaw tradition of, 306.

Drunkenness: 78, 105, 145. See also Prohibition, Whiskey.

Duels: Choctaw, 141-43.

Du Pratz, Le Page: quoted, 440, 473.

Durant, Alexander: 349.

Durant, Ellis: 349.

Durant, Louis: 331-32, 344-46, 349.

Durant family: 349.

Dutch Johnnie: 238-42.

Dwellings: of Choctaws, 173, 311; of Chickasaws, 394-95, 414, 432; of Natchez, 441.

Eaton, John: 414, 427.

Eclipses of sun: belief of Choctaws, 229-31, 308; of Chickasaws, 410.

Economic life: Choctaw, primitive, 190-91. See also Agriculture, Cotton picking, Domestic manufactures, Dwellings.

Education: vocational, 386, 432-33. See also Schools.

Elections: Choctaw, 112. See also Government.

Eliot Mission: 71-85, 95-100.

Emmaus Mission: 86.

English: machinations among Choctaws, 28-29, 33-36, 41, 243ff, 364-85 passim; Chickasaw friendship for, 36, 41, 364-79; Chickasaw asylum in Carolinas, 380.

Fables: Choctaw, 164-65.

Factions: among Choctaws, 34-35. See also Civil War, Choctaw.

Factories: 386-87.

Family life, Chickasaw: 395-96, 435. See also Children, Marriage, Women.

Family life, Choctaw: matrilineal descent, 59n, 87, 300; harmony, 90, 122; mother-in-law avoidance, 144. See also Children, Marriage, Women.

Festivals: Natchez, 444-46.

Hebron Mission: 7, 114, 159, 182, 202-3, 279, 328, 470.

Himarkubih, Choctaw chief: 133, 135.

Hinds, Thomas: 57, 60, 67.

History: injustice to Indians, 15, 38-40, 192-93. *See* also Cushman, Horatio Bardwell, aims in writing.

Hitchitees, Indian tribe: 13-14.

Hittites: relation of Choctaws to, 13-14.

Hodgson, Adam: quoted, 79-82.

Holubi Miko, Choctaw chief: 163.

Hoomastubbee: *see* Moshulatubbee.

Hooper, William: 82, 102.

Hospitality: of Choctaws, 122, 136.

Houses: *see* Dwellings.

Human sacrifice: by Taensas and Natchez, 437-39.

Humphries, David, 358-59.

Hunting: Choctaw skill in, 118-20, 138-39. *See* also Wild animals.

Hypnotism: among Choctaws, 307.

Ibanowa Miko, Chickasaw chief: 234.

Iberville, Pierre Le-moyne, Sieur de: 18, 41, 227, 437.

Imperial designs: *see* English, French, Spanish.

Indian Territory: liquidation of Indian tribes of, 8, 43-44 and notes, 361n, 364n, 412-13; white settlement of, 54n, 363n. *See* also Oklahoma, Removal.

Infanticide: by Choctaw women, 88.

Inheritance laws: Chickasaw, 403.

Intermarried white men, with Chickasaws: 414. *See* also Colbert, Logan; Gunn, James; Harris, Daniel; Love, Thomas; McGee, Malcomb.

Intermarried white men, with Choctaws: 312-15, 331. *See* also Cravat, John; Crowder, Eli; Durant, Louis; Folsom, Ebenezer; Folsom, Edmond; Folsom, Nathaniel; Harkins, John; Le Flore, Louis; Le Flore, Michael; Mitchell, Samuel; Nail, Henry; Perry family; Pitchlynn, John.

Intruders: white, 49, 157-58, 396.

Ishtehotopa, Chickasaw chief: 403-4, 429.

Jackson, Andrew: 390, 425; negotiated Treaty of Doak's Stand, 57, 60-69; Choctaws fought under, 59, 262, 267-68; Pushmataha's arguments with, 60-69, 263-64; Peter Pitchlynn's relations with, 334.

Jesuits: 438, 472, 486.

Jewell, Moses: 72, 96.

Kerlerec, French governor: 35, 384-85.

Kingsbury, Cyrus: work among Cherokees, 71; among Choctaws in Mississippi, 71-88, 95-100, 103-4, 107, 290-93, 335; family, 72, 85; removal to West, 116; death, 83-85.

Kingsbury, Sarah Varnum: 72, 85.

Kiowas: 147.

Lafayette, Marquis de: Pushmataha's conversation with, 270.

La Harpe, Bernard de: quoted, 30.

Land, Chickasaw: aboriginal domain, 21, 192-93, 362, 378-79, 392-94, 413; in severalty, 412-13.

Land, Choctaw: aboriginal domain, 41-42, 51-70, 163-64, 192-93, 292; native ownership system, 178; in severalty, 43-45, 58, 67.

Land, Natchez: aboriginal domain, 163, 438, 440.

Language, Choctaw: changes in, 16-17; studied by misionaries, 90, 96, 136; retention of: 160.

La Salle, Robert Cavelier, Sieur de: 17.

Lawgiver: Natchez, 442-43.

Laws: Choctaw, 88-89, 300, 312-15, *see* also Punishments: Chickasaw, 402-3; Natchez, 442-43.

Le Flore, Basil: 191, 343-44, 347-48.

Le Flore, Forbis: 343-44, 347-48.

Le Flore, Greenwood: 235, 277-85, 343, 347.

Le Flore, Louis: 331-32, 342-47, 349, 352.

Le Flore, Michael: 331, 343-46, 348-49.

Le Flore, Michael, Jr.: 348.

Le Flore, Thomas: 348.